LORD

[Handwritten inscription:]
To Richard,
with very best wishes
and regards,
A. Tink
8/12/11.

Until March 2006, Andrew Tink was shadow attorney-general and shadow leader of the House in the New South Wales Parliament. After a year studying in the United States, he graduated in Arts and Law from the Australian National University and practised as a barrister before being elected to the Legislative Assembly in 1988. Since stepping back from active politics, Andrew has concentrated on two of his great passions – writing and history. He is a visiting fellow at Macquarie University's law school. Andrew's first book, *William Charles Wentworth*, was published in 2009. For this, the first comprehensive biography of Wentworth, Andrew was awarded 'The Nib' CAL Waverley Award for Literature in 2010.

LORD SYDNEY
[the life and times of Tommy Townshend]

Andrew Tink

AUSTRALIAN SCHOLARLY

© Andrew Tink 2011

First published 2011 by Australian Scholarly Publishing Pty Ltd
7 Lt Lothian St Nth, North Melbourne, Vic 3051   TEL: 03 9329 6963   FAX: 03 9329 5452
EMAIL: aspic@ozemail.com.au   WEB: scholarly.info

ISBN 978-1-921875-43-4

ALL RIGHTS RESERVED

Design and typesetting Art Rowlands   *Printing and binding* BPA Print Group

The main chapters of this book are typeset in Adobe Garamond Pro 11/16 pt

For my wife, Kerry, whose support for me during my battles with cancer has allowed me to see Sydney's story through to publication

Contents

Acknowledgements ix
Preface xiii

1 Republicans and royalists 1
2 Young Tommy Townshend 7
3 The parliamentary apprentice 12
4 Cousin George and the conquest of Quebec 18
5 George III and Tommy's Whig inheritance 24
6 The American Stamp Act 28
7 Cousin Charles and his tea tax 34
8 Wilkes and Liberty – Tommy's defence of dissent 41
9 Opposition 49
10 The dye is cast 57
11 At war with America 65
12 At war in Parliament 74
13 Britain on the brink 83
14 Cousin Cornwallis and Yorktown 90
15 Oh God! It's All Over! 100
16 Tommy re-enters the ministry 107
17 The American peace talks 114
18 Strachey strikes the peace with America 122
19 Tommy's defence of the peace 130
20 Aloft in a storm 138
21 Family and friends 148
22 The golden age of Irish government 156
23 From Nabobs to Nootka 164
24 Loyalists transform Canada 175
25 Dorchester upon the spot 183
26 Nelson, Bligh and Phillip 192
27 Sydney, the soft touch 203
28 Transportation where? 211
29 The First Fleet 218
30 Sydney Cove 228
31 First news of Phillip 235
32 Madness and regency 241
33 A good retreat 251
34 Give me my draught… 259

Notes 265
Bibliography 299
Index 309

Acknowledgements

My obsession with Lord Sydney began about six months before the Sydney 2000 Olympic Games. Sydney, it seemed, was everywhere and nowhere. While his name was on just about every billboard, nothing much was known about the man himself.

Historians were quick to point out that Sydney had only ever had the cove around which the Sydney CBD now nestles named after him; the rest had happened by custom. And most saw Arthur Phillip's naming of the cove itself as little more than his thankyou to the man who had appointed him governor.

With encouragement from antiquarian bookseller Derek McDonnell, I wrote a piece on Sydney's life which was duly published in the *Sydney Morning Herald* on 30 June 2000, the bicentenary of Sydney's death. This caught the attention of a Reuters correspondent, Brian Williams, who wrote an article expressing astonishment that 'Pete Townshend, a founder member of the famed rock group The Who, is far better known in the host city for this year's Olympic Games than his 18th century namesake Tommy Townshend [Lord Sydney]'. The Williams' piece was then reproduced around the world in publications as diverse as *The Indian Express* and *CNNenEspanol.com* while my *Herald* article was republished in the *Cape Breton Post*, a paper circulating in Sydney, Nova Scotia, a city also named after Lord Sydney.

There was no biography of Sydney. And based on the international response to Williams' article, I decided to fill the gap, assuming that publication would follow if I could put a workmanlike book together.

One of the only major Australian historians to take Sydney seriously has been Alan Atkinson. In volume 1 of his book, *The Europeans in Australia*, Atkinson places Sydney at the centre of the decision to send convicts to Botany Bay. I therefore arranged to meet up with him. And so began a number of meetings, telephone conversations, emails and ultimately, manuscript edits without which I could not have written this book. Crucially, Alan advised that Sydney's personal papers had been sold off in 1915 and that most of them were now held by the William L. Clements Library in Ann Arbor, Michigan – a library which specialises in the collection of papers of British politicians and military men of the American Revolutionary War.

As my parliamentary duties allowed, I consulted all the sources I could find and I am especially grateful to the then NSW Parliamentary Librarian, Greig Tillotson, and Research Director, David Clune, for introducing me to some of the Library's earliest holdings, such as *The Parliamentary History of England* and the various journals and memoirs of Horace Walpole.

At the Mitchell Library, I very much appreciated the assistance of the Dixson Librarian, Mark Hildebrand, who directed me to microfilms of documents relating to the foundation of the Botany Bay penal colony.

By this time, I was able to order second-hand books over the internet, rapidly accumulating a guide to Sydney's life and times. These confirmed that if I was going to make a research trip anywhere, the Clements Library was the place to go.

During a mid-year parliamentary break in 2004, I spent a month at the Clements going through what the Library's catalogue described as 'Sydney Papers 1665–1828, 6 feet'. This was a huge job and I am particularly indebted to the Library's then Director, John Dann; Curator of Maps, Brian Dunnigan; Curator of Manuscripts, Barbara De Wolfe; Curator of Graphic Materials, Clayton Lewis; Research Specialist Janet Bloom; the late John Harriman and more recently to the current Director, J. Kevin Graffagnino, for their patient advice and assistance. Access to the University of Michigan's Hatcher Library with its Canadian collections, and to the then recently published *Diplomatic History of the Foreign Relations of the United States under the Articles of Confederation 1780–1789*, also proved invaluable. It was at the Clements that I began to fully understand Sydney's key roles in determining the boundary between the United States and Canada and in resettling loyalist refugees.

Unable to find the time to get to London, I am particularly grateful to Dr Andrew McDonald for accessing the records of the Royal College of Physicians on my behalf. These reveal the substantial role Sydney played during King George III's bout of madness in 1788–89 and form the basis of Chapter 32 'Madness and regency'.

Acknowledgements

By the beginning of 2005, a massive manuscript began to emerge which in various drafts was read by David Clune, Brian Fletcher, Ian Hancock, Bruce Kercher, Ken Turner and, on no less than three occasions, by Alan Atkinson. Suffice to say that the manuscript going to press is about half the length of the first draft.

At the end of 2005, Lyn Tranter agreed to be my literary agent. Her indefatigable belief in Sydney's story is what, six years later, has got a manuscript which Australian publishers have repeatedly said was 'not Australian enough to be published' to the point of publication. Apart from Lyn, the constant support of Alan Atkinson, Derek McDonnell and my family, Kerry, Michael and Peter, has kept me going.

To Vice-Chancellor Steven Schwartz, Emeritus Professor Bruce Kercher and Professors Andrew Buck and Peter Radan, my thanks are due for the courtesies they have extended to me as a Visiting Fellow at Macquarie University's Law School.

Finally, I would like to thank Fred Anderson, Andrew Bamjii, John Bennett, Paul Binsted, Tim Castle, Kate Curr, Peter Dadswell, Senator Concetta Fierravanti-Wells, Peter FitzSimons, Pamela Forde, Russell Grove, Rt Hon William Hague MP, Penny Hatfield, Geoff Lindsay SC, Glenn Mitchell, Viola Porcari, Derek Townshend, Michael Waterhouse and Scott Whitmont for their advice and encouragement.

[Preface]

Although primarily responsible for the first European settlement of Australia and the Great Lakes' boundary between the United States and Canada, Lord Sydney is now remembered, if he is remembered at all, through the cities which bear his name. Known for most of his life as Tommy Townshend, 'Sydney' is the title Tommy chose in remembrance of his kinsman, the seventeenth-century republican martyr Algernon Sidney, whose writings inspired America's founding fathers.

Born in 1733 to a family at the centre of British politics, Tommy Townshend was just twenty-one when he entered the House of Commons. From there he witnessed his country triumph over France and Spain during the Seven Years' War. But Britain struggled to govern its massive new territories in North America. And Tommy's first ministerial appointments coincided with a turbulent time, during which there were seven prime ministers in just ten years.

Full of bumptious ambition and self confidence, Tommy held a succession of minor portfolios until, in 1768, he was pitched into fourteen years of lonely opposition after losing out in a factional dispute. The born-to-rule self-assurance of a gilded youth gave way to a much more mature politician as Britain slid towards a full-scale civil war with her American colonies. Tommy was one of just a few parliamentarians who supported the Americans. Variously accusing the war-time British government of corruption and treachery, he was counted lucky by his contemporaries not to be locked up in the Tower of London. But he had his revenge when he helped defeat that government on the floor of the Commons, following the surrender of a British army at Yorktown in 1781.

At the age of 49, Tommy soon became secretary of state for home affairs in the new administration, with ministerial responsibility for the American peace negotiations. Largely as a result of his efforts, modern-day southern Ontario, including what is now Toronto, is part of Canada rather than the United States. Following America's independence, Lord Sydney, as Tommy became in 1783, had to deal with a flood of loyalist refugees who were resettled in Canada. And when the Americans refused to take any more British convicts, Sydney was instrumental in redirecting them to New South Wales. During the 1780s, he was also involved in decisions that would briefly bring parliamentary independence to a united Ireland and steer India away from the East India Company towards direct British rule.

After a fiery career in opposition, where he was noted for his hot temper, Tommy approached the high cabinet office he finally achieved with considerable restraint. His personal diffidence and offsetting determination are captured in his letter to one of his peace envoys:

> I have no knowledge of any [of the American negotiators] except Dr Franklin ... I am not vain enough to suppose that any public conduct ... of mine should have attracted much of his notice. But I believe he knows enough ... to be persuaded that no one has been more averse to ... this unhappy contest or a more sincere friend to ... reconciliation than myself. If he does me the justice to believe these sentiments ... he will be convinced that I shall show myself ... an unequivocal and zealous friend to pacification upon the fairest and most liberal terms.[1]

Even so, Tommy's return to government saw his principles tempered by the realities of office. There were sometimes frustrating delays in his ministerial decision-making. But these must be weighed against his heavy responsibilities which spanned every inhabited continent in an age when return communications occasionally took years. And Tommy's work, whether it related to the peace with America or the settlement of Canada and Australia, played an important role in shaping the English-speaking world.

'Aloft in a storm' was a phrase Tommy used at a time of political chaos when, in December 1783, he agreed to join a new cabinet shortly after King George III had sacked the previous ministry. But the phrase equally describes most of Tommy's career and those of his first cousins, George and Charles Townshend and Charles Cornwallis. Prickly and eccentric as they may have been, they were all pivotal figures and always in the thick of the action in government, opposition or combat during one of the most turbulent periods in the history of the English-speaking people.

Preface

In the two centuries since Tommy's death, his legacy has been assessed largely through the eyes of his strongest contemporary critics including Oliver Goldsmith, Nathaniel Wraxall and William Smith. As a result, Tommy's reputation has suffered at the hands of historians, most recently Alan Frost, who concludes that 'Sydney was manifestly not up to his work'. However the brief biographies by John Brooke in the *History of the House of Commons* and by Ian Archer in the *Oxford Dictionary of National Biography* hint at much more. And Alan Atkinson, who has written extensively about Tommy in *The Europeans in Australia*, reveals a much more influential person than previously understood.[2]

Still, no full biography of Tommy has been written before. Perhaps this is because his greatest achievements occurred during the seven years that separated the American and French revolutions – a period the British prefer to forget following their defeat at Yorktown, and one the Americans like to celebrate with their own heroes. My hope is that this life of Sydney will put to rest many of the misconceptions about his competence and demonstrate that he was the moving force behind the British Government's decision to send the First Fleet to Botany Bay.

Andrew Tink
October 2011

[*One*]

— Republicans and royalists —

When the prisoner was asked if he had any last words he replied: 'I have come not to talk but to die'. After handing a paper to his executioner, he placed his neck on the block. Suppressing a shiver in the freezing conditions, he steadied himself for the axe. Just days later, a document entitled *The Very Copy of a Paper delivered to the Sheriffs upon the Scaffold on Tower-hill on Friday December 7, 1683 by Algernon Sidney before his execution there*, was circulating all over London. In it, Sidney asserted as if from the grave:

> God had left nations unto the liberty of setting up such governments as best pleased themselves [and]
> Magistrates were set up for the good of Nations, not Nations for the honour and glory of Magistrates.

These radical claims, that ordinary people should decide the fate of kings, were directed at Charles II who had come to assert that he ruled by divine right – by the will of God alone. Little could Algernon Sidney have dreamt of the impact his paper would have after his beheading on that bitterly cold London morning. But soon copies were crossing the Atlantic to the president of Harvard College and other influential Americans.[1]

The infamous Judge Jeffreys had sentenced Algernon to be hung, drawn and then cut open while still alive so he could see, feel and smell his insides being pulled out and burnt. After that, he was to be beheaded and what was left of his body was to be chopped into four pieces. He was to suffer a traitor's death for his role in the Rye House Plot, an attempt to overthrow Charles II. But in an act of leniency, the king reduced this sentence to beheading alone. Still, one of his many loyalist supporters, Horatio Townshend, congratulated Charles on his firmness. A century later, however, Horatio's great-grandson, Tommy Townshend, looked up to Algernon Sidney as a hero. And despite the slightly different spelling, Tommy took the title of Lord Sydney in memory of his distant uncle whose sister, Lucy Sidney, was Tommy's great-great-grandmother.[2]

This is the story of Tommy Townshend, whose mixed political inheritance from Algernon Sidney and Horatio Townshend played out in a parliamentary career spanning almost half a century, including a critical period between the American and French revolutions when the destiny of the English-speaking people was being decided in America, Canada, Ireland and Australia.

An ancient Norfolk family, the Townshends traced their ancestry to Lodvae, a 'Noble Norman' who came to England in the early twelfth century. Sixteen generations separate Tommy Townshend from Lodvae and the modern history of the Townshend family begins with Tommy's great-grandfather Horatio. Elected to Parliament during the Commonwealth Protectorate of Oliver Cromwell, Horatio alternated between the royalist and commonwealth sides as the new regime began to unravel under Cromwell's son Richard. Having gained a reputation as a political chameleon, Horatio finally settled on the royalists, helping to orchestrate Charles II's return to England as king in 1660. Although he was rewarded with a peerage and appointed lord-lieutenant of Norfolk, Horatio was an argumentative character who was eventually dismissed from his post. In an attempt at rehabilitation, Horatio signed *The Address of Norfolk* which congratulated the king on crushing the Rye House Plot.[3]

Algernon Sidney, who was beheaded for his part in this plot, was a lifelong republican who had served as a colonel in Parliament's army during the English Civil War. Later elected to the House of Commons, Algernon's high intelligence, 'ungovernable pride' and 'turbulent' temperament combined to produce a prickly public personality, one he celebrated by incorporating a porcupine in his coat of arms. Critical of the commission set up to try Charles I for treason, Algernon declared: 'the King cannot be tried by any Court and no man by this one', to which Cromwell growled, 'I tell you we will cut off his head with the Crown upon it.' Appalled by Cromwell's use of force to shut down the Parliament, Algernon sat 'grimly' in his place as troops tried to pull the speaker out of his chair. So after Cromwell's death, when another civil war threatened and Parliament invited Charles II to assume the throne on agreed terms as a unifying figure, Algernon reluctantly accepted him as a constitutional monarch.[4]

As the years passed however, Charles II began challenging Parliament's power and asserting his own divine right to rule. Arrested in the aftermath of the Rye House Plot, Algernon had been caught drafting a rebuttal to *Patriarcha*, a book which defended the divine right of kings. So he was charged with writing a treasonable libel. And fired up by Judge Jeffreys, who had been promoted lord chief justice to deliver Algernon's head, the jury took only a quarter of an hour to deliver its verdict. For writing: 'the power originally in the people of England is delegated into the Parliament [and] ... we may therefore change or take away kings', Algernon was convicted of an act of treason. 'Is writing an act?' Algernon demanded. 'Yes', replied the judge. 'It is agere' (to put in motion).[5]

Fifteen years later, Algernon's manuscript was published as *Discourses Concerning Government*, a substantial work which asserted that:

> All just magisterial power is from the people.
> Government is not instituted for the good of the governor but of the governed.
> That which is not just is not law and should not be obeyed.
> Laws were made to direct and instruct Magistrates and if they will not be directed to restrain them.
> Free nations have a right of meeting when and where they choose.
> The general revolt of a nation cannot be called a rebellion.
> The rigour of the law is to be tempered by men of known integrity and judgment.[6]

Over the next eighty years, these radical ideas rippled through the American colonies. In 1749, Benjamin Franklin insisted that copies of *Discourses* be displayed on the shelves of his Philadelphia academy. And in *Poor Richard's Almanac*, he repeated Sidney's claim that 'God helps those who help themselves'. Among Sidney's other devotees were John Adams and Thomas Jefferson, who recommended *Discourses* to friends at 15 shillings. '[It is] a rich treasure of republican principles,' Jefferson said, 'and probably the best elementary book on ... government.' Sidney's posthumously published writing was also influential in England, not least on his distant nephew Tommy Townshend.[7]

Following Algernon's execution, his body was released to his younger brother, Henry, who survived the remainder of Charles II's reign by going overseas. However, Charles's successor, James II, fell out with Parliament too, when he dislodged his Protestant daughters Mary and Anne as his heirs with the birth of his Catholic son, James. Henry Sidney joined others in writing to Mary and her husband, William of Orange, that most Englishmen 'would join with ... [William] if he invaded England'. So it was that on 5 November 1688 Henry returned as a senior officer in William's invasion force, which soon swept all before it. As a reward, Henry was created Viscount Sydney when William and Mary ascended the English throne as joint monarchs.[8]

Tommy Townshend's political legacy from Horatio Townshend was rather different, involving an ever-growing web of interlocking political influence based around the family's Raynham estate at Norfolk. Shortly before his death in 1687, Horatio had appointed a prominent Norfolk squire, Robert Walpole, to look after his family's interests, including those of his son, Charles, born in 1674. Although Charles was two years older than Walpole's eldest son Robert (who would later be Britain's longest serving prime minister) the two boys attended Eton and Cambridge together, becoming firm friends. At the age of 24, Charles married Elizabeth Pelham who was the grand-daughter of Algernon Sidney's sister, Lucy; Elizabeth's half-brothers, the Duke of Newcastle and Henry Pelham, would also become long-serving prime ministers.[9]

Soon after taking his seat in the House of Lords in 1697, Charles Townshend abandoned his father's Tory belief in the divine right of kings. Instead, he joined the Whigs – those who believed that the power of the king had to be balanced by the power of Parliament. Charles's first major foray into national affairs was as one of the commissioners who, in 1706, negotiated a treaty of union between England and Scotland. Then three years later he was sent to The Hague to help negotiate a peace with the French. From there, Charles also assisted thousands of Palatine war refugees displaced from the Lower Rhine, to migrate to England, supporting some of them out of his own pocket. It has been claimed that these refugees included members of the Phillip family whose descendant, Arthur Phillip, was to command the First Fleet to Botany Bay.[10]

The bishop of Salisbury described Charles Townshend as 'a man of great integrity ... free from all vice'. Nevertheless, he turned out to be a poor peace negotiator, with a reputation for being 'impatient of contradiction... and often perplexed in argument'. Ongoing difficulties with the French negotiations led to a change of ministers in 1710 and Charles found himself out of office. However, Queen Anne's death four years later triggered the so called Act of Settlement whereby her closest Protestant relative George Louis, elector of Hanover, became king ahead of Anne's Catholic half-brother, James Stuart. Before long, this new king, George I, was at loggerheads with his Tory ministers who had worked hard to put James Stuart on the throne. As a prominent Whig, Charles Townshend was soon returned to office, helping the king put down a rebellion of James's supporters in Scotland.[11]

Following his wife Elizabeth's death, Charles had married Robert Walpole's sister, Dorothy. By now, Walpole was also a leading Whig politician and the political partnership between these brothers-in-law soon became known as 'the firm of Townshend and Walpole'. For a time, Charles was pre-eminent. But the Earl of Chesterfield noted that although Charles 'spoke materially, with argument and knowledge... he never pleased [because] his diction was... inelegant... frequently ungrammatical [and] always vulgar: his cadences false; his voice unharmonious and his actions ungraceful'. And Walpole, who was in the Commons, began to dominate the partnership as the importance of the lower House grew. Describing him as 'the ablest manager of Parliament that I believe ever lived', Chesterfield remarked on Walpole's ability to clearly state 'the most intricate matters... [so] that while he was speaking the most ignorant thought they understood what they really did not'.

Walpole's ascendancy became apparent when he seized the initiative by proposing legislation to deal with the South Sea Bubble financial crisis which had threatened public credit. And it was not long before he became known disparagingly as 'prime minister' – Britain's first. The firm now became known as 'Walpole and Townshend' and tensions developed, especially after the death of Charles's wife Dorothy. The accession to the throne in 1727 of George II, who got on better with Walpole than with Townshend, was another factor, not least because his wife, Queen Caroline, also preferred Walpole.[12]

Many years later, Tommy Townshend, who took a keen interest in his family's tales of political intrigue, wrote of a dispute which broke up his grandfather Charles's firm. Apparently Walpole and another brother-in-law, the Duke of

Newcastle, had outmanoeuvred Charles over some negotiations with Spain. And during a discussion over parliamentary tactics at the home of Tommy's maternal grandfather, John Selwyn, Walpole sneered at Charles: 'There is no man's sincerity which I doubt more than yours.' Furious, Charles called Walpole a 'brute' whereupon they laid hands on their swords, prompting Selwyn's wife to summon the guards. Although the two men had been separated by the time help arrived, the damage was done.

Tommy attributed their 'unusual want of temper' to the fact that they 'had some deceit which they had agreed to keep to themselves but had both imparted in confidence to the Queen'. Envious of their close relationship, the queen had thought that making them jealous of each other might also make them more manageable. She had let each of them know that the other had trusted her. Apparently Walpole had arrived at Selwyn's house after discovering this. Later, the queen was mortified to hear of the violent confrontation she had triggered, but now forced to choose she did not hesitate to back Walpole. And when Charles attempted to establish an independent relationship with the king, 'Her Majesty ... overthrew the whole tactic'.[13]

Retiring from politics, Charles withdrew to his Raynham estate. There he experimented with crops including a four-course rotation of cereal, turnips, cereal and grasses to get the best out of the poor Norfolk soil. As a result, these soils were 'turned into gold'. And by the time of his death in 1738, Charles 'Turnip Townshend' was at the forefront of England's agricultural revolution.[14]

[*Two*]

— Young Tommy Townshend —

The entry in the *Gentleman's Magazine* was short and to the point: 'the Lady of the Hon. Thomas Townshend, Esq; second Son of the L'd Visc. Townshend, deliver'd of a son'. Born in London on 24 February 1733, Thomas Townshend the younger was a first-born child – known from his earliest days as 'young Tommy' to differentiate him from his father.[1]

Thomas the elder, who had been born in 1701, was the second son of Charles, Viscount Townshend and his first wife Elizabeth Pelham. Like the sons of many Whig families, Thomas was educated at Eton and King's College, Cambridge. Then, at the age of just 21, he was elected to the House of Commons where he soon became his father's under secretary, accompanying him on trips to Hanover with the king. In 1727, Thomas switched constituencies so he could represent Cambridge University, a Whig stronghold controlled by his uncle, the Duke of Newcastle.[2]

Young Tommy's mother, Albinia Selwyn, was only sixteen when she married Thomas in 1730. Her father, John, represented Gloucester in the Commons while her mother, Mary, had been a woman of the bedchamber to Queen Caroline. Described as 'a beautiful and amiable lady to whom … [Thomas] was tenderly attached', Albinia bore him five children before dying at the age of 25. For Thomas, the trauma of his wife's early death was offset by the generosity of his father-in-law. Although Albinia had two brothers, their father settled the moated manor of Scadbury in Chislehurst, Kent, upon Thomas because the Selwyn boys were seen as nothing but eccentric wastrels. The strange ways of Albinia's brother, George, centred on his morbid interest in public executions. When George was chided for watching a condemned man's head being chopped off, he replied: 'Why? I made amends by going to the undertaker's to see it being sewn on again'. Of John Selwyn's children, Albinia was the sensible one.[3]

Thomas's occupation of Scadbury was fortuitous because as a younger son he had no claim to his father's title or to Raynham, his Norfolk estate. His plan had been to rebuild the Scadbury manor house. But overcome by his wife's death, Thomas soon took over the next door Frognal mansion, 'a fine old brick house of the Stuart period', which was to remain the seat of his descendants for over a hundred and fifty years. As much an academic as he was a politician, with a special interest in Latin, Thomas was well suited to represent the University of Cambridge whose five hundred electors comprised those with higher degrees. Although he rarely spoke in Parliament, Thomas attended to Cambridge's interests, introducing legislation to crack down on people who sold liquor in the university's cellars without the chancellor's permission. Shortly after Thomas's death in 1780, the vice-chancellor wrote that he had been one of the first and most elegant scholars of his age. 'His cheerfulness and serenity of temper', the vice-chancellor said, 'gained…[Thomas] universal affection and respect'.[4]

Britain's three dominant prime ministers during the first half of the eighteenth century were Robert Walpole 1721–42, Henry Pelham 1743–54 and the Duke of Newcastle, 1754–56 and 1757–62. Thanks to the fact that Pelham and Newcastle were his uncles and Walpole was his 'step uncle', Thomas enjoyed the post of teller of the exchequer, one of the greatest sinecures in government. Even so, he was not above sharing some barbed poetry with one uncle, Pelham, at the expense of the other two. Perhaps referring to their double-cross of his father over those negotiations with Spain, Thomas wrote:

> Profound yet empty shallow yet obscure…
> [Newcastle] thinks himself a mighty politician
> Say how the coxcombe plays the fool abroad
> As Robin Walpole plays the rogue at home.

Thomas was due to be promoted chief secretary to the lord-lieutenant of Ireland. But when his wife died, possibly from a complicated pregnancy, he turned the job down. A widower at the age of 38 with five young children to look after, Thomas was now content to remain an exchequer teller and the squire of Frognal mansion with its magnificent formal gardens, stables and out-buildings.[5]

Young Tommy was just six when his mother passed away in 1739. And within two years, he was packed off to his father's alma mater, Eton. Leaving his childhood playground of moats, terraced landscapes and ornate fountains to his younger siblings – Charles, Henry, Albinia and Mary – young Tommy took up lodgings in a private boarding house adjacent to his school. In the 1740s, Eton's curriculum focused on Latin and Greek verse composition and rote learning. French could be taken as an extra and Tommy's later proficiency in that language suggests he studied it. Tommy and his father enjoyed swapping Eton stories. One involved an old lady, Sarah Bramston, who sold pies at the school. Nicknamed 'the Dame', Sarah was a strong supporter of the Stuart pretenders to the British throne. Despite her politics, the Dame somehow managed to survive at this great Whig school. And after her death in 1765, Tommy wrote to his father: 'Dame Sarah ... was equally famous for her politics and pastry'.[6]

Of all his relatives, it was his eldest cousin, George Townshend, who cut the most dashing figure during young Tommy's school years. Almost ten years older, the handsome George had first seen active service in 1743. This was thanks to his great-uncle, Newcastle, who got him a staff job in time for the battle of Dettingen, at which an army under the direct command of King George II defeated the French. 'The enemy ... [was] received with great firmness', one report said, 'and so great was the slaughter that they ... were obliged to scamper'. In a rematch at the battle of Fontenoy, the British, now led by the king's son, the Duke of Cumberland, were the losers. Still, George Townshend fought well and was promoted to command a company.[7]

In the spring of 1745, with nearly all regular British troops away in Flanders and George II in Hanover, the Stuart pretender, Bonnie Prince Charlie, judged the moment right to attack England from Scotland. The early battles went well for the Prince who had a major victory at Preston Pans. This created alarm in London as the rebels advanced halfway through England. According to the *Gentleman's Magazine*:

> They marched about a mile from Derby ... ordered a very large sum of money to be raised instantly ... and threatened destruction to the whole town if they

did not raise more. They seemed to be extremely out of humour and stripped some persons of their clothes.

For young Tommy, still a boarder at Eton, it was an exciting and unsettling time. Cousin George was among the English troops rushed back from Flanders to meet the threat head on. Under Cumberland's command, the English pursued the rebels deep into Scotland, crushing them at the bloody battle of Culloden, the last to be fought on British soil. But George's regiment, which was in the second line, suffered only minor losses.[8]

Returning to Flanders with Cumberland, who was now referred to behind his back as 'the butcher', George again saw action during the battle of Laffeldt. Standing next to a German officer when the poor fellow's head was blown off by a shell, George wiped the mess from his coat. 'I never knew Scheiger had so many brains', he said. This crazy-brave attitude enhanced George's career and he was soon promoted to lieutenant-colonel and elected to the House of Commons. But the battle itself was another defeat for 'butcher Cumberland' and hastened a negotiated peace with France.

At home, this conflict saw the political emergence of William Pitt the Elder who had been brought into government by Prime Minister Pelham because he had been so troublesome in opposition. '[Pitt] commands the passions with a sovereign authority and...is a consummate orator', one contemporary noted. 'He has courage of every sort...is imperious, violent and implacable; impatient of even the slightest contradiction and under the mask of patriotism has the despotic spirit of a tyrant'. This charismatic force of nature made an unforgettable impression on young Tommy as he prepared to leave Eton for Cambridge. By now full of bumptious ambition and self-confidence, Tommy was a stark contrast to his father who, for a politician, was modest and retiring.[9]

The sense of family tradition young Tommy felt at Eton was even stronger at Cambridge where his father was a graduate, the local member and the donor of annual prizes. But unlike Thomas who had attended King's College, young Tommy opted for Clare Hall which, being founded in 1326, was just within the bounds of acceptable family rebellion. Although he was not like his father an 'elegant scholar', Tommy was no fool. And in later public life, he demonstrated an impressive knowledge of constitutional history and command of French.[10]

After graduating Master of Arts from Cambridge in 1753, young Tommy took the Grand Tour of Europe, then a rite of passage for wealthy Englishmen. Keeping up a constant correspondence with his father, brothers and sisters, Tommy wrote from Lausanne that he and his boon companions were 'very apt to herd with the Frenchmen'. Even so, value for money was his constant preoccupation. 'One month at Paris', he noted, 'will be as expensive as two at Turin'. Moreover the difference between hiring a chair (a seat closed to the weather and carried by two bearers) in Turin and in Paris was so great, Tommy said, that 'they must not be compared together'. Keen to get to Turin to take dancing lessons, Tommy was excited to find a bargain. 'The [dancing] Academy is certainly the cheapest place', he said. His concern for economy aside, the highlight of young Tommy's tour was herding with Frenchmen.[11]

As his Tour wound up, Tommy noted that more than half his English friends had already gone home. They were accompanied by some 'fearless Frenchmen', he said, including the Comte de Gisors, a striking young man who was later to die leading a celebrated charge against Prussian troops. '[Gisors] is not so prejudiced against us as ... his countrymen are', Tommy noted glibly, 'and is not afraid of being burned ... by an English mob which ... most Frenchmen think [is] a necessary consequence of going to England'. This naïve self-assurance which appears in Tommy's letters is also captured in a portrait of him as a young man. Standing with his hand on his hip in a typically haughty, born-to-rule Townshend manner, there is just a hint of unease in his pose which is totally missing from similar portraits of his cousins George and Charles Townshend. Inheriting his mother's rounded forehead and long facial features, rather than the more aquiline and handsome Townshend profile, young Tommy reveals the beginnings of a paunch which was to become more noticeable in middle age.[12]

Young Tommy, or just plain 'Tommy' as he was increasingly being called, now stepped forward for a career in the House of Commons.

[*Three*]

⸺ The parliamentary apprentice ⸺

Like his father before him, Tommy Townshend was just 21 when he first entered the Commons following the general election of 1754. As his father's nominee, Tommy was elected unopposed in Whitchurch, a borough electorate of 70 voters whose special property holdings, known as burgages, gave them the right to cast a ballot. But these rights could be bought, sold and controlled by one patron, sometimes for as much as 10,000 pounds, when the land they were attached to was worth just 100 pounds. Even so, Tommy's father did not have to pay a penny, having inherited the patronage of one of Whitchurch's two Commons' seats from his father-in-law, John Selwyn, who had passed away in 1751. Although such seats were supposedly safe, they still required careful political management. Houses were kept empty until shortly before an election when the patron would convey them to friends, to be returned to him after the ballot. In 1752 Tommy's father received a bill for 66 pounds to repair such a house which had been 'almost wholly pulled down by the mob'.[1]

The Commons Tommy joined consisted of 558 members. But the distribution of electorates was uneven, ranging from 20,000 voters in Yorkshire to just seven, in Old Sarum. And the parliamentary building, described by one observer as a 'venerable rabbit-warren', was as ramshackle as the system that selected the members to sit in it. According to one contemporary inspection report, 'the House of Commons... is an ancient building... so surrounded by [others]... as the expose the whole to a general conflagration'. Occupying St Stephen's Chapel, which fronted a garden alongside the River Thames at Westminster, the chamber itself was a room about 58 feet long by 33 feet wide and 30 feet high. The speaker's chair, which was backed by ornately carved white painted timber, trimmed in gold and surmounted by a crest, was placed on the altar steps, while the clerks' table had replaced the lectern in the middle of the choir. During the day, the chamber was sunlit by three large fanlight windows behind the speaker. For evening debates, members relied on a series of lamps, the largest of which, resembling a cross between a collection of mushrooms and a chandelier, hung from the ceiling. Members sat in collegiate stalls fixed in rows along the walls. Overhanging them on three sides were galleries supported by thin columns. Still, the chamber was far too small to seat all the members at one time. So debates were intimate and personal.[2]

As a new member, it is unlikely that Tommy got to witness the king's message being read shortly after Parliament re-opened on 31 May 1754. But there was not much to hear. Indeed because the king did not 'think it proper now to lay before [Parliament] any points of general business', the Commons adjourned for six months. None of the members then assembled could have known that just days beforehand, Major George Washington of the king's Virginia militia had ambushed a mixed force of French and Indians some 3,000 miles away in the American backwoods. Later, this was to be acknowledged as the opening skirmish of a seven-year-long world war which would lead to the American and French revolutions. However, it was over a month before news of Washington's ambush reached London and much longer before its significance was understood, even by senior ministers. When the Duke of Newcastle was told that Annapolis (Maryland) must be defended, he replied, 'to be sure Annapolis must be defended – where is Annapolis?'[3]

During Tommy's early years in Parliament, if someone had called out 'Townshend with an h' on the floor of the Commons, so as not to confuse those Townsends without an 'h', up to six heads might still have turned in acknowledgment. Apart from Tommy and his father Thomas, his younger brother Henry represented Eye, cousin George represented Norfolk, cousin Charles represented Saltash and another cousin Charles, nicknamed 'Spanish Charles' because of his embassy service in Madrid, represented Great Yarmouth. In addition, Tommy's uncle George Selwyn was member for Gloucester, while Tommy's brother-in-law George Brodrick, husband of Tommy's sister, Albinia represented Ashburton.

As members of a family close to the centre of political power, they would all have mourned the death of their relative, Prime Minister Pelham, on 6

March 1754. Yet they would all have been comforted that Pelham's brother, the garrulous Duke of Newcastle, soon replaced him. To his family, the Duke was 'generous... free from pride [and] attached to his King and... country'. But Newcastle was renowned for his eccentricities, including a propensity to weep, which led his enemies to describe him as 'the most curiously ridiculous being ... the falsest of politicians, the most imbecile of all political Dukes'. And King George II was unsettled by the change. During Pelham's nine years as prime minister, it was said that a bird might build a nest in the speaker's chair and no debate would disturb it. On hearing of Pelham's death, the king fretted 'now I shall have no more peace'.[4]

Although Tommy represented a safe seat, this did not guarantee him peace as a local member. In May 1755, he received a disturbing report from a supporter, Thomas Bingham, of violent local opposition led by a Mr Portal who had resolved to oppose Tommy on all occasions:

> Last night [Portal] came into our room where the club were met unsent for and... I thought it not safe to continue in his company... whereupon [he] brake out into such volley of oaths as I've scarce overheard from a gentleman... that I could not bear it.

Located in Hampshire on the Test, one of England's finest trout rivers, Whitchurch's bucolic isolation was threatened in the mid-eighteenth century by 'turnpike mania' when networks of new, high speed, tolled roads sprang up all over Britain. These allowed super-fast 'flying machines' to replace much slower stage coaches, cutting some longer trips from six days to two. Even so, there were demonstrations against these roads and a suspicion that they were designed only for wealthy travellers. Divided by the east-west road from London to Exeter and the north-south road from Oxford to Southampton, Whitchurch flourished. But not everyone was happy with this progress. And Thomas Bingham complained to Tommy that his parish would be 'very much oppressed' by a Turnpike Bill then before the Commons.[5]

Tommy's parliamentary peers immediately pigeonholed him as a Whig in the Townshend family tradition. But just about every ambitious new member identified himself that way and the government's problem was 'to find enough pasture for the beasts ... [to] feed'. There were only about 100 Tory members and they were not organized. Prime Minister Newcastle was more likely to face opposition from within his own party. Keen to enlist the support of his relatives to entrench his position, Newcastle soon appointed Tommy as a clerk of the household to George, Prince of Wales. Ambitious and self confident, Tommy welcomed this position which placed him at the centre of court intrigue during the dying days of George II's reign.[6]

The prince had turned eighteen on 4 June 1756 and so it had become necessary to establish a separate household for him. The king had had a bad relationship with his own son, Frederick, and had called him 'no son of mine'. This in turn had soured the king's relationship with his daughter-in-law and also with her son, Prince George. Frederick had been the king's heir apparent. But he had died in 1751 after being hit by a cricket ball. Concerned now that the young Prince George might shortly become king himself, Newcastle prevailed on an elderly George II to appoint John Stuart, the Earl of Bute, to head up the prince's household. While Newcastle was keen to accommodate this 'most ardent request' of the prince, he also had misgivings. Lord Bute was descended from a bastard branch of the Scottish royal family. And with the best legs in London, he was rumoured to be having an affair with the prince's widowed mother. Newcastle therefore appointed Tommy and some other young Whigs to Prince George's household to keep an eye on things. But the young prince's defiance grew. 'I have too much spirit to accept the Crown and be a mere cipher', he told Bute – an ominous signal for Newcastle and the Whigs who had been treating George II as a cipher for years. Nevertheless, their most immediate problem was the widening war with France.[7]

French retaliation over Major Washington's ambush had led to a swift escalation in hostilities and Newcastle dispatched Major-General Edward Braddock to take command. After leading his men through the American wilderness as if they were marching from London to Windsor, Braddock was ambushed. Mortally wounded, his last words were 'we shall know better how to deal with them next time', while Washington barely escaped with his life. For Newcastle the news was no better at sea when Admiral Byng failed to engage a French fleet off the Mediterranean island of Minorca, forcing the British garrison to surrender. In an attempt to divert the angry public reaction to this news and mindful of the popular rhyme, 'hang Byng or take care of your King', Newcastle had Byng court-martialled and shot dead on the quarterdeck of a warship in Portsmouth harbour. But this was not enough to save Newcastle. He was forced to make way for a shaky alliance between the Duke of Devonshire as nominal prime minister and William Pitt, who wielded the real power.[8]

It was soon clear, however, that this combination would not work. And so Newcastle returned as prime minister to fund the war, while Pitt stood by his side as secretary of state, to run it. 'The Duke of Newcastle and Pitt jog on like man and wife, seldom agreeing [and] often quarrelling', the Earl of Chesterfield said, 'but by mutual interest upon the whole, not parting'. Years of political hostility between these two, during which Tommy had felt obliged to support his distinguished relative, came to an end – replaced by a messy partnership. Nevertheless, it was an arrangement which allowed Tommy to embrace his political hero without offending his great-uncle.

Although Newcastle was prime minister of the new wartime government, Pitt was in charge – the Winston Churchill of his day. 'The Treasury, Admiralty and War Office all obeyed ... [Pitt's] orders with prompt and implicit submission', one parliamentary observer noted, 'and although Newcastle often complained, he always complied'. King Frederick of Prussia was characteristically blunt: 'England has been in travail a long time; at last she has brought forth a man'.[9]

Although Tommy looked up to Pitt, he was no slavish disciple. And when Pitt introduced a Bill prohibiting newly elected members from taking their seats until they had sworn that they met a property test 'in a full House with the Speaker in the Chair', Tommy waded in. Pitt's proposal was unworkable, he said, because members had to take their seats before a speaker was chosen. It was a good point. But a more prudent junior member might have remained silent. However, this was not to be Tommy's style. With a passion still bordering on bumptiousness, Tommy continued to present a stark contrast to his gentlemanly father.[10]

Tommy was a strong supporter of Pitt's plan to ally himself with King Frederick of Prussia. As Pitt saw it, Frederick would pin down the French in Europe, allowing the British to pick off far-flung French colonies. But the financial cost of this strategy was huge, involving direct subsidies to Frederick of 670,000 pounds per year, together with payments of 1,200,000 pounds a year to King George's Hanoverian army. And along the way there was humiliation for the king when the French overran most of Hanover, his birthplace. In London, Tommy received regular reports from those on active service including his brother, Harry, and his cousin, Charles Cornwallis, son of Thomas Townshend's sister Elizabeth. 'I have been appointed aide-de-camp to your friend Granby', Cornwallis wrote, 'and beg when Harry comes home covered with laurels… you will ensure him of my sincere joy'. On 1 August 1759, Charles and Harry accompanied Lord Granby, a renowned cavalry commander, at the battle of Minden in North Germany. Described by an old Etonian classmate as 'very handsome, very good natured, clever and spirited – in short a noble creature', Harry was wounded. But the battle was a great victory for the combined British–Prussian force of 30,000 which routed a French army more than twice its size. This was despite the British commander, George Sackville, ignoring his Prussian commander-in-chief's direction that Granby's cavalry be given the order to charge. Jealous that such a charge would deliver Granby all the glory, Sackville was court-martialled and only narrowly avoided the death penalty, being dishonourably discharged instead. Now known as the 'coward of Minden', Sackville set about restoring his reputation. So began a process, including a name change to George Germain, which many years later would lead to his appointment as secretary of state for America.[11]

Of France's far-flung colonies, Canada topped Pitt's target list as he planned a multi-pronged attack on his enemy's North American strong-points. Lieutenant-General Jeffrey Amherst was to sweep up Lake George and Lake Champlain to Montreal, where Major-General James Wolfe was to meet him after taking Quebec to the east. But Quebec was the biggest target because it controlled access along the St Lawrence River to the interior of French North America.[12]

[*Four*]

Cousin George and the conquest of Quebec

Tommy Townshend's cousin George was the eldest son of the third Viscount Townshend and his wife, Audrey Harrison. Renowned for her beauty, wit and sexual promiscuity, Audrey's superior contempt of reputation was inherited by her son. After falling out with his commander, the Duke of Cumberland, over the need for legislation to raise a militia, George Townshend drew cartoons of the morbidly obese duke 'which adorned the shutters, walls and napkins of every tavern in Pall Mall'. It mattered not that the duke was the king's son. Full of his mother's contempt for authority, George savagely lampooned Cumberland as a 'prodigious mass' of royal flesh. So bad did this feud become, that George was forced to leave the army in 1750. And even the promotion of his younger brother, Roger, was affected.[1]

Turning to a career in Parliament, George was described by one of his Commons' colleagues, Horace Walpole, a renowned writer and son of the former prime minister, as 'a very particular young man... with great fickleness, greater want of judgment and with still more disposition to ridicule'. When his ally, William Pitt, formed a parliamentary alliance which included the Duke of Cumberland's friend, Henry Fox, George had stormed off, calling it 'a ridiculous and dishonest arrangement of men'. But these very same men were now waging a war which George desperately wanted to fight in.[2]

It was Pitt's 'patriot program' of mobilization that led to George's military salvation. Both were agreed on the need for a strong local militia to free up the army for fighting abroad. So George's bill to expand the militia, which had met such stiff resistance from Cumberland because he thought it would siphon off army resources, was now championed by Pitt. And it duly became law. Moreover, Butcher Cumberland's string of defeats in battle had worn down his father, the king, who replaced him as commander-in-chief. So when George wrote to Pitt on 27 August 1758 volunteering for service 'as a Colonel in the line', the de facto prime minister agreed.[3]

Restored to his former rank of lieutenant-colonel, George was soon seeing action in raids along the French coast which were part of a hit-and-run strategy Pitt had devised. But the centre piece of Pitt's ambition was to humble France by conquering Canada, where a British force had captured Fort Louisburg which guarded approaches to the St Lawrence River. Brigadier James Wolfe had distinguished himself in this battle. So as a reward, Pitt promoted Wolfe, just 32, placing him in command of the planned attack on Quebec. When the Duke of Newcastle told George II that Wolfe was mad, the king replied, 'Mad is he? Then I hope he will bite some of my other generals'. To serve as Wolfe's three brigadiers, Pitt nominated Robert Monckton, George Townshend and James Murray with seniority in that order. 'Ambition, activity, industry and passion for service were conspicuous in Wolfe', Horace Walpole said. 'To him was associated George Townshend whose proud, solemn and contemptuous temper never suffered him to wait for thwarting his superiors'.[4]

George's brother Roger was already in Canada, advancing on Montreal as part of Lieutenant-General Amherst's force. Aware that George's North Atlantic crossing to Nova Scotia in the early spring of 1759 would be bitterly cold and debilitating, Roger had ensured that 'a large quantity of vegetables and roots' would be available when his brother landed, to help him regain his strength. But they would not meet again. Just weeks later, Roger was fatally wounded by a cannon ball during an attack on Fort Ticonderoga. And George worried that their mother would now 'start at every knock at the door'.[5]

Quebec was a natural fortress protected by 300-foot high cliffs. The fast running St Lawrence River, 1,300 yards wide, stood in the way of its southern approaches, while to the east, it was shielded by the Montmorency River which included a 200-foot high waterfall. Moreover the talented French commander, Louis-Joseph de Montcalm, had fortified these natural assets, entrenching his 14,000 troops. The only lightly defended area was to the west of Quebec where Montcalm thought that the river cliffs leading to the Plain of Abraham were too steep to climb. Wolfe, who had only 9,000 regular soldiers including

George Townshend's brigade of 1,487, took up a position at Point Levi on the south side of the St Lawrence River and began to bombard Quebec. To break what was otherwise a stalemate, Wolfe settled on a plan to attack the French troops dug in on the western side of the Montmorency River. George was to lead a force of 2,000 across the mouth of this river, to support Monckton and Wolfe who were to land much closer to the French lines.

For reasons best known to Wolfe, the attack did not begin until 4.00 p.m. on 31 July. Still, George's force crossed the Montmorency River and marched along the beach in good order towards the French. But contrary to Wolfe's expectations, the enemy did not leave their fortified positions to fight in the open. Instead, they raked George's exposed troops with withering fire from their trenches. Wolfe therefore ordered a retreat. And although George's force managed to do so, again in good order, the British suffered 443 casualties.[6]

Wolfe's reputation among his troops was now badly shaken. And George began caricaturing him as savagely as he had Cumberland. One cartoon depicted Wolfe responding to a deputation of Canadian women who were begging for mercy: 'That depends, my pretty ones. Write more petitions. Send fifty beautiful virgins to me at once.' Wolfe retaliated by criticizing George's fortifications, claiming also that his troops were too slow to make camp on new ground. When George reported to Wolfe that he had observed Montcalm through a telescope aiming extra artillery in his direction, Wolfe laughed him off. Furious, George now formed a cabal of other high-born officers including Murray. 'Some difference of opinion upon some military point termed slight', Wolfe noted in his dairy, 'and ... the commander-in-chief is threatened with a Parliamentary inquiry'.[7]

All the French had to do was to sit tight and let the fast-approaching Canadian winter defeat the British for them. 'Unless Wolfe lands above the town and forces me to battle I am safe', Montcalm noted. 'Strange if Wolfe didn't do something ... he is obliged to make one final effort'. Now seriously ill with kidney disease, Wolfe called a council of war to get the advice of his three brigadiers. This, he hoped, would lock in George's cabal, giving him some insurance against a possible parliamentary inquiry. Wolfe then proposed another advance from the east, an idea his brigadiers rejected out of hand. Instead, they advised:

The most probable method of striking an effectual blow is to ... carry the operations above the town. If we can establish ourselves on the north shore ... Montcalm must fight us on our own terms. We are between him and his provisions and between him and the French army opposing General Amherst. If he gives us battle and we defeat him Quebec and probably all Canada will be our own.[8]

Accepting this, Wolfe set off in a little boat on 10 September to study the north shore of the St Lawrence, upriver from Quebec, in the area that the French thought was impregnable. With him, disguised in grenadiers' greatcoats, were Monckton and Townshend. From a vantage point on some high ground west of Quebec, they could see that the Plain of Abraham was lightly defended in the vicinity of the Anse au Foulon Cove at Sillery. Their little boat then drifted downstream, allowing a detailed study of the cliffs above this cove, which was further down river than Pointe aux Trembles, the landing place proposed by the brigadiers. Close inspection of the Foulon cliffs revealed a very steep path to the plain that was blocked in numerous places. Wolfe then made his decision, at first keeping it to himself. But when the brigadiers demanded to know the 'the places we are to attack as we should be sorry to commit any mistakes', Wolfe told them, 'the place is called Foulon distant upon 2 miles ... from Quebec'.[9]

The British assault force took to the water on the evening of 12 September 1759, drifting down river with the advantage of a moonless night. Along the way, an enemy sentry challenged 'Qui vivre?' to which a Captain Frazer replied 'la France et vivre le Roy'. Although the sentry was satisfied, the rapidly running tide created another problem, carrying an advance party beyond the intended landing place. In one of the other leading barges, Wolfe himself landed in the right spot, with Monckton, Murray and their regiments close behind. Their boats then went back for George and his regiment while the advance party, which had managed to land downstream, back-tracked. Soon an enemy battery opened up and Wolfe ordered a halt to further landings. But his command was ignored and George's troops were brought across. The battery was quickly silenced and before long Wolfe had 4,828 men lined up on the Plain of Abraham. 'I see them where they ought not to be', Montcalm said. 'This, my friends, is a serious business'.[10]

Townshend's regiment had formed up on the left flank, furthest away from the St Lawrence River. Next in line was Murray's regiment with Wolfe in the centre, while the right-hand flank closest to the river was covered by Monckton's men. Being on the landward side, Townshend's light infantry was engaged early, repelling the enemy's attempts to slip behind the British line and attack them from the rear.[11]

By the time the main battle commenced at 10.00 a.m. on 13 September, Wolfe had already been wounded in the wrist. The British held their fire until the enemy was just forty paces away. Then Wolfe's men fired a massive volley, advanced and fired again. When the French wavered under shock of this onslaught, Wolfe gave the order to charge. Almost immediately, he was fatally hit. 'They run, they run', someone shouted. 'Who run?' the mortally wounded Wolfe asked. 'The enemy sir. Egad! They give way everywhere'.[12]

As the British charge progressed, individual soldiers began pursuing the French helter-skelter back towards the enemy's fortified lines. The order of the British regiments quickly disintegrated and Wolfe's second in command, Monckton, was hit by a musket ball which penetrated his lungs. All the while the danger grew that a French reserve force, under the command of Colonel Louis Antoine de Bougainville and encamped further up river, might arrive behind the British lines. It was at this precarious time that George Townshend took control of all the British forces. He immediately ordered all battalion commanders to stop their pursuit of the enemy and reform their units. This was none too soon as George later wrote:

> Bougainville with about 2,000 men ... appeared in our rear – I advanced two pieces of light artillery and two battalions towards him but upon two or three shots he retired ... it was not my business to risk the fruits of so glorious a day and to abandon so commanding a situation to give fresh enemy battle on his terms and in the woods and swamps.[13]

Montcalm had also been mortally wounded and, when Bougainville retreated, the battle was effectively over. During the next few days, as George prepared to bombard Quebec itself with his land and sea batteries, the French decided to surrender. And so on 18 September George Townshend countersigned the French articles of capitulation. These guaranteed that the French-Canadians would be 'preserved in the possession of their houses, goods...and privileges...and that the exercise of the Catholic...religion shall be maintained' – they would be allowed to keep their laws and religion.[14]

After dispatching news of the victory to Pitt, George sailed for London on 18 October. Although Britain rejoiced, George's political enemies were circling. '[Townshend] and his friends...attempted to ravish the honour of the conquest from Wolfe', Horace Walpole charged, 'and indirectly assume the glory'. This was a reference to George's claim that 'we determined on 13 September to do what we ought to have done in the beginning'. Many now alleged that George was diminishing the martyred Wolfe's role in order to boost his own.[15]

Although George's career never fully recovered from this attack on his reputation, historians have acknowledged his role. 'The merit of...[Wolfe's] daring plan belongs to Colonel George Townshend', one of Canada's foremost historians, George Warburton, wrote, 'although long disputed or withheld by jealousy or political hostility'. And later historians are unanimous in emphasizing that George's prudence in reforming the British battalions to face Bougainville was of supreme importance to the outcome. But the French army was not destroyed and on 28 April 1760 the battle of Quebec was fought in reverse against Murray, by this time holed up in the remains of the French trenches. However, the British noose was tightening and on 8 September the French surrendered Montreal and with it all of French Canada – an enormous area stretching up from the Mississippi River to lands under the control of the Hudson's Bay Company in the far north.[16]

For so long as the French colonists in Canada and Louisiana had hemmed in the British colonies along the North American seaboard, the king's subjects on both sides of the Atlantic had been united against their ancient enemy. But once 'relieved from the dread of France', the American colonists assumed a much more spirited and independent identity. Henceforth, 'any provocation to the Colonies was doubly dangerous'.[17]

[*Five*]

George III and Tommy's Whig Inheritance

By the beginning of 1760, Britain's church bells had been 'worn threadbare with the ringing of victories' in North America, India and Europe. William Pitt was at the peak of his popularity and power. Then, on 25 October that year, George II died of a heart attack and his grandson, the Prince of Wales, assumed the throne as George III. 'Born and educated in this country', the new king told Parliament, 'I glory in the name of Briton'. As the first English-born monarch in almost half a century, George III was determined to stamp his authority on his Whig ministers who had dominated his German-born grandfather. And the young king's head of household, Lord Bute, was keen to help.[1]

George III's initial clash with his senior ministers arose over what he proposed to say at his first formal cabinet meeting. A draft speech, prepared by Lord Bute, referred to 'a bloody and expensive war' and to the need for 'an honourable and lasting peace'. For William Pitt, these words amounted to a repudiation of his victories over the French. And after a day of aggressive lobbying Pitt managed to get them changed to 'an expensive, just and necessary war' and 'an honourable peace in concert with our allies'. But in return, the king insisted that Lord Bute be made a senior minister.[2]

Meanwhile, the Whig government, still nominally led by the Duke of Newcastle, gave Tommy Townshend a modest promotion, making him a clerk of the board of green cloth – a minor treasury position. This left him with enough time to sponsor a bill enabling the naturalization of foreign Protestants who had served in the Royal American Regiment, many of them under his cousin George at Quebec.[3]

The young king's desire for an end to the war was popular with the public and so William Pitt turned his mind to peace negotiations. But the discovery of a secret agreement between France and Spain made Pitt reconsider. Now convinced that war with Spain was inevitable, he proposed that Britain should strike first. This Lord Bute opposed, while the Duke of Newcastle sat on the fence. Pitt's brothers-in-law, who were also ministers, were divided too; George Grenville supported Bute while Lord Temple backed Pitt. In the end, Lord Bute had his way. And on 5 October 1761, Pitt and Temple resigned in protest.[4]

The following January, Britain did go to war with Spain. Continuing Pitt's policy of attacking the colonies of her European enemies, she won a string of further victories in the West Indies, Havana and Manila. But in Europe it was a different story. Having described his late grandfather's birthplace, Hanover, as a 'horrible electorate', George III was unwilling to adopt Pitt's policy of subsidizing the Germans to fight the French on the continent. And when the Duke of Newcastle proposed raising 2,000,000 pounds a year to assist Frederick the Great of Prussia, Lord Bute opposed him. In this dispute, which was widely debated beyond cabinet, Tommy Townshend sided with his great-uncle. 'Is there a nation on earth that will trust you again', one of Tommy's supporters asked, 'if you carry on your wars in this uncertain manner?' When Lord Bute prevailed, the Duke of Newcastle resigned. And a furious King Frederick never did trust Britain again.

On 7 May 1762, George III appointed Lord Bute to fill Newcastle's place. The man, who until recently had been head of the young king's household, was now his prime minister. Bute's parliamentary allies, George Grenville and Henry Fox, became secretary of state and leader of the House of Commons respectively. But even though the Whigs' long hold on power collapsed, Tommy Townshend clung to office as a treasury clerk.[5]

Meanwhile Tommy's relations had continued on active service in Europe. After a successful action against the French at the battle of Vellinghausen, George Townshend saw out the remainder of the war as a lieutenant-general in the army of Britain's ally, Portugal. Tommy's younger brother, Harry, by now a colonel, was less fortunate. As Harry's mentor, Tommy had obtained James Wolfe's counsel in 1756. To succeed in the army, Wolfe had advised, twenty-year-old Harry should study mathematics. But Harry also studied Wolfe's pursuit of glory in combat, emulating his hero at the battle of Wilhelmstaal in June 1762. 'He lost his life seeking the post of honour that his duty did not require', the regimental record said. 'He was the only officer of rank killed in this action'. Among Tommy's papers at the William L. Clements Library in Michigan is the following tribute to his younger brother:

> Like Wolfe, a patriot and a generous friend –
> Alas! Too like that warrior in his end.[6]

From as early as November 1761, Lord Bute had been in secret negotiations with the French. Now as prime minister, he had to settle a peace acceptable to the cabinet, the Parliament and Britain's allies. All the while, the political ghost of William Pitt hovered in the background. For the return of Havana to Spain, the cabinet insisted on obtaining Florida and Puerto Rico, fearing a furious political reaction from Pitt if they settled for anything less. However, it turned out that Britain gained enormously from the treaty, obtaining all Canada, all Spanish and French lands east of the Mississippi except New Orleans, some West Indian and West African colonies, confirmation of Indian gains, the recovery of Minorca, the evacuation of the French from Prussia and the restoration of Hanover, Hesse and Brunswick in Germany. Indeed, on hearing of Bute's sweeping success, Pitt suffered a debilitating gout attack.[7]

The peace treaty ending the Seven Years' War was signed on 3 November 1762. But it had to be ratified by the British Parliament. And although the treaty was popular, Lord Bute's government was not, because most people credited William Pitt with the territorial gains. Bute's leader of the House of Commons, Henry Fox, left nothing to chance. 'A shop was opened at the pay office', Horace Walpole wrote, 'whither members flocked and received the wages of their veniality in bank bills even to so low a sum as two hundred pounds for their votes on the Treaty'. Unable to say anything negative about the territorial gains, Pitt alleged instead that Britain had abandoned its allies, especially King Frederick of Prussia. Although racked with gout, Pitt remained on his feet in the Commons for three and a half hours. It did not matter that Frederick was being unreasonable, Pitt said, only that he was unhappy. Furthermore George III had dishonoured his pledge to make an honourable peace 'in concert with our allies'.

In this confrontation, Tommy Townshend backed his political hero, supporting Pitt's view that 'America had been conquered in Germany', which is to say that Britain had beaten France in Canada because her German allies had kept French troops tied down in Europe. As Tommy was still a government office-holder, his support of Pitt was an act of considerable political courage. And when the peace was ratified by 227 votes to 63, it was clear that Tommy's stand would have consequences. On hearing that the treaty had been approved, George III's mother said, 'now my son is king of England'.[8]

To ram home their advantage, Bute and Fox wreaked vengeance on those government office-holders who had voted against the treaty. 'Having used political rewards [Fox] now doled out the political punishment', Horace Walpole said, 'and a more severe political persecution never raged'. After backing Pitt, Tommy stood no chance and was dismissed as a Treasury clerk 'without the smallest notification'. His cousins who had supported the treaty were, however, rewarded. Charles Townshend was appointed to head the Board of Trade. And not long afterwards, George Townshend became master-general of ordnance – the senior minister in charge of army supplies. The Townshend family, which had symbolized the power of the Whigs for seventy-five years, now reflected its disintegration.[9]

Although Tommy's Whig career-path had been destroyed, he found a new freedom, being one of those members of the Commons who was energetic and ambitious enough to adapt. It was Tommy and other young members such as George Onslow, nicknamed 'cocking George' because of his love of cock fighting, who attempted to constitute an opposition in the form of a political club. But the Duke of Newcastle, who had been so long in power that he did not believe in opposition, was appalled to hear of a meeting at Onslow's on 21 December 1762. 'They were all … violent for a club … [and] said there was nothing to be done without it; that they must collect their friends', Newcastle complained. 'I opposed to the utmost these clubs … that carried much the air of faction'. And thanks to Newcastle's objections, no coordinated opposition was formed until January 1764.

Despite his dismissal, Tommy's growing political ability was being recognized. 'As he was distinguished by steady abilities and was a bold, able and unembarrassed speaker in Parliament', historian John Jesse wrote, 'these qualities added to his family influence rendered him a valuable acquisition to his party'.[10]

[*Six*]

— The American Stamp Act —

All George III and William Pitt could agree on about the Seven Years' War was that it had been 'expensive'. By March 1763, Britain's national debt stood at 141,000,000 pounds compared to its annual tax revenue of just 10,000,000 pounds. Struggling to pay off even the interest, Prime Minister Bute proposed a new tax on cider. But still smarting over his fall from power, William Pitt stirred up fierce public opposition. And Tommy Townshend joined in, exploiting the fact that most of the MPs who represented the 'cider counties' were government supporters. Although a majority of them ended up supporting the tax, a surprisingly high number voted against it.

On-going unrest over the cider tax contributed to Lord Bute's resignation and he was replaced by George Grenville. One of his supporters described the new prime minister thus:

> His skill upon all matters of finance, of commerce, of foreign treaties and above all the purity of his character gave him weight ... An Act of Parliament was in itself entertaining to him, as was proved when he stole a turnpike bill out of somebody's pocket at a concert and read it in a corner despite all the efforts of the great singers to attract his attention.

Obsessed by detail, Grenville overlooked the bigger picture, ignoring former Prime Minister Walpole's warning about taxing Americans. 'It must be a stronger man than himself', Walpole said, '[to] ... venture such an experiment'.[1]

America was a taxation target because of the huge added expense to Britain of administering her newly conquered territory there. The removal of the French threat along the Ohio and Mississippi Rivers encouraged swarms of Anglo-Americans to push west. Violent clashes ensued with a number of

Indian nations under the leadership of Chief Pontiac, who overran all but three of the posts that the British had captured from the French, west of the Appalachians. Aged just 25, the new president of the board of trade, Lord Shelburne, faced the following questions about North America:

> What new courts should be established there? What form should be adopted for such a government?
> What military establishment will be sufficient? What new forts should be erected? In what way least burdensome and most palatable to the Colonies can they contribute towards the support of the additional expense which must attend their civil and military establishments?[2]

By a proclamation of 7 October 1763, the Grenville government established the new colonies of Quebec out of lands taken from the French, and East and West Florida out of lands ceded by Spain. Settlement west of a 'proclamation line', running from Georgia to Canada along the watershed between the Mississippi and the Atlantic, was prohibited. And immigrants were redirected to Quebec and Florida. George Washington and many of his soldiers, who had been promised lands in the Ohio Valley in return for their war service, were now prohibited from occupying them.[3]

In March 1764, parliamentary resolutions to levy a stamp duty in America to pay for 'defending, protecting and securing British Colonies' there, attracted very little comment in the Commons. The peacetime British army in America was 10,000 strong and the proposed stamp duty which targeted printers, lawyers and publicans, was projected to raise 100,000 pounds, less than one third of the amount required to support those troops. However, the necessary legislation, which provided that a duty would be levied in America as it had been in Britain for a century, was delayed, and the British government cracked down on tax avoidance at home. Writing to his uncle in November 1764, Tommy Townshend noted:

> The strictness of the Custom House officers still continues. Mr Rigby brought one fine suit of clothes which he saved by wearing when he landed. Mr Elliot saved a coat and a waistcoat by the same means but not having taken the precaution for breeches, they were seized and burnt.[4]

Finally, in February 1765, Prime Minister Grenville introduced the American Stamp Bill. Among other things, it provided for stamps of two pounds for college degrees, ten shillings for a pair of dice and one penny for a sheet of newspaper. Grenville explained that the delay of eleven months had been to give the colonists an opportunity to comment on Parliament's earlier resolutions. But he then dismissed the colonists' plea 'not to be taxed but by their representatives' with the response that 'all Colonies are subject to the dominion of the mother country' and commended the bill to the House. Tommy Townshend hotly disputed the prime minister's assertions, seconding a motion to adjourn the proceedings. After mustering only 49 votes out of the 300-odd members present, Tommy ploughed on in the main debate. Described by one observer as a 'champion for the colonies', Tommy argued that the duty 'was treating the Americans with levity and insult'. And on 30 April he 'battled clause by clause' Grenville's American Mutiny Bill which required soldiers to be accommodated in private houses. Nevertheless, both bills became law. But before the full impact of these new measures was felt, a crisis over regency legislation had undermined George Grenville.[5]

Because his son was not yet three, the king consulted his prime minister about planning for the possibility that he might die before his heir was old enough to take over. George III then asked Parliament to determine whether he should be able to nominate a regent who would assume the powers of the Crown if this possibility eventuated. The mere suggestion of such a proposal drew immediate fire from some younger members of the Commons, including Tommy Townshend who 'dropped some severe sentences'. Concerned that the king might name his mother to be regent, allowing her 'close friend' Lord Bute a back-door return to power, Tommy argued that this was 'seeking to re-establish the empire of the Princess and the Favourite'. And he supported an amendment that the regent be nominated by Parliament. But this was defeated. And the king got to 'fill up the blanks' on the regency nomination form as he had requested. Despite his victory, George III felt humiliated, he said, by the 'insults offered to his mother'. Ignoring Tommy's jibes in the House, the king blamed Grenville for placing the royal family in such an embarrassing situation in the first place. And many felt that it was a major cause of the prime minister's dismissal a few weeks later.[6]

George III had already begun to tire of Grenville. 'When he has wearied me for two hours', he said, 'he looks at his watch, to see if he may not tire me for an hour more'. So on the young king's behalf, his uncle, the Duke of Cumberland, began consultations to find a new prime minister. After Pitt declined for family reasons, Cumberland approached the leading Whigs, including the Dukes of Newcastle and Grafton, as well as the Marquess of Rockingham. Before responding, they in turn consulted their more energetic younger colleagues, among them Tommy Townshend. He was by now active in a political club called 'the Coterie', a clique which had been formed in January 1764. 'The new club', Horace Walpole had noted then, 'makes the Ministry very uneasy'. And indeed, its members were now meeting to consider a new ministry. At Thomas Wildman's home in Albemarle Street, Mayfair, they agreed that Rockingham should be prime minister; Grafton, secretary of state; and Newcastle, lord privy seal. Tommy and George Onslow were to be lords of the treasury. 'Fond of talking business but dilatory in its execution', Horace Walpole said, '[Rockingham's] single talent lay in attracting dependents'. As such a dependent, Tommy was happy with the changes. But his cousins, George and Charles Townshend, still strong supporters of George Grenville, were not.[7]

Shortly after the Rockingham ministry assumed office on 10 July 1765, alarming reports reached London about the American colonists' reaction to the new Stamp Act. Tommy made a note of them at a meeting with his fellow treasury lords:

> Letters of 24 and 25 August from Mr Oliver distributor of Stamps at Boston relative to the late outrages in that country with copys of Proclamations Resolutions of Council etc. Gov: Bernard [Governor of Massachusetts] must take care of the stamps. A new distributor to be appointed. Mr Oliver having resigned. The account to be sent to the Privy Council.[8]

In a half-hearted response, cabinet ordered the colonial governors to preserve the peace and to apply to Major-General Thomas Gage, the British commander in America, for military assistance if necessary. But the reports from Gage, which also landed on Tommy's desk, confirmed his worst fears:

> The resolves of the Assembly of Virginia gave the signal for a general outcry: The general scheme seems to have been to oblige the stamp officers to resign; in which they have generally succeeded and next to destroy the stamps on their arrival… [they] also rose their mob and not only forced the stamp officer to promise not to act but destroyed the houses of the two persons who had written and talked in defence of the Act and obliged them to fly on shipboard… it is not to be doubted that a considerable body would have approached the fort with arms which would have brought on an open rebellion and the city would have been in great part destroyed.[9]

Like his fellow ministers, Tommy's opposition to the Stamp Act now placed him in a dilemma. The Act had been strongly supported by the king and both Houses of Parliament. There was no guarantee that the new government could muster the votes to repeal it or that the king would consent to any such repeal. And to simply not enforce the law, would set a bad example for Britain's other colonies. All the while, former Prime Minister Grenville enjoyed 'the distress of his adversaries'.[10]

To strengthen the government's hand against Grenville, Tommy was dispatched to sound out William Pitt on a return to the ministry. According to Prime Minister Rockingham, 'No one could… talk with Mr Pitt on the present important matter… better than young Thomas Townshend'. And he duly reported back from Bath that Pitt was ready to accept. However, the king would have none of it. 'So loose a communication as that of Mr Pitt and Thomas Townshend is not sufficient to risk either my dignity or continuance of any administration by a fresh treaty with that gentleman', the king said, 'for should it miscarry all public opinion of this Ministry would be destroyed.'[11]

The crisis over the American Stamp Act therefore dragged on into 1766. And when the Commons met on 14 January, Tommy, who was by now playing a leading government role, was accused of 'a lack of resolve' against the colonies. The authority of Parliament itself was now in question, opposition members claimed. Rallying to Tommy's defence, William Pitt replied that 'the Commons did not represent… America and had no right to lay an internal tax upon… [her]'.[12]

The following month, the government came up with a compromise plan: to repeal the Stamp Act while at the same time declaring Britain's right to tax her American colonies. When Grenville and his supporters furiously opposed this plan, Tommy responded that even Governor Bernard of Massachusetts, a Grenville favourite and a supporter of British colonial authority, backed repeal. Still, it took another strong speech from William Pitt to win the repeal vote for the government.

Next came the Declaratory Bill, which asserted that the British Parliament 'had, hath and of right ought to have, full power…to make laws…to bind the…people of America…in all cases whatsoever'. This bill Pitt opposed. And it was feared that he might combine with Grenville to defeat it. But the concern was unfounded. The Declaratory Bill became law. And the door was left open for the British Parliament to impose further taxes on Americans.[13]

[*Seven*]

Cousin Charles
and his tea tax

Charles Townshend, known to history as the man who sparked the Boston Tea Party, was the second son of the third Viscount Townshend and Audrey Harrison, the brother of George Townshend and the first cousin of Tommy Townshend and Charles Cornwallis. Born in 1725, Charles was first elected to Parliament in 1747 where he was described by Horace Walpole as follows:

> A young man of unbounded ambition and ... abilities capable of satisfying that ambition ... yet to such parts and such industry he was fond of associating all the little arts and falsehoods that always deprecate though so often thought necessary by a genius ... His figure was tall and advantageous, his action vehement, his voice loud, his laugh louder. He had art enough to disguise anything but his vanity. He spoke long and with much wit.

Charles's early parliamentary career, however, did not meet his expectations. Suffering from severe epileptic fits, he behaved so erratically that one contemporary called him a 'splendid shuttlecock who laughs at the Ministry at night and assures them in the morning that he is entirely theirs'. At other times, his progress was retarded because of the feud between his brother George and the Duke of Cumberland. By the mid-1760s, Charles had advanced to the post of paymaster-general, a lucrative but not senior ministry.[1]

The king, meanwhile, had never fully accepted Prime Minister Rockingham's decision to repeal the Stamp Act. Under pressure, Rockingham sidelined one of his key ministers, the Duke of Grafton, who retaliated by calling for the return of William Pitt to lead the government. Keen to have Pitt back, but not as prime minister, Rockingham dispatched Tommy Townshend a second time to try to persuade his hero to rejoin the ministry. The Duke of Newcastle, who still fancied himself as a Whig power-broker, was not consulted. And when Tommy returned with the news that Pitt would not join any ministry in which Newcastle was a member, the old duke felt humiliated. 'Such harsh terms can never be justified', he said, 'and ... my nephew Tommy Townshend should have excused himself from carrying such a message ... so offensive to his own uncle'.[2]

Rockingham refused Pitt's ultimatum, however, and insisted that Newcastle remain a minister. Unhappy with this stand-off, the Duke of Grafton then resigned his government positions. But Pitt refused to take Grafton's place, claiming the political situation was not yet 'ripe' enough. Instead, he waited for the king to offer him government on his own terms. Forced to choose between Pitt and Newcastle, the king 'sent for Mr Pitt'. And Newcastle's ministerial career, which had begun in 1717, now ended on a bitter note. 'I was the first sacrificed to ... [Pitt's] boundless ambition', the old Duke said, 'whose first view was to debauch and detach my nearest relations ... in order to make me less able to resist his power'.[3]

Having obtained government on his own terms at the end of July 1766, Prime Minister Pitt vowed 'to take the best men without distinction of parties' to form a ministry. Grafton was appointed first lord of the treasury, Henry Conway became leader of the Commons and Charles Townshend became chancellor of the exchequer, thereby assuming responsibility for taxation, including the taxation of America. Tommy Townshend continued as a lord of the treasury.[4]

To the astonishment of just about everybody, William Pitt now accepted a peerage which disqualified him from leading the Commons, his greatest source of strength during his years as war minister. As the Earl of Chatham rather than 'the great commoner', he lost his popularity both at home and in America. Pitt had been 'sold for a title', Horace Walpole said. Splits soon emerged in the government and a number of ministers resigned. Tommy, for one, was tempted. 'Old Tommy Townshend will not suffer his son to resign', Newcastle observed, 'even if he was disposed to do it'. And young Tommy stayed, for once taking his cautious father's advice.[5]

In his quest for revenue to pay for the debts he had incurred as war minister, Lord Chatham eyed off India where, thanks to a British victory in 1757, the East India Company had increased its financial gain by 2,000,000 pounds a year. Chatham therefore proposed that in return for being allowed to administer its Indian territories, this British company should surrender its territorial rights and a large slice of its revenue to the British state. Chatham's problem was that his revenue minister, Charles Townshend, owned a large quantity of East India shares. And even Tommy had a modest stake.[6]

When the company increased its dividend from six to ten percent, speculation in its shares prompted Chatham to call a parliamentary inquiry. But this strategy posed a threat to Charles's shareholding and he was able to undermine it with a proposal, endorsed by Parliament, whereby the company would pay an annual fee to the government in return for extending its charter and territorial rights. In this way, Lord Chatham's attempt to reduce Britain's war debt by using East India Company revenue was sabotaged by his chancellor, who had a financial stake in the outcome. At the height of this crisis, Charles had entered the Commons' chamber 'half drunk with champagne'. According to Walpole:

> Townshend powered both a torrent of wit, parts, humour, knowledge, absurdity, vanity and fiction heightened by the graces of comedy the happiness of allusion and quotation and the buffoonery of farce... He excited such murmurs of wonder, admiration, applause, laughter, pity and scorn that nothing was so true as the sentence with which he concluded... Government [had] become what he himself had often been called; a weathercock.

All members could ask each other for some days afterwards was 'Did you hear Charles Townshend's champagne speech?' Lord Chatham's chancellor was the original 'Champagne Charlie'.[7]

With his government in disarray, a severely stressed Chatham succumbed to a life-threatening gout attack, combined with what appeared to be a mental illness. He removed himself to his country estate, Burton Pynsent, in Somerset. Even there, he could not bear to be under the same roof as his children and took four or five houses successively to ward off ordinary neighbourhood noises. So bad did his condition become that his wife wrote his letters for him and left his meals at a hatch. One critic described him as 'a lunatic brandishing a crutch'. And his ministers complained bitterly about how inaccessible he was. One commentator noted that of those left to step into Chatham's shoes, Grafton was incapable, Conway was incompetent and Charles Townshend was irresponsible.

In short, the British government was dysfunctional and Charles Townshend was left to his own devices in his search for new taxation targets.[8]

It was Benjamin Franklin who sowed the seeds of Charles Townshend's taxation plan. In evidence before a parliamentary committee on 17 January 1766, Franklin had drawn a distinction between 'internal taxes' such as a stamp duty on newspapers and 'external taxes' on imported goods such as tea:

> You say the colonies have always submitted to external taxes and object to the right of Parliament only in laying internal taxes; now can you shew that there is any kind of difference between the two taxes?
> The difference is very great. An external tax is a duty laid on commodities imported; that … makes a part of the price. If the people do not like it at that price … they are not obliged to pay it. But an internal tax is forced from the people without their consent, if not laid by their own representatives.

As Chatham had expressed similar views, Charles began formulating a new plan to tax the Americans, something left open to him by the Declaratory Act.[9]

On 26 January 1767, in answer to a parliamentary question on army expenditure, Charles bragged that he had come up with a new tax, without providing any details. But the embittered former prime minister, George Grenville, pounced immediately. And he forced Charles to commit himself to whatever this new tax might be, before he had consulted his ministerial colleagues. As Grafton put it:

> Townshend chose to boast … that he knew the mode by which a revenue might be raised in America without giving offence. Mr Grenville fixed him down directly to pledge himself on the declaration which was received with such welcome by the bulk of the House as dismayed Mr Conway who stood astonished at this unauthorized proceeding of his vain and impudent colleague.

The question was in fact the first part of an ambush organized by Grenville. Charles's fellow ministers were furious with him for the way he had responded. But none of them had the authority to recommend his dismissal. And nothing less could have stopped what now followed.[10]

The second part of Grenville's ambush took place a month later when Charles proposed to the Commons the 'usual rate' of land tax at four shillings in the pound. After he had completed the standard homily that he hoped in future to be able to take a shilling off the rate, one of Grenville's supporters moved to do just that immediately. No doubt motivated by Charles's assurance a month earlier that he had a new source of revenue in America, the House duly voted to reduce the land tax to three shillings in the pound. And as a result, the British government's revenue estimates were slashed by 500,000 pounds. To cover this shortfall, Charles now had to make good on his boast.[11]

On 1 June 1767, Charles Townshend proposed legislation to impose new levies on glass, paint, paper and tea imported into the colonies. The tea duty, of three-pence a pound-weight, was calculated to raise 20,000 pounds, while the duties on the remaining commodities were projected to return a further 20,000 pounds. Still a lord of the treasury, Tommy Townshend was apparently content to let the legislation through, as was every other member. There was no call for a formal vote over a tax that the Americans themselves seemed prepared to put up with. However, as Charles planned the establishment of a customs board in America, he privately ridiculed Benjamin Franklin's distinction between internal and external taxes.[12]

'[Charles Townshend] had every great talent and every little quality', Walpole said. 'His vanity exceeded even his abilities'. Aged just 42, Charles died on 4 September 1767. A 'putrid fever' had claimed his life before the disastrous consequences of his new taxes emerged. Still, it was not long before opposition to the so-called 'Townshend Duties' had spread from Massachusetts to Georgia. And even Benjamin Franklin joined these protests. The British government reacted strongly, establishing a new department and a new cabinet post – secretary of state for American affairs. British troops were withdrawn from America's western forts, where they had been fending off Indian attacks, and redeployed to eastern cities, to put down demonstrations against the Townshend Duties. And income from these duties was used to pay Crown office-holders, to make them independent of America's colonial legislatures.[13]

In protest, the American colonies imposed a trade boycott and, by the beginning of 1769, the duties raised had slumped to just 11,000 pounds. But the cost of lost business to British exporters was estimated to be 700,000 pounds. So in May that year Prime Minister Grafton proposed the repeal of all Townshend Duties, but he was rolled in cabinet by Lord North who insisted that the tax on tea should remain in place. Soon afterwards, Grafton resigned. And on 5 March 1770, Lord North, by now prime minister himself, proposed that all Townshend Duties be repealed, except the tea tax.[14]

As a member now in opposition, Tommy Townshend voted to remove this tax on tea as well. To justify his apparent about face, Tommy told the House:

> By repealing those duties now and tea next year, you will do what… [the Americans] want, but you will not have the credit of doing it for their good. If there had been a vote upon the question, I should have opposed those duties. It was not the humour of the time to oppose them.[15]

Still, the tax on tea continued in force. For a while Prime Minister North's concession of removing the other duties worked to undermine the colonies' trade boycott. But Charles Townshend's tea tax remained a time bomb that was activated when Lord North took steps, in 1773, to assist the East India Company. A decade of mismanagement was by then threatening the company's future and the Tea Act was passed to give the company the exclusive privilege of selling tea in America. Britain's export tax of one shilling was waived but America's import tax of three-pence per pound-weight remained. This discrimination fired up the colonial agitators. On 16 December 1773, colonists disguised as Indians boarded a number of the East India Company's ships and dumped 10,000 pounds worth of tea into Boston harbour. After digesting this news about what had quickly been dubbed 'the Boston Tea Party', Lord North told the Commons: 'we are now to establish our authority or give it up entirely'.[16]

North attempted to re-establish Britain's authority by championing the Coercive Acts of 1774. These Acts provided that the port of Boston was to be closed until the dumped tea had been paid for. They also empowered the new governor of Massachusetts, Major-General Gage, to appoint colonial legislators and judges and to take over buildings to house troops. And they allowed the prosecution of colonists to take place in England to avoid hostile American juries. Tommy Townshend's reaction was mixed. He had no problem with English jurors hearing colonial cases. 'Whether… [a juror] wears a red coat or white coat', he said, 'is a matter of indifference to me'. But it was with 'a great deal of concern and anguish' that he supported the closure of Boston's port. And like his father Tommy argued that the tax on tea should be repealed. 'Why keep up this duty', he asked. 'Merely to show you ought to keep up the subject of the contest?'[17]

The Coercive Acts transformed American colonial resistance into a world-historical revolution. And the Townshend tax on tea was a prime cause of the trouble which led to their enactment. Nevertheless, Tommy attempted a defence of his cousin, arguing that he had relied on Benjamin Franklin's evidence before the parliamentary committee in 1766:

> [Charles] desired taxes agreeable to the Americans... He flattered himself too far... he was misled by the Americans themselves who told him, 'take the tax, let it bear the appearance of port duties, it will not be objected to'. A Chancellor of the Exchequer at that time who had not attempted something of the kind would have been looked upon as blameable.[18]

[*Eight*]

Wilkes and Liberty! – Tommy's defence of dissent

In the lead-up to the American Revolution, 'Wilkes and Liberty!' was the rallying cry of those who felt that the British political system was corrupt. John Wilkes's notoriety began when he defamed George III in a way that was widely condemned as outrageous. But the response to Wilkes was so mismanaged by successive British governments, the legal system and the Parliament itself that it spawned a reformist political movement which 'carried across the Atlantic to sweep away half the British Empire'. For supporting Wilkes, Tommy Townshend was to be stripped of the lucrative post of paymaster-general and cast down into fourteen long years of opposition.[1]

Edward Gibbon, the author of *The Decline and Fall of the Roman Empire*, described Wilkes, the cross-eyed agitator:

> He has inexhaustible spirits, infinite wit and humour and great knowledge; but a thorough profligate in principle as in practice; his character is infamous, his life stained with every vice, and his conversation full of blasphemy and bawdy. These morals he glories in, for shame is a weakness he has long since surmounted.

First elected to the House of Commons in 1757, Wilkes fell out with the prime minister, Lord Bute, in 1762. To attack Bute, Wilkes began publishing what even Horace Walpole described as a 'most virulent weekly paper'. It was called the *North Briton*, a title intended to emphasize the prime minister's Scottish origins, at a time when the battle of Culloden was still a recent memory. Before long, the *North Briton* was implying that Bute and the king's mother were lovers.[2]

But it was not until shortly after George Grenville had taken over from Bute as prime minister that the young king finally exploded. On 23 April 1763, the *North Briton* No. 45 alleged that George III had betrayed his country by agreeing to a peace treaty 'at the dictate of the King of Prussia'. The paper thereby inferred that the king and Bute had been parties to a treasonous conspiracy to end Britain's seven years' war with France and Spain. Legal advice to George III was that, apart from being a seditious libel, the No. 45 was a breach of the peace. As such, the immunity from arrest that Wilkes enjoyed as an MP, would count for nothing.[3]

On 26 April, Secretary of State Halifax issued a general warrant for the arrest the No. 45's 'authors, printers and publishers'. Wilkes was duly arrested and imprisoned in the Tower of London. But within days he was released after a finding that his conduct had only *tended* to breach the peace. Sensing overwhelming public support, Wilkes counterattacked with a warrant to search the secretary of state's home. And in a further act of aggression, he reprinted the No. 45.[4]

These provocations could not be ignored. So Prime Minister Grenville transferred the fight with Wilkes to the floor of the Commons. There Grenville asserted that the No. 45 was a 'false, scandalous and seditious libel' and a breach of parliamentary privilege. Despite the best efforts of about a hundred members, including Tommy Townshend, who argued that what was at stake was the liberty of free speech, the Commons backed Grenville with two-to-one majorities. And it voted overwhelmingly that a copy of the No. 45 be symbolically burned by the public hangman. After the magistrates had duly assembled in front of a large crowd at the Royal Exchange on 3 December 1763, the executioner set fire to a copy of the paper. But this sparked a great riot. 'The paper was forced from the hangman', Walpole said, 'the constables were pelted and beaten and ... one of the sheriffs ... was wounded in the face ... by a billet snatched from the fire ... and thrown at him'. The furious mob's cry was 'Wilkes and Liberty!'[5]

Unable to prove that Wilkes had been the author of the No. 45, the king's lawyers changed tack and prosecuted him on a charge of reprinting it, whereupon he fled overseas. In his absence, a large majority of his colleagues voted to expel him from Parliament. But Wilkes's case triggered another debate – about whether an arrest warrant should be required to specify the name of the person to be arrested. Was it good enough simply to refer to 'authors, publishers and printers'? Or should each suspect be individually named? It was one of the great eighteenth-century constitutional debates, and it split the Townshend family.[6]

In the presence of 450 members crammed into every corner of the chamber and overflowing outside, the debate got underway on 13 February 1764. From the beginning, Tommy strongly backed Wilkes. When George Townshend moved to adjourn after a long sitting, Tommy rounded heatedly on his cousin. 'The House had voted the expulsion of ... [Wilkes] at 4 in the morning', Tommy thundered. 'Would not they proceed to hear his complaint at 11 pm at night?' George could only muster 31 votes and so the debate continued, but many members then drifted off to nearby coffee houses and, forty-five minutes later, the government was able to sneak through an adjournment.[7]

Next day, the debate focused on precedents. It was noted that the second Viscount Townshend, 'a zealous, bold and authoritative Minister', had made 'free use of' general warrants. In the end, what the House had to decide was whether 'a general warrant for seizing authors and papers of seditious libel is not law'. And although George Townshend had opposed Wilkes, his brother Charles Townshend now sided with Tommy in a speech 'as well acted as ever Garrick did Othello'. Even so, the government scraped home by 232 votes to 218. However, the lord chief justice provided some consolation to Wilkes's supporters when he ruled that arrest warrants must name the person sought. As for Wilkes himself, after being found guilty of the reprinting charge, he failed to appear for sentencing. Still at large overseas, he was declared an outlaw. And as the months and then years passed, public interest in him faded.[8]

After Charles Townshend's death in September 1767, Lord North, whose courtesy title allowed him to sit in the Commons, took Charles's place in cabinet. North's half of the paymaster-general's portfolio, a ministerial position which he had jointly shared with George Cooke, passed to Tommy Townshend, who also became a privy councillor. From Treasury, the joint paymasters received money in bulk for the whole army. And it was quite legal for them to personally pocket the huge interest payments earned by investing the regimental balances. The ministerial reshuffle which handed Tommy this financial bonanza was part of a desperate deal with a faction led by the Duke of Bedford. It was an arrangement designed to shore up the government whose absent leader, Lord Chatham, appeared by then to be barking mad. Unknown to Tommy, however, there was a side deal in which the cabinet had promised one of Bedford's organizers, Richard Rigby, that he would be made sole paymaster 'at the first opportunity'.[9]

All the while, American affairs were descending into crisis. And nothing could hide the lunatic in Chatham or Grafton's inability to stand in for him. 'All that I dread for myself', Grafton said, 'crowded at once on my mind'. Under pressure from the Commons, George III was forced to take the extraordinary step of appointing three commissioners to exercise Chatham's powers, news of which appeared in the *London Gazette* of 2 February 1768. Just nine days later, the Massachusetts Legislature resolved to oppose the Townshend Duties.

On 11 March, Parliament was dissolved for a general election whereupon John Wilkes emerged from exile to stand as a candidate in London. Claiming that he 'must raise a dust or starve in jail', Wilkes polled last. As elections then continued over a number of days, Wilkes flowed on to Middlesex, whereupon the government factions split over what to do about him. Tommy's Chatham faction was sympathetic to Wilkes, but Richard Rigby's Bedford faction was hostile. Hopelessly divided, the government did nothing. Wilkes was elected with the support of the mob. Still an outlaw, he then cheerfully surrendered himself to the authorities. Furious at Wilkes's impudence and electoral success, the king pressured the government to move again for his expulsion from Parliament.[10]

To consider the king's demand, a meeting of the 'principal parts' of the government outside the cabinet was held on 12 May, and a fierce argument ensued. The Chatham faction was 'violently' opposed to Wilkes's expulsion, while the Bedford faction was just as violently in favour of it. As a privy councillor, Tommy had sworn an oath to oppose 'anything done…against His Majesty's…dignity royal'. His continuing support for Wilkes, who had so offended the king, would have consequences, and when the Bedford faction prevailed, Tommy's ministerial future looked shaky. But the decision to expel Wilkes could not be acted on until the Parliament resumed in November.[11]

However, not long after the government decided to expel Wilkes, Tommy's joint paymaster, George Cooke, died, and Richard Rigby moved swiftly to claim the whole of the paymaster-general's portfolio for himself, pursuant to the factional promise he had extracted six months earlier. 'Rigby's severity is infinitely more rude and direct', the *English Chronicle* noted, 'than that of any other individual in the House'. Already on the outer for opposing moves by Rigby and the Bedford faction to expel Wilkes, Tommy stood no chance of holding on to his half share of the pay office. In a spirit of compromise, Grafton, as the acting prime minister suggested that Tommy become vice-treasurer of Ireland, the post Rigby was about to vacate. With his mentor Chatham incapacitated, Tommy turned to his father for advice. 'I…wish to be allowed a little time to consider your Grace's proposal', Tommy told Grafton. 'My father who will be in town today is not yet arrived: and I cannot with any degree…of decency come to a final resolution…without a communication with him'. What then happened between father and son is unknown, but according to some accounts, Tommy was 'woefully angry at Rigby's preferment' and refused to be 'turned backwards and forwards every six months'. As always, Horace Walpole had something to say: 'I find Townshend has been very ill treated and I like his spirit in not bearing such neglect and contempt though wrapped up in 2,700 pounds a year'.[12]

However it came about, Tommy's departure from the ministry was a huge blow to his career. He would not be a minister again until 1782, going out of office at the age of 35 and not returning until the age of 49. At the time of his departure, he was described as rating highly within the second-rank of speakers in the Commons, being 'indefatigably industrious'.

Tommy expressed his feelings towards the political intriguer, Rigby, and his patron, the Duke of Bedford, in verse. Focusing on Bedford's coat of arms which incorporated a goat, a lion and an antelope, Tommy's poem was addressed rhetorically to the Duchess of Bedford who, he believed, was a power behind the scenes:

> The goat an emblem of yourself we trace
> The horned beast the image of his Grace
> Whilst in the lion's rough vigorous mein
> Adopted Rigby's brawny strength is seen.

When it was all said, the Marquess of Rockingham best picked Tommy's mood and future direction. 'I saw him for a few minutes soon after the event and he was in exceeding good spirits and well satisfied with what he had done', Rockingham noted. 'He will try to appear moderate when the session begins but I don't think [this] will continue.' So it was that Tommy Townshend went into opposition over the Wilkes affair and soon became a key opponent of the American war.[13]

Meanwhile the situation in America continued to deteriorate, at one stage forcing a British admiral, Samuel Hood, to retake key parts of Boston. Although, as Hood put it, he was able regain 'possession of Faneuil Hall School of Liberty from the sons thereof without force', Chatham still begged the king to let him surrender his seals of office. Finally George III relented and Acting Prime Minister Grafton assumed full responsibility for leading the government. Some suspected that Chatham had used his illness as an excuse to avoid responsibility for the growing American crisis which he knew he could not control. And by the summer of 1769, Chatham had made 'an astonishing one might say miraculous recovery', whereupon he and Tommy 'entered into violent opposition to the Government'.[14]

In Prime Minister Grafton, the king had a political weakling. 'He neglected everything', Walpole said, 'and when pressed to be active, threatened to resign'. It therefore came as no surprise that after Wilkes petitioned the Parliament for redress, Grafton tried to appease him by proposing that he withdraw his petition, apologize to the king and make some token submission. In return, Wilkes would be released from prison and the motion to expel him as the member for Middlesex would be dropped. But Wilkes was a stubborn contrarian and he published yet another libel, this time in the *St George Chronicle*, relating to the quelling of a riot. Wilkes called this incident the St George's Fields 'Massacre' and alleged that the government had planned the slaughter of a number of the rioters. Grafton therefore pushed ahead with the expulsion motion, and it was carried by a two to one majority, despite the best efforts of Tommy Townshend and Wilkes's other supporters.[15]

When a writ was issued to elect a replacement for Wilkes in Middlesex, he promptly re-nominated. And he was re-elected after the government was unable to find anyone to stand against him. He was expelled again and another by-election was called. But Wilkes nominated once more, and despite being opposed, this time by a popular war hero, Henry Luttrell, Wilkes won the ballot. The government therefore moved a motion to declare Luttrell duly elected, claiming that the dignity of Parliament was at stake. For Tommy and Wilkes's other supporters, however, Parliament would have no dignity if the representatives of electorates with as few as seven voters could combine to expel a man who had been elected by a thumping majority of almost one thousand. If Wilkes could be expelled, so could any member of the opposition. As Tommy later put it:

> The members of this House must not ask whether the man whom the electors have chosen is fit company for them; he acquires an indisputable title to admission by that election and that election alone. His title is that he is chosen by his constituents not that he is adopted by the House, deriving his full power from those who sent him.

Despite evidence that Wilkes had polled almost four times more votes in Middlesex than Luttrell, the government used its parliamentary majority on 8 May 1769 to have Luttrell declared elected.[16]

Tommy remained angry about Middlesex for a long time. As late as December 1771, he informed the House that he would not pay tax on his property in the County of Middlesex, which gave him a right to vote there, because the county was not legally represented in the Commons. The speaker coolly responded that this was a question of law and Tommy later had some of his property seized for failing to pay his taxes. But a grateful Wilkes warmly approved of Tommy's 'excellent speech', the 'justice and merited severity' of which were 'truly striking'. When he finally returned to the Commons in 1774, he and Tommy swapped poems, including a satirical election advertisement describing the sort of member who had voted to expel Wilkes:

> Permit me good people to now recommend
> This very good lord and my very good friend…
> I know him that's all He will stick to his plan
> Like a harmless obnoxious pretty sort of man.[17]

In 'raising a dust' John Wilkes had stirred up fundamental issues which laid bare the shortcomings of the British constitutional system. And the

American colonists saw not only that they were unrepresented in Parliament but so too were the voters of Middlesex. 'Will any man deny', Chatham asked, 'that discontents... in many parts of his Majesty's dominions... arise from the proceedings of the... Commons touching the declared incapacity of Mr Wilkes?'[18]

[*Nine*]

Opposition

The Commons' motion to declare Henry Luttrell elected, even though John Wilkes had won the popular vote, brought the opposition factions together. On 9 May 1769, the day after the motion had been passed, a cross-factional dinner was held at the Thatched House Tavern. Belying its name, this 'tavern' was located in St James's Street, the address of London's best-known gentlemen's clubs. And in its massive dining-room, lit by chandeliers and decorated by portraits in gilt frames, the seventy-two well lubricated attendees noisily expressed their disgust at the Luttrell declaration. Those present included the former prime minister George Grenville, the renowned philosopher Edmund Burke, the staunch Rockingham supporter John Cavendish, and Tommy Townshend. A total of twenty-one toasts were drunk that night, among them to 'the rights of electors', to 'freedom of debate within doors and freedom of election without', and to 'our next happy meeting'.[1]

In the autumn of 1769, Tommy followed up with an attempt to unite the left-leaning Rockingham faction, which included Edmund Burke, with the middle-of-the-road Chatham faction to which George Grenville was now associated. As a Chatham supporter, Tommy approached his friend Burke, who duly reported to Rockingham. Tommy was 'a very safe and honest man', Burke said; 'But past experience had informed us of … [Chatham's] enmity to your whole system of men and opinions.' Rockingham agreed, making it clear that he was not prepared to give Chatham and Grenville the senior roles they would demand in a coalition.[2]

On 22 January 1770, this disorganization within the opposition's ranks spilled out on to the floor of the House. Following the speaker's sudden death, the government nominated an eminent lawyer, Sir Fletcher Norton, to replace him. Despite being known around the courts as 'Sir Bullface Doublefee', it was expected that Norton would be elected unopposed. Then, without any prior warning, John Cavendish nominated Tommy Townshend. '[He] has parts, temper and constitution', Cavendish said, '[and an] honesty...which prompts a man to do what he might lawfully...leave undone'. Seconding the motion, George Sackville added that while Norton had been 'practicing in the Courts below,' Tommy has been 'learning the business of...the House'. Shocked, Tommy responded. 'I had not the least knowledge...of being proposed', he said. 'I am equally unfit for the duties and unworthy of the honour'. Still, when Tommy polled a respectable 121 votes, it was clear that many of his colleagues thought otherwise. The untidy way in which Tommy had been nominated was however, a sign of the opposition's ill-discipline.[3]

On the government side, the Lutttrell affair hastened Prime Minister Grafton's political demise and he was replaced by Lord North. Although North was the king's seventh prime minister in ten years, he had already proven his ability to manage the Commons. And just as importantly, he was happy to do the king's bidding. Horace Walpole described him thus:

> North had two large eyes that rolled around to no purpose (for he was utterly short sighted), a wide mouth, thick lips and inflated visage, which gave him the air of a blind trumpeter. A deep untuneable voice, which instead of modulating, he enforced with unnecessary pomp, a total neglect of his person and ignorance of every civil attention disgusted all who judge by appearance. But within that crude casket were enclosed many useful talents – wit, good humour, natural sense, assurance and promptness.[4]

The king instructed his new man to obtain the opposition factions' 'absolute submission'. North used the long parliamentary break between May and November to entrench his government. Meanwhile Tommy kept up regular contact with Chatham, but on the very day that Parliament resumed, their faction suffered a severe blow when George Grenville died – a post-mortem revealing that his skull bones had corroded. Now deeply pessimistic about the crisis 'in the interior of the thing called Opposition', Chatham was 'determined to be found...[at his] post'. A parliamentary assault was therefore mounted against the government for allowing Spain to seize a British port in the Falkland Islands. This seizure had prompted an angry public reaction, and in the Commons, Tommy indignantly demanded the tabling of all government papers relating to the fiasco. But following diplomatic negotiations, the port was handed back and North found himself being thanked by the public for avoiding a war. 'The only question the Opposition acted together on was the Falklands', one observer said, 'and here their violence defeated their objects'. After Grenville's death, many of his followers had begun to waver and the outcome of the Falklands' crisis pushed them into the arms of the government.[5]

What was left of the opposition factions next attempted to attack the government over the role of juries, especially in libel cases. An anonymous pamphleteer, who used the pen name 'Junius', had likened George III to the Stuart kings, inferring that he might share their fate. Unaware of Junius's real identity, which remains a mystery to this day, the king sued the pamphlet's printers and publishers. A jury was duly empanelled to decide whether the words the king complained about had been published, and, if so, by whom. But the lord chief justice would not let the jury decide whether those words were libellous; that, he ruled, was a question he alone would decide. The jury had other ideas, returning the verdict 'guilty of printing and publishing only'. A former lord chancellor backed them, arguing that if judges were left to decide whether something was defamatory they would likely stifle criticism of the government which appointed them.[6]

The opposition factions now fell over themselves to defend the role of juries, but in doing so, they split. While the Rockingham faction supported the immediate reform of jury laws, the Chatham faction wanted an inquiry into 'the administration' of libel laws. In late 1770, each faction put up a motion advocating its point of view, and each boycotted the other's vote. As a result, both motions were lost. In fact, the government's numbers were soft, and had the opposition factions combined, they might have prevailed.

However, their disarray continued into the New Year with a further motion, a further split and a further defeat. By March 1771, Prime Minister North was able to report to the king 'the friends of Government sat still and let the Opposition debate it amongst themselves'. Tommy had been a leading speaker for the Chatham faction in the Commons. And despite the chaos on the opposition benches around him, he managed to make an important statement:

> The liberty of the press and the institution of juries are the two grand palladiums of the constitution... But will anyone pretend to tell me that the liberty of the press remains entire and undiminished when a judge, when any single man is to determine what is or is not a libel... who is biased by his own interest and solicited by a promising court... Our ancestors foreseeing this danger, instituted juries who could be under no temptation to incline to any side but to that of equal and impartial justice.

This strong defence of juries might appear inconsistent with his later support of a law that provided for American colonists to be tried in England, but Tommy saw the concept of the jury, rather than any local connection with the defendant, as the key.[7]

Following the jury debates, the gulf between the supporters of Rockingham and Chatham widened. The opposition's dwindling relevance was typified by petty priorities, including a spat between the two Houses about the etiquette of sending formal messages back and forth. When Lord George Germain (formerly Lord George Sackville) declared that it was all a matter of honour, a fellow opposition member, George Johnstone, questioned what Lord George would know about honour. Taking this to be a reflection on his alleged failure to order a cavalry charge at the battle of Minden, Germain challenged Johnstone to a duel. Duelling was then often resorted to as a means of defending one's reputation, and it involved the antagonists facing off against each other with equally matched pistols. It was a measure of Tommy's standing that he was asked to act as a second (supporter) for both men, who proceeded to blast away at each other in Hyde Park. Neither was seriously injured, and in successfully fighting for his reputation Germain cleared the way for his appointment as American secretary four years later.[8]

As Prime Minister North increased his grip on the Commons, the Marquess of Rockingham seemed more interested in his racehorses and considered boycotting Parliament altogether. But he was unsure about whether other opposition members would join him and asked Burke to take soundings. 'Neither of the Townshends the father or the son would enter into it', Burke reported back, '[being] contrary to the opinions of both and to all the feelings of the younger and more active of the two'. Although any idea of a formal boycott was abandoned, opposition numbers in some important votes between 1771 and 1774 fell to as low as 20. All the while, Tommy remained an active debater on topics as diverse as the East India Company, mad houses, royal marriages, dog stealing and America. For Burke, the self-styled 'philosopher in action', who had recently published *Thoughts on the Causes of the Present Discontents*, such parliamentary opposition seemed tiresome:

> There is no dignity in carrying on a ... [teasing] and vexatious sort of debate without any other effect than fretting Ministers now and then and keeping honest gentlemen from their dinners; while we make trifling and ineffectual divisions in the house and the nation quietly acquiesces in those measures which we agitate with so much eagerness.[9]

Still, Tommy persisted, and in December 1772 he took up the cause of the Carribs, 'the last of the Aborigines from South America'. On the island of St Vincent, a military expedition had been mounted against these indigenous people, who had resisted British planters' attempts to take over their traditional lands. Tommy described the expedition against the Carribs as 'a breach of national honour' and the commanding general admitted that the Carribs had been 'ill-used'. Tommy moved to condemn the expedition as one 'undertaken without sufficient provocation' by those who wanted the Carribs exterminated, but these arguments counted for little in the face of the government's numbers and Tommy's motion was defeated.[10]

Throughout his parliamentary career, Tommy Townshend supported Algernon Sidney's political legacy. 'A drop of the blood of Sidney is in my veins', he once proudly informed the House. Sidney's legacy was never more important than during the 1770s when George III and Prime Minister North came to dominate the Parliament to a degree not experienced since the revolution of 1688. During one debate, King Charles I, who had been executed after losing the English

Civil War to Parliament's army, was lauded as a 'Royal Martyr'. But Tommy's response was sharp. 'The persons who first took up arms against... [Charles] were... praiseworthy', he said. 'Had... I lived [then] I should not have hesitated to take up arms likewise'.[11]

Outside Parliament, pamphleteers and propagandists also argued about the legacy of the 1688 revolution. Had it been glorious? Or had it amounted to a Dutch takeover of the British throne? One of the king's propagandists, Dr Samuel Johnson, was so effective that he was paid a secret pension. Now best remembered for his dictionary, Johnson was also known in his own day as a 'notorious Jacobite' who believed that the king should dominate the Parliament. A bitter critic of Algernon Sidney, Johnson had spoken lightly of the irregularities in Sidney's treason trial (the guilty verdict in which had later been overturned by Parliament) calling him a 'rascal' anyway.[12]

On 16 February 1774, the House of Commons had under consideration a pamphlet that some argued was 'a libel on the Glorious Revolution of 1688'. When his turn came to speak, Tommy rounded on Johnson by disclosing his secret pension to the House:

> The revilers of the revolution... have been applauded, revered and even pensioned... Dr Johnson wrote a pamphlet in which he advanced notions which deserved punishment. Dr Johnson was pensioned by the administration. Dr Johnson published a second pamphlet of the same stamp with the first. The administration... had his pension doubled.

As someone who reported on parliamentary proceedings for *The Gentleman's Magazine*, Johnson may have been in the public gallery at the time. Whatever the case, word of what Tommy had said spread quickly.[13]

Johnson certainly discussed it with Edmund Burke and Oliver Goldsmith, his regular dining companions at St James's Coffeehouse, a popular literary haunt located near the Thatched House Tavern. Tommy might have counted Edmund Burke as a friend, but on this occasion, Burke sided with Johnson, arguing that the pension had been granted 'solely for literary merit'. However Goldsmith went further. Terminally ill, the famous writer was digesting the following lines Burke had written about him:

> Here lies Nolly Goldsmith, for shortness called Noll
> Who wrote like an angel but talked like poor Poll.

So in a poem appropriately entitled 'Retaliation' he hit back at Burke, now adding Tommy's name as payback for his attack on Johnson:

> Here lies our good Edmund whose genius was such
> We scarcely can praise it or blame it too much
> Who born for the universe narrowed his mind
> And to party gave up what was meant for mankind
> Though fraught with all learning yet straining his throat
> To persuade Tommy Townshend to lend him a vote.[14]

Of these lines, which became some of the most quotable in the English language, Johnson's biographer James Boswell wrote:

> I am well assured that Mr Townshend's attack upon Johnson was the occasion of his 'hitching a rhyme'; for that in the original copy of Goldsmith's character of Mr Burke in his retaliation another person's name stood in the couplet where Mr Townshend is now introduced.

Goldsmith hitched Tommy to the poem and his reputation has been stuck fast there ever since. Following his death in 1800, Tommy became known as 'the Tommy Townshend of Goldsmith's *Retaliation*'. In 1892, William Pitt the Younger's biographer wrote that Tommy 'is now chiefly remembered by Goldsmith's famous line'. And in his multi-volume *History of Australia*, Manning Clark used the line to claim that, in Goldsmith's eyes, Tommy was 'exclusively a dispenser of political interest' in a rotten political system.[15]

The true nature of Johnson's pension was disclosed when details of the king's seventeen categories of secret pensions were made public in the early 1780s. It had not been paid under category five –'Literary and University' – but under category sixteen – 'Political or more properly Political Hacks'. As Horace Walpole observed, 'Johnson had prostituted his pen to party even in a dictionary and had afterwards for a pension contradicted his own definitions'. Johnson was especially tough on the Americans, and his argument that their hostility should be answered by arming Indians and encouraging slaves to plunder plantations appalled even Boswell.[16]

As the failure of the Coercive Acts became painfully apparent, the king's pensioned political hack turned out increasingly bitter diatribes against the revolting colonists. In stark contrast, a small band of parliamentarians turned their backs on British government policy and soon took up key elements of the American cause. One of the most vocal was Tommy Townshend.[17]

[*Ten*]

~ THE DYE IS CAST ~

'The dye is cast', Lord North told the king. 'The [American] Colonies must either submit or triumph.' For Tommy Townshend, the dye had been cast four months earlier, in May 1774, when he had led opposition to North's Quebec Bill.[1]

This bill proposed a special system of government for George III's Canadian subjects. It was the brainchild of the British governor of Quebec, Sir Guy Carleton. And it incorporated the principles behind the surrender terms of 1759. Quebec's hundred thousand mostly French-speaking inhabitants would be allowed to live under their traditional law and to continue practicing their Catholic religion. They would also be exempt from English law and jury trials. But Quebec's growing minority of English-speaking inhabitants would be subject to French law too.

The Americans were furious. In 1765 they had drawn up a Declaration of Rights which listed trial by jury as the inherent right of every British subject, a right Tommy Townshend strongly supported. He saw North's bill as a betrayal of the great principles behind the revolution of 1688 because in Quebec, an all-powerful governor would make laws by decree. Supported by Edmund Burke, Tommy made a strong speech in the House:

> The Council is ... the legislative authority ... [but] the Governor can appoint suspend and turn [it] out at his pleasure ... [while] in leaving the inhabitants the civil law of France ... you take away trial by jury in civil matters and you cut off the Habeas Corpus from them ... [depriving] many British born subjects ... of the dearest birthrights of Britons.[2]

During the bill's committee stage, Tommy relied on his schoolboy French to cross examine a French-Canadian witness, a Monsieur de Lothbiniere:

> [Are] Canadians... desirous of having an assembly?
>
> They are very desirous of it.
>
> Why have they not made representations?
>
> Because... if they were gratified with an assembly they would... have the expenses of the government to support.
>
> Have they been displeased with the English law?
>
> They like the English judicature very well.[3]

After the debate on the bill itself resumed, Tommy accused Lord North of making a public show of agreeing to a former governor of Quebec being called before the committee, knowing all along that this witness was unavailable. When the prime minister shot back 'had Murray been available, [you] would have heard him', Tommy attacked him again. According to Walpole, 'North fell into the most ridiculous passion for which he was severely handled by Townshend'. This clash was a foretaste of the parliamentary battles that were to rage between these two throughout the American war. And the three-to-one majority in favour of the Quebec Bill was a foretaste of the government's iron control of the Commons itself.[4]

Soon after the Quebec Bill became law, Prime Minister North called an early election, bringing to an end a Parliament which had first convened in 1768. During that time, Tommy had spoken on no less than 380 occasions, a record bettered only by Lord North, Edmund Burke and William Dowdeswell, another leading member of the Rockingham faction. By contrast, Tommy's father, who was retiring on account of his age and health, had hardly spoken at all. During its last session, this Parliament had goaded the American colonies into combined action. After convening at Philadelphia, the first Continental Congress issued a fresh Declaration of Rights on 14 October 1774. The Quebec Act, it proclaimed, was 'impolitic, unjust, cruel and unconstitutional'. But if American opinion was running strongly against the king, the British people were just as strongly behind him.[5]

In all, there were contests in 95 constituencies during the general election of 1774, from which the North government emerged just as strong, while the opposition factions remained just as weak. One of the new members was Tommy's nephew, George Brodrick, who had been elected as the other member for Whitchurch; Tommy himself never faced a contested election during his 29 years as an MP.[6]

For a short time after the 1774 election, the king appeared to be in a conciliatory mood. In late October, the first Continental Congress addressed a public letter to 'the Oppressed Inhabitants of Canada' denouncing the Quebec Act for not providing an elected assembly, jury trials or habeas corpus. And on 3 January 1775, George III instructed Governor Carleton to reconsider the introduction of each of these in Quebec. But by the time Carleton received the king's letter, he was already digesting Major-General Gage's reports of a full-blown rebellion in Massachusetts.[7]

The flexibility George III displayed towards the Canadians had not been extended to his other North American subjects. In November 1774, he told Prime Minister North that 'blows must decide whether … [the Americans] are to be … independent', describing General Gage's idea of suspending the Coercive Acts, which had attempted to reassert Britain's authority in the wake of the Boston Tea Party, as absurd. 'We must either master them', the king said, 'or leave them as aliens'. Soon afterwards, the Rhode Island Legislature voted to purchase 300 barrels of gunpowder, 3 tons of lead and 40,000 flints.[8]

Not everyone in Britain was as eager for a showdown with the Americans as the king appeared to be. London's merchants, fearful that a war would ruin their businesses, petitioned the House of Commons in January 1775. And as the *Evening Post* reported, Tommy Townshend championed their cause:

> Distress … must fall on the commerce, the landholder, and the stock holder; but the place holder … will batten in the sunshine of his country's ruin; no distress of the public can affect him … The contractors of every kind may pant for a civil war; but … violent councils must shake to its very foundations the public credit on which everything depends.

Displaying his 'usual manly spirit and good sense', the paper noted that Tommy had 'argued with great force of reason with wit and with spirit'. Indeed he had argued 'with everything but effect on his audience'. And the vote went 250 to 89 the government's way. Still, the debate seemed to have an impact on Lord North who proposed a compromise plan to the Commons a month later. Should any single colony undertake to provide for the common defence and civil governance and should their plan be approved by Parliament, Britain would abstain from imposing any taxation within that colony. Although Tommy dismissed this idea as 'impracticable whether it meant to enforce obedience or effect reconciliation', North's vote was higher than before. But the prime minister's plan had created great tension behind the scenes, with the anti-American Bedford faction almost deserting the government in protest. And of the colonies, only Nova Scotia took up the offer.[9]

The central role of Parliament in North's compromise plan did not impress the Americans because, from their point of view, it did not represent them. There were only four members of the Commons who had been born and nurtured in America. In the colonies themselves, Americans voted and exercised rights of the traditional English type in far greater numbers than Englishmen did in England. Only one in six Britons had the right to vote for an MP whereas two out of three Americans were eligible to vote for a representative in their colonial legislatures. Moreover, Rhode Island and Connecticut were effectively republics, electing their own governors and owing only a vague allegiance to the British Crown. Of those who did have the vote in Britain, one constituency had just seven voters whilst others contained up to twenty thousand; some of the fastest growing areas, such as Manchester and Birmingham, had no representation at all. In America, by contrast, representation in proportion to population was entrenched. The British theory that Manchester, Birmingham and the American colonies were 'virtually' represented in the Commons by other members who each represented the whole Empire just did not wash with most Americans. They placed a premium on local representation.[10]

As a representative of a small borough constituency, Tommy Townshend was in no hurry to change the way he was elected, but he had supported some reform, including a proposal to permanently transfer the hearing of election petitions from the whole of the Commons to a special committee of thirteen. In a rare defeat for Lord North, Parliament had approved this modest change in February 1774. Even so, Tommy lashed out at the conduct of members who brought parliamentary debates into disrepute on both sides of the Atlantic:

> [Often] only twenty or thirty members [attended] and possibly half those

[were] asleep during examination of evidence… [When called to vote] down stairs came tumbling members who had not heard a word… and whose only excuse was that they were not in their senses.[11]

Leading American thinkers including Thomas Jefferson and John Adams now argued that only the separate American legislatures were sovereign in America, that Parliament had no authority there and that the only link to Britain was via the king. As the French writer Alexis de Tocqueville later put it, 'the monarchy was still the law of the State but the republic was already vigorous in every township'. In Britain, many remained convinced that 'Englishmen are still Englishmen and the ferrying of them across the Atlantic does not alter their nature', but this was no longer true. As far back as 1755, Benjamin Franklin had calculated that only 80,000 of the estimated 1,000,000 American colonists were immigrants and many of those were from countries other than Britain. The American colonies were, in substance, nations. With greater ease than many of his countrymen, Tommy Townshend was able to apply Algernon Sidney's dictum that 'free nations have a right of meeting when and where they choose'.[12]

The failure of Prime Minister North's compromise plan strengthened the hand of the government's anti-American faction. The concerns of London's merchants were ignored and a bill was introduced to restrain the trade and commerce of America's New England colonies. As always, Tommy Townshend and Edmund Burke were loud in their opposition, but many of their parliamentary allies were not. 'In the case of this Bill', the king noted, 'the languor of Opposition arose from feeling the sense of the Nation warm in favour of this proposition'. The bill duly sailed through the House.[13]

The rising tide of public opinion in favour of taking stern measures against the Americans did not deter Tommy from repudiating his earlier support for the Coercive Acts:

'[They] made no discrimination between innocence and guilt, which starved all alike and which [fixed] an eternal hatred of this country and its legislature in the minds of the Americans… Britain's violation of these privileges first produced the disobedience and then the disobedience was punished in the most cruel and unnatural acts.

From the king's point of view, this speech was little short of treasonous. A French secret agent predicted that 'seven or eight members of the Opposition would probably go to the Tower'. During the last Commons' debate but one on American affairs before a fateful clash of arms at Lexington, Tommy gave a prophetic warning to the prime minister. 'Though the present measures were adopted by a large majority of Parliament', he said, 'if they did not succeed the noble lord [North] would find himself responsible'.[14]

News of what was quickly dubbed the 'battle of Lexington' on 19 April 1775, during which Paul Revere's minutemen attacked a British force on its way to Concord to destroy military stores, took some time to reach London. There, divisions in the opposition factions had been plumbing new depths over a grant of 100,000 pounds to the king for the renovation of Somerset House and what is now Buckingham Palace. Edmund Burke eagerly supported this display of 'splendour', while Tommy Townshend sharply criticized its extravagance. 'There was no concerted action or lasting union in the Opposition', one of its senior members, Lord Shelburne, observed. 'Sometimes the leaders would not lead and sometimes the followers would not follow'.[15]

Less than a month after Lexington, which had cost 273 British and 95 American lives, the second Continental Congress approved the Olive Branch Petition which professed loyalty to the king. It pleaded with him to separate himself from his ministers who it blamed for the conflict. However, news from America usually took a month to reach London, while dispatches going the other way could take up to four, depending on the weather, allowing the British government no time to evaluate the petition and send instructions back to its commanders before news arrived of the next clash, at Bunker Hill. If the petition had been a serious attempt at conciliation, it was overtaken by events.[16]

At the battle of Breed's (Bunker) Hill near Boston on 17 June, the British suffered a thousand casualties. '[The Americans] conceal themselves... till an opportunity presents itself of taking a shot... which done they immediately retreat', one redcoat said. 'What an unfair method of carrying on a war'. While the British abandoned Boston for Halifax, Nova Scotia, the Continental Congress proceeded to create an army and to appoint George Washington as its commander. Then, on 23 August, the King formally proclaimed the Americans to be rebels and the opposition 'made no noise on this stretch of power'. One pro-American member of the Commons, Sir George Yonge, wrote to Tommy: 'the storm gathers every hour and this country is hastening to its fate by its own hands...with indifference and a satisfaction that is equally astonishing and unexplained'.[17]

The king was no mere figurehead. He encouraged Prime Minister North to use 'every means of distressing America'. And he attempted to micro-manage the war, giving directions for the deployment of individual regiments. Having impressed George III a year earlier with a call for resolute action against mob violence in Boston, Tommy's old friend Lord George Germain became secretary of state for the American Department. 'He had all the requisites of a great minister', Germain's secretary observed, 'unless popularity and good luck are to be numbered among them'. As American secretary, Germain now stepped forward to help the king wage war, a task Lord North shrank away from. In the meantime, Major-General Gage's replacement, William Howe, had been developing a plan to link New York and Canada via the Hudson Valley, thereby isolating the rebellious New England colonies, but he needed more troops. With a total military strength of 48,650, Britain was stretched thin throughout her Empire. Germain therefore set about recruiting a new Army of 20,000.[18]

Britain's use of German soldiers was long-established and Germain recruited 10,000 of them to fight the American rebels. It was a move which appalled Tommy Townshend. 'While foreigners were taken into the British pay in every war since the Revolution [of 1688]', Tommy told the Commons, 'it made a great difference in hiring them to fight our battles on the Continent...and introducing them in to the British Empire'. In a trans-Atlantic civil war between British subjects, Tommy's concern was that such troops 'cannot esteem your laws; they know not your constitution; they cannot respect it'.[19]

Prime Minister North had not totally given up on negotiating a settlement. At his urging, William Howe was appointed to lead a peace commission to negotiate directly with the colonies. Germain's insistence that this commission could not come to terms with any colony unless it recognized the supremacy of the British Parliament soon proved to be a major obstacle, but it was the Americans' fury at the British use of German troops which would finally tip the colonists over the edge. Tommy might have opposed the foreign component of the new army and its strategic purpose, but he did not oppose the government's plan to pay for it, and when a 25 per cent increase in land tax was moved in the Commons he told the House: 'as the Army and Navy were voted, they must not be starved'.[20]

On 3 July 1776, William Howe began landing his army at Staten Island in preparation for an attack on New York; the very next day, Congress approved the Declaration of Independence. Nevertheless, Howe published his powers as peace commissioner. He offended George Washington, however, by addressing a copy to him as a private citizen, and when the congressional leaders told Howe that they were from 'the Independent States of America', he replied 'then I cannot receive you'. In New York, the rebels began melting the king's statue for bullets; its bronze head was saved and smuggled to England, eventually ending up under a sofa in George Townshend's London home.

A parliamentary report noted that on 22 May Tommy had told the House:

> What Parliament... resolved... was of very little consequence for [the] administration would act just as they liked. Parliament... was at length degraded into a mere engine of government one day to bully another to conciliate and the next he foresaw would be to sue for terms with America.

The very next day, Parliament had commenced its long summer break, seeing no need to return until 31 October.[21]

[*Eleven*]

AT WAR WITH AMERICA

The American Declaration of Independence was an act of high treason. Its author, Thomas Jefferson, had drawn inspiration from the works of Algernon Sidney, who had been beheaded for asserting the people's right to 'take away kings'. And now by this declaration the second Continental Congress was attempting to take away kings in America. As Benjamin Franklin put it, 'we must all hang together or ... we shall all hang separately'.[1]

Thomas Jefferson freely acknowledged Algernon Sidney's influence. It can also be seen by comparing extracts from Sidney's *Discourses on Government* with passages from the Declaration itself. In *Discourses*, Sidney wrote: 'Man is naturally free ... [and] cannot justly be deprived of his liberty without a cause ... nothing can be more evident than that if many [men] had been created they had been all equal'. In the Declaration, Jefferson asserted: 'We hold these truths to be self evident; that all men are created equal; that they are endowed by their Creator with certain inalienable rights; that among these are life liberty and the pursuit of happiness'. And Sidney's conclusion that 'we may therefore ... take away kings', is reflected in the next part of the Declaration: 'Wherever any form of government becomes destructive of these ends, it is the right of the people to alter or abolish it'.[2]

Much of the declaration was personally directed at George III with no less than eighteen specific charges against him. Jefferson had already rejected the notion that the British Parliament had any authority over the colonies, maintaining that the only link to Britain was via the king. To ground a reason for independence, it was therefore necessary to demolish the link with George III himself. This the declaration proceeded to do by accusing the king of waging war on his American subjects: 'He is at this time transporting large armies of foreign mercenaries to complete the works of death, dissolution & tyranny, already begun ... and totally unworthy of the head of a civilized nation'. Although Tommy Townshend had also objected to the use of mercenaries from Hans towns, 'which were known to be the asylum of all the rogues and vagabonds of the rest of Germany', he did not agree with the Declaration's most fundamental assertion – that of complete independence for the colonies.[3]

George III had proclaimed his Declaration of Rebellion almost a year before, and the civil war, which had existed in reality ever since, was now formally recognized on both sides of the Atlantic. Those who signed the American declaration understood that whilst they could assert independence, the king would only accept it if forced to do so. Like those who had rebelled against Charles I during the English Civil War just over a century earlier, the American rebels were fighting the whole apparatus of state, including many ordinary people whose history, language and heritage they shared. But unlike the English Civil War, which was fought among Englishmen, and the American Civil War of the 1860s which was fought among Americans, the revolutionary civil war, which lasted until the intervention of France turned it into a world war in 1778, was fought within the transatlantic community of English-speaking peoples.[4]

Because the war was a civil war, there were splits, misgivings and divided loyalties everywhere. 'We cannot forget', said one British general, 'that when we strike we wound a brother'. And on hearing a suggestion that church bells might be rung to celebrate a victory, even George III was moved to say that 'notes of triumph would not have been proper when the successes are against subjects, not a foreign foe'. In America, Benjamin Franklin was celebrated as a patriot. But his son, William, the governor of New Jersey, remained fiercely loyal to the king throughout the war. Across the Atlantic, the Townshend family was also divided. George, by now the fourth viscount, and 'Spanish' Charles remained active members of Britain's wartime government. However, George's son, Lord Ferrers, declared on his first day in Parliament that he 'should oppose all measures of the Court but out of respect for his father would not begin on that day'. And Tommy Townshend continued as one of the British government's most bitter critics. By contrast, his cousin Charles Cornwallis, who as an MP had opposed taxing the American colonies, felt that as a professional soldier he could not decline a command, sailing for America on 10 February 1776.[5]

Now a major-general, Cornwallis first saw action with General Howe in August that year when, following the collapse of Howe's peace commission, the British army clashed with General Washington's forces on the outskirts of the city of New York. During an attack on Fort Washington near the top of Manhattan Island, Howe restrained his troops, telling them 'to treat our enemies as if they might one day become our friends'. Then, after capturing the fort and 3,000 rebels, Howe and Cornwallis chased Washington across the Hudson River into New Jersey. On 19 November, when a breathless junior officer told Cornwallis that Washington's troops were in sight, the general replied, 'let them go my dear Ewald … we do not want to lose any men'. Reflecting on this later, Captain Ewald said: 'now I perceived what was on foot. We wanted to spare the King's subjects and hoped to terminate the war cordially'. Later, at Princeton, the American commander was only an hour ahead of Cornwallis. But further pauses in the British advance kept Washington just out of harm's way, allowing him to escape across the Delaware River. Even so, the British now occupied New York, a superb port which dominated inter-colonial communications to the north, south and west.[6]

When the Commons finally reconvened on 31 October 1776, concern over the Declaration of Independence had been offset by news of the capture of New York. And by the end of the year, the opposition was under more pressure than the government. After an opposition motion for 'the revisal of all laws by which the Americans think themselves aggrieved' was defeated by a margin of two to one, the Rockingham faction ceased to attend Parliament altogether and 'dispersed to their estates to go fox hunting'. But Tommy Townshend refused to join in the boycott, saying the he 'was much strengthened and confirmed in his own view by the authority of Lord Chatham'. And Chatham's faction also continued to attend Parliament.[7]

In days when holding an office of profit under the Crown did not disqualify a person from taking his seat in Parliament, many soldiers and sailors were members. Between 1754 and 1790, a total of 208 army officers and 79 navy officers sat in the Commons. During the revolutionary war, these members included key commanders such as Generals Burgoyne, Clinton, Howe and Vaughan and Admirals Hardy, Howe, Keppel and Palliser. In Parliament, Tommy Townshend had been on friendly terms with most of them. But as a strong critic of Britain's war effort in the early days when the war was popular, Tommy often found himself misrepresented in the press. On 7 November, he was forced to write to his friend, General Clinton, who had taken part in the New York campaign. 'Your behaviour in Long Island ... [does] you honour', Tommy said. 'However the erroneous retailers of our debates in the papers have made me ... censure you very unjustly when I know you deserve every mark of esteem'.[8]

By early 1777 it had become clear to the British government that this transatlantic war would be long and bitter. In consequence, it introduced a bill to suspend habeas corpus for people suspected of high treason in North America, allowing rebels there to be seized and detained indefinitely. 'This was ... arming Ministers with a power ... unknown to the constitution', Tommy responded, 'dangerous in itself and alarming to the last degree'. For him, it rekindled memories of the way John Wilkes had been targeted in general warrants. It amounted to a full-scale attack on the British constitution. But with the Rockingham faction continuing its parliamentary boycott, the remainder of the opposition went down to a crushing defeat.[9]

On 11 September, Howe began an advance on the rebel capital, Philadelphia. During a set-piece battle against Washington, Cornwallis was detached with a strong corps. And two days later he caught up with the rebels on the Brandywine River, routing them in the woods nearby. Although Washington again escaped, Cornwallis had the satisfaction just under two weeks later of entering Philadelphia unopposed, the second Continental Congress having fled just a few days before. What appeared to be a major symbolic victory for the British, though, was already contributing to a strategic disaster. Howe's original plan had been to drive north from New York to meet up with a British force advancing south from Canada. The goal was to isolate the New England colonies which the British considered to be the most rebellious. However Howe's Philadelphia campaign had seriously reduced the number of troops available for this second operation, which had already begun.[10]

The governor of Quebec, Sir Guy Carleton, a general who had repelled a rebel attack on Canada, was the obvious choice to command the Canadian end of the operation to isolate New England. But years before Carleton had fallen out with Lord George Germain following the battle of Minden and Germain was now the secretary of state for America. To Carleton's intense annoyance, his subordinate, John Burgoyne, was appointed instead. 'I hear Carleton has assured Burgoyne that he will give him every assistance', Tommy observed, 'but has asked for leave to return home'. A playwright, gambler and all-round colourful member of Parliament, 'gentleman Johnny' Burgoyne was described by Walpole as 'a vain very ambitious man with a half understanding which was worse than none'. Burgoyne's objective was to drive south from Canada to join up with Howe or at the very least to 'get possession of Albany and open communication to New York'.[11]

Lieutenant-General Burgoyne's force of 7, 000 had begun its advance south down Lake Champlain in June 1777. On reaching Ticonderoga, Burgoyne had with little difficulty driven out the American garrison. But from there to his next goal, Fort Edward, he chose a winding trail to the east of Lake George. This route slowed his progress, burdened him with supply problems and allowed the rebels to regroup. He then compounded his difficulties by dispatching 800 men on a supply raid to Bennington where they were cut up by a growing band of rebels. Forced to garrison Ticonderoga with a further 900 men, Burgoyne's main contingent was weakened just as the rebels' strength was swelled by volunteers from the surrounding countryside. The disintegration of a mixed British and Indian diversionary force at Fort Schuyler was a further blow. Faced with the decision as to whether to go forward to Albany or back to the safety of Ticonderoga, the gambler Burgoyne gambled all and advanced across the Hudson River, thereby cutting his supply line. Before long, he was greatly outnumbered. With no hope of relief, he surrendered at Saratoga on 13 October.[12]

Parliament resumed on 18 November 1777 and in the absence of any news about Burgoyne's defeat the king's speech was 'all adulation'. Unimpressed, Tommy attacked the government's war budget 'on the simple principle that it was in support of a war he detested and abhorred'. Put on the defensive over his campaign to isolate the New England colonies, Lord Germain justified his choice of Burgoyne by criticizing Carleton, the man he had passed over. Tommy 'vindicated' Carleton by claiming that he had been 'dishonourably superseded'.

The first rumours of Burgoyne's surrender came via Paris. A Commons debate soon followed, although absolute confirmation of the disaster was still some days off. Ever ready to blame the government rather than its generals, Tommy 'condemned the whole expedition, spoke very favourably of General Burgoyne and imputed his want of success to the ignorance and incapacity of those who directed him from hence'. He was particularly hostile about the use of Indian 'savages' against the rebels at Fort Schuyler. Almost rejoicing at the failure of this largely Indian expedition, which would have resulted in 'a diabolical system of blood and carnage', Tommy's comments again bordered on treason.[13]

After receiving an assurance from the prime minister that he 'would not abandon' him, the king canvassed the creation of a new army to make up for Burgoyne's loss. And he demanded a plan from North to 'repel' the opposition's parliamentary attacks, especially those which called for the tabling of embarrassing government papers. No sooner had he done so than the opposition moved for all papers relating to the deployment of Indians, prompting a sharp exchange between Tommy and Lord Germain. While the government comfortably defeated this motion, behind the scenes it was on the brink of imploding.[14]

On 29 January 1778, the prime minister canvassed various peace proposals with the king. One exempted from parliamentary taxation any colony which renounced independence while another repealed the tax on tea. Concerned about an adverse public reaction, George III demanded that full details be put to cabinet, allowing Lord Germain to vent his furious opposition. Nevertheless, three weeks later, North introduced bills to authorize the appointment of peace commissioners and to abandon Britain's right to tax the colonies, while maintaining the Navigation Act to regulate trade.

Heard 'in dull and melancholy silence', the prime minister was soon under attack from Tommy who targeted the peace package at its weakest point:

> When your Commissioners have caused hostilities to cease by sea and land: what will become of your Navigation Act? For suppose contrary to the provisions of the Act, an American ship should be found trading and be made a prize of; then the colonies will tell you that you have broke the truce and hostilities will commence on their part.[15]

Although Lord North won the debate, he was so unnerved that he proposed a new cabinet with Lord Chatham in charge. Appalled, the king demanded that the prime minister remain at his post. 'Nothing can ever make me address myself for the assistance of Lord Chatham or any other branch of the Opposition', he fumed. 'I would rather lose the Crown I now wear than bear the ignomiuy of possessing it under their shackles.' While North's parliamentary influence would remain significant, the king was now head of government as well as head of state, relying on his American secretary, Lord Germain. and his first lord of the admiralty, Lord Sandwich, to help run the ever widening war.[16]

Despite his increasingly strident criticism of the British government, Tommy continued his good relations with its generals. When one of his Selwyn relatives was shot through the arm and lungs during a duel aboard a troop transport, Tommy did not hesitate to lobby General Clinton:

> Mr Selwyn ... at present eldest Lieutenant in the 7th Regiment ... returned with your leave for a chance of recovering his wound ... (not brought on by any misbehaviour of his) ... Now I am to request of you that he may not be set aside when promotion falls to him.

Although his nephew's recovery took more than two years, Tommy was finally able to write to Clinton on 23 December 1780 expressing his 'very sincere thanks for your protection of my relation Captain Selwyn'.[17]

Even though George III was by now a complete affront to the Whig concept of a constitutional monarch, this did not unite the opposition. It split in both Houses over the issue of American independence. In the Lords, the Duke of Richmond, described by one colleague as a 'plaguing fellow' for his incessant stream of opposition motions, moved that the king withdraw his forces from America and bring about a reconciliation that implied independence. On hearing this, Chatham roused himself from his sick bed to proclaim that he would never consent to independence, before collapsing on the floor of the chamber. Meanwhile, in the Commons, a motion proposing negotiations with America 'to declare the independency of that country' was supported by Charles Fox. Originally a follower of Lord North, Fox had crossed the floor in support of the Americans and soon began dressing in a buff waistcoat and blue overcoat – aping George Washington's uniform. Less enamoured of the rebels than Fox, Tommy Townshend 'thought the motion premature' and managed to get it adjourned. Chatham, Tommy and Lord Shelburne were opposed to

American independence while Rockingham, Fox and Richmond supported it. On this issue, the opposition was in disarray.[18]

As a young man, Lord Shelburne had seen his precocious ministerial career shattered by the political turmoil of the mid-1760s, prompting him to say then of William Pitt 'tis you sir alone in everybody's opinion can put an end to this anarchy'. And now Shelburne thought that Chatham in power might have been able to preserve the link between Britain and the colonies by 'repealing at one stroke all the vexatious legislation'. But Chatham never recovered from his collapse, dying on 11 May 1778.

As he rose to speak on a motion praising his late mentor, Tommy was at first so emotional that he had to resume his seat, though he was composed enough to act as a pallbearer at Chatham's huge public funeral. Almost two hundred years later, Winston Churchill wrote 'to weld all [England's] resources of wealth and manhood into a single instrument of war which should be felt from the Danube to the Mississippi; to humble the House of Bourbon, to make the Union Jack supreme in every ocean to conquer, this was the spirit of Pitt'. After the funeral, Tommy helped to arrange for Chatham's debts to be paid and for his next of kin to receive a generous pension. 'Your invariable... goodness to me and my family [is] such as I can find no words sufficient to acknowledge', Lady Chatham wrote, '[and] your friendship to me and my family [is] the most valuable thing we can be possessed of'. Like Tommy, Chatham was an Eton old boy. A congratulatory letter from the school's former headmaster, Edward Barnard, warned him that he might pay a price for his generosity. 'Your attention to the family of your country's deceased friend does you honour and ought but I fear will not recommend you', Barnard wrote. 'The age did not know how to estimate him, it was unworthy of him tho' it owned his excellence by its envy'.[19]

Chatham's hope had been to settle with the rebels in such a way that they would again become part of the British Empire. In early 1778, the North government's peace commissioners, led by Lord Carlisle, offered Congress a union under a common sovereign, whereby Britain and America would act together in equal freedom for mutual safety. However, Congress replied that, having affirmed a 'perpetual union between the thirteen states' in a 'confederacy' to be known as 'The United States of America' in late 1777, it would not negotiate unless Britain recognized the United States or withdrew its Army. Talks with the British commissioners were therefore abandoned and Congress duly solemnized the thirteen states' perpetual union on 9 July 1778.[20]

[*Twelve*]

⸺ At war in Parliament ⸺

Saratoga was like Quebec in 1759, a small battle that changed the course of history. Following Quebec, French forces had departed North America. After Saratoga, they returned. On 6 February 1778, France signed treaties of 'commerce and alliance' with the rebels, receiving Benjamin Franklin six weeks later as ambassador for 'the United States of America'.[1]

The intervention of France gradually turned what had been a civil war into a world war. This time, unlike the Seven Years' War, Britain did not have Prussia as an ally to keep France busy in Europe. King Frederick had not forgotten his humiliation at the hands of Prime Minister Bute in 1763 and now 'beheld with satisfaction [Britain's] augmenting embarrassments'. With a beachhead in New York and often hostile country beyond, the British army needed to source many stores from home, notwithstanding a sizeable number of loyalist Americans in its ranks. The rebels, by contrast, were largely self-sufficient. As a result, the British navy was stretched to the limit on convoy duty, while at the same time patrolling the American coast and the rest of the Empire. Around Britain itself, the home fleet had to be on constant alert to counter any attempted French invasion. The French navy, on the other hand, was free to target Britain's three-thousand mile supply line and to make mischief wherever else it chose.[2]

In November 1777, Tommy Townshend had been sceptical of Vice-Admiral Hugh Palliser's assurance on behalf of the Admiralty that the British navy was more than a match for those of France and Spain combined. After France entered the war, Tommy's scepticism turned to fury. As early as 1769, his friend Edmund Burke had commented on his almost manic temper. 'Had there been fuel enough ... to feed [Tommy's] fire there would have been a dreadful conflagration', Burke said, 'but there wants a sufficient staple in his mind'. And his anger was made worse by the government's naval incompetence.[3]

A French fleet based at Toulon had long been viewed as a serious threat to Britain and in April 1778 rumours flew that it was about to sail for America under the command of Admiral Charles d'Estaing. Despite the fact that a British fleet under Admiral Augustus Keppel was then at Spithead, Prime Minister North lamented that no squadron was available to mount a challenge. Furious at North's inaction, George III personally intervened, demanding that Keppel 'beat this Frenchman before he passes... Gibraltar'. In fact d'Estaing had departed two days earlier, on 13 April, with eleven ships of the line and numerous supporting frigates, as well as a French minister accredited to the Continental Congress. Keppel's poor relations with the first lord of the admiralty, Lord Sandwich, contributed to d'Estaing's escape, as did Sandwich's strange combination of efficiency and dilatoriness. 'If any man will draw up his case and put his name at the foot of the first page, I will give him an immediate reply', Sandwich said. 'Where he compels me to turn over the sheet, he must wait my leisure'.[4]

During a parliamentary debate over this débâcle three weeks later, Horace Walpole noted that 'T. Townshend, Charles Fox and Mr Burke attacked the Ministers with great warmth'. Tommy began sensibly enough, demanding to know why the British fleet had been kept idle at a naval pageant when 'the Ministers ought to have dispatched a sufficient force to... put it out of the power of d'Estaing to elude us', but then he worked himself up into a manic temper charging the ministers with 'ignorance, laziness, incapacity and treachery' lamenting that 'while our pageant... streamers were wantoning in the wind at Spithead... our coasts were insulted'. Struggling to explain why Keppel was *still* in port, the prime minister said Tommy would not so hastily condemn the ministry when he knew the full extent of the fleet's preparations. That very same day, the king had stormed off down to Portsmouth, which he refused to leave until the fleet had sailed. In reply to North, Tommy accused the ministry of being 'scandalously' negligent. 'Was it possible for Ministers to be awake?' he demanded.[5]

With the first lord of the admiralty a member of the House of Lords, it was George Germain along with the prime minister who bore the brunt of his attacks in the Commons. They grimly held to the government line that the navy was in a 'formidable state'. Behind the scenes, Germain was so dissatisfied with North that he threatened to resign. Privately, the prime minister begged to do likewise. 'Nothing can prevent the utmost confusion and distress but a material change in the Ministry', he pleaded. 'If your Majesty does not allow me to retire you and this country are ruined'.[6]

Despite everything the government said publicly, d'Estaing's escape was a disaster, compounded by his reappearance off North America on 20 August. 'The arrival of the French fleet upon the coast of America', George Washington observed, 'is a great and striking event'. Thanks to d'Estaing, Britain was unable to blockade America's coast and lost its mastery of the Western Atlantic and Caribbean. As a result, 55,000 British troops dotted around the Americas and dependent on the Royal Navy for support were now isolated from each other. So concerned was General Clinton about this that he retreated to New York from the rebel capital, Philadelphia.[7]

Meanwhile, Gentleman Johnny Burgoyne had returned to England in May. 'He is desired not to come to Court', Tommy told his father, 'and a Board of General Officers is to examine…his conduct'. But nothing prevented the defeated general from attending the Commons where he was a serving member. He duly turned up to defend his actions at Saratoga, demanding a parliamentary inquiry. When this was refused, he joined the opposition. Burgoyne wanted Parliament to sit through its traditional summer recess, reasoning that its 'occasional sanctions' would give 'fresh energy' to the Crown. Predictably adverse to such scrutiny, the government ridiculed the idea. Tommy's old nemesis, Richard Rigby, was especially harsh, prompting Tommy to defend the 'unfortunate general' who was 'labouring' for his reputation. But the ministry was not finished with Burgoyne. On parole as a prisoner of war, Gentleman Johnny was ordered back to America to join his troops in captivity. This order he refused to obey, claiming that it was no more than a clumsy tactic by the government to silence a strong critic. He was forced to resign his commission. Grateful for Tommy's support, he wrote 'If my conduct is thought worthy of the esteem of men like you, the situation I resign is much overpaid'.[8]

After finally leaving Portsmouth, Admiral Keppel and his fleet of twenty ships of the line had engaged a French fleet of twenty-seven on 22 July 1778. During this battle off Cape Ushant on the east coast of Brittany, Keppel had tried to re-form his fleet so as to re-engage the enemy after their first clash, but Keppel's vice-admiral, Hugh Palliser, did not comply with his orders and the French fleet escaped. Some claimed that Palliser's ships had been damaged. Others said he was incompetent and worse. Similar accusations were made against Keppel, whose notable fighting spirit had been tempered in later years by the legacy of a fever he had contracted as a young officer. 'In self possession, judgment, superior maritime skill and presence of mind; in all those endowments of a great commander which ensure victory', one colleague said, 'I have always found him deficient'. Tommy, however, seemed untroubled by the actions of either man, writing to his uncle eleven days after the battle:

> We were tantalized here last night with an account of a complete victory over the French fleet which today does not seem so considerable... However if our advantage is not great thank god our loss is very small... No one can doubt but that Keppel and his officers did their best.[9]

All the while, Parliament had been in recess. Surrounded though he was by the magnificence of Frognal's gardens in summer, Tommy could not take his mind off the ever-widening war. Hostilities with Spain were almost certain and another 10,000 men had been earmarked for American service. 'If we had not been so mad already about America', Tommy wrote, 'I should say this was impossible to be true'. In London, Vice-Admiral Palliser's conduct off Ushant had come under attack in the *General Advertiser*, a paper sympathetic to the opposition. Believing that the *Advertiser*'s attack had been inspired by Admiral Keppel, Palliser retaliated in the *Morning Post*, a paper sympathetic to the government. So concerned were the king and the first lord of the admiralty about the potential for matters to boil over politically, that they compiled a list of Keppel's captains and their political allegiances, among them:

> Captain Hood – very adverse to Admiral Keppel.
> Captain Jervis – a good officer but turbulent and busy, and violent as a politician attached to Mr Keppel.
> Captain Cosby – connected with opposition and on that account led to favour Mr Keppel.[10]

Both admirals were members of the House of Commons, Keppel being associated with the opposition and Palliser with the government. When Parliament resumed in December 1778, a parliamentary clash seemed likely. 'I am sorry to find', the king said, 'the strange managed dispute between the two Admirals is to be canvassed in the... Commons'. At first, this contest was confined to the admirals themselves. Keppel, on Palliser's demand, was court-martialled but acquitted, whereupon Palliser was forced to hide from the mob. Then several admirals and captains petitioned the king for Palliser's dismissal, and he too was court-martialled and acquitted. By now their dispute, which had progressively dragged in more and more MPs on both sides of the House, was a direct fight between the government and the opposition.[11]

On 3 March 1779 Charles Fox and Tommy Townshend pushed for a motion censuring the Admiralty for sending Keppel into battle with an inadequate fleet. This prompted an ugly clash with the prime minister, who had used the word 'side' when referring to factional divisions in the navy. '*Side*' should not have been used in a debate about national safety, Tommy thundered. But now that the prime minister had used the word:

> *That side* [North's side] had sent out... [Admiral Keppel] with an inferior force; *that side* had refused to thank him for saving his country... *that side* had depreciated the victory of 27 July and called it a defeat; *that side* had instituted an ill founded and malicious prosecution against him... *that side* had... shewn every mark of approbation to the accuser and... *that side* was determined to drive the Hon. Admiral for ever from the service of his country.[12]

To a point of order, Tommy argued it was 'to the highest degree absurd' that Admiral Keppel's evidence to the Commons could not be recorded. A by-now furious North contemptuously replied that the speaker had already ruled against recording this evidence. The House backed the speaker, but the vote was 208 to 169 – a heartening result for the opposition and one which the prime minister had difficulty explaining to the king. '[It was] the very bad [Government] attendance that the Opposition have conceived great hopes upon', North said. 'Mr Thos. Townshend spoke to order and was violent'. One government numbers' man noted that the opposition was now 'very full of spirits and presumption'.[13]

Just over two weeks later, the opposition pressed its advantage with a motion for the removal of Sandwich as first lord of the admiralty. Tommy accused Sandwich of bias against any naval officer who disagreed with him. 'My eye on my captains', Sandwich had once boasted, 'frightened them more than the enemy'. And now, Tommy predicted a deal in which the first lord would get a 'corrupt majority' to defeat the motion before resigning in favour of another 'land lord-admiral'. In time of war, Tommy charged, this was nothing more than an attempt to keep naval patronage in the hands of men who would do the government's bidding. 'If you can devise any means I can personally take to assist in getting persons to ... [vote]', the king told North, 'you will find me most ready to adopt it'. Armed with this ultimate offer of patronage, the prime minister rounded up the numbers to support Sandwich, who then remained first lord for the remainder of the war.[14]

No sooner was this debate over than a Commons committee began an inquiry which pitted the Howe brothers and Burgoyne against the North government. In the aftermath of Saratoga, General William Howe had resigned his command to General Clinton and returned to London, claiming that the secretary of state for America, George Germain, had failed to reinforce him. Like Burgoyne, General Howe and his brother Richard, until recently Britain's commanding admiral in America, were also MPs. During the Keppel – Palliser debates, the king had offered to make Richard Howe first lord of the admiralty to stop him siding with the opposition. Howe had declined; he was no land lord-admiral.[15]

At the outset, Prime Minister North attempted to knobble the 'Inquiry into the American War' as it was known. When Lieutenant-General Cornwallis was called to give evidence in support of the Howe brothers, the government moved to block his testimony. 'The Commons is a very improper place to have the conduct of military men enquired into', the prime minister argued. 'A court martial was the only tribunal'. Supporting the moves to have his cousin called, Tommy Townshend expressed astonishment at North's 'total want of memory' of earlier occasions during which officers' conduct had been debated:

> Was [North] asleep when [Admiral Howe] was impliedly censured [in Parliament] ... for returning to New York ... thereby permitting d'Estaing to escape from him in to Boston? Did [North] forget the direct charges [also

in Parliament] against... [General Howe] for going southward [from New York to Philadelphia] instead of favouring another General's [Burgoyne's] operations from Canada?[16]

Apart from this, Tommy continued, the prime minister and Germain had paid for pamphlets full of 'artful invectives' against General Howe. When on half a dozen occasions North rose to defend himself, the Commons refused to hear him; he was obliged to resume his seat. In the end, the motion to call Cornwallis passed the Commons, which then sat riveted by his evidence. British forces were too small to prevail against the rebels, Cornwallis said. The almost universal hostility of Americans was making it difficult to get supplies. And British spies were reduced to smuggling rebel newspapers in pies and shoes. After concluding that 'it was impossible for the army to carry on its operations at any distance from the fleet', Cornwallis returned to America. 'Howe's examination has taken a disagreeable turn in the House', North told the king. 'Declarations concerning the impracticability of the war have made such an impression it will be very difficult to get the better of it'.[17]

The inquiry continued badly for the government when General Carleton, who had every reason to dislike Burgoyne for superseding him in command, exonerated his rival's conduct before his Saratoga surrender. However in a blunder which eclipsed anything he was accused of on the battlefield, General Howe was not present in the Commons' chamber when his business was called on. This would not have surprised one of his staff officers, Major Wemyss. 'However fit to command a corps... [Howe] was unequal to the duties of a Commander-in-Chief', Wemyss said. 'His manners were sullen and ungracious, with a dislike of businesss and a propensity to pleasure'. In Howe's absence, the committee was dissolved without the ministry being held to account. As Tommy put it:

> The Committee was concluded without any propositions being drawn from it; and the Ministers were silent when two of the greatest officers said there were imputations thrown upon their conduct, which prevented them from serving their country, and yet denied the justice of refuting them.[18]

In wider debates about the war during 1779, Tommy bombarded North with fundamental policy questions. 'What was the present object of the war with America? How was it to be carried on? Was unconditional surrender still an object of the Administration?' Strongly denying that it ever was, the prime minister nevertheless sought a vote of credit for another 1,000,000 pounds, which suggested otherwise. Despite growing outrage at the government's conduct of the war, no one, not even Charles Fox or Tommy Townshend, voted against providing the extra money. For one thing, the war now involved Britain's ancient enemy, France, with the risk growing every day that Spain would also side with America. Still, Tommy hoped for a separate peace with the rebels and proposed that Parliament should continue to sit during the summer of 1779. 'Ministers had asserted that the majority of America wished for an accommodation', he said. 'If that was the case it was a very strong argument for Parliament to continue sitting that they might co-operate in the much wished for work of peace'.[19]

On 15 June, Tommy's motion to continue sitting over summer was defeated. Perhaps it was his frustration at this result which, six days later, triggered his next parliamentary outburst, his most furious yet:

> So complete a scene of misfortune and national ruin ... could [not] have owed its origin to mere incapacity and want of sense; there was treachery and corruption in the case ... there was something about the Court and the Cabinet that bought and sold; some black traitor whose base purpose it was for a stipulated price to undermine and destroy the very existence of Britain.[20]

Although the prime minister denied these sweeping charges, he was greatly upset and began crying. His closest supporters claimed that it had something to do with the recent death of his two-year-old child; he appeared to be 'quite unhinged'. The king was furious with North's 'inexplicable' conduct. 'Yet', he said, 'I will do all I can to push him on'. Despite the fact that it was Tommy's 'violent attack' which had contributed to the prime ministerial break-down, the king did not hold him responsible. George III seems to have respected Tommy, even at his most rebellious.[21]

Whatever relief the government felt when the House of Commons was finally adjourned on 3 July 1779 was short-lived. That same day, Spain joined France and the American rebels, promptly attacking the British possessions of

Minorca and Gibraltar. A war that had begun 3,000 miles away at Lexington was about to land on Britain's doorstep. France and Spain had about 80 ships of the line between them for home service compared to Britain's 55. And as about 30,000 troops massed on the north-west coast of France waiting for the order to invade Britain and seize the Portsmouth area, the combined fleet moved into the Channel unopposed to cover their crossing. The outnumbered British fleet, under Admiral Hardy, was far to the west. For the first time in almost a century, an enemy fleet was in possession of the English Channel.[22]

When the enemy appeared off Plymouth and fired at a straying British ship, many shopkeepers and their families fled inland. A royal proclamation was issued that all horses and cattle be driven from the coast. According to some, this state of affairs had no parallel since the Spanish Armada. The Townshend family was as confused as everyone else about what was going on. 'Some report that the French and Spanish fleets have stood out to sea; others that the *Ardent* is taken in her attempt to join Hardy', Tommy's brother Charles wrote on 20 August. 'But so many contradictory reports are given every hour that we can depend upon nothing'. Three days later, Charles noted: 'the enemy's fleet quitted its station and sailed to the westward'. By 4 September, he was reporting that 'Hardy is safe at anchor at Spithead'. As quickly as the threat of invasion had blown up, it had died down. The enemy fleet had been ordered back to France after illness swept its ships.[23]

Despite the outcome, the threat of invasion had been real. It highlighted the transatlantic problems faced by the British navy, rent as it was by political factions. In the face of Admiral d'Estaing's threat, the British abandoned their base at Rhode Island. This gave the French fleet a foothold on the American coast and was, according to a senior British admiral, George Rodney, 'the most fatal measure that could possibly have been taken'. Britain's effort to supply her army in America from the other side of the North Atlantic, a logistical feat which would have no parallel until 1944, was now under grave threat. Indeed, this French naval presence was to play a major role in Britain's ultimate defeat at Yorktown.[24]

Tommy Townshend in 1754 (Mitchell Library, Sydney)

Full of bumptious ambition and self-confidence, Tommy Townshend was just 21 when he was first elected to the House of Commons. As one of two members for Whitchurch, a constituency controlled by his father, Tommy never had to face a contested election during his 29 years in the Commons.

Algernon Sidney in 1663 (National Portrait Gallery, London)
Beheaded in 1683 for writing 'the power originally in the people…is delegated into the Parliament [and]…we may therefore… take away kings', Sidney was an inspiration to America's founding fathers and to his distant nephew Tommy Townshend, who took a variation of Sidney's name – Sydney – on becoming a member of the House of Lords.

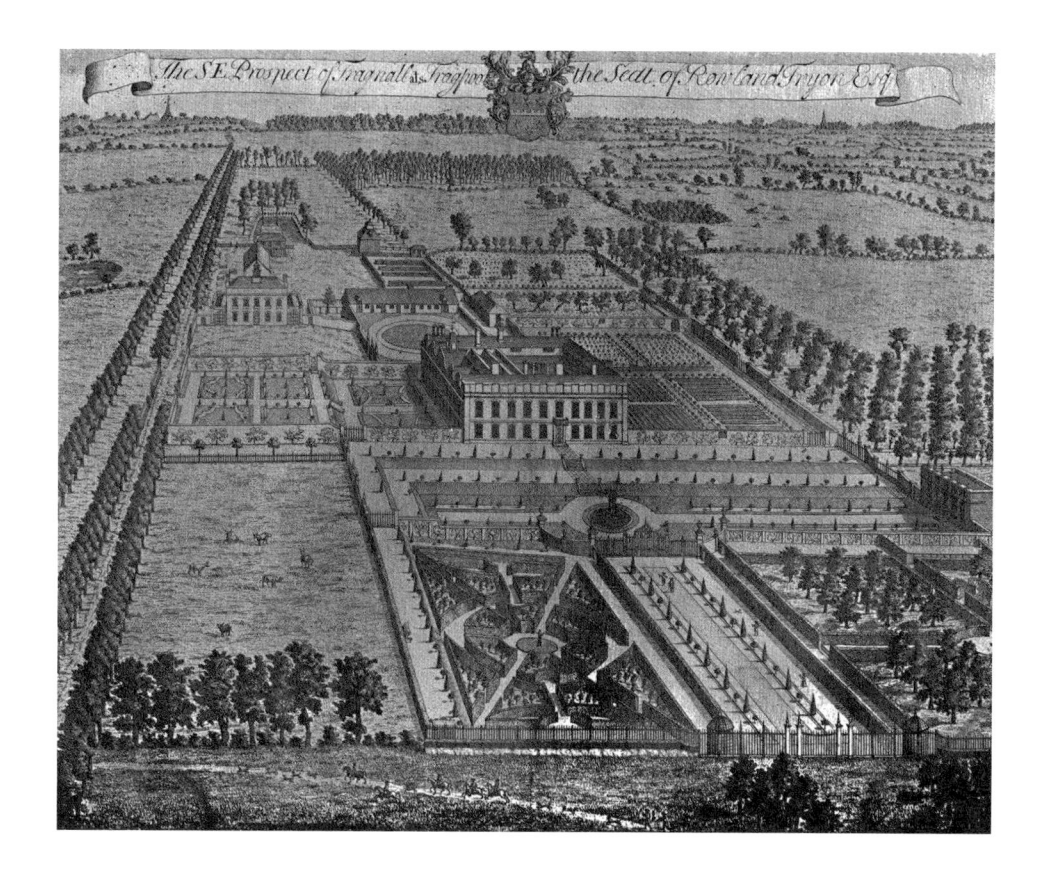

Frognal mansion (public domain)

Frognal was the country seat of Tommy Townshend's family for over 150 years. Tommy entertained many house guests there, none more important than William Pitt, 1st Earl of Chatham and his son William Pitt the Younger – two of the most powerful and influential prime ministers in British history.

George Townshend in 1760 (National Portrait Gallery, London)
Tommy Townshend's first cousin, George, took over command of British troops from the mortally wounded James Wolfe at the battle of Quebec in 1759. Won by the British, this battle triggered the end of French rule in North America. Tommy and George would later clash in the House of Lords, most notably over the madness of King George III.

A Townshend Caricature (National Portrait Gallery, London)

George Townshend was infamous for his caricatures, in this case of George II's son, the Duke of Cumberland, 'that prodigious mass of royal flesh'. This image of Cumberland, who was also the commander-in-chief at a time when George was a junior officer, 'adorned the shutters, walls and napkins of every tavern in Pall Mall'.

William Pitt, 1st Earl of Chatham in 1772 (National Portrait Gallery, London)

A charismatic force of nature, Pitt was described by Winston Churchill as having welded all England's 'resources of wealth and manhood into a single instrument of war which…[was] felt from the Danube to the Mississippi…[making] the Union Jack supreme in every ocean'. Pitt was Tommy Townshend's political hero and mentor.

Monday Oct: 7.

1. Mem: of Prussian Minister in favour of a Subject of his Master — rejected

2. Letter from Mr. de Blosset to Mr Lowndes.

3. Petition of John Earl of Breadalbain for an Exchange of Lands with the Commr: of annexed Estates.

4. Letters, of 24th & 25th of Aug: from Mr Oliver Distributor of Stamps at Boston relative to the late outrages in that Country, with Copys of Proclamations, Resolutions of Council &c. — Gov: Barnard must take care of the Stamps. A new Distributor to be appointed. Mr Oliver having resigned. The Acct &c. to be sent to the Privy Council.

Treasury Minutes, 7 October 1765 (W. L. Clements Library, Michigan)

As a lord of the treasury, Tommy Townshend wrote these minutes of a meeting with his fellow treasury lords. Item 4 recorded 'the late outrages' in Boston, protesting Britain's attempt to introduce an 'internal' Stamp Tax in America. 'Gov: Barnard [the British Governor of Massachusetts] must take care of the stamps', the minute noted.

Charles Townshend in 1766 (National Portrait Gallery, London)

As chancellor of the exchequer, Tommy Townshend's first cousin, Charles, introduced a tax on American tea. Eventually, it triggered the Boston Tea Party. Believing that the Americans had no objection to this 'external' tax, Tommy at first supported it. Later he tried unsuccessfully to have it repealed.

Benjamin Franklin in 1778 (National Portrait Gallery, London)

In 1766, Benjamin Franklin told a British parliamentary committee that 'the colonies have always submitted to external taxes and object...only...[to] internal taxes'. Tommy Townshend later defended his cousin's tea tax: 'He [Charles] was misled by the Americans themselves who said "take the tax, let bear the appearance of import duties" '.

Samuel Johnson in 1769 (National Portrait Gallery, London)
A bitter critic of Algernon Sidney, Johnson was attacked in the Commons by Tommy Townshend. So Johnson's friend Oliver Goldsmith included Tommy in a famous poem called *Retaliation*. Two of Goldsmith's lines suggested that Tommy was corrupt, a baseless charge which has nevertheless haunted Tommy's reputation ever since.

Thomas Jefferson in 1797 (National Portrait Gallery, London)

Author of the Declaration of Independence, Jefferson acknowledged Algernon Sidney's influence. In *Discourses Concerning Government*, Sidney had written 'nothing can be more evident than that if many [men] had been created they had all been equal.' Jefferson later asserted: 'We hold these truths to be self evident; that all men are created equal'.

King George III in 1761 (National Portrait Gallery, London)

As his prime minister shrank from the task of waging war on America, King George III became de facto head of government. Although a bitter opponent of this wartime administration and sympathetic to the Americans, Tommy Townshend managed to maintain good personal relations with the king.

Frederick North, 2nd Earl of Guilford in 1773 (National Portrait Gallery, London)
While he was an astute manager of the House of Commons, Lord North had little stomach for the war against America. And he repeatedly begged King George III to let him resign his prime ministership. One of North's most bitter critics in the Commons was Tommy Townshend, who often let fly with venomous attacks on the prime minister.

The House of Commons in 1794 (National Portrait Gallery, London)

Although Tommy Townshend had become a member of the House of Lords eleven years earlier, this image of the Commons with William Pitt the Younger on his feet, captures the chamber's atmosphere as Tommy would have known it. Far too small to seat all 558 members at one time, debates in this converted chapel were intimate and personal.

Charles Cornwallis in 1783 (National Portrait Gallery, London)

Defeated by George Washington at Yorktown in 1781, Tommy Townshend's first cousin, Charles, was nevertheless highly regarded. 'Judgment with moderation, simplicity of manners and incorruptible integrity were in Cornwallis united', one contemporary said. Tommy prevailed on Cornwallis to accept an appointment as governor-general of India.

The taking of Yorktown 1781 (Library of Congress)
Outnumbered three to one, Cornwallis's troops came under enormous pressure. A week before capitulating to George Washington, Cornwallis wrote 'Last evening the enemy carried my two advanced redoubts on the left by storm…[and] we shall soon be exposed to an assault in ruined [earth] works….with weakened numbers'.

Establishment of the Office of His Majesty's Principal Secretary of State for the Home Department.

Secretary of State Lord Sydney			
Total Salary	5580	Nett	3960 9
Patent Salary	100	Nett	84 6
	£5680		4044 15
Under Secretaries			
Hon. J. T. Townshend	500	Nett	
Evan Nepean Esq. } Salary	500	Nett	
		& Fees of Office	
Clerks.			
First Clerk Mr. William Pollock	No Salary – but Fees of Office		

	Salary	Parliamentary allowance	Total
2 Mr. Charles Brietzcke	175	190	365
3 George Randall	130	105	235
4 William H. G. Higden	120	95	215
5 George William Carrington	65	85	150
6 Thomas Daw	65	75	140
7 Eardley Wilmot	60	60	120
8 James Nassau (Collector)	45	55	100
9 Mr. Richard Chetwynd	45	45	90
10 George Lewis Patman	50	40	90
11 Thomas Chapman	50		50
	805	750	1555

Chamber Keepers		
William Kirby	20 16	} and Fees of Office
John Doudiet	20 16	
Necessary Woman		
Elizabeth Emmett	48	
	£894 12	
Messenger *Porter*		
Charles Henry	No Salary	Paid for Postage &out of Contingent Account

Home Department Establishment (W. L. Clements Library, Michigan)

Tommy Townshend became Secretary of State in July 1782. To assist him in running the British Empire and much of the internal government of Britain, Tommy had a total of just seventeen departmental staff to help him. These included two under secretaries, a necessary woman (tea lady/cleaner) and a porter.

The Montagu Lodgings (author's copy from Dugdale)

Originally a private residence on Whitehall, the Montagu lodgings housed the home secretary, Tommy Townshend, and his departmental staff who occupied just four rooms on the first floor. From there during the 1780s, decisions were made which affected every inhabited continent on the planet.

A draft of Article 5, 1782 (W. L. Clements Library, Michigan)

As home secretary, Tommy Townshend was responsible for peace negotiations with the Americans. This draft of article 5 of the Peace Treaty in Tommy's handwriting, attempts to protect loyalists – those Americans who had fought for George III. The fate of the loyalists was the major sticking point in negotiations with the Americans.

John Adams in 1800 (W. L. Clements Library, Michigan)

The toughest of the American peace negotiators in Paris was John Adams. 'There is but one way to negotiate with Englishmen [and] that is clearly and decidedly', he said. 'Their fears only govern them – if we entertain an idea of their generosity or benevolence towards us we are undone. They hate us universally from the throne to the footstool'.

Henry Strachey in 1782 (Sotheby's, New York)
Sent to Paris by Tommy Townshend to stiffen up the British peace negotiators, Strachey was described by John Adams as 'the most eager, earnest, pointed spirit who is artful and insinuating and who pushes every point as far as it can possibly go'. In frustration, the American negotiators nicknamed him 'Mr Stretchy'.

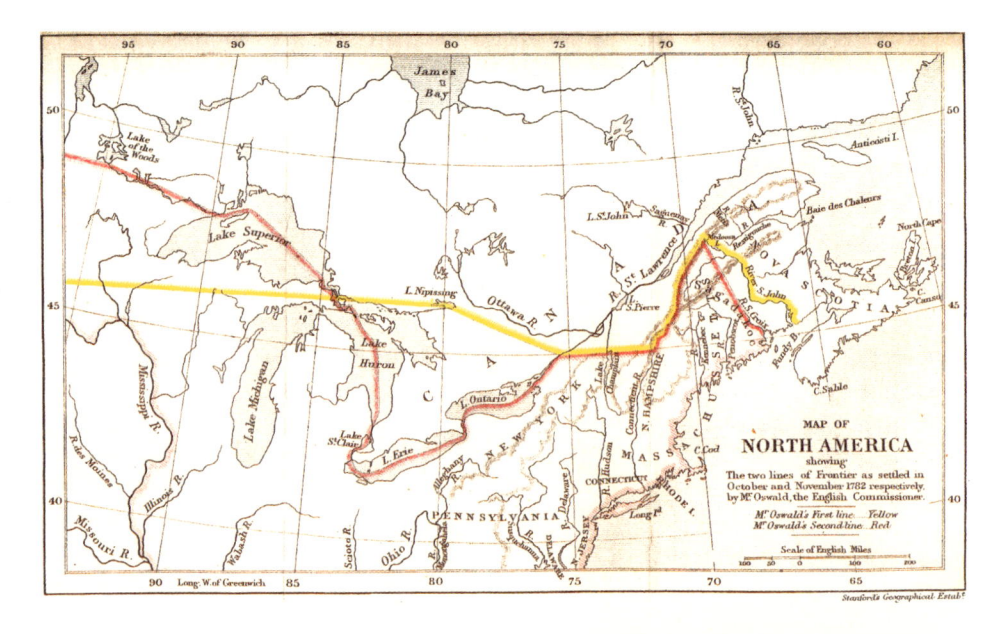

North American Boundaries in 1782 (public domain)

With Tommy Townshend's enthusiastic backing, Henry Strachey fortified the waning resolve of Britain's lead negotiator, Richard Oswald. As a result, the Americans retreated from the yellow line proposed by Congress and accepted the British red line. This means that today Toronto is located in Canada rather than in the United States.

The House of Lords in the early eighteenth century (public domain)
This is how the Lords' Chamber would have looked in Lord Sydney's time, physically separated from the Commons by a court complex and a garden. As the Lords' most junior member, Sydney at first felt far removed from the political action. But within a year, he was leader of the government there.

Copyright ,1905, by John D. Morris & Company
SIGNING THE PRELIMINARY TREATY OF PEACE AT PARIS, NOVEMBER 30, 1782, BY THE JOINT COMMISSIONERS OF THE UNITED STATES AND ENGLAND. JAY AND FRANKLIN STANDING AT THE LEFT OF THE PICTURE
Painting by C. Seiler

Signing the Preliminary Articles of Peace (Library of Congress)

On 30 November 1782, Articles of Peace were signed in Richard Oswald's suite at the Grand Hotel Muscovite, Paris. With their faces visible are the Americans; John Jay and Benjamin Franklin are standing while John Adams is seated. The British negotiators, not individually identifiable, are Richard Oswald, Henry Strachey and Alleyne Fitzherbert.

Lord Sydney in 1785 (Mitchell Library, Sydney)

For securing the peace with America, Tommy Townshend was created Baron Sydney of Chislehurst in March 1783. This portrait, painted two years later, shows a John Bull-like character. Most striking is Sydney's plain dress, a stark contrast to the ermine and gold decorated red robes most of his fellow nobles would have insisted on wearing.

The Rt. Hon: Thos. Townshend Creation of Baron Sydney

	£	s	d
Receipt	5	5	—
Depy. Purse	2	2	—
Kings Household	109	5	6
Earl Marshall	5	—	—
Garter	20	—	—
English Heralds	16	—	—
Scotch Do.	16	—	—
Principal Usher	6	13	6
Crown Office	9	13	6
Divd. Docqa.	2	7	—
Private Seal	2	—	—
Lord Chancr. Gent	6	—	—
Porter	1	1	—
Deputy	5	5	—
Ingrs. Clk.	1	1	—
Hanaper	24	13	6
Deputy	1	1	—
Sealer & Chaffwax	2	5	—
Deputies	1	1	—
Gilt Skin	6	—	—
Stamps	6	1	—
Boxes	1	1	—
	£249	16	—
Exped	2	2	0
	£251	18	0

6th March 1783 Received the above

Densam

Baron Sydney's fees (W. L. Clements Library, Michigan)

Taking his title in remembrance of his martyred kinsman Algernon Sidney, Lord Sydney had to pay a bill totalling 251 pounds and 18 shillings, before he could take his seat in the Lords at the lower end of the Barons' bench. Among others, the king's household received almost 110 pounds while the principal usher received six and a half pounds.

Lord Sydney in 1784 (National Portrait Gallery, London)

Caricatured here in more formal attire than he chose for his official portrait, Sydney had just come through a bruising political battle. Reluctant to return as Pitt's home secretary following the sacking of Charles Fox's government, Sydney said 'I am looked upon as one who is ready to go aloft in a storm…[so] I thought it my duty to undertake the task'.

Pitt and Fox in the Commons – 1785 (National Portrait Gallery, London)

Prime minister at the age of just 24, William Pitt the Younger, standing, confronts Charles Fox, seated at the right. Lord Sydney's daughter, Mary, married Pitt's elder brother, the 2nd Earl of Chatham. 'The 2nd Earl inherited his illustrious father's form and figure but not his mind', Wraxall said. 'That present of nature fell to the second son'.

The India Board of Control (National Portrait Gallery)

Lord Sydney was president of this Board which had ultimate responsibility for India. But one of William Pitt's drinking companions, Henry Dundas, a Scottish MP, wielded the real power. Here Dundas (seated left) fends off some of his bedraggled, job-seeking constituents while Pitt (centre) and Sydney (right) play push-pin.

Joseph Des Barres (Library and Archives Canada)
Appointed lieutenant-governor of Cape Breton Island by Lord Sydney in 1784, Colonel Des Barres fell out with his superiors in Halifax, Nova Scotia after accusing them of being jealous of his efforts to develop the Island. Described by his biographer as being 'pig headed, irascible and litigious', Des Barres was recalled by Sydney in 1787.

Sydney Cape Breton in 1784 (Library and Archives Canada)

Joseph Des Barres founded what became the capital of Cape Breton in the early 1780s, naming it 'Sydney' in honour of the home secretary. This painting of Sydney town was later presented to Lord Sydney by Cape Breton's provost marshal. At the time this image was painted, Sydney had a population of about 1,000.

[*Thirteen*]

Britain on the brink

On the eve of Parliament's resumption in late November 1779, Lord North warned the king that 'the great and increasing opposition added to the disunion amongst ourselves will break up the government'. However, Charles Jenkinson MP, for the king, was more optimistic: he estimated that the government could still muster 230 votes in the Commons, compared to the opposition's 180.[1]

Tommy Townshend began the new session with one of his by-now trademark tirades against the ever-widening war:

> [It was] impossible we could ever have been brought into [this] calamitous state... if, to the inability of our Ministers base treachery was not added; treachery... was somewhere lurking in our councils and had surrounded the throne.

Although the government won the motion Tommy had been speaking to by a bigger margin than Jenkinson had predicted, the prime minister again threatened to resign. And Tommy's attack gained traction with the wider public. A merchant wrote to him two days later:

> I was in the gallery the other night and heard you make a charge of treachery against the Ministers... Nine tenths of your fellow citizens believe the charge to be well founded. I hope... you will... proceed to bring those that merit it to condign punishment.[2]

The merchant was particularly angry that off Yorkshire in September the rebel raider John Paul Jones had attacked a convoy of British merchant ships. The first lord, Sandwich, had provided only one frigate to protect these ships even though he knew that Jones was nearby in the *Bonhomme Richard*, accompanied by a squadron of Franco-American privateers. At the time, Sandwich claimed there were no more warships available to protect the convoy. But no sooner had Jones captured the frigate *Serapis* than Sandwich ordered no less than ten warships to hunt him down. The merchant now accused the first lord of being a traitor. 'Had one of those ships been added to the convoy when first applied for', the merchant charged, 'Paul Jones would have been brought into the Thames instead of his carrying the King's ships into the Texel'.[3]

The Jones fiasco was a major factor behind the Reverend Christopher Wyvill's decision to petition the House of Commons for an inquiry into 'all sinecures... unmerited by public service'. Wyvill was a talented activist who was campaigning for 'the restoration of national morals, then sinking under the... [Government's] debasing influence'. Sandwich's blundering in particular was seen by many as the result of a corrupt system in which incompetents could purchase key public service positions. And within weeks, Wyvill's petition had ignited a huge protest movement across England, providing a uniting cause for an opposition which, until then, had been hopelessly divided discredited and ignored. Now there were hopes of better things.[4]

At first, Prime Minister North was able to stall a parliamentary inquiry. He achieved this by relying on the 'corrupt majority' Tommy had referred to during an earlier debate, which had attempted to remove Sandwich from the Admiralty. About a hundred members could be counted upon to support the prime minister solely because they held government offices, commands or contracts. 'There were only 30 admirals in the last war', Tommy told the House, 'but now there are upwards of 60. Of that number, 40 have been created in [Sandwich's] time... not more than 20 [of whom] were employed'. Such appointments extended the government's reach to the votes of naval contractors and employees who returned MPs in coastal constituencies.[5]

What forced the government's hand was the appearance outside Parliament of 3,000 'Wyvill' petitioners. On 2 February 1780 they met with Tommy and a number of opposition members at Westminster Hall. Nine days later, the Commons agreed to appoint a committee, including Edmund Burke, Charles Fox, Tommy Townshend and a former solicitor-general, John Dunning, to prepare a bill 'for the limitation of pensions and the suppression of sundry, useless … and expensive places'. The keeper of the fire-buckets and the groom of the confectionary were just two examples.[6]

But Edmund Burke also had some bigger targets in mind, including the position of secretary of state for America, occupied by George Germain. Speaking strongly in support of Burke's motion to abolish his old friend's job, Tommy argued that it was about lessening Crown influence by doing away with places such as Germain's, which 'was a new and useless office'. In the end, the American secretary's position survived by just seven votes, although the Board of Trade was abolished by eight.[7]

On 13 March the prime minister tried to regain control of the reform agenda by proposing a public accounts' commission, independent of Parliament. This was a direct insult to the House, Tommy said. '[It] impeached at once the integrity and abilities of members … implying either … that half a dozen gentlemen could not be selected out of 558 … equal to the task or that being equal to it they were not to be trusted'. Nevertheless Lord North got his way and General Carleton, recently returned from Canada, was appointed to head the commission.[8]

The prime minister had claimed all along that the power of the Crown was not increasing, but his resolution to establish the commission suggested otherwise. It confirmed Tommy's view that the extra appointments associated with Britain's growing war machine increased the Crown's power by allowing it to trade jobs for votes. As opposition members considered the petitions of thousands of angry taxpayers, they resolved to back a simple, yet profound, motion proposed by John Dunning 'that the influence of the Crown has increased, is increasing and ought to be diminished'. Many other members, fed up with high wartime taxation, also backed the motion and it passed by 233 votes to 216. This win so stunned and confounded the government that the prime minister begged once more to resign.[9]

The government's defeat dramatically raised the expectations of petitioners across Britain. The opposition attempted to follow through with specific reform Bills. One of these targeted the 'free exchange' of Cinque Ports, constituencies which were under the direct control of the king. Tommy noted that when the secretary at war became unpopular in his electorate, he had 'skipped away to Hastings' (a Cinque Ports constituency). The bill was narrowly defeated.

Another, to prohibit government contractors from sitting in Parliament, passed the Commons but was defeated in the Lords. The opposition therefore reverted to its proven method of obtaining a majority by proposing another simple motion – not to dissolve Parliament 'until Measures had been taken to reduce the Influence of the Crown'. Despite Tommy's warning that the House must adopt the motion or 'drive the people to desperate measures', it was defeated by 51 votes. Within weeks, London was in flames.[10]

What triggered the conflagration was a petition bearing 120,000 signatures. It demanded the repeal of the Catholic Relief Act which had abolished penal provisions aimed at Catholic priests and schoolmasters. The president of the Protestant Association, Lord George Gordon, a man one of his contemporaries noted had 'a twist in his head, a certain whirligig which ran away with him if anything relative to religion was mentioned' told a large public meeting that if less than 20,000 petitioners attended Parliament, he would not present their petition. 'The only way to stop Popery', he thundered, 'was to ... [show] ... they were determined to preserve their religious freedom with their lives'. On 2 June 1780, an angry crowd of 60,000 accompanied Gordon to Parliament. As members arrived, they were attacked. After being roughed up, George Townshend was sent into the Lords with his hair hanging loose on his shoulders. Lord Stormont, who was in the hands of the mob for half an hour, had his coach reduced to matchwood. Even so, Gordon's motion to consider the massive petition was overwhelmingly defeated.[11]

Outraged by this, tens of thousands of angry petitioners began a frenzy of rioting and looting which was to rage for days. Nathaniel Wraxall, a member of the Commons and noted political diarist, described an attack on the lord chief justice's residence:

> The door of Lord Mansfield's house burst open ... and in a few minutes, all the contents of the apartments being precipitated from the windows were piled up and wrapped in flames. A file of foot soldiers arriving drew up near the blazing pile but [did not] attempt to quench the fire or to impede the mob who were indeed far too numerous.

Wraxall watched as a brewery owned by a Catholic 'threw up a pinnacle of flame resembling a volcano', while on approaching Blackfriars Bridge, he 'beheld the King's Bench Prison completely wrapped in flames'. The prime minister was dining at Downing Street when the adjoining square became thronged with people. But reinforcements soon arrived and the immediate danger passed. After finishing their meals, North and his guests 'mounted to the top of the house where [they] beheld London blazing in seven places and could hear the Platoons firing in various directions'.[12]

'Had the mob been competently led', Wraxall said, 'London would have been effectively overturned that night'. But the king kept his head. While Lord Mansfield dithered over whether the formalities of the Riot Act had been complied with, the attorney-general advised that military force could be used. 'Then let it be done', the king replied. Cavalry patrols with orders to shoot were dispatched throughout the West End. By the eighth day, with an official death toll of 285, the riots died down. Charged with high treason, Lord George Gordon was sent to the Tower of London.[13]

Under military guard, Parliament had resumed on the riot's fourth day and some members criticized the government's handling of the crisis, but the opposition was in more trouble. For one thing, the riots had deterred moderates from pursuing reform. The Duke of Richmond, who had just proposed 'one vote, one value', now thought again. And while Rockingham strongly backed the government's tough action against the rioters, Shelburne, who was anti-Catholic, sat on the fence. These two leading opposition members were now barely on speaking terms.[14]

Despite the tumult in London, things had been going better for the government in America where a strategy to focus on the weakly defended southern colonies had resulted in the British capture of Charleston, South Carolina. Even so, the riots and Prime Minister North's pleas to retire prompted George III to explore changes to the ministry. Negotiations were opened with Rockingham. While he did not seek any office for himself, Rockingham wanted to be able to convey offers to key members of the opposition. The Dukes of Richmond, Portland and Manchester must be included, he said, along with Charles Fox, Edmund Burke and Tommy Townshend. Richmond and Fox should be secretaries of state, Rockingham advised, with Tommy as chancellor of the exchequer. Furthermore, Admiral Keppel should succeed Sandwich at the Admiralty.[15]

Citing his 'unremitted personal ill conduct to me', George III refused point-blank to include Charles Fox, who had said of him 'it is intolerable that it should be in the power of one blockhead to do so much mischief'. The king was even less happy about Richmond and refused to remove Sandwich, who had 'now got out the finest fleet this country ever possessed'. But his Majesty was a lot more positive about Portland and Manchester and positively glowing about Burke and Townshend, who would be 'real acquisitions'. At first sight, Tommy's inclusion seems strange. He had fought just as hard against the government as Fox had done and a great deal harder than Richmond. The difference between them was that Tommy was careful to keep his criticism directed at the king's ministers while Fox and Richmond had, by word or deed, personally criticized the king – in Richmond's case by refusing to attend court. In the end, these negotiations came to nothing and the government called an early election for 9 September.[16]

Having turned his back on a compromise ministry, George III was determined that Prime Minister North would be re-elected with the strongest possible majority. The king had personally been saving 1,000 pounds per month towards this contest since November 1777 and he now pulled out all stops. In total, the government spent 80,000 pounds in 87 contested constituencies with 8,000 pounds spent in the electorate of Westminster alone. As a prominent opposition member in a safe seat, Tommy was returned unopposed in Whitchurch, along with his nephew, George Brodrick.[17]

Overall, the results were disappointing for the king who saw the government's majority fall significantly. But he had wins against some of his strongest critics, including General Howe, who withdrew in Nottingham because 'half the town abhorred him for going to America and [the other] half for doing so little there'. Edmund Burke lost in Bristol although he was later returned in Malton. And Admiral Keppel, George III's local member, was beaten in Windsor although he was also later returned in Surrey. New members who joined the opposition included John Townshend (George's second son) and Richard Sheridan. A man of literary and theatrical gifts, Sheridan was soon savaging the ministry, saying of Lord Sandwich that he was 'born for the destruction of the British Navy'.

Although John and Tommy Townshend were in opposition, this did not necessarily mean that they saw eye to eye, with John firmly in the Rockingham faction and Tommy still leaning towards the Chatham camp, now led by Lord Shelburne. A mix up in invitations to a factional dinner revealed the sensitivity. 'There is to be a dinner here tomorrow', the hostess said, 'Derbys, Burgoynes, Burkes, Sheridans, Hares etc. A card was sent to Jack Townshend but by mistake was taken to Tommy; will he be pleased or awkward?'[18]

Whilst parliamentary numbers were tight for the government after the 1780 election, the victory at Charleston, the searing memory of the Gordon riots and the split between Rockingham and Shelburne meant that it was still well-placed. From 'a union of birth, connections, talents and eloquence', Charles Fox became leader of the opposition in the Commons, but most of his followers were lethargic. At the end-of-year adjournment it was noted that hardly any bothered to turn up, 'scarce anybody but Charles Fox and T. Townshend'. Meanwhile the British government had picked yet another fight, declaring war on the Dutch because their ships carried rebel goods.[19]

In November 1780 Tommy spoke on a vote of thanks to Generals Clinton and Cornwallis for their victory at Charleston. 'Of Earl Cornwallis', he was proud to say, 'he was not indeed an impartial judge…his good conduct and great bravery certainly merited every mark of…respect…provided always that it should not be understood that by this support, he gave any countenance to the American war'. Tommy sent a copy of his speech to Cornwallis and to his nephew, Harry Brodrick, who was the general's aide de camp. After thanking 'Dear Thomas' for his support in the Commons, Cornwallis continued, 'I send you H. Brodrick with [news of] another victory [at Guilford Courthouse]. Whether it may be of advantage to the public or not I trust it will prove useful to him'.[20]

[*Fourteen*]

Cousin Cornwallis and Yorktown

The battle of Guilford Courthouse was no real advantage, as it turned out. Seven months later, Charles Cornwallis surrendered to George Washington at Yorktown, a capitulation which led to the British recognition of the United States of America.

Like his cousin Tommy Townshend, Charles Cornwallis, who was about five years younger, attended Eton and then Clare Hall, Cambridge. At Eton, a future bishop of Durham hit Cornwallis in the face with a hockey stick, leaving him with a permanent squint. Far from disfiguring him, this injury made him look worldly wise, which compared to his cousins, he probably was. At the end of 1756 Cornwallis was commissioned into the army and saw active service in Europe. Four years later, he replaced Tommy's brother Harry as a member of the Commons. There, he strongly opposed the British government's scheme for taxing the American colonies. On the outbreak of hostilities with the American rebels, he accepted a senior British command, believing it was his duty to do so, even though he thought the conflict was unjust. Devastated, his wife claimed to be dying of a broken heart and passed away soon afterwards.[1]

In America, Cornwallis had played prominent roles in the capture of the rebel capital, Philadelphia, and in the capitulation of Charleston. Following Charleston's occupation in May 1780, General Henry Clinton returned to New York, leaving Cornwallis in charge of the military government. With 4,000 soldiers under his command, Cornwallis was expected to recruit local loyalist sympathizers and to pacify the countryside as he advanced north. The strategy he was to implement was what remained of a plan drawn up in 1779. On the assumption that the southern colonies were more sympathetic to George III, the plan had proposed splitting them away from the more rebellious colonies to the north. This involved attacking a middle colony with an army of 12,000 men and a small naval force to 'penetrate to the heart of Virginia or Maryland'. A fundamental assumption was that Washington's army was shrinking.

With a much smaller force than originally planned, Cornwallis was now starting much further to the south. The idea of creating a split by attacking a middle colony had been abandoned. Instead, Cornwallis would have to conquer all the territory between South Carolina and Virginia, knowing that if the country he passed through was not also pacified the rebels would rise again, as they had in New Jersey. Everything hinged on the expectation that many southern colonists would fight for the British and supply them as well.[2]

As early as 10 June, Cornwallis was complaining that prior to his return to New York General Clinton had been too generous in granting protection to rebels who claimed to be the king's faithful subjects. The result was that loyalist units had become infested with spies and stirrers who made it their business to undermine Cornwallis at every opportunity. Still, there was an early success. When news arrived on 9 August that the rebel general, Horatio Gates, was moving on Camden 150 miles north-west of Charleston, Cornwallis went out to confront him. And with a force half the size, he routed the rebels.[3]

To capitalize on this victory, Cornwallis decided to advance into North Carolina, but a rebel ambush of 1,000 loyalists at King's Mountain on the Carolinas' border forced him back. The savage treatment of loyalist prisoners by the rebels prompted a protest to their commander. 'The hanging of poor old Colonel Mills who was always a fair and open enemy to your cause', Cornwallis wrote, 'was an act of the most savage barbarity'. Equally disturbing was the number of militiamen who had sworn allegiance to the king and now deserted to the rebels.[4]

Keen to resume offensive operations, Cornwallis sought Clinton's permission for 'a diversion in the Chesapeak', a massive bay surrounded by the colonies of Virginia and Maryland. And Clinton appeared to agree, replying that this was the principal object of Cornwallis's expedition. Despite the setback at King's Mountain, the plan was still to consolidate the south whilst at the same time moving north into Virginia. There, Cornwallis hoped to meet up with

British reinforcements. But Cornwallis's progress was soon being hampered by the 'Swamp Fox' – the rebel colonel, Francis Marion. 'By the terror of his threats...the cruelty of his punishments and...the promise of plunder', Cornwallis warned Clinton, 'there is scarcely an inhabitant between the Santee and the Pedee [Rivers] that is not in arms against us'.[5]

As he again advanced north towards the Carolinas' border country, all the while harassed by the Swamp Fox's guerrilla tactics, Cornwallis was threatened by more conventional soldiers led by General Daniel Morgan. On 17 January 1781, Cornwallis detached 700 infantry and 350 cavalry under the command of Colonel Banastre Tarleton to engage Morgan's troops at Cowpens. Although the rebels were greater in number, their line at first gave way, and then did an about face and fired on the pursuing British troops. '[This] occasioned the utmost confusion in the first line', Cornwallis told Clinton, 'and Tarleton could not prevent the panic from becoming general'. The British lost 600 soldiers, the rebels just 100. Cowpens was Britain's worst defeat since Saratoga and it crippled Cornwallis's ability to manoeuvre for the remainder of the war.[6]

However, this did not stop Cornwallis advancing through North Carolina, almost to the Virginia border. And on 15 March, it did not prevent him from routing a force of 6,000 rebels led by General Nathaniel Greene at Guilford Courthouse. But it did stop him from pursuing the enemy, and Greene remained free to harass the British at every opportunity. Although Cornwallis now believed that 'the Chesapeak may become the seat of the war even at the expense of abandoning New York', he nevertheless turned away from Virginia and away from Chesapeake Bay, marching 200 miles southeast to Wilmington near the Atlantic Coast. Harassed by Greene's rebel forces, which were growing more numerous every day, Cornwallis was desperate to improve communication with New York and London, necessitating access to shipping.[7]

Once better communications had been established, Cornwallis dispatched Tommy's nephew, Henry Brodrick, with a report to the secretary of state for America, Lord Germain, in London. In it he confirmed that 'a serious attempt upon Virginia' was still 'the most solid plan'. Cornwallis also wrote to Clinton on 23 April describing his progress, which was coming to resemble Burgoyne's descent to Saratoga. 'I have experienced the dangers and distresses of marching some hundreds of miles in a country chiefly hostile', he said, 'without one active or useful friend, without intelligence, and without communication with any part of the country'. However there was no direction from New York where Clinton enjoyed a cosmopolitan life style and gave no sign of taking any initiative. Increasingly frustrated, Cornwallis wrote to one of his colleagues:

> Now my dear friend what is our plan? Without one we cannot succeed and I assure you that I am quite tired of marching about the country in search of adventures. If we mean an offensive war in America, we must abandon New York and bring our whole force into Virginia: we then have a stake to fight for and a successful battle may give us America.[8]

On 25 April, British forces under Lord Rawdon beat Cornwallis's chief tormentor, General Greene, near Camden. That this fight took place near the site of a much earlier battle underscored the ducking, weaving and backtracking nature of the British campaign. In the absence of any specific instructions from Clinton, Cornwallis himself backtracked from Wilmington, arriving at Petersburg, Virginia, on 20 May. Cornwallis could claim Clinton's general endorsement for an advance into Virginia at some stage. And George Germain approved too. 'Cornwallis's opinion entirely coincides with mine', he said, '…of pushing the war…[into] Virginia with all the force that can be spared until that province is reduced'. But Cornwallis's march to Petersburg had not been specifically approved and Clinton was later highly critical of it.[9]

In London, many could sense Cornwallis's deteriorating situation. During a Commons' debate on 12 June 1781, Tommy Townshend summed up his cousin's plight. 'Cornwallis could not effect the reduction of America', Tommy said, 'because he could not effect impossibilities…with timid friends, inveterate enemies…[and] cut off from all resources indispensably necessary for the support of an army in the heart of hostile country'. In fact not all resources had been cut off. After arriving at Petersburg, Cornwallis joined up with British reinforcements led by the rebel turncoat, Benedict Arnold. But the enemy strength was increasing at a greater rate. The French general, Marie-Joseph La Fayette, was not far away, soon to be joined, Cornwallis thought, by the rebel general Anthony Wayne. And word came from Clinton that a French fleet carrying 2,500 troops had sailed from Rhode Island. Keen to dislodge La

Fayette before he could be reinforced, Cornwallis left Petersburg and crossed the James River, executing a series of manoeuvres around Richmond before ending up down the Virginia Peninsula between the James and York Rivers, at the old colonial capital of Williamsburg.[10]

Clinton meanwhile was worried about the possibility of a rebel attack on New York and on 26 June he demanded that Cornwallis send troops north to reinforce him there. Concerned about the growing number of rebels he would have to confront if he attempted to send those reinforcements by land, Cornwallis searched for a deepwater embarkation point instead. During this search, he examined Yorktown. Although it was further down the narrow peninsula than Williamsburg, it was on the York River and not far from the sea. On closer inspection, however, Cornwallis was unimpressed. 'It far exceeds our power consistent with your plans', he told Clinton, 'to make safe defensive posts there and at Gloucester [across the York River] both of which would be necessary for the protection of shipping'. He therefore re-crossed the James River and marched south-east 40 miles to an alternative deepwater port at Portsmouth, near Norfolk.[11]

Now in regular communication with Clinton by sea, Cornwallis soon learned that his commander-in-chief disapproved of just about everything he had done since the battle for Guilford Courthouse on 15 March, including his advance from Wilmington into Virginia. 'I am conscious that my judgment is liable to error', Cornwallis replied. 'Perhaps...at Wilmington the measure which I adopted was not the best; but I have at least the satisfaction to find by the intercepted letters of 14 May from General Greene to Baron Steuben that it was not agreeable to his wishes that I come in to Virginia'.[12]

Clinton's next dispatch sharply criticized Cornwallis's march to Portsmouth. According to the commander-in-chief, Cornwallis should have taken up a defensive position at either Williamsburg or Yorktown. Cornwallis's concerns that Williamsburg had no harbour and Yorktown would take 'a great deal of time and labour to fortify' had been swept aside. So severe was Clinton's censure that Cornwallis felt he had no choice but to evacuate Portsmouth and fall back to Yorktown, which at least had deep water access. On 22 August, he was able to report the complete evacuation of Portsmouth, noting nevertheless that Yorktown's defences would take another six weeks to complete. By following

Clinton's orders and digging in at Yorktown on the Virginia Peninsula, Cornwallis knew that his only escape from enemy encirclement was by sea. Still, he assumed that the British navy would be able to come to his rescue, but just seven days later there was a dramatic turn for the worse with the arrival of Admiral Francois-Joseph de Grasse and the French West Indies fleet, whose movements had been coordinated with those of General Washington. '[Cornwallis's] Army had the goodness to quit a situation from whence it might have escaped', Benjamin Franklin said, 'and [placed] itself in another from whence escape was impossible'.[13]

The appearance of Admiral de Grasse was the most dramatic evidence yet of how the French navy had seized the initiative in American waters. It had begun with the arrival of Admiral d' Estaing three years earlier and had been followed up with the opening of a French naval base on Rhode Island. By late August 1781, the British admirals Thomas Graves and Samuel Hood were searching for a French fleet commanded by Admiral Jaques-Melchoir Barras, which had left Rhode Island for an unknown destination. Rumour had it that Barras was on his way to Chesapeake Bay. Graves and Hood went there in search of him, and upon arrival found not Barras but de Grasse, who had 24 ships of the line, compared to their nineteen. In naval terms, the battle which followed on 5 September was a draw, but with the arrival of Barras eight days later the combined French fleets were strong enough to block Chesapeake Bay. This blockade forced Graves and Hood to return to New York, cutting off Cornwallis's escape route by sea. Tommy Townshend's worst fears about the French naval threat had come to pass.[14]

The bad news for the British at sea was compounded by alarming intelligence that General Washington was advancing on Yorktown with a combined army of almost 17,000, comprising 7,800 Frenchmen and 8,800 rebels. Cornwallis's only consolation was word from Clinton that 4,000 British troops were on-board ship and would reinforce Yorktown as soon as the British navy judged it prudent to do so. 'This place is in no state of defence', Cornwallis replied. 'If you cannot relieve me very soon, you must be prepared for the worst'. Rattled, Clinton called a council of war to cover himself. One subordinate officer said of Clinton that he was 'fool enough to command an army when he [was] … incapable of commanding a troop of horse'. The five generals and four admirals in attendance at the council resolved to send what now amounted to 5,000 troops and 23 ships of the line on 5 October. Admiral Hood insisted that only a major fleet action could save Cornwallis. But his superior, Graves, was unenthusiastic.[15]

Arriving back in New York after a pleasant Atlantic crossing, Cornwallis's aide-de-camp, Harry Brodrick, wrote to his uncle Tommy about the news from Yorktown:

> Cornwallis has ... 5000 fine troops and 1200 seamen. Washington is at Williamsburg twelve miles from York with about 20,000 men ... We receive letters every now and then from Cornwallis by small vessels which pass the French fleet in the night ... he says he can hold out to the middle of November; he is not afraid of their attacking him but unless he is relieved by that time, he will be reduced to lay down his arms for want of provisions so that it is reduced to this alternative – either to risk an action at sea against a force infinitely superior or to suffer a very fine army to lay down their arms without firing a shot.

One other Townshend cousin was in New York at this critical time. Cornwallis's brother William was captain of the *Canada*, a 74-gun ship of the line which had joined Hood's squadron in August. 'Poor Captain Cornwallis as you may easily suppose is very anxious', Brodrick told Tommy, 'and abuses the Navy very much for their unnecessary delays'.[16]

On 3 October, the enemy had completed two redoubts within 1100 yards of Cornwallis's defences. And by the 11th, they were just 300 yards away. Now under constant fire from 40 heavy cannon and sixteen mortars, Cornwallis was losing men fast. 'Nothing but a direct move to York River which includes a successful naval action', he told Clinton, 'can save me'. Four days later, Cornwallis outlined how desperate his position had become:

> Last evening the enemy carried my two advanced redoubts on the left by storm ... My situation here becomes very critical; we dare not show a gun to their old batteries and I expect their new ones will open up tomorrow morning ... our fresh earthen works do not resist their powerful artillery so that we shall soon be exposed to an assault in ruined works, in a bad position

and with weakened numbers ... I cannot recommend that the fleet and army should run great risk in endeavouring to save us.[17]

Only one slim hope remained and that was to try and escape north across the York River to Gloucester. Sixteen large boats were loaded. But then the weather changed to 'a most violent storm of wind and rain' and these vessels were swept away. When this attempt failed, Cornwallis wrote to Washington on 17 October proposing a ceasefire to settle surrender terms. He had no choice. Facing a combined enemy force now swelled to around 18,000 as well as the French navy, Cornwallis had just 4,000 fit troops left. At Yorktown there were 5,014, with 3,273 fit for duty and another 1,714 present but sick, while at Gloucester there were 936, with 744 fit for duty and 192 present but sick. Although there were also some sailors present, those who could fight were out of cannon balls and reduced to sheltering behind crumbling trenches.[18]

The articles of capitulation, signed on 19 October, stipulated that Cornwallis's men would emerge from behind what was left of their barricades 'at two o'clock precisely, with shouldered arms, colours cased and drums beating a British or German march'. The one chosen was *The World Turned Upside Down*, first performed in one of gentleman Johnny Burgoyne's operas:

> If ponies rode men, and if grass ate cows,
> And cats should be chased into holes by the mouse...
> If summer were spring, and the otherway'round,
> Then all the world would be upside down.

Cornwallis refused to take part, claiming he was ill. Brigadier-General Charles O'Hara was sent out in his place. Upon approaching the French commander to formally capitulate, O'Hara was directed to George Washington 'by a gracious inclination of the eyes'. Washington in turn directed O'Hara to surrender his sword to Major-General Benjamin Lincoln, the vanquished defender of Charleston. That same day, Clinton's reinforcements for Cornwallis set sail from New York.[19]

An intelligence report received in New York on 24 October was the first indication there that something was seriously amiss:

> Jonas Rider a black man says he left Yorktown on Thursday the 18th to make [his] escape as it was said the troops were going to give it up. There had been no firing for a day and a half before he left and it was reported that Cornwallis was making terms.

By the following day, Admiral Hood for one was in no doubt, lamenting 'the hard fate' of Cornwallis and his troops. 'I shall without ceasing grieve that we were not in the Chesapeak ten days ago', Hood wrote to Clinton, 'which I very much flatter myself we should have been'.[20]

While Cornwallis's troops were taken into custody for what was left of the war, Cornwallis himself was released on parole. Although he was free to return to England, he could not take any further part in the American conflict and was subjected to an open-ended recall by the rebels.[21]

Arriving back in New York on 19 November, Cornwallis fell into a dispute with Clinton over three issues. The first was over the decision to march into Virginia; the second was whether Clinton had ordered Cornwallis back to Yorktown; and the third was whether Cornwallis should have held out longer there, on the promise of relief. In Clinton's papers, there is a sixteen-page document containing extracts from Cornwallis's letter explaining his defeat. And scribbled all over it are Clinton's comments and rebuttals. Cornwallis began with:

> I never saw [Yorktown] ... in a very favourable light. A successful defence however in our situation was perhaps impossible. For the place could only be reckoned an entrenched camp [with] ... the ground so disadvantageous that nothing but the necessity of fortifying it as a post to protect the navy could have induced any person to erect works upon it.

And Clinton responded:

> [Cornwallis] never made a report to [me] ... of the defects of the ground or gave [me] ... the least hint of its being disadvantageous before his letters ... were received about the time of and after the capitulation.

In fact since July Cornwallis had been sending dispatches to Clinton expressing concerns about the problems with Yorktown. On and on it went, tit for tat. Clinton later bitterly complained to Lord North that Cornwallis's version had been published in the *Parliamentary Register* without his own version also being included.[22]

Both men understood the historical enormity of what had happened and both scrambled to protect their reputations, often at the expense of the truth. Clinton was never employed as a commander again. But Cornwallis was welcomed at court by the king. The British government's plan to appoint Cornwallis supreme commander in America was foiled only by the terms of his parole.[23]

[*Fifteen*]

— Oh God! It's all Over! —

Because it took some days for news of the Yorktown surrender to seep through Franco-American lines to General Clinton, Paris received formal word of Cornwallis's capitulation ahead of London. Nevertheless, wild rumours had swept through Whitehall, causing rampant speculation on the stock market. Everyone feared the worst, but the news when it did come was a severe shock. Waving his arms and beating his chest, Prime Minister North cried out to no one in particular: 'Oh God! It's all over! Oh God! It's all Over!' With Parliament due to resume almost immediately, the North government was widely expected to seek terms with the American rebels.[1]

However, George III was 'not inclined to give up', willing the prime minister and the whole nation to continue the war, and Britain was by no means defeated. She still had 30,000 troops in North America and still occupied the strongholds of New York, Savannah and Charleston in the thirteen United States, as well as St Augustine in Spanish Florida. Although General Washington was keen to move against these, he could not do so without the French fleet, which now had obligations elsewhere. After some fierce verbal skirmishing in the Commons, it was clear too that a majority of members still supported the conflict. The state of war between Britain and America continued.[2]

Britain was forced to the negotiating table not by the rebels, but by a pack of parliamentarians. They waged 'incessant warfare' on the government with a barrage of increasingly tough Commons' resolutions which finally forced Lord North from office. Prominent in this pack were Charles Fox, Tommy Townshend and Henry Conway, whose career in both the military and Parliament stretched back forty years. Now in opposition, General Conway had long condemned the American war and 'the butchery of his fellow subjects'. As another longstanding opponent of the war, Tommy Townshend was incensed that the prime minister would not give in. He now went after North personally, with brief, venom-laden contributions that wore the prime minister down. As always though, Tommy was careful not to personally target the king.[3]

Prior to the news of Yorktown reaching London on 25 November 1781, the government had maintained its strong position, thanks largely to the British victory at Charleston. 'Our opposition is scattered and runs wild…under no leader', one of its members said. Moreover the king's opening address to Parliament on 27 November, which proposed continuing the war 'with vigour', was carried by 218 votes to 129. This was because many of the opposition had stayed away; the news of Cornwallis's surrender had arrived too late for them to change their plans. But as usual, Tommy Townshend did attend and did defend his cousin. 'Cornwallis was constrained to surrender', Tommy said, 'because his first concern was to preserve the fleet upon which he knew the very existence of this country depended'. The king, meanwhile, took great comfort in his 89-vote margin, directing his secretary of state for America, George Germain, to come up with a fresh plan for conducting the war.[4]

An opposition re-energized by the Yorktown surrender was also making fresh plans. On 12 December its motion asserting that 'all attempts to reduce the revolted colonies to obedience are contrary to the true interests of this Kingdom' was defeated by just 41 votes. While this result reflected renewed interest in Parliament from those opposition members who had been absent on 27 November, it would take a great deal more to end the war with the rebels. To pass a binding resolution on the government to end the conflict, the opposition's leaders had to ensure that all their members turned up to vote, that 'swinging votes' were won over, and that as many of the prime minister's supporters as possible defected. The king and his ministers were ultimately subject to the will of the Commons. What was needed was sufficient support for a form of words which would make it a treasonable act to continue the fight.[5]

Of all the ministers in the Commons, George Germain was most strongly in favour of continuing hostilities against the rebels. Tall and powerfully built with alert and unforgiving facial features resembling those of a bird of prey, Germain was a force to be reckoned with. Frustrated by Clinton's inaction, Germain encouraged loyalist Americans to harass the rebels. The former governor of New Jersey, William Franklin, became leader of the Loyalist Association which sponsored guerrilla raids to do what the British army would not. Prime Minister North, however, was less enthusiastic. The Commons' debate of 12 December had laid bare a growing rift between Germain, who wanted America to remain 'dependent', and North, who was searching for some alternative approach without splitting the cabinet. Even so, two days later Germain claimed that the ministry was unanimous against abandoning America. 'All the Ministers had come to their senses', Tommy Townshend replied, 'except the Secretary for the American Department'.[6]

George Germain's future was decided not in the Commons but by the king. Unable to appoint Cornwallis to succeed Clinton as commander-in-chief in America, George III chose General Carleton instead. 'The country will have more confidence in a new man', the king told Germain. '[And] the man who... the Army... [would look] on as the best officer is Sir Guy Carleton... [whose] uncorruptness is universally acknowledged'. Carleton had, however, long despised Germain for his 'cowardice' at the battle of Minden and the feeling was mutual. The American secretary's position was untenable, and the king let him retire with a peerage.

Despite their growing differences over the war with the rebels, Germain and North had made a formidable team in the Commons. Severely short-sighted, the prime minister had relied on Germain to survey the opposition benches 'to see who attended as well as who was absent... [forming] his conclusions accordingly on the business of the day'. With the eagle-eyed Germain now in the House of Lords, North faced the opposition's onslaughts in the Commons like a blind man.[7]

On 22 February 1782 Tommy Townshend foreshadowed a motion 'respecting the continuance of the American War', followed by Henry Conway who moved that 'public tranquility be restored... with the revolted colonies'. Replying, the new American secretary, Welbore Ellis, pleaded with the Commons to 'make allowance' for his ministerial inexperience. Cornwallis's captured army, he said:

> formed a part of 73,000 men voted for the American service... [but] the American war... was the French war because Washington's army was fed,

clothed and paid by France so it was France not the Congress that was fighting in America.

Showing no mercy towards the hapless Ellis, Tommy Townshend counter-attacked:

> It had been thrown out in debate that it was not now an American war, but a French war … what then could be inferred but that France with 3,400 men in America had done more that England had with 73,000?[8]

And when Conway's motion was put to the vote, the government scraped home by just one vote. Charles Fox therefore demanded that the motion be recommitted, prompting relations between Tommy Townshend and the prime minister to boil over. After Lord North described one opposition member as 'uncivil, brutal and insolent' for calling him 'the scourge of the nation', Tommy objected to the prime minister's 'total disregard of decency'. North was attacking a colleague who was simply exercising his right of free speech, Tommy said. Claiming that Tommy 'was addicted to treating him with … particular harshness', North refused to apologize. The speaker ordered him to do so – a sure sign that the prime minister's authority was slipping, and North admitted as much three days later. When Conway gave notice of an almost identical motion on 25 February, North confided to the king 'Conway has too much prospect of success.' No longer able to consult George Germain in the Commons' chamber, the prime minister was now struggling with his parliamentary tactics.[9]

Two days later, Henry Conway upped the ante by moving 'against the further prosecution of offensive war with America'. Needing extra votes to get a decisive result, the opposition targeted the swinging votes of the so-called 'country gentlemen'. Although generally supportive of the king, these members were taxpayers who had become deeply troubled by the cost of the war. Increasingly difficult for the government to manage, country gentlemen such as Sir William Dolben were just as tricky for the opposition. As Dolben himself said, 'he went to act his humble part … [in Parliament] free from all attachments'. After supporting Conway's first motion, Dolben announced that he would vote against this second one, because the attorney-general 'had mentioned an intention' of introducing a bill for a truce with the rebels. If Dolben's attitude was widely shared by other country gentlemen, Conway's latest motion would be defeated, thereby frustrating the opposition's ultimate goal – a complete change of government. As the next speaker, Tommy Townshend had the key task of demolishing Dolben in the eyes of his country colleagues. This Tommy did by attacking 'with the utmost severity the inconsistency of the hon. Baronet who in the course of a few days gave two different votes on the same question although there had not been the least change in affairs to warrant such conduct'.[10]

Those who spoke after Tommy, including the leading country gentlemen Gilbert Elliot and Thomas Powys, followed his cue. Sensing that the government was in trouble with other swinging voters as well, the attorney-general moved to adjourn the debate, which had continued to rage well beyond midnight. He was soundly defeated. And soon afterwards, the main motion against further prosecution of the war was carried on the voices. Again the prime minister pleaded to resign. However, the king was determined to struggle on, even though he was 'much hurt at the success of Mr Conway's motion'.[11]

In answer to what was now a Commons' resolution, the king said simply that he would 'take such measures as shall appear to me to be most conducive to the restoration of harmony between Great Britain and the revolted Colonies'. And the attorney-general proved equally evasive about the workings of a bill he now introduced to conclude a peace with the rebels – ignoring Tommy Townshend's demands that he explain the details. Moreover, behind the scenes the king commissioned the lord chancellor to see whether any alternative prime minister could be found who would 'keep our present possessions in North America and attempt a negotiation with any separate provinces or even districts'.[12]

To nail down the king, Henry Conway put up a further motion on 4 March. Declaring 'the advisers of the further prosecution of offensive war in America to be enemies to the King and Country', this motion passed without any opposition at all. Although its wording was directed at everyone but the king, the motion was intended to bind him by prohibiting his ministers, admirals and generals from prosecuting the war. Only after this further setback did the government allow the Commons to consider the attorney-general's bill in detail.[13]

Still trying to avoid the inevitable, the king now changed tack, attempting to form a new ministry in consultation with former Prime Minister Grafton, who was 'the most temperate of all the Opposition'. But the key opposition leaders wanted no less than a clean sweep of all ministerial positions and the king soon found that Grafton had no power to negotiate on their behalf. Indeed, the opposition were intent on keeping up the pressure on Prime Minister North. On 9 March a thinly disguised no confidence motion 'that the calamities... of the times had proceeded from want of... abilities in the Ministers' was defeated by just ten votes. 'It is totally impossible', the prime minister advised, 'for the present Ministry to conduct His Majesty's business any longer'. Nevertheless, the king continued his search for a compromise ministry. However neither of the two most likely prime ministers, Lord Shelburne and the Marquess of Rockingham, would agree to the king's terms.[14]

To force the king's hand, the opposition next prevailed on Sir John Rous, a country gentleman and until recently a supporter of the prime minister, to move a motion of no confidence in the whole ministry. On 15 March Rous duly moved 'for withdrawing the Confidence of Parliament from His Majesty's Ministers'. In the desperate debate which followed, Tommy Townshend ridiculed the ministers' excuses for leaving Britain without allies, charging that 'if the greatness of our power had raised up enemies against us, that greatness, thanks to the Ministers was no more but still we were without allies'.[15]

Although the government defeated this motion by nine votes, the king's man in the Commons, John Robinson, was pessimistic. 'The rats are very bad', he advised the king next morning. 'I fear they will increase before Wednesday, when Mr Fox has given notice... [the Opposition] will attack again'. Emboldened by his opposition colleagues, who had finally resolved to stand united behind him, the Marquess of Rockingham now demanded that 'the King must not give a veto to the Independence of America'. He insisted also that George III agree to specific electoral reform and to regulation of his civil list (a personal budget which allowed the King to dispense patronage far and wide). Only then would Rockingham agree to any request to lead a government.[16]

Deeply insulted at Rockingham's unprecedented attempt to dictate the terms upon which he would become the prime minister, George III continued to hold out. The opposition renewed its assault with a motion that 'it is contrary to the interests of His Majesty to continue the management of public affairs in the hands of the present Ministers'. In the face of this ultimate parliamentary threat, which was due to be debated on 20 March, the king did one final whip around for support. The message came back 'we shall certainly be beat tomorrow'. The prime minister had real concerns for George III should his cabinet be taken by storm and he wanted to negotiate a surrender. Finally, the king began to listen.[17]

On 20 March the Commons met in circumstances of high drama. A record number of MPs overflowed beyond the floor of the chamber and into the galleries above. When the speaker called on the day's business at 4.15 p.m., Charles Howard, the son and heir of Britain's leading peer, stood up to move the opposition's no confidence motion. Amid scenes of great confusion with points of order taken on both sides, Howard was immediately challenged for the speaker's eye by the prime minister. 'His Majesty had come to a full determination to change his Ministers', North said, 'and his Majesty's Ministry … [is] at an end'. To an astonished Chamber, North then said: 'Goodnight gentlemen – you see what it is to be in on the secret'.[18]

[*Sixteen*]

— Tommy re-enters the ministry —

Although the opposition members' meeting to approve the new cabinet list was held at Tommy Townshend's London house, Tommy himself had to settle for a junior ministry. He had last been a minister in 1768. And after fourteen brutal years in opposition, he had expected something more than being put in charge of the army, as secretary at war. While he gave the impression that he was happy with his new post, his uncle George Selwyn was sure he was not.

Nathaniel Wraxall, a North supporter in the Commons, described Tommy, now almost 50:

> [He is] a man of very independent fortune and of considerable Parliamentary interest, present as well as prospective … which greatly contributed to his personal as well as political elevation: for his abilities though respectable scarcely rose above mediocrity … yet as he always spoke with facility sometimes with energy and was never embarrassed by any degree of timidity, he maintained his place in the front ranks.

Tommy's boisterous ambition in opposition, it seems, had run ahead of his talent – at least in the eyes of his senior colleagues. The new ministerial pecking-order also reflected the fact that the Rockingham faction and Charles Fox, rather than Tommy's ally Lord Shelburne, had the numbers in the new government. Finalized on 27 March 1782, the cabinet was led by Rockingham as prime minister with Shelburne and Fox as secretaries of state for home and foreign affairs respectively. But Rockingham was a physically frail figurehead and the real power was soon delicately balanced between Fox and Shelburne.[1]

Claiming that this sudden change had totally incapacitated him from either conducting the war or obtaining peace, the king drafted a message of abdication.

It was never acted on, and before long, George III was grudgingly working with his new ministers as they implemented their agreed reforms to electoral laws and the civil list. In the Commons Tommy Townshend played a supporting role to Charles Fox, the senior minister in that chamber. Long used to seeing Lord North in prime position on the treasury benches, Nathaniel Wraxall now found it difficult to pick him out among the opposition members, who dressed all alike in simple great coats, frocks and boots. By stark contrast, Tommy and his new ministerial colleagues had 'thrown off' such clothes and were 'now ornamented with the appendages of dress... decorated with swords, lace and hair powder'. The ministers' baubles barely disguised the differences within the government, however, and when young William Pitt, Chatham's second son, moved for a wide-ranging inquiry into electoral reform, divisions among government MPs defeated his proposal.[2]

The government split again over the attorney-general's bill requiring former paymasters to repay soldiers' money they had invested during their terms of office. After fourteen years in the job, Richard Rigby owed 1,100,000 pounds. Tommy had already repaid his own more modest obligation of 13,171 pounds. And with malice directed at his old nemesis, Rigby, Tommy claimed that it would be 'shameful' for such a massive sum to remain in private hands. He received no thanks from his Commons' leader, Charles Fox. Having inherited what was left of the 248,394 pound windfall his father had earned as paymaster during the Seven Years' War, an amount he would now be required to repay in full, Fox ensured that the attorney-general's bill was defeated.[3]

On 26 April 1782, Tommy rose in the House to address the first item of business in his portfolio – the army's accounts. Affecting a disarming, deferential and matter-of-fact manner in sharp contrast to his bombastic opposition performances, Tommy's tone was captured by a parliamentary reporter:

> He was unequal to the task of speaking fully on the... accounts as from the short time he had been in office it was impossible to be fully acquainted with them... He therefore shortly stated that the sum wanted... would be 3,436,399 pounds... Large as the sum wanted this year was, it was less than that of last year by 28,562 pounds.[4]

After a debate which included no less than three speakers going on about the cost and carriage of oats for cavalry horses, the sum sought was agreed to. Parliament took its role of overseeing the army very seriously and Tommy faced a formidable array of army officer MPs ready to buy into any debate. A little book called *Advice to Officers of the British Army*, first published that year, suggested to commanders-in-chief that if they served a minister wanting to make budget cuts, they should:

> make a great bustle about retrenchment... The subaltern officers and private soldiers... will of course make such complaints... it will render your economy the more conspicuous... You must [also]... so interlard your letters with technical terms that the Minister... will [not] understand them.[5]

By now only technically at war with the rebels, Britain was still very much at war with France, Holland and Spain. As the government moved to redeploy its troops, Tommy was swept up in a cabinet resolution that directed the new commander in America, General Carleton, to withdraw from New York, Charleston and Savannah to Halifax, Nova Scotia. Estimates indicated that this evacuation would require 85,000 tons of shipping, three times the amount then available. Prime Minister Rockingham was soon hounding Tommy and the Admiralty to muster all available transports, beginning an operation which would last until November 1783, involving a total of 183 ships moving in excess of 50,000 people from New York alone, to Canada, the West Indies and Britain.[6]

Tommy's responsibilities for the army were global and Gibraltar, then as now, was a key British outpost. During a long siege by the Spanish, Gibraltar's commander, General George Eliott, also fought his deputy, Lieutenant-General Robert Boyd – over a delivery of ham. Thanks to Boyd, who had been a colleague of Tommy's late brother Harry, this dispute soon ended up on the secretary at war's desk in Whitehall. In February 1782, Boyd had received twelve Lamego leg hams which were immediately confiscated by his commander. A furious Boyd then complained about 'a late malicious insult offered to me by General Eliot [sic]... concerning a parcel of hams which were seized and put up at auction'. Whatever the outcome of this complaint, Eliott made a second seizure four months later, this time of Boyd's wine. 'I have … met such malicious attempts to make my situation disagreeable', Boyd complained to Tommy, 'that I can assign no other motive … than an intention to drive me from Gibraltar'. Notwithstanding these trivial disputes over ham and wine, Eliott and Boyd combined to mount a heroic defence of Gibraltar. They were able to keep the Spanish at bay and later earned Tommy's praise during a parliamentary vote of thanks.[7]

Disputes at the highest levels of government had more serious consequences. 'Daily jealousies' between Fox and Shelburne over their reform agenda blew wide open over the future of America. On 30 June 1782, Fox brought matters to a head by arguing that the rebels ought to be granted immediate and unconditional independence. And when cabinet insisted that independence could only be resolved as part of an overall peace treaty, Fox declared his intention to resign. The very next day, Prime Minister Rockingham died.[8]

Any hopes Charles Fox had of being prime minister were now dashed by George III, who still hoped that America might somehow remain part of the British Empire. The king approached Shelburne, who accepted the prime ministership without first consulting his ministerial colleagues. A furious Fox immediately resigned, taking the chancellor of the exchequer, Lord John Cavendish, as well as the junior ministers Edmund Burke, Richard Sheridan and the Duke of Portland, with him. Tommy Townshend had hoped that his friend Burke would stay, expressing his 'warmest wishes for everything that contributes to your continuance in office'. But when Parliament resumed, Burke sat on the opposition benches. However, his reply to Tommy was friendly and he hoped that 'our political differences, great as they are, will not weaken my private influence with you'.[9]

In the major ministerial reshuffle which followed, there was some talk of Tommy being appointed chancellor of the exchequer. Instead, he replaced the new prime minister in the then more prestigious position of secretary of state for home affairs. The king had hoped that Shelburne would propose the emerging political genius, William Pitt the Younger, just 23, for this post, but Tommy's length of service in the Commons prevailed. 'Undoubtedly … [Pitt] may now take the lead as Chancellor of the Exchequer which Mr Townshend cannot object to', the king said. 'And perhaps considering his youth the arrangement may appear better as necessity has decided it'. Young Pitt himself bore no grudge, expressing his 'infinite satisfaction' about Tommy's new portfolio. So it was that alongside Lord Grantham as the new foreign minister, Tommy Townshend finally entered cabinet as the new home secretary. 'I will say nothing of politics', Charles Cornwallis wrote in a congratulatory note, 'concluding that you have had a full dose'.[10]

Not long after Tommy Townshend took over the Home Office on 10 July 1782, he received advice from the attorney-general. 'The two Secretaries of State are his Majesty's principal Secretaries of State and the distinction of Home and Foreign are mere arrangements of office', the attorney said. 'But either of them may as I apprehend do any part of the duty'. Even so, these 'mere arrangements' in Tommy's department, newly created following the abolition of the American Department, were enormous. They involved whatever related to the internal government of Britain (comprising England, Scotland and Wales) as well as Ireland, the Channel Islands, the Isle of Man, the North American colonies, the West Indies, the East Indies, Africa and Gibraltar. Tommy was responsible for correspondence with governors, Crown grants, army commissions, church appointments and the militia. His portfolio included diplomatic relations with the four Barbary States of Morocco, Tripoli, Algiers and Tunis as well as business relating to criminals, including correspondence with magistrates on the preservation of public order. Tommy was also in charge of the Secret Service, which used everything from coffee house gossip to agents based in the Channel Islands, to spy on France.[11]

Even the king's description of Tommy as 'Secretary for the Home Department and British Settlements', did not fully cover his responsibilities, which also included a supervisory role over other departments. In relation to colonial affairs, Tommy issued instructions to the Admiralty concerning ships, personnel and supplies; convicts housed in navy hulks came under his jurisdiction too. On behalf of the king himself, Tommy received letters begging for mercy, addresses from universities, applications to ride in royal parks and requests for audiences. The Home Office also supervised personnel as diverse as secretaries, translators, decipherers, the king's messengers, the Signet Office and the *London Gazette*. On 12 December 1782, during a Commons vote of thanks to the feuding Gibraltar generals, Tommy had to explain how General Eliott's official praise of Lieutenant-General Boyd had been left out of the *Gazette*.[12]

Waiting in Tommy's new office on the first floor of the Montagu lodgings, a modest split-level former residence in Whitehall, was a 'Memorandum to Mr Townshend'. In it, his predecessor Lord Shelburne posed literally dozens of questions under the headings 'East Indies', 'West Indies', 'North America' and 'Africa', for Tommy's urgent attention. To assist him, Tommy had just seventeen staff, including two under-secretaries, ten clerks, a doorman and a necessary woman (a housekeeper). While he and his two under-secretaries each had separate offices, the clerks shared a single room. In total, the Home Office occupied just four rooms of the Montagu lodgings. The senior clerks had separate desks but the others sat at a long table where they copied documents with quill pens. Evan Nepean, who had joined the department as the permanent under-secretary to Lord Shelburne from day one, came with a reputation for 'unremitting diligence and integrity'. Tommy's eldest son, John, who had joined as non-permanent (later parliamentary) under-secretary in February 1784, was just nineteen, and noted for his family connections alone.[13]

Although the official business hours of 10.00 a.m. to 3.00 p.m. might have suggested otherwise, the Home Office was frantically busy. During a meeting with Evan Nepean, New York's former chief justice William Smith observed that 'there were 20 interruptions... so it always is and for this reason business is so greatly retarded'. While some evidence suggests that Tommy himself could be a late riser, his official diaries are full of breakfast and dinner appointments on most week days, and for urgent business, Tommy would be at his desk before dawn. At 5.57 a.m. one day, Tommy wrote to the king seeking a cabinet meeting to approve a commission for a new governor; the king's permission was obtained at 8.46 a.m. and the cabinet meeting was held at 1.00 p.m.[14]

As regular visitors, William Smith and General Frederick Haldimand, the former governor of Quebec, often passed each other on the stairs to Tommy's office. Sometimes Haldimand just 'paid a visit', on the off-chance of a meeting with the secretary of state. Tommy could get flustered when things were busy and Smith noted that he suffered from 'an obstructed utterance that... [did not] arise from the fault of the tongue but a scattered mind and impotence of language. Yet there is some sense in all he says'. After many years in opposition, where it had been all care and no responsibility, Tommy now found himself at the centre of government. With the prime minister a member of the Lords,

Tommy became government leader in the Commons. He was also part of Shelburne's kitchen cabinet alongside William Pitt, Lord Ashburton (formerly John Dunning) and Lord Grantham. When the pressures of office abated, Tommy could be charming. At one Saturday morning meeting, Smith observed:

> nobody present and he is in temper and at ease. I had a conversation with him for half an hour uninterrupted … he was calm and more serene than I have ever found him before and we had on the whole a very agreeable half hour.

Tommy's son was a different story. According to the chief clerk, 'all the work of the office was thrown on Nepean…and [John Thomas] Townshend did nothing', preferring foreign travel instead. After completing the Grand Tour of Europe, the non-permanent under-secretary departed again – for a leisurely tour through Switzerland on horseback. Although his father had also done the Grand Tour, he had not been a government office-holder at the time.[15]

[*Seventeen*]

⸺ The American peace talks ⸺

Negotiating a peace treaty with the 'revolted American colonies', as George III liked to call them, was the most pressing item of business for the new home secretary, Tommy Townshend. The Rockingham government's agreed position, that the king 'should not give a veto to the Independence of America', provided no guide as to how and when independence should be granted. Prime Minister Rockingham and Charles Fox had wanted to acknowledge the colonies' independence immediately and unconditionally; Lord Shelburne and Tommy had wanted it to be linked to an overall peace settlement. At one stage, they even contemplated a loose federal arrangement that might have kept America within the Empire. Although Tommy had strongly sympathised with the American rebels in their fight against the North government, he remained lukewarm about their Declaration of Independence, especially when the rights of American loyalists remained unresolved.[1]

These cabinet disagreements were aggravated by the distribution of ministerial duties. As foreign secretary, Charles Fox had responsibility for negotiations with France, Spain and Holland, while the home secretary, Lord Shelburne, was in charge of negotiations with the revolted colonies so long as they remained, in British eyes, part of the Empire. Once their independence was recognized, however, Fox would assume responsibility for relations with the new nation.[2]

Despite these differences, the Rockingham cabinet met on 11 April 1782 and agreed to recognise America's independence 'upon Great Britain being restored to the situation she was placed in by the Treaty of 1763'. Independence was to be part of an overall settlement with France and Spain, scheduled to be hammered out at peace talks in Paris. Charles Fox duly appointed 27-year-old Thomas Grenville (son of the former prime minister) to represent him at these talks, while Lord Shelburne appointed 77-year-old Richard Oswald. Although the cabinet had insisted that Grenville and Oswald jointly negotiate with the American peace commissioners, Shelburne instructed Oswald to tell one of them, Benjamin Franklin, that he wanted a federal union with America. Franklin, however, had a totally different agenda, asserting that 'there would be no peace while… [Canada] remained an English colony'. Such was the diplomatic mess that landed on the new home secretary's desk. Now in opposition, Charles Fox, who believed that Britain should immediately recognise American independence, waited to see what Tommy would do.[3]

Complicating any talks with the Americans was the fate of tens of thousands of British troops and the loyalists – those Americans who remained loyal to George III. And at the New York coffee house in London, merchants trading with America fretted over what would become of their property. As secretary at war, Tommy had been involved in the withdrawal of troops from New York, Savannah and Charleston. Now as home secretary, he had the commander-in-chief in America, General Carleton, reporting directly to him about loyalists and merchants as well. On 14 August 1782, Tommy instructed Carleton to be 'guided by circumstances on the spot'. But that very same day in New York, Carleton, whose expectation that he would be negotiating the peace from there had been dashed, was penning his letter of resignation.[4]

Meanwhile, on 11 July, the day after the Shelburne ministry had been finalised, Parliament was dissolved until 3 September. During its dying days, the North government had passed a special Act 'to enable his Majesty to conclude a Peace or truce with certain colonies in North America', and to disregard any existing legislation to the contrary. But the Enabling Act did not refer to the United States, and it only empowered George III 'to treat for reconciliation and amity with the Colonies' – a limitation the king personally supported. As Tommy began supervising negotiations with the rebels in the king's name, and Grantham, the new foreign secretary, did likewise with Britain's European enemies, Shelburne loomed large over both ministers. The prime minister often bypassed the cabinet, his secretaries of state and the British negotiators in Paris, at one stage entering into secret and direct talks in London with the lead French negotiator, Joseph Gerard de Rayneval. A highly intelligent man who had first achieved cabinet rank in 1763 at the age of 25, Shelburne had a reputation for deceit. 'His falsehood was so constant and notorious', Walpole said, '…that he could deceive only by speaking the truth'. And as early as 27 July, Tommy was venting his frustrations about Shelburne's go-it-alone approach:

> I feel anxious at the thought of sending the Instructions to Paris without the opinion of a Cabinet. Your Lordship may think me too cautious but I feel the great importance of the measure…ought to have the formal sanction of the Cabinet or at least as many as can be conveniently collected.

Adding to Tommy's angst was an unauthorized concession young Thomas Grenville had already made to the American peace commissioners: that Britain would recognize the colonies' independence before a treaty was signed. Although Grenville had later been recalled and replaced by Alleyne Fitzherbert, it was not anticipated that this personnel switch would undo the damage that Grenville, now best remembered for his book-collecting, had caused to Britain's negotiating position.[5]

As the Shelburne government saw it, Grenville's concession had breached the Enabling Act, which provided only for negotiations with the colonies, not with the independent United States. To amend this Act, Parliament would have to be reconvened, allowing Charles Fox and his growing band of opposition supporters to threaten the government's existence. For Fox, the government's interpretation of the Act was simply pedantic, but it was of vital importance to loyalists and merchants. As Tommy Townshend well knew, they feared that their legal rights in America would disappear if independence was conceded before a comprehensive settlement was reached. Unlike the English and American civil wars, which had ended with one side completely vanquished, the revolutionary civil war had ended with both sides legally intact. So to preserve their rights in America, the loyalists and merchants began lobbying and litigating in London. The home secretary was their prime target, so much so that when the treaty was finally signed one British negotiator said: 'This will relieve Mr Townshend from another set of solicitors'.[6]

Because Richard Oswald had been appointed by Lord Shelburne, he remained in place as the chief negotiator with the Americans after his sponsor became prime minister. 'You will not be a loser by the Minister you will have to correspond with', Shelburne told him. 'You will find in Mr Townshend great habits of business joined to the most honourable principles.' Oswald himself had been a successful international businessman for many years. Although forced to sell up his property in Virginia during the war, Oswald's priority at the peace talks was to encourage thriving commercial relations with America, and he was not troubled by independence or boundaries per se. He was highly thought of by the American peace commissioners, who no doubt saw him as a soft touch.[7]

The prime minister told Oswald that his official correspondence would 'of course' be with the home secretary, but Shelburne immediately undermined this arrangement by writing to Oswald in secret. To cover his own back, Tommy began a direct communication with the Foreign Office negotiator, Allcyne Fitzherbert, who was a friend of the Townshend family.[8]

Writing from Paris on 10 July, Oswald advised his new home secretary of Benjamin Franklin's first offer. The American commissioner proposed four 'necessary' and four 'advisable' articles for a treaty. The necessary articles included independence for the thirteen colonies and the withdrawal of British troops, a boundary settlement, confinement of the Canadian boundaries by cession of 'the backlands thereof', and fishing rights off Newfoundland. The advisable articles included indemnification of Americans whose property had been destroyed, a public apology, American and British shipping to be on an equal footing and 'giving up every part of Canada'. In March 1781, the second Continental Congress had ratified articles of confederation creating the United States of America. These articles made specific provision for Canada to be admitted as a member state, but Nova Scotia was also on Franklin's list because the Americans had long assumed that if they won independence, they would automatically acquire that province as well – giving them the whole of British North America.[9]

On 25 July, Tommy Townshend signed a commission pursuant to the Enabling Act giving Richard Oswald the authority to conclude preliminary articles of peace with the 'Commissioners … named … by the said Colonies'. This commission was supposed to be sealed in the presence of the lord chancellor who was, however, out of town. In his absence, Tommy sent a copy of the commission to Oswald in Paris, hoping that it would be sufficient. It turned out that Benjamin Franklin raised no objection; having been advised by his friend David Hartley MP that 'a more honourable and honest man [than Townshend] does not exist', Franklin never doubted the home secretary's integrity.[10]

Oswald also received secret instructions to protect the loyalists by proposing 'a restoration of all rights and a general amnesty for all offences'. He was further instructed that 'if the American Commissioners are not at liberty to treat on any terms short of independence, you have our authority to make that concession'. But it was made clear to Oswald that he had no authority to acknowledge independence before a peace treaty had been agreed to.[11]

During the first half of August, Oswald was optimistic about his discussions with Franklin, 'finding no alteration...from the usual good natured and friendly way...he had formerly behaved to me'. However, the Foreign Office negotiator, Alleyne Fitzherbert, was less sanguine, writing privately to Tommy Townshend on 8 August:

> Notwithstanding the unfeigned desire which Dr Franklin has expressed of a cordial reconciliation with England and notwithstanding all that Mr Oswald has said to me on the same subject...I am very much inclined to doubt of the American Minister's sincerity in these expressions.

In fact Franklin's fellow commissioner, the flinty New York lawyer John Jay, was pressuring him to be tougher. Franklin had been in France since 1776, and while this might have made him 'the world's foremost American', Jay worried that he had been seduced by the French view that American independence should await an overall peace settlement. To make his point, Jay had gone so far as to draft a *British* Declaration of American Independence. If taken seriously, Jay's proposal would have required Parliament to pass new legislation. Stopping short of this, Franklin nevertheless now pressed for Britain to recognize America's independence as a condition precedent to a treaty, claiming that Thomas Grenville's concession had amounted to an order 'to grant it in the first instance'. And the future of the loyalists, Franklin argued, was a matter not for Congress but for each individual American state. It followed, he said, that, as a commissioner appointed by Congress, he had no power to make binding promises about loyalists' rights.[12]

Apparently unperturbed by Franklin's tougher stance, Oswald hinted that Britain would happily surrender Canada to the Americans. When Franklin said there could be no peace while Canada 'continued under a different Government as it touched their States in so great a stretch of frontier', Oswald replied that 'Canada should be given up...as it would prevent future differences and was worth nothing'. Indeed, Oswald had first recommended ceding Canada when Rockingham was still prime minister, at which time neither he nor Shelburne had objected. 'I soon learned there was a disposition in England', Franklin observed, 'to give us Canada and Nova Scotia.'[13]

Alarmed by Oswald's view that Franklin and Jay were 'entirely friendly to us', Fitzherbert sent a second private warning to Tommy Townshend on 17 August. Because Oswald was the prime minister's appointee, Tommy needed strong ministerial support to enforce a tougher line against the Americans. And so, on his recommendation, an urgent cabinet meeting was called. In this, Tommy was strongly backed by George III. 'The dispatches from Mr Oswald which Mr Townshend has sent me fully shew that all Dr Franklin's hints were only to amuse', the king wrote to Shelburne. 'I do not possibly see how the present Ministry can consent to independency but as the price of a certain peace'.[14]

The cabinet duly met on 29 August 1782 with everyone present except Admiral Keppel. As was the custom, Tommy took the minutes because it was the business of his department which was under discussion. The ministers felt that any recognition of independence prior to an overall peace settlement was beyond the power granted by the Enabling Act. With the rights of tens of thousands of loyalists hanging in the balance, Tommy's cabinet minute noted that:

> If the [American] Commissioners should refuse to treat without the previous acknowledgment of independence...Mr Oswald should inform them that he has no power under the [Enabling] Act to conclude upon that footing but that Your Majesty will recommend it to Your Parliament to acknowledge the Independence of the thirteen Colonies absolutely and irrevocably.

On 1 September, Tommy duly advised Oswald that it was beyond the king's power to recognize America's independence ahead of a general peace treaty, without a further Act of Parliament. With cabinet concern growing every day about Charles Fox's increasing popularity, there was little appetite among the ministers to test their numbers in the Commons; Parliament, which had been scheduled to sit again on 3 September, was further prorogued (suspended) until 26 November.[15]

Tommy Townshend now tried to change the focus of Oswald's negotiations so that Parliament would not have to meet. 'If the American Commissioners are ... sincerely disposed to a speedy termination of the war', Tommy told Oswald, 'they will not ... embarrass the negotiation by refusing to accept ... independence as an Article of the treaty'. He then suggested that Oswald refocus on to the 'necessary' articles which had been proposed by Benjamin Franklin. This meant, Tommy said:

> Independence full and complete to the Thirteen States and all troops withdrawn from thence;
> Settlement of the boundaries of their Colonies and the Loyal Colonies;
> Confinement of the boundaries of Canada at least to what they were before the last Act of Parliament;
> A freedom of fishing on the banks of Newfoundland.[16]

To tackle the hard American, John Jay, Tommy primed Oswald with diplomatic precedents to demonstrate that recognizing independence prior to a final treaty being signed was unnecessary. Tommy mentioned the way the Spaniards and the Dutch States had negotiated firstly a truce, and then a treaty, in 1607, referring Oswald to the '*Corps Diplomatique* and other books on the subject'. But still the Americans held out as Jay's resolve was stiffened by John Adams. Originally appointed by Congress to be its sole negotiator, Adams, another flinty lawyer, was so tough that the French had insisted Franklin and Jay be appointed to act as moderating influences. Adams took rebel propaganda that the king could ignore Parliament if he wanted to, at face value. He encouraged Jay to remain firm:

> There is but one way to negotiate with Englishmen [and] that is clearly and decidedly. Their fears only govern them – if we entertain an idea of their generosity or benevolence towards us we are undone. They hate us universally from the throne to the footstool.

Whatever moderating influence Benjamin Franklin may have had on these two was impeded by what Oswald described as 'a severe fit of gravel in the kidneys'. Jay drafted a letter to Oswald 'objecting to entering with you into negotiations for peace on the plan proposed'. There was now a real likelihood that the peace talks would fail altogether.[17]

[*Eighteen*]

STRACHEY STRIKES THE PEACE WITH AMERICA

John Jay only softened his stand after discovering that his French allies were secretly talking to the British behind his back. Fearing that the French might undermine him, Jay was now keen to break the stalemate. First, though, he had to convince John Adams to soften his position. He revisited a letter Adams had written on 13 August in which he had refused to negotiate with the British 'until we see a minister authorized to treat with the United States of America *or* with their ministers'. Taking up a variation of Adams's second option, Jay proposed that Richard Oswald be authorized to negotiate with the 'Commissioners of the United States of America', rather than the thirteen colonies referred to in the Enabling Act. On 10 September 1782, Oswald duly communicated this idea to the home secretary.[1]

After obtaining legal advice from Lord Ashburton that there was no difficulty negotiating with the Americans 'under whatever name they chose', Tommy Townshend persuaded his colleagues that no amendment to the Enabling Act was necessary, recording cabinet's decision of 19 September as follows:

> A new Commission be made ... enabling Mr Oswald to treat with the Commissioners appointed by the Colonies under the title of Thirteen United States inasmuch as the Commissioners have offered under that condition to accept the Independence of America as the First Article of the Treaty.[2]

With these preliminaries out of the way, work began in Paris on a draft treaty. Although the Americans now withdrew their territorial demand for the whole of British North America, John Jay proposed a southern boundary for Canada through Lake Nipissing. This would have placed all of modern-day southern Ontario, including Toronto, within the United States. While Oswald was happy with this compromise, Tommy Townshend was not. The territory Jay was demanding was some of the finest in Canada, and if the Americans refused to guarantee the rights of loyalists, this land would be needed for their resettlement – under the protection of the British Crown. Tommy requested another cabinet meeting for 17 October.

After resolving firstly to oppose American calls for Newfoundland fishing rights and secondly to demand the free navigation of the Mississippi, the ministers turned their attention to boundaries. Complicating their discussion was an about-face by the prime minister. Having originally acquiesced in Oswald's idea of giving up Canada entirely, Shelburne now wanted to fence the Americans in behind his Proclamation Line of 1763, that is to say within their existing areas of settlement. All the while, Oswald had maintained his generous attitude, writing to Tommy about raising money 'out of what is cutt of [sic] from Canada'.

Tommy himself was searching for a middle way. Attempting to fence in the Americans as Shelburne suggested had been one of the factors leading to the war in the first place. As Tommy had pointed out in 1774, the western forts upon which the 'fence' would have relied were already a proven failure. 'They are incapable of defending the inhabitants', he had said then, '[and] they are incapable of attacking the Indians'. But Oswald's view was equally distasteful to the home secretary, who insisted that the loyalists must be provided for. In the end, cabinet directed Oswald to 'insist upon as large an extension as can be obtained to the south west of Nova Scotia'. And in relation to the lands west of the Appalachian Mountains, Tommy's minutes noted:

> [Oswald] should state your Majesty's right to the back country and urge it as a means of providing for refugees saying however that your Majesty is willing to recede from the same upon condition that the United States make a just provision for the refugees.[3]

The prevailing cabinet view was that Oswald had been prepared to give too much away. '[He has been] a great deal too easy upon these subjects', Tommy said, 'so as to appear... quite in the hands of Mr Franklin and Mr Jay'. As the Foreign Office negotiator Alleyne Fitzherbert observed, Oswald never understood that he was 'bound to consider what his instructions are, not what he thinks they ought to be'. As Oswald was the prime minister's hand-picked envoy, Tommy could not simply dismiss him, but he dispatched his own assistant, Henry Strachey, to stiffen him up. The boundary negotiations had raised many questions about vast tracts of land which had not yet been closely mapped; when Oswald asked Tommy for the most up-to-date maps he could provide, the home secretary sent the 45-year-old Strachey to Paris to deliver them.[4]

Born in humble circumstances, Strachey had begun his career as a clerk at the War Office. Because of his outstanding work there, he had been recommended as a secretary to Robert Clive, the founder of the British Empire in India. '[Without Strachey's] abilities and indefatigable industry', Clive later said, 'I could never have gone through my great and arduous undertaking'. With Clive's help, Strachey had been elected to Parliament in 1768, where he generally supported the government. In 1776 he had been appointed secretary to William Howe's unsuccessful peace commission in America. In spite of his support for Prime Minister North, Rockingham had appointed him secretary to the treasury following the change of government in March 1782. When Rockingham died a few months later, his successor, Shelburne, transferred Strachey to the Home Office, where he began a close working relationship with the new home secretary, Tommy Townshend. 'I was never a party man', Strachey later said, 'but from habit, I am fond of business'.[5]

After being fully briefed by the cabinet, Strachey arrived in Paris in late October with secret instructions to intervene in the negotiations if necessary. The prime minister told his envoy Oswald:

> Mr Strachey is the confidential secretary of Mr Townshend. He is a most amiable and well intrusted man and it was judged proper that some person should be sent to explain the boundaries... I thought it very lucky for your sake and for that of the great object we have all in view that Mr Townshend's choice fell upon him... He will share the responsibility with you which is great.

As it turned out, Oswald welcomed Strachey, admitting that he might have gone too far, too fast and conceding that some issues should be taken up anew.[6]

The Americans were left in no doubt about Strachey's importance. 'The confidential situation in which … [Strachey] stands with me', Tommy wrote to Benjamin Franklin, 'makes me particularly desirous of presenting him to you'. And John Jay clearly acknowledged that Strachey had the authority to negotiate a treaty. Moreover, the Americans soon noticed a tougher British stance. John Adams described Strachey as 'the most eager, earnest, pointed spirit who is artful and insinuating and who pushes every point as far as it can possibly go'. Benjamin Franklin complained that the talks were 'not likely to be soon ended'. At one point, Franklin threatened that if the British persisted in a compensation claim for loyalists, a counterclaim would be submitted by the Americans for the destruction of their property by the British. In frustration, the Americans nicknamed their new opponent 'Mr Stretchy'.[7]

What frustrated the Americans delighted their British counterparts; Alleyne Fitzherbert wrote to Tommy:

> Nothing could exceed the uncommon vigilance and dexterity which he [Strachey] showed in seizing upon and turning to the best advantage every opportunity that offered in arguing the stipulations we wished for nor the indefatigable perseverance with which he disputed inch by inch those parts of the ground which we were finally obliged to recede from.

Even Oswald was happy, conceding that Strachey had revisited arguments afresh, sometimes stirring up 'insinuations of menace' from the American commissioners. Among other things, Strachey extracted a concession that no impediment could be placed on debts contracted on either side of the Atlantic before 1775.[8]

It was a map accompanying the second draft treaty which revealed the full extent of Strachey's gains, Benjamin Franklin noting that 'we had much contestation about the boundaries'. Although Strachey modestly wrote to Tommy Townshend on 8 November that these revised boundaries were 'better than the original line as well in respect to Canada as Nova Scotia though neither of them equal to your hopes', they included vital new lands suitable for resettling the loyalists. The boundary between Nova Scotia and what is now Maine was extended to the western side of the Bay of Fundy as far as the St Croix River's source, the Americans abandoning their claim to a boundary running down the middle of the St John River. But the most important change placed all modern southern Ontario in Canada, with the boundary line running through the middle of the Great Lakes, rather than Lake Nipissing. In agreeing to this, the American commissioners ignored the boundaries suggested by the Continental Congress, and as a result Toronto is today a Canadian city.[9]

On 8 November, these proposals arrived on Tommy's desk with a request from Strachey that they be written up in a 'regular form'. This involved a furious round of drafting during which Tommy took expert legal advice, especially on article 5 relating to the confiscation of loyalist property. He then went through the draft treaty 'line by line' with each senior minister, also making presentations to the full cabinet on 11, 14 and 15 November. The result, 'such a Treaty as we can sign' was given to Strachey to take back to Paris on 19 November. Tommy made clear that he was prepared to let the negotiations fail altogether if the loyalists were not adequately provided for. Apart from that, Oswald was empowered to sign a binding agreement after consulting Strachey and Fitzherbert. When Tommy asked the king if he wanted to see the dispatch to Oswald, George III replied:

> Mr Townshend cannot be surprised at my not being over anxious for the perusal of them, as Parliament having to my astonishment come into the ideas of granting a separation to North America, has disabled me from longer defending the just rights of this Kingdom.[10]

Although a settlement in Paris was now close, both sides remained under pressure; the British because Parliament was just across the Channel, the Americans because Congress was on the other side of the Atlantic. For the American commissioners, this meant that they were unable to get any updated instructions from Philadelphia during the second half of 1782. Moreover, the home secretary had been taking advantage of the Americans' extended lines of communication to intercept their secret dispatches to Congress. By contrast, the problem for Tommy was that if Parliament met again as scheduled on 26 November Charles Fox would attempt to embarrass the ministry with claims that it was selling out the loyalists. At Tommy's urging cabinet again postponed the next meeting of the Commons to 5 December.[11]

For the British, the future of the loyalists was *the* political issue. During surrender negotiations at Yorktown the previous year, George Washington had ignored Charles Cornwallis's pleas not to punish loyalist soldiers. And while the Americans' first-draft treaty, which made no mention at all of the loyalists, had been amended, the amdendment only allowed them six months to evacuate. Indeed, Oswald warned Tommy that Jay and Franklin 'would never forgive' some loyalists, whose lives would be in danger if they remained in the United States. When Strachey presented the American commissioners with the latest British draft on 25 November, he thus warned that:

> The restitution of the property of the loyalists is the grand point upon which a final settlement depends – if the Treaty breaks off now the whole business must … take its chance in the Parliament where … the warmest friends of American Independence will not support the confiscation of private property.[12]

Support for the British draft was also delicately balanced in cabinet where Lord Camden, an elderly former lord chancellor, and the Duke of Grafton were 'ill at ease', while Admiral Keppel and the Duke of Richmond were 'inclining to cut loose'. Apart from Tommy, only the prime minister and William Pitt remained strongly in favour of an immediate settlement. Over the next four days, there was a final flurry of talks in Paris. After hearing the Americans' final offer on the loyalist question, the British deliberated. 'Mr Fitzherbert, Mr Oswald and Mr Strachey retired for some time', John Adams noted. 'Returning, Mr Fitzherbert said that upon … weighing everything as maturely as possible, [he and] Mr Strachey … had determined to advise Mr Oswald to strike with us'. Writing to Tommy at 11.00 p.m. on 29 November, Strachey advised that the treaty would be signed the following day. 'The 5th article regarding the refugees is different to any of the modifications you left to our choice', Strachey advised, 'but we think it will meet with your approval'.[13]

The negotiators duly reconvened on 30 November in Richard Oswald's magnificently mirrored and gilt-decorated suite at the Grand Hotel Muscovite. At the Americans' request, Oswald agreed to one last-minute change – 'British troops should carry off no negroes or other American property'. Then Adams, Franklin, Jay, and Oswald signed the preliminary articles of peace whereby Britain recognized the United States of America. Among other things, Britain agreed to withdraw her troops and to exchange prisoners; to a border with Canada through the Great Lakes; to an enlargement of Nova Scotia to the St Croix River source; to an unmolested right to take fish from traditional fishing grounds; and to free navigation of the Mississippi on the basis, wrongly as it later turned out, that its headwaters were located in Canada. However, the Americans had remained adamant that it was beyond the power of Congress to guarantee the loyalists' rights. Still, in article 5, they committed Congress to 'earnestly recommend' to the thirteen state legislatures that provision be made 'for the restitution of all estates, rights and properties which have been confiscated ... and for a reconsideration of all laws to render [them] consistent with a spirit of reconciliation'.[14]

The American commissioners wrote to their foreign minister that article 5 had been 'among the first discussed and the last agreed to'. After finding it impossible to accept the British concept of 'honour' on this question, they had decided to take a 'middle line'. Meanwhile Strachey returned to London to find that his conduct had given Tommy Townshend 'perfect satisfaction'. Having earlier noted that 'it is impossible to suppose the Americans so blind to their real interest as wantonly to proscribe so large a number of their fellow citizens', the home secretary remained optimistic that the thirteen states would respect loyalists rights. Apart from Tommy, those cabinet ministers who supported Strachey's work included the prime minister, Lord Grantham and William Pitt. But the Duke of Richmond and Admiral Keppel were 'highly displeased' with article 5.[15]

The Home Office arranged a passport for the American ship *Washington* so it could safely transport a signed copy of the treaty to Philadelphia, where it arrived in early March 1783. Generally the articles were well received by Congress, but there was concern about the loyalists. The future president, James Madison, predicted that the thirteen states would not comply with article 5. 'It had the appearance of sacrificing the dignity of Congress', Madison said, 'to the pride of the British King'.[16]

Although a treaty had been concluded with America, its operation was suspended until Britain could finalize a peace with France and Spain. Paroled prisoners like Charles Cornwallis, now in London, therefore remained liable to be recalled to the United States. Cornwallis had been casting about for a suitable American prisoner to exchange for himself, the obvious choice being the president of Congress, Henry Laurens, who had been captured at sea. In May 1782 the British had released Laurens from the Tower of London, whereupon he and Benjamin Franklin agreed that Cornwallis be allowed 'full liberty... until the pleasure of Congress shall be known'. Although Laurens acknowledged that Tommy Townshend had treated him with 'candor, politeness and consideration', Congress had other ideas about Cornwallis. He was ordered to return to America as a prisoner of war. Over Christmas 1782 and into the New Year, Tommy tried to come to some arrangement with the Americans still in Paris, on behalf of his anxious cousin.[17]

Meanwhile, the news that the Americans had come to terms, when added to Britain's naval victory at the battle of the Saintes and her successful defence of Gibraltar, convinced France and Spain to do likewise. On 20 January 1783 they signed a peace treaty with Britain which provided for the immediate exchange of all prisoners, including Charles Cornwallis. As the historian Vincent Harlow noted, 'the treaties closed a period of humiliation [for Britain] on terms that might well have been worse'.[18]

[*Nineteen*]

— Tommy's defence of the peace —

After stalling for months, the government finally reconvened Parliament on 5 December 1782. Members were told that George III had offered to declare America 'free and independent' in a treaty to take effect as soon as a settlement was reached with France. Knowing that as leader of the government in the Commons he would be spearheading a defence of these treaties, Tommy Townshend attempted to lower expectations. 'We could not expect to procure terms as advantageous as we might have done in...a triumphant...war', he said. The opposition leader, Charles Fox, assumed that Britain would recognize America's unconditional independence, and former Prime Minister North took it for granted that there would be a reciprocal concession by the Americans relating to the loyalists.[1]

The cabinet, meanwhile, had been in uproar over the negotiations with France and Spain. Ministers were especially angry that Prime Minister Shelburne had run roughshod over his foreign minister, Grantham, and his envoy, Fitzherbert, at one point holding secret talks with the French negotiator, Joseph de Rayneval. Kept in the dark, senior ministers fumed. 'Shelburne continues to withhold those communications and schemes for the Government', Grafton wrote, 'which I am vain enough to think I am entitled to receive from any Minister, especially him'. While Tommy ensured that every article of the American treaty had been discussed in cabinet, only Grantham knew of Shelburne's concessions to France. All that stopped Grafton now resigning was the fear that Admiral Keppel and the Duke of Richmond would follow him, thereby bringing down the government.[2]

The ministers' pent-up frustration boiled over on 3 December at a cabinet meeting to decide Gibraltar's future. The fact that Shelburne and Rayneval had already privately discussed its fate only added to the tension. After eight hours of 'violent altercations' a majority agreed to return 'the Rock' to Spain in a swap for Minorca and the Bahamas. Tommy Townshend supported this decision. He was concerned that the price of keeping Gibraltar in British hands would include the surrender of Florida, where a legislature had just been set up. Among the strong dissenters were Admiral Keppel and the Duke of Richmond: to abandon Gibraltar, they argued, would be seen as a betrayal of the heroic efforts Generals Eliott and Boyd had put into its defence.

A few days later, after France came up with some further proposals, the dissenters relisted Gibraltar's future for further discussion. On 11 December the ministers met again with some claiming that the prime minister was afraid to attend at all. Amid scenes of great acrimony, the cabinet reversed itself, agreeing to retain Gibraltar, while offering Minorca and the Floridas to Spain instead. As a result, Tommy now had the unpleasant task of informing Florida's governor that almost 6,000 loyalist refugees, who had just moved from the United States, would have to move again. The king had other concerns. 'Richmond, Grafton, Camden, Keppel and Conway... [will] fight the whole peace over again', he said, '... [forming] fresh cabals'. Gibraltar, he added, would fuel a 'constant lurking enmity' with Spain.[3]

During this eight-day cabinet brawl Tommy had been put on the spot in the Commons. Did the agreement with the United States recognize its unconditional independence? Or was it was conditional on peace with France and Spain, Charles Fox demanded to know. Tommy replied that the provisional treaty with America would only take effect when agreement was reached with the Europeans. Nevertheless, soon afterwards William Pitt told the House that 'the clear indisputable meaning of the provisional agreements... was the unqualified recognition of... [American] independence'. Supposedly on side, Pitt had inadvertently handed the wily Fox an advantage. 'Dark, harsh, and saturnine', like Charles II from whom he was descended, Fox's features 'derived... a sort of majesty', Wraxall said, 'from the addition of two black and shaggy eyebrows, which sometimes concealed... the workings of his mind'. Having previously expressed support for the king's address on 5 December, Fox now claimed to 'detest and despise it'. And he charged Tommy with 'shifting the responsibility of recognizing [America's] independence... from himself to Parliament'.

Edmund Burke joined in, accusing his old friend and young Pitt of 'talking the double language of the serpent'.[4]

A treaty was finally signed with France and Spain on 20 January 1783, whereupon Admiral Keppel resigned. Although the Dukes of Grafton and Richmond remained ministers, they now boycotted cabinet meetings. Mutinous thoughts, moreover, were not confined to the administration. On 28 January London received news of an army mutiny in Portsmouth involving the death of a soldier and the wounding of an officer. Tommy's immediate response was to issue orders separating and confining the troublesome regiments. Then he fixed the underlying problem by publicly proclaiming that 'no soldier would be constrained to serve on any other terms but on those on which he was attested'. Unrest in cabinet and in Parliament, however, was not so easily resolved.[5]

As the day fixed for parliamentary debate on the peace treaties loomed, a concerted effort was made to strengthen the government. The two leading parliamentary figures outside the Shelburne cabinet were Charles Fox and the former prime minister, Lord North. Putting to the backs of their minds the unpleasant debates just weeks earlier, the ministers sounded out both men. Fox insisted that the choice of prime minister be made by the cabinet rather than the king; the king insisted that Shelburne remain as prime minister; and Fox refused to rejoin the cabinet. Tommy Townshend therefore tried to find a compromise with North's supporters, but William Pitt blamed the former prime minister for the American war and blackballed his return to the ministry. 'The proscription of Lord North by Pitt and of Shelburne by Fox', Nathaniel Wraxall said, 'drove those two excluded Ministers into each other's arms'.[6]

With the enemy gathering all around, a cabinet meeting was convened at the prime minister's house on 13 February to settle just how the treaties would be presented to Parliament. Any note of triumph, it was agreed, would be inappropriate. There was to be 'no flattery of the King's servants', Tommy stressed. Next day, Lord North's supporters also met, resolving 'to join with Mr Fox and his party in opposing the peace'. And the day after that, Fox and North agreed they would act together. The ultimate goal of these two was to form a government with the Duke of Portland, a shy public speaker, as nominal prime minister, but the real power would be shared equally by Fox and North. Such was the formidable team, hungry for office, which Tommy Townshend would now have to face when he defended the peace treaties in the Commons.[7]

Debates in both chambers began on 17 February. In the Lords, Tommy's cousin, George, censured the boundaries and claimed that the loyalists had been deserted. Taking a savage swipe at Tommy, Viscount Townshend charged that the treaties had been concluded in the 'most gross and unpardonable ignorance... with the most criminal inattention to the interests of the Empire'. Among the other speakers attacking the government were Admiral Keppel and the Duke of Richmond, who was still a minister. In a spirited defence, however, Prime Minister Shelburne posed a number of rhetorical questions:

> Were we not in the extremity of distress? Did not the boldest cry out for peace? Was not the independence of America solemnly recognized by Parliament? Had we scarce one taxable article that was not already taxed to the utmost extent? Were we not 197 millions in debt and had we not the enormous sum of 25 millions unfunded?

Finally at 4.30 a.m. on 18 February a vote to approve the treaties was called. More peers were present for this ballot than anyone could remember and the government won by 69 votes to 55.[8]

In the Commons, Tommy Townshend had moved simply that the House 'assure his Majesty... we have considered [the Treaties] with the most serious attention'. Unwisely, some government speakers then attacked the former prime minister by referring to the American war as 'Lord North's war'. But although this riled Lord North, Charles Fox could not count on his unconditional support. After North made it clear that he 'would oppose any vote of censure but could not concur in a vote of approbation', everything depended on the motion's precise wording. One of Fox's supporters moved a 'gentle' amendment that the House 'will proceed to consider' the treaties. This challenged Tommy's motion which implied the treaties' approval with words which hinted at their deferral. The amendment was, said one member, 'very soft [and] calculated for the squeamish stomachs'. But it was enough to throw the debate wide open.[9]

Taking Fox's bait, Lord North went on the attack; the treaties were too generous to France and Spain and they abandoned the loyalists. 'Never was the honour of a nation so grossly abused', he claimed, 'as in the desertion of those men who are now exposed to every punishment that desertion and poverty can inflict'. The former prime minister proposed an amendment to further protect them, but he lied about his arrangement with Fox, claiming that he was 'neither a Minister nor a candidate to become a Minister'. As he did so, a stray dog entered the chamber. 'I was interrupted by a new speaker', he said after the dog barked, 'but as his argument is concluded I will resume mine'.[10]

When Tommy Townshend finally entered the fray, he defended the concessions to France and Spain as a 'prudent adjustment' to the 'humiliating terms' forced on them after the Seven Years' War. As for the American treaty, Tommy reminded the House of its resolution the previous year, which had declared that any admiral or general who waged offensive war on America would be a traitor. 'A padlock had been put on the British sword', he said, 'and it thence became the duty of Ministers to conclude a peace with America as soon as possible'. It was in Britain's interest, he added, to establish 'a close commercial connection' with the United States. While he claimed that the Americans' just expectations should be met, he foresaw that they might not reciprocate with the loyalists. 'I trust that should the recommendation of Congress to the American States prove unsuccessful, this country will feel itself bound ... to make them full compensation for their losses.' And on the Canadian boundaries question, he pointed out that any attempt to enforce the old colonial borders of 1763 'would have revived that spirit of resentment which it is now our business to quiet'. Tommy concluded by offering to support the former prime minister's amendment if he, in turn, supported the government's motion. But Lord North declined.[11]

By now, word had filtered across from the House of Lords that the government had prevailed there. Concerned that a government win might also be looming in the Commons, Charles Fox now revealed his plan. For him the debate was not about the treaties so much as about gaining power. 'The American war was the cause of the enmity between ... [North] and myself', he told the House, '[but] the American war and the American question is at an end'. This was enough for North and his supporters to fall into line, and when the vote was finally taken at 7.30 a.m. on 18 February the government went down to the combined forces of Fox and North by 224 votes to 208.[12]

Tommy had done well to get the support of 87 independents, compared to Fox and North, who had only managed a total of 38 between them. Even Nathaniel Wraxall, who had voted with Charles Fox, was unstinting in his praise:

> Mr Townshend as Secretary of State excelled himself in his defence of the peace and may really be said to have in some measure earned on that night the peerage which he soon afterwards obtained. I never saw him display so much animation nor hear him manifest such ability.

And William Pitt's biographer later described Tommy's contribution as having been 'clear and full', but it had not been enough.[13]

Emboldened by their combined win and encouraged by the growing disarray within cabinet, Fox and North piled on the parliamentary pressure to force a change of government. A motion was moved censuring the peace terms. Even so, the mover had only praise for Tommy himself. 'He could not bring himself to believe that anything had been done under ... [Tommy's] direction with a view to any other purpose than what he might have considered really and essentially necessary for the purpose.' Still, Tommy now found himself justifying the peace by revealing British intelligence that, had the war continued, the Americans might have seized Quebec. The fact that he was forced to make this disclosure to answer Charles Fox, that erstwhile supporter of unconditional American independence, showed just how naked Fox's grab for power had become.[14]

After his government lost this motion by 207 voted to 190, Shelburne advised the king that 'any further attempt to carry on ... would be in vain'. Tommy Townshend and William Pitt agreed, he added. On 24 February, Shelburne stepped down, recommending Pitt for prime minister and the 'steady and honest Thomas Townshend' for a peerage. Tommy accepted, Pitt declined, and Britain was without a prime minister for the next six weeks.[15]

In accepting a peerage, Tommy relinquished his constituency of Whitchurch which he had represented for 29 years. When asked what name he would like to go with his title, Tommy first proposed Lord Sidney in honour of his martyred kinsman Algernon Sidney. However, after discovering that 'the elder branches' of his family might have a claim on it, he suggested Sydenham, the name of a village near his home in Kent. Finally, as he explained to the King, he settled on Lord Sydney:

> The consideration of the title itself occupies my thoughts no farther than to avoid taking any one which might clash with the pretensions of any other family... If your majesty... will allow me to change the title to Sydney of Chislehurst... neither of which are claimed by anybody and to which I am allied... by the Sydneys and the Veres I hope my relatives will be satisfied and that I shall offend no one else.[16]

Tommy's distant kinsman, Henry Sidney, had been created Viscount Sydney of Sheppy in 1689, but this title had lapsed on Henry's death in 1704, and there seemed to be no claim on it now.[17]

On 6 March 1783, 'Thomas Townshend esquire, being by Letters Patent... created Baron Sydney of Chislehurst' was introduced to the House of Lords. After taking the oaths and paying the customary gratuity of four pounds and four shillings to the door keepers, he was placed at the lower end of the Barons' Bench as the Lords' most junior member. Dressed in a magnificent full-length scarlet robe, his junior status was denoted by two guards (stripes) of ermine topped with gold lace, higher ranking peers being entitled to more stripes. No less striking was the Lords' chamber itself. Housed in a modest medieval hall, its high concave ceiling was intricately patterned while sumptuous tapestries decorated the full height and length of its walls. Tommy received many congratulatory messages on his elevation to this place. None was more pleasing than a letter from the Dowager Lady Chatham. His peerage, she said, recognized 'his zeal and labour for restoring the peace and prosperity to this unfortunate country'.[18]

Tommy had first known Lady Chatham as Hester Pitt, wife of his mentor and hero, William Pitt the Elder, who had led Britain during the Seven Years' War. Indeed, by the time William Pitt the Younger was born in 1759, Tommy and the elder Pitt had been friends and colleagues for five years. So close were their families that Tommy had literally seen young William and his siblings John, James, Hester and Harriet grow up. However it was young William who stood out. His tutor wrote of him when he was just seven that he 'continues to surprise and astonish... his steady attention and sage remarks... frequently throw light upon the subject and strongly impress it on my memory'. His mother noted that 'he does not intend to be a sailor but a William Pitt in the House of Commons'. Following his father's death in 1778, William had kept in touch with Tommy, writing to him from Exeter whilst on circuit as a junior barrister.

First elected to the House of Commons in 1781, young William had sided with Tommy and Shelburne, his father's political disciples. After becoming a member of Shelburne's cabinet with Tommy eighteen months later, he had helped them to defend the peace treaties. But with Shelburne now gone, having been preceded by a number of his colleagues, William and Tommy were just about all that was left of the government.[19]

[*Twenty*]

Aloft in a storm

After Tommy Townshend's elevation to the House of Lords as Baron Sydney, William Pitt became government leader in the Commons. There the 23-year-old conducted business with such ability that George III asked him to be prime minister, and Pitt accepted. But within 'a few hours', as Walpole put it, he changed his mind, apparently uncertain of support from Camden and Grafton, who had helped to bring Prime Minister Shelburne down. 'The ball seems to be absolutely at his feet', an astonished Sydney said of his young friend's hesitation. With Pitt wavering, the king searched for someone else; 'for Mr Thomas Pitt or Mr Thomas anybody', Shelburne said. The only person who seemed to have support in the Commons was the Duke of Portland, who was the nominee of the Fox/North coalition – a 'desperate faction', the king said, 'into whose hands I will never throw myself'.[1]

Meanwhile, faced with an outbreak of rioting in Newcastle over corn prices, Lord Sydney, still home secretary, had ordered a call-out to preserve the peace. Although a number of troublemakers were arrested, the riots spread to Liverpool, forcing him to send troops there too. With much of the fleet being paid off now that peace was at hand, there were also growing rumours of unrest among the sailors. Without a prime minister, Sydney worried that the remains of the Shelburne cabinet might not cope with this widening security emergency. He urged the king that a new administration 'be speedily formed'.[2]

Despite a motion in the Commons 'for an Administration entitled to the confidence of the people', the king continued to stall, demanding that Portland submit a plan of his proposed cabinet. To this Portland replied that no such plan would be submitted until the king agreed to his becoming prime minister. Negotiations were broken off; the Commons formally demanded a new administration; and the king renewed his offer to William Pitt. In the knowledge that Portland was no more than a puppet of the Fox/North coalition, George III pleaded with Pitt to 'stand forth against the most daring and unprincipled faction this Kingdom has produced'. However, Pitt again declined.[3]

Finally, on 1 April 1783, the king gave in, after withstanding the Fox/North coalition until, as he said, not a single man was willing to come to his assistance. When Fox presented himself at court, one witness noted that his Majesty 'turned back his eyes and ears, like a horse intent on throwing a new rider'. Portland became prime minister while Fox and North became secretaries of state for foreign and home affairs respectively. Cousin George, Viscount Townshend, again became master-general of ordnance; his son, John, a lord of the admiralty, and 'Spanish Charles' Townshend, treasurer of the navy. Sydney's cousins were in. And he was out.[4]

For a second time, the king considered abdicating, but he was prevailed upon to stay rather than risk 'the dissolution of all Government'. On reflection, he could see that the Fox/North coalition was inherently unstable and that the new administration might not last long. As the American minister in London, John Adams, put it:

> The Coalition is a rope of sand. Mr Fox... has justly excited so many jealousies of his sincerity that no confidence can be placed in him by us... Shelburne, Townshend, Pitt and [their] Administration... seem to have been the only ones who for a moment had just notions of their Country and ours.[5]

A coalition split soon occurred, over William Pitt's Bill to reform the Commons by abolishing a hundred 'rotten borough' electorates. Although this had Fox's support, North was opposed to it. In the House of Lords, meanwhile, the slower pace of business took its toll on Lord Sydney. Separated from the Commons by a large court complex and outdoor garden area, the Lords' chamber seemed both physically and symbolically removed from the main political game. It had less than half the membership of the Commons and many of its members were politically inactive. 'Down to the last evening that he remained... [in the Commons] Tommy Townshend displayed very considerable talents', Nathaniel Wraxall said. 'Lord Sydney when removed to the upper house... seemed to have sunk into an ordinary man'. This most junior peer now seemed content to rest on his laurels – his political ambition spent. However a bill to examine abuses by senior public officials fired Sydney up into a confrontation with his cousin George. As a longstanding minister in the North government, Viscount Townshend worried about what any examination of his own conduct might uncover, and when Sydney pushed hard for the tabling of papers which might authenticate abuses, including Lord North's misuse of a stationery allowance, Prime Minister Portland blocked him. A reform proposal had divided the new government, but a cover-up had reunited it.[6]

Although the new administration's priority was to reform government in India, the finalization of peace with America, France and Spain also had to be attended to. The king left the government in no doubt about his continuing unhappiness: 'I have signed a Warrant for the Heralds to proclaim peace', he said, 'and [I] am glad it will be on a day when I am not in town'. When the final treaties came before Parliament, Charles Fox tried to argue that they were completely different from those he and North had conspired to defeat at the beginning of the year. But Nathaniel Wraxall, who had supported their coalition then, noted now that 'Fox's supposed differences were minor', and John Adams described them to the president of Congress as 'but a Confirmation or Repetition of the Provisional Articles'. As far as Charles Fox was concerned, those earlier peace debates had never been about peace; they had always been about seizing power.[7]

§

For many members of Parliament, the East India Company had long seemed more powerful than the British government. As the largest multinational corporation of its day, the company's influence was exercised through its clout with British investors, its capacity to dispense patronage and its direct support in Parliament. It had its own army and its own governors, running large parts of India like a company-owned plantation. As home secretary, Sydney had already had a confrontation with the company's proprietors, who had ignored a parliamentary committee's direction to recall the governor of Bengal, Warren Hastings, over alleged mismanagement involving millions of pounds. The proprietors' dispatches, ordering their Indian employees to ignore the committee's direction, had been forwarded to Sydney for approval, but the then home secretary had found them 'so opposite to the sense of the Commons' that he would 'not suffer them to be sent out to India'. The company's supporters complained to the then prime minister, Shelburne, that 'your worst enemy could not have given you more pernicious advice', before publishing their objections all over England. Their aggressive stance, however, could not hide a growing concern that the company's regime in India 'was a government of anarchy and confusion'. Indeed Shelburne had proposed that a powerful governor-general be placed in charge of the company's Indian possessions, floating Charles Cornwallis's name for the job. But the prime minister had resigned before the idea could be taken further. Now it was Charles Fox's turn to confront the East India Company.[8]

Like young Pitt, Fox had been marked out for greatness from an early age. In 1771, Horace Walpole had said:

> Bold, spirited and confident, ... [Fox] behaved as if already in possession of all the triumphs he aspired to, and familiarized himself with pre-eminence before he was known enough to have published even his pretensions. Thus at twenty-two he acted and was hated as a leader of a party; his arrogance, loquacity, and intemperance raising him the enemies of a minister before he had acquired the power of one.

So it came as no surprise that on 18 November 1783 Fox introduced a bill which stripped the East India Company of its entire Indian administration and directly threatened the powers of George III himself. In his bill, Fox proposed that a board of commissioners, nominated by Parliament and independent of the Crown, would have absolute power over the company's office-holders to administer its Indian possessions as they saw fit. The company's supporters loudly complained that their chartered rights, fundamental to English law, were being trampled on. And the king was furious that the bill, which proposed extending the commissioners' appointments beyond 'the power of the Parliament then sitting', was intended to 'disable ... [him] for the rest of his reign'. But despite strong opposition from William Pitt in the Commons and the growing concerns of the nation at large, Fox's bill passed the lower

House by 208 votes to 102. Adamant that this bill would not become law, the king began to plan for Fox's removal and replacement.[9]

By the time the India Bill had reached the House of Lords on 9 December, carried there by Charles Fox 'and an immense body of members', the king's numbers man in the Commons, John Robinson, had all but convinced William Pitt that he could survive if appointed prime minister. Public concern about Fox's high-handed tactics was beginning to tell. Meanwhile, George III authorized Lord Temple to say that 'whoever voted for the India Bill...would be considered by him as an enemy'. Contemptuous as always of such threats, one of Fox's supporters, Viscount Townshend, noted that the company's lawyers had been standing at the bar of the Lords' chamber a full hour 'as little regarded as a couple of hackney coach horses at an alehouse door'. Speaking against his cousin, Lord Sydney argued that Fox was trying to place himself above Parliament by extending the commissioners in office beyond the parliamentary term. In the end, thanks in no small part to the king's threats, the House of Lords rejected Fox's India Bill by 95 votes to 76.[10]

When the bill was reconsidered by the Commons, the key issue was the king's interference in the Lords' vote. A motion was passed declaring that anyone who used the king's opinion to influence members would be guilty of a high crime. It was followed by another: 'that the house will consider as an enemy to this country any person who shall...advise his Majesty to prevent or...interrupt the...consideration of a suitable remedy for the abuses...in the British East Indies'. Charles Fox was behind both motions and he sensed that the king would soon sack his coalition government; he thought that anyone who volunteered to replace him would have to be mad, vowing 'we shall destroy them as soon as they are formed'.[11]

The very next day, George III dismissed his ministers. According to Nathaniel Wraxall, 'never did any King of England contest for such a stake since Charles I'. Fox and North were refused an audience and ordered to leave their seals of office with the permanent heads of their departments. As other members of the cabinet did likewise, the king's table soon presented an 'extraordinary spectacle', covered with the seals, wands, gold sticks and other badges of office. More junior ministers, such as 'Spanish Charles' and John Townshend, were notified by letter. Viscount Townshend received one on 19

December: 'His Majesty has no farther occasion for your Lordship's services as Master General of Ordnance', was all it said.[12]

That same day, 24-year-old William Pitt was appointed prime minister, supported by Lord Temple, who agreed to be secretary of state for both home and foreign affairs on a temporary basis. A desperate attempt was then made to form a new cabinet, but the most likely candidates – Camden, Cornwallis, Grafton, Grantham and Richmond – all refused to join what was already being called the 'mince pie Administration' because no one thought it would last beyond Christmas. And Lord Temple refused to stay on, bruised by the violent reaction to his aggressive lobbying on the king's behalf against Fox's India Bill. As for Shelburne, he was 'blackballed' by the king for 'selling out the Colonies'.[13]

With Pitt himself now predicting that his new government might last less than a week, Lord Sydney was approached to again be home secretary. And on 22 December 1783 he accepted, writing to Shelburne two days later:

> You will perhaps be surprised to find me dating a letter from the Offices to which your lordship first introduced me. Your astonishment cannot exceed mine. I certainly never wished and I have done all I could to avoid returning to it. But I am looked upon as one who is ready to go aloft in a storm. Under the present circumstances, I thought it my duty to undertake the task.[14]

Sydney's cousins were out, and, reluctantly, he was back in. His concern about rejoining the cabinet in such desperate circumstances may have been magnified by the strain his previous ministerial duties had placed on old friendships. Eleven months earlier, he had been forced to refuse gentleman Johnny Burgoyne's request to leave his military post in Ireland, prompting Edmund Burke to observe:

> I see they have put our unfortunate friend Tommy Townshend on all the odious service they can find for him. I forsee they will be fond of making such men ... the instruments of their malice against their old friends. I wish I could have saved the poor man in question from his share of this disgrace.[15]

The sacking of the Fox/North coalition government badly split Sydney's immediate family too, and he ended up in the doghouse with his sister, brother, in-laws and nephew. His aunt, the dowager Lady Cornwallis, lamented the state of the Townshend family. 'Mary and Charles Townshend and all the Brodricks talk violent opposition language', she said, 'and Lord Middleton has voted in all the violent questions against Lord Sydney'.[16]

The remainder of the new cabinet comprised Lord Carmarthen as secretary of state for foreign affairs, Lord Thurlow as lord chancellor, Lord Howe as first lord of the admiralty, the Duke of Rutland as lord privy seal and Lord Gower as lord president of the council. Out of this group, Sydney was made leader of the government in the Lords which, as in the Commons, involved planning tactics, making key interventions in debates, organizing speakers and ensuring a 'a good attendance' in the chamber. Having been content to sit on the Lords' backbench as its most junior opposition member, Sydney was now in charge. His challenges were nothing compared to those faced by the new prime minister; with just two years' parliamentary experience, Pitt was now the only member of the cabinet in the Commons, where Fox and North, furious at their dismissal, were waiting to confront him.[17]

The king, supported by Gower, Carmarthen and Sydney, wanted to dissolve Parliament immediately. 'We must be men', he said, 'and cut the threads that cannot be unravelled'. Pitt and a narrow cabinet majority were for holding on. So on Christmas Eve, George III assured a suspicious Commons that it would not be dissolved. And on 12 January 1784 the MPs reconvened. Wraxall described the prime minister's arrival thus:

> From the instant that Pitt entered the doorway of the House of Commons, he advanced up the floor with a quick and firm step, his head erect and thrown back, looking neither to the right nor to the left; nor favouring with a nod or a glance any of the individuals on either side ... It was not thus that Lord North and Fox treated Parliament; nor for them would Parliament have so patiently endured it: but Pitt seemed made to command, even more than to persuade or to convince, the Assembly that he now addressed.

Despite Pitt's apparent command, Fox and North still had the numbers. The new government proceeded to lose a string of Commons' votes on key issues. Finally, on 2 February, a motion 'against the continuance of the present

Ministers in their offices', passed by 223 votes to 204, but Pitt did not resign and the Commons resolved next day, by 211 votes to 187, to lay the no-confidence motion before the king.[18]

However much confidence the young prime minister displayed in the Commons' chamber, behind the scenes the combined effect of these motions was taking its toll. The king therefore looked to the government leader in the Lords for support:

> For Lord Sydney's private ear Mr Pitt seemed rather this day to despond this will be by his friends I hope combated: his career has been handsome as yet and he ought to see whether the spirit of the Lords may not a little startle the Commons; those who have deserted him in that House from fear may from the same motive return.[19]

The Lords' spirit was soon tested over resolutions, already passed by the Commons, which attempted to stop treasury officials from carrying out their statutory obligation to pay certain India accounts. These resolutions had been championed by Fox and opposed by Pitt; a great deal was at stake because no government could survive comprehensive defeat in both Houses of Parliament. Moreover, the Lords' vote was not a foregone conclusion for Pitt. The Duke of Grafton and other influential peers who had supported him were becoming increasingly hostile as details leaked of the precise circumstances surrounding the dismissal of the Fox/North government. So to oppose the resolutions targeting treasury officials, Sydney argued that the Commons could not simply resolve to suspend the law. No less than an amending act agreed to by both Houses would be required. And after some spirited support from Lord Gower the new government won by 100 votes to 53; a triumph compared to their vote of 95 to 76 on Fox's India bill back in December.[20]

With a government majority of 'near two to one' in the Lords, the support of his 'subjects at large in a much more considerable proportion' and an opposition majority in the Commons of no more than 25, the king looked to form a compromise administration that included Pitt and his predecessor, Portland. 'The only person I can think from his office as well as personal character proper to be sent by me', the king told Pitt, 'is Lord Sydney'. And so on 15 February, Sydney attempted to convince Portland to '[heal] the present divisions by ... [forming] a new Administration on a wide basis'. But the former prime minister's entirely predictable reply was that 'the confidence of the ... Commons [was] indispensably necessary to any arrangement'. And it was therefore impossible to discuss any compromise ministry with Pitt. In these circumstances, a special cabinet meeting at Sydney's home decided that 'no further steps could be taken towards a negotiation'. As Charles Cornwallis put it: 'The Ministry was determined not to resign but was willing to treat, while the Opposition was determined to enter no treaty till the Ministry had resigned'.[21]

Fox's majority on 3 February of 24, as it turned out, had been his high point. On 1 March, when a vote was taken on a motion demanding that the king sack his ministers, Fox's majority was twelve. Just a week later, when Fox sought the Commons' support on a complaint to the king about 'the state of public affairs', he won by a single vote. According to Cornwallis, this dramatic slide in Fox's support 'totally disconcerted the ... opposition'. Sensing the government's growing strength, the East India Company forwarded their minister some suitable reading material. 'The Chairman and Deputy Chairman ... present their compliments to Lord Sydney', they said, 'and furnish [him] with a printed copy of several charters granted to the Company'.[22]

Despite his earlier promise not to do so, the king could not help himself, and on 25 March 1784 he dissolved the Commons altogether. With three years of the fifteenth Parliament yet to run, the country went to the polls. And Cornwallis's observation that 'the mass of the people is certainly with the present Ministry' turned out to be spot on. Factors contributing to William Pitt's landslide win included a belief among ordinary voters that 'Mr Fox was attempting to dethrone the King and make himself Oliver Cromwell'. Moreover, Fox's personal life only made things worse. 'He loved only ... women, play and politics', one of his gambling companions said. 'Yet he [never formed] a creditable connection with a woman ... lost his whole fortune at the gambling table and with the exception of about eleven months [was] always in Opposition'.[23]

The election was a disaster for the Fox/North coalition, and as Fox's biographer noted, 'it determined for more than forty years the question of the government of England'. Over 160 of Fox's supporters lost their seats and only 40 survived. 'Spanish Charles' Townshend lost his seat of Yarmouth and William

Pitt defeated John Townshend in Cambridge. The new Parliament met on 18 May 1784. Pitt soon asserted his dominance with votes as high as 282 to 114 as he turned his attention to the pressing priorities of public finances and India.[24]

[*Twenty-one*]

Family and friends

Angry at losing his Cambridge constituency to William Pitt, John Townshend joined with fellow victims of the 1784 election landslide to compose *The Roillad*, a satirical poem aimed at the victors. A combination of Pitt's youth and ability rankled with those who had lost their seats:

> A sight to make surrounding nations stare
> A Kingdom entrusted to a schoolboy's care.

And it was no doubt John Townshend who took aim at the long chin of his father's cousin, Lord Sydney, using it to poke fun at the home secretary's colonial responsibilities:

> Oh had by nature but propitious been
> His strength of genius to his length of chin
> His mighty mind in some prodigious plan
> At once with ease had reached to Hindoustan.[1]

Although aged 50, Sydney was still the fourth youngest in a cabinet of seven when he returned to office in December 1783. Gower was 63, Howe 58 and Thurlow, 53. Only Rutland and Carmarthen, 30 and 33 respectively, were anywhere near the age of the prime minister, who was still just 24. Gilbert Stuart, who painted portraits of George Washington, John Adams and Thomas Jefferson, also painted Sydney in 1785. The most striking thing about this official portrait is Sydney's simplicity of dress – a plain black coat – a stark contrast to the ermine-striped scarlet robes most peers would have insisted on wearing. Otherwise, the home secretary is depicted as a beefy, almost John Bull-like character, one who bears a determined look on his face. It is the image of a heavy set, still agile man, whose facial colouring suggests a quick temper. Sydney's smooth hands, however, indicate that his battles had been fought in the Commons, not at sea or on horseback. The Townshend haughtiness captured in a portrait of him as a much younger man has been replaced by the knock-about look of a politician who had spent fourteen long years in often lonely and aggressive opposition. Portraits of his cousins George, Viscount Townshend and Charles Cornwallis in later life provide an interesting contrast. The viscount, now haughtier than ever, is painted in a full suit of armour, while Cornwallis, who had spent most of his life in the saddle, bears the world-weary look of a pro-consul.[2]

Sydney's rough-and-tumble political career was balanced by what appears to have been a tranquil family life. On 19 May 1760, almost six years exactly after he entered Parliament, Sydney had married Elizabeth, eldest daughter and co-heir of Richard Powys of Hintlesham, Suffolk, and his wife the former Lady Mary Brudenell. Through her mother, Elizabeth was a grand-daughter of the third Earl of Cardigan and very well connected to court life through her uncles. The Brudenells, who were Tories, had once been Catholic and presumably Jacobite. Unfortunately no correspondence between Sydney and his wife appears to have survived. But given that they came from very different political backgrounds and that he had a lifelong reputation as a family man, it is reasonable to assume that their marriage was a love match. And a clearly indulgent Sydney put up with his wife's expensive taste. 'Elizabeth desires me to ask you to bring her a black silk winter cloak about the value of two guineas', Sydney wrote to his uncle, George Selwyn, in Paris. 'She says the French ones are much better than the English'. Noting that this cloak 'was trimmed with lace', Sydney's unmarried sister, Mary, added pointedly, 'the English manufacturers content me for my wearing apparel'.[3]

Three years Sydney's junior, Elizabeth bore him six sons and six daughters. But only seven, Georgiana, Mary, John, Frances, Harriett, William and Horatio, are known to have survived infancy in an age when the mortality rate of children under two was especially high. On 9 December 1777, for instance, his brother Charles noted that Sydney's wife 'is brought to bed and is very well: the child died three hours after she was born'.[4]

Elizabeth apparently contributed no fortune to the marriage, but thanks largely to his father's inheritance of Chislehurst from the Selwyns, Sydney and his family were wealthy. This wealth, later augmented by a bequest from Sydney's second cousin, Lady Exeter, of 70,000 pounds, allowed Sydney and his wife to entertain in style at Frognal, their country home on the Chislehurst estate in Kent. For most of the 1770s, when Sydney had languished in lonely opposition, the most important house guests had been Lord and Lady Chatham and their children. 'We are never so well pleased', Sydney said, 'as when ... [we] have the honour of receiving at Chislehurst any part of [Lord Chatham's] family.'[5]

During Sydney's years in the Commons, Parliament would commence sitting in autumn and continue over winter into the late spring when the long summer recess would begin. Sydney's habit was to divide his time between his family estate in Kent, when Parliament was not in session, and his London townhouse, when it was. At Frognal, Sydney saw a great deal of his sisters, including his unmarried sister, Mary, who, along with another sister, Albinia Lady Midleton, carried the load of caring for their father, Thomas. 'My father and I accompany Lady Midleton to Pepper Harrow tomorrow', Mary wrote within months of his retirement. 'I shall deposit ... [him] under her care and make my escape for a few days'. Unlike Sydney, Mary was a lively correspondent of modest ambition, who relied on another brother, Charles, in financial matters. 'The affair of the mortgage I trust entirely to Charles', she wrote in 1780. 'I still should like a bit of land for my potatoes'. While parliamentary business often prevented Sydney spending time with his family, he helped where he could. 'I am going to nurse my sister [Albinia] who has miscarried in the country', he wrote just before Christmas 1764, 'and my stay there depends on her health'. Ten years later, Albinia's son, George, was returned as a member of the Commons for Whitchurch on the interest of his uncle. And later still, Sydney also helped another nephew, severely wounded in a duel, to advance in rank from lieutenant to captain.[6]

Sydney's wife, Elizabeth, was close to her sister, Mary, who had married an Irish nobleman, James, second Earl of Courtown. Sydney's sons John, William and Horatio Townshend had attended Eton and, when the Courtown boys were enrolled there, Sydney's sister, Mary, noted the effect this had on Elizabeth. 'My brother and his family are gone to town to visit Lord and Lady Courtown who are come to England to put their sons to Eton', Mary said, 'which gives great joy to Mrs Townshend'. From 1784 to 1793, Lord Courtown was treasurer of the royal household, a position which no doubt facilitated the appointment of his wife and Lady Sydney as ladies-in-waiting to the queen. Elizabeth's connections at court through her own family, the Brudenells, had already shaped Sydney's habit of targeting Prime Minister North, rather than George III, over Britain's war with America. His personal relationship with the king, which had remained cordial, was now enhanced by his wife's proximity to Queen Charlotte who, among other things, gave Elizabeth a Louis XIV gold music-box.[7]

As home secretary, Sydney was responsible for most people's access to the king and for organizing what went on in his name both at home and in the colonies. He was also responsible for George III's most intimate affairs, including medical access to his person when he went mad, and whether the body of his late aunt, Princess Amelia, should be embalmed. Aspinall's *Later Correspondence of George III* reveals that there was no more frequent a correspondent with the king than his home secretary, Lord Sydney. Apart from weighty matters of state, the letters cover topics as diverse as taking a madman into custody at the king's Kew residence, firing the Tower guns on thanksgiving days and the king's indisposition caused by a nettle rash. The correspondence reveals a close but proper relationship between the two, with Sydney displaying a slightly pedantic and bustling approach to business, a characteristic he shared with George III.[8]

The personal and business relationship between king and subject enhanced Sydney's influence across government where one of the home secretary's roles was to co-ordinate other departments for major and special projects, the largest of which was to be the first European settlement of Australia. Another major source of Sydney's power was his control of the Secret Service. From time to time, this allowed him to keep an eye on a diverse range of people including the Prince of Wales, Charles Fox, Lord North, Benjamin Franklin, the directors of the East India Company and Lord George Gordon. Britain's traditional enemies, France and Spain were not forgotten. And even three years after his retirement Sydney still had intelligence sources reporting to him about the payment of a large sum of money from Ireland to France.[9]

Less clandestinely, Sydney and his wife were at the centre of London's social life. They were regulars on the charity circuit where Sydney was a steward of the

Sons of the Clergy, who performed charity concerts at St Paul's Cathedral. A wide circle of friends kept the home secretary abreast of events as far away from each other as Kent and Botany Bay. At Frognal, Lord and Lady Sydney were noted for their hospitality, including dinners where the local gentry were invited to join Prime Minister Pitt when he stayed overnight, continuing a tradition he had first enjoyed there as a young boy. Although Sydney allowed his neighbours to kill game on his property as they pleased, there were more partridge in 1789 than in any preceding season. This *The Times* attributed to Sydney's gamekeeper, who could not 'take down a bird'. The following year, there were even more birds because Sydney allowed every local gentleman 'liberty to shoot', which made them all anxious to deter poachers. But allowing his neighbours to hunt on the Frognal estate was not without its risks. On one occasion, Sir John Dyke's hounds chased a fox which 'made up to [Sydney's] House and leapt at the windows', breaking a pane. According to *The Times*, 'had not the blind been up, [the fox] would have entered the window with the whole pack of hounds'.[10]

Thanks to Sydney's longstanding friendship with William Pitt the Elder, the first Earl of Chatham, their respective children had become good friends. On 27 June 1782, William Pitt the younger wrote to his mother 'of a match of which the world here is certain but of which [my older brother John] assures me he knows nothing between himself and the beauty in Albemarle Street'. The second Earl of Chatham's reputation for punctuality was such that he was known as 'the late Lord Chatham' and his marriage to Sydney's daughter, Mary Elizabeth, did not take place until July the following year. 'Lord Chatham inherited his illustrious father's form and figure but not his mind', Nathaniel Wraxall observed. 'That present of nature fell to the second son'. The Pitt–Townshend marriage produced no children and the Earldom of Chatham became extinct on John's death in 1835 – Mary Elizabeth having predeceased him in 1821.[11]

Sydney continued his close personal relationship with the prime minister whose biographer noted that Sydney 'once his [Pitt's] father's friend and now his own continued to act with him on the most cordial terms'. This relationship, together with Sydney's friendship with George III, allowed the home secretary to smooth things between the warm-tempered king and his young prime minister, who was a cold fish. 'Awkward and ungraceful in his person, cold and distant in his manners, reserved and sometimes stately in deportment', Wraxall noted,

'Mr Pitt is not formed to captivate mankind by the graces of external figure or address'. During the early days of minority government in late 1783, the king had relied on Sydney to keep Pitt's spirits up in the face of relentless pressure from Charles Fox. And after Pitt's decisive election victory the following year, when the king stood back from the day-to-day affairs of government, Pitt relied on Sydney to brief George III on many matters which would previously have required the prime minister's personal presence.[12]

In 1785, Sydney averted a showdown between the two. On 14 March, the prime minister proposed major electoral reform and threatened to resign if George III instructed his 'Household brigade' of parliamentary supporters to vote against it. In a strongly worded draft reply, the king angrily questioned Pitt's honesty whereupon Sydney intervened to reassure him that the prime minister's motive had been entirely honourable. This defused the confrontation. The proposal, which involved compensating electors in small constituencies who were willing to surrender their voting rights, was then debated by the Commons. There, to Sydney's relief, it was defeated by members who represented small borough electorates like Whitchurch, in which he still held an interest.[13]

After the 1784 election, Pitt's relationship with his cabinet changed. He now held a great deal of the decision-making tightly to himself and was tardy with his voluminous correspondence, leaving his ministers to complain of his 'chronic want of communication'. As a confirmed bachelor, the prime minister could only unwind with his closest friends, spending a lot of his time drinking at the Wimbledon house of his crony, Henry Dundas. 'No men in high office since Charles II's time', Wraxall said, 'drank harder than Pitt's companions'. While Sydney was a convivial host who would have his cabinet colleagues around to his London home for dinner during parliamentary adjournments, he was not 'one of the boys'. Like George III, he was circumspect in his personal behaviour.[14]

During 1784, rumours grew that Sydney might be shifted out of the Home Office. He had developed 'a frightful and alarming disorder in his eyes' and could not read or write. 'Should it grow worse', one colleague said, 'Sydney must bid adieu to all business.' But he recovered, becoming one of the most active cabinet members. Having volunteered to go aloft in a storm, Sydney remained fully involved in cabinet unlike some of his colleagues. On 10 January 1787, for example, *The Times* reported that only Sydney and the foreign secretary, Carmarthen, had bothered to attend a cabinet meeting in the prime minister's office. The work habits of Sydney and his son John continued to provide a contrast as the young man's official duties clashed with his grand tours of Europe. As his father had done with him, so Sydney corresponded with young John during these tours, addressing him as 'My Dear Jack'. Warning him not to stay too long in Paris, Sydney said 'H.M. would not I think like it in your present situation [as under secretary]'. However, as for shopping there, Sydney told his son 'not to trouble... about ducks... [But] as to the claret, I should be glad to try a hogshead'.[15]

What of Sydney the administrator? His energy as a minister has been questioned largely as a result of some bile-filled comments William Smith, the former chief justice of New York, committed to his diary. At the time, Smith was angry because he thought the delayed settlement of his loyalist compensation payments was an 'American matter', falling within the jurisdiction of the Home Office. In fact it was the head of treasury, George Rose, who had held things up. But soon after Sydney informed him of this, Smith, described by his own detractors as 'a snake in the grass', wrote:

> Sydney has a bad utterance and but a moderate understanding. I should imagine him very unfit for his present situation. His thoughts are on the surface very scattered. He seems to be candid, he is reputed to be honest but I can't believe him industrious or vigilant, certainly not profound and he wastes time at all his audiences by talking himself on subjects not relating to business.[16]

Others had a different view. 'I should be much concerned to lose Lord Sydney', the lord-lieutenant of Ireland remarked in 1784. 'He is most practicable, punctual and good-humoured correspondent'. Even so, there was self-doubt in Sydney's makeup, exacerbated by the stress of a heavy workload, which sometimes left a negative impression. Perhaps this reflected the fact that he had spent most of his career in robust opposition and was never comfortable wielding executive responsibility. But wield it he did, as he determined vital policies relating to the United States, Canada, Australia and Ireland, and persevered in choosing key personnel to carry them out. As the editor of the *Historical Records of Australia* put it, 'Sydney appears to have possessed the rare faculty of perceiving intuitively, the latent powers in the men with whom he came in contact'.[17]

Prime Minister Pitt's priority was to fix Britain's finances and Sydney was generally left to his own devices at the Home Office. But when Pitt did intervene, in India and Ireland, Sydney stepped back. Still, his influence remained important as when he refused to transmit East India Company dispatches to Bengal because they ignored a parliamentary direction to recall its governor. Even Charles Fox praised this precedent. As Fox's biographer later acknowledged, it showed the way forward:

> The real supremacy of the Ministers usually kept in the background but always ready to be exerted has kept in check the administration of the Company and placed the affairs of India under the guarantee of Ministerial responsibility by which all things in Great Britain are ordered and controlled.[18]

Such decisive action, combining boldness and restraint, was fundamental to good constitutional government. It leveraged off Sydney's very strong relationships with the king and with Pitt. And it became a hallmark of his Home Office administration during the 1780s in British North America, in New South Wales and in Ireland, where he was instrumental in establishing the so called 'golden age' of Irish government.[19]

[*Twenty-two*]

The golden age of Irish government

Tommy Townshend's family had been involved in governing Ireland for well over a century by the time he assumed responsibility for it as home secretary in July 1782. The key issue for Tommy, as it had been for his predecessors, was the loyalty of predominantly Catholic Ireland in any fight between Protestant England and Catholic France and Spain.[1]

During the English Civil War, the Parliament in London had placed Ireland under the control of Philip Sidney as lord-lieutenant, while his brother, Algernon, was appointed governor of Dublin. Without adequate troops to back them, these arrangements were short lived, and for the next 40 years, Catholics and Protestants vied with each other for control. This tussle came to a head at the battle of the Boyne in 1690 when Protestant forces, led by King William III, defeated the Catholics, led by King James II. As a consequence, Catholics were excluded from the Parliament, the army and the legal profession. Two years later, Philip and Algernon's younger brother, Henry, who had been one of King William's principal officers, was appointed lord-lieutenant. Henry's tolerance of Catholics upset Ireland's Protestant Parliament, however, leading to his recall the following year.[2]

In February 1717, Tommy's grandfather Charles, second Viscount Townshend, was appointed lord-lieutenant of Ireland as a consolation prize, following his removal as secretary of state, but his ongoing disagreements with the British government saw him dismissed from his new post just eight weeks later. At that time, the Irish Parliament's duration between elections was absurdly long, its meetings short and infrequent and its powers severely limited. Moreover its key members, known as 'undertakers', ensured that the British government got its way in return for the right to dispense royal patronage.³

This system was still operating when Tommy's cousin George, fourth Viscount Townshend, was appointed lord-lieutenant in August 1767. As Ireland's chief executive, George Townshend immediately set about reform, managing to cut the duration of the Irish Parliament from the life of a monarch, which could last 30 years, to a set period of eight years. The added accountability brought about by more frequent elections helped to break the power of the undertakers and George's carriage was drawn through Dublin by a joyous mob. However, when the newly invigorated Irish MPs rejected a budget bill, George attempted to regain control by dispensing patronage; now acting like an undertaker, his conduct contributed to his recall five years later. Nevertheless, one of Ireland's greatest patriots, Henry Flood, said that 'the period of Lord Townshend's administration was universally allowed to be the springtime of a practical adaptation of the British constitution to Ireland'. But one reform had been beyond him – the repeal of Poyning's Law which required all Acts of the Irish Parliament to be approved by the British government. 'The rights of the Crown in Great Britain ... [under] Poyning's Law', George was instructed, '[are] upon no account to be given up'.⁴

Prior to becoming home secretary, Tommy Townshend's interest in Ireland had been limited to parliamentary debates about relieving the 'famishing condition' of its inhabitants. In January 1779, Tommy had advocated the removal of 'those partial restraints on trade which ... [were] the cause of her distress'. Noting that 'by a narrow policy America had been lost', he had warned the House to beware of losing Ireland. And indeed, for so long as Britain's fight had been with America alone, the leading Irish politician of the day, Henry Grattan, had been sympathetic to the rebels, but when Catholic France and Spain joined the Americans, Grattan and his Protestant supporters swung behind Britain. Their about-face was made easier by Prime Minister North's decision, at the end of 1779, to grant Ireland broad trade concessions. Now encouraged by the British government, Grattan's supporters formed an 80,000-strong volunteer militia to take on the defence of Ireland.⁵

Before long, these volunteers were calling for sweeping constitutional reform. In April 1782 the Parliament in Dublin endorsed Henry Grattan's demand for

Irish legislative and judicial independence. The British government agreed to this, in return for Ireland supplying 20,000 sailors for the Royal Navy. Britain's Parliament then resolved that the King 'take such measures... most conducive to the establishing by mutual consent, the connection between this Kingdom and the Kingdom of Ireland upon a solid and permanent basis'. In Dublin, this news was greeted by bells and bonfires. After being informed by Grattan that the British Parliament 'had concurred in a resolution to... gratify your every wish', its Irish counterpart purported to repeal Poyning's Law and to secure the independence of Irish judges.[6]

Although Grattan's chief political rival, Henry Flood, welcomed these developments, he argued that the repeal of the Act asserting Britain's right to make laws for Ireland 'was a simple repeal without the renunciation of the principle'. The British Parliament, he said, would have to pass a special Act to renounce any claim to legislate for Ireland and to acknowledge the independence of Irish judges. With the backing of the Irish Parliament, Grattan hotly denied this was necessary. Even so, the volunteers supported Flood. Outraged at being upstaged in this way, Grattan accused Flood of being 'intemperate, corrupt and seditious'. Grattan was a 'mendicant patriot', Flood replied.[7]

In the autumn of 1782, an Irish case came before an English judge, Lord Mansfield. Although for technical reasons Mansfield was correct to hear it, his decision gave the appearance of being a breach of the resolutions acknowledging Irish judicial independence, and the case was widely misrepresented in Ireland as proof that Flood was right and Grattan was wrong. Adding to this impression was a new British Act which prohibited the export of calico printing blocks to Ireland. It seemed to affirm another of Flood's claims – that Britain's right to legislate for Ireland, at least externally, had been left unchanged.[8]

The intensifying contest between Grattan and Flood coincided with a change to the personnel responsible for Britain's Irish policy. Shelburne replaced Rockingham as prime minister, Tommy Townshend replaced Shelburne as home secretary, Lord Temple replaced the Duke of Portland as lord-lieutenant and William Grenville became Temple's chief secretary in Dublin. As sons of former Prime Minister George Grenville, Temple and Grenville were first cousins of William Pitt whose mother, Hester, was George Grenville's sister. On 27 November 1782, Grenville came to London and spent some time briefing Tommy Townshend on Irish affairs. Although he was preoccupied by the American peace negotiations, the home secretary made it clear that cabinet would give 'every support' to Grenville and Temple. 'Where there was not some marked difference of opinion', Tommy said, 'the Lord Lieutenant should be left to himself without however being abandoned'. Then Grenville raised concerns over how a speech the king was going to deliver referred to 'the liberal spirit' of new measures governing commerce with Ireland, without referring to 'rights'. Tommy accepted the need for an amendment and, although Prime Minister Shelburne was initially unenthusiastic, he grudgingly gave way. When the speech was delivered on 5 December 1782, it referred to 'the liberal principles adopted by [Parliament] with respect to the rights and commerce of Ireland', referring also to 'our two Kingdoms' – thereby implying equality of constitutional status.[9]

The home secretary next turned his attention to Henry Flood's demand for an Act of the British Parliament which would positively renounce its right to legislate for Ireland. But the prime minister was, again, unenthusiastic. 'Shelburne was much more disposed to narrow than to extend the rights and concessions yielded to Ireland by Britain', Grenville said. At best, the prime minister seemed disinterested. '[Townshend] acted the most friendly and honest part … and sacrificed his time to me for an hour or an hour and a half for several days', Grenville noted, 'while during the fortnight I have been here I haven't seen Shelburne for 20 minutes whole'. Although Grenville was now based in Ireland, he remained a member of the House of Commons. And so as leader of that House, Tommy allowed Grenville to do some kite flying, to bring Irish affairs to a head. With William Pitt's concurrence, Grenville proposed a bill 'putting to an end every idea of legislation and jurisdiction over Ireland'. It was designed to pressure Prime Minister Shelburne, who as a member of the Lords was unable to immediately respond. 'By giving such a notice speaking from the Treasury bench in the hearing of and backed by … [Townshend] and Pitt', Grenville said, 'I have most undoubtedly pledged the Government to do something'.[10]

Following a discussion between Tommy Townshend and Shelburne on Christmas morning 1782, Grenville felt confident that the prime minister would support his proposed bill. Then a hostile lord chancellor intervened and Shelburne deferred any action into the New Year. Finally in January 1783

Sydney, Pitt and Shelburne began work on a draft bill. But the legal cross-checking proceeded at a snail's pace because too many government lawyers, the prime minister claimed, were still on their Christmas holidays. However, the home secretary soon tired of Shelburne's stalling and on 19 January 1783 a delighted Grenville noted that 'he [Townshend] will on Tuesday move for leave to bring in a Bill'.[11]

So it was that on 22 January 1783 Tommy introduced the Irish Judicature Bill to remove 'all doubts... concerning the exclusive rights of the Parliament and Courts of Ireland in matters of legislation and judicature'. The home secretary noted that although the British Parliament had taken steps to do this the previous year, Lord Mansfield's decision to hear an Irish case in England 'had excited jealousies in the breasts even of the best intentioned men in Ireland'. Tommy therefore explained to the House why it must act again:

> To lull these jealousies; to lay all doubts and disputes about constitutional points asleep so that they might never wake again was the object and he hoped Ireland would rest satisfied that... England... [surrendered] all legislative and judicial authority over Ireland.[12]

After a short debate, Tommy Townshend's bill passed the Commons without opposition. But in the House of Lords, it ran into trouble when Lord Bellamont, an Irishman, claimed that it 'did not answer the purpose' and that the whole of Ireland would be 'thrown into flame'. Then further debate was interrupted as Parliament began its consideration of the American, French and Spanish peace treaties. By the time the Lords returned to the bill in April, the Fox/North coalition was in government while Tommy Townshend, by now Lord Sydney, sat on the opposition benches. There he was joined by Lord Temple, who before resigning his lord-lieutenancy had 'cordially' acknowledged Sydney's 'very steady [and] honourable... support' over Ireland 'in the complicated scene of the four winter months'.[13]

Despite the change of government, Temple's younger brother, William Grenville, remained keen on reform. He urged Sydney to take up the Irish Judicature Bill in the Lords, but Sydney wanted first to see what the new prime minister, Portland, would do. When the Lords met on 11 April, Portland's reluctance to take up the bill himself soon became obvious. Every peer, he said, was equally entitled to move for it to be considered. Sydney therefore seized the moment:

> The Bill was certainly a measure of infinite importance and as he had not only the honour of moving that it be read a first time by their Lordships but had originally introduced it into the other House of Parliament, if any one Lord was more answerable for its contents than any other, it was himself.

So it was that Sydney found himself in the extraordinary position of moving this key bill in both Houses – once from the government benches in the Commons and once from the opposition benches in the Lords.[14]

As the Lords' debate on the bill got under way, the prime minister's disinterest was matched by that of his predecessor, Shelburne, while other influential Lords, such as the Duke of Richmond and the lord chancellor, were openly hostile. But for once, Viscount Townshend supported his cousin. As a former lord-lieutenant of Ireland and senior member of the new coalition government, Townshend's views carried weight. The Lords, he said, had to pass Sydney's bill to show the sincerity of 'their ... two resolutions of 17 May last [urging] the necessity of ... doing Ireland the fullest justice'. And after a tortuous debate, the bill was approved.[15]

Sydney's legislation confirmed new constitutional arrangements for Ireland which were to continue until 1800. It was the last time the whole country was to have a single Irish-based Parliament, albeit under a Protestant minority, which made laws for all 32 counties. Described as 'a golden age of Irish government', Britain and Ireland co-existed as two independent kingdoms under the same Crown. What had been achieved was a form of self-government within the Empire. Although this model had been offered by the British peace commissioners and rejected by the Americans in 1778, it was a formula that in a modified form would later be adopted by Canada, Australia and New Zealand. In Ireland's case, the link to the British government remained the lord-lieutenant, who still wielded enormous executive power and patronage. It was this which would ultimately bring Ireland's legislative independence undone.[16]

Towards the end of 1784 the British prime minister expressed support for an Irish proposal that Britain's remaining restrictions on Irish imports be eliminated. Pitt insisted, in return, that Ireland pledge to help defend the Empire. Following intense discussions, Sydney received cabinet approval for the lord-lieutenant to make a declaration 'in favour of a final settlement of all commercial questions between the two countries'. However, the Irish Parliament was due to be prorogued within days, and the efforts made to deliver this declaration before that happened drew comment from the press. 'In case the messenger [to Dublin] be detained by contrary winds or any untoward accident', *The Times* reported, 'Sydney sent a duplicate of the speech by another messenger who is to travel through Scotland and cross over from Port Patrick to Donaghadee in Ireland'.[17]

In declaring its support for 'a final settlement', the British cabinet had left the details to be negotiated, but over the next six months, it gradually became clear that they were insurmountable. In Britain, the prime minister faced fierce opposition from Charles Fox. And in Ireland, Henry Grattan had to stare down Henry Flood. Arguments raged over whether a defence contribution was necessary in peace time and whether equalizing duties between the two kingdoms might have serious consequences. In the end, the Irish proposals were so severely amended in London that the Parliament in Dublin rejected them. Despite the legislation of 1783 which had established the broad principle of parliamentary co-existence, it was beyond the two Parliaments to agree on terms that would allow for an autonomous Ireland within what was then a mercantile rather than a free-trade empire.[18]

Meanwhile, Lord George Gordon, who had set London aflame in 1780 with the worst anti-Catholic riots in living memory, remained a menacing presence in Anglo-Irish relations. Sydney had him tailed by the Secret Service, twenty-four hours a day, seven days a week. The fact that Sydney's spy watched Gordon's house from a Catholic shopkeeper's window across the road may have unnerved the target, and in July 1785, he complained to Sydney about a 'desperate villain' from Dublin employed by the Catholics to assassinate him. But Sydney kept up the surveillance. 'Gordon cannot be too closely watched', he said. 'If an opportunity of raising a disturbance of any kind should present itself, his activity and ingenuity will never suffer it to slip by him.'[19]

Up until Sydney's retirement as home secretary in June 1789, relations between Britain and Ireland were generally smooth – the exception being during the regency crisis. But during the 1790s, when Britain was again at war with France, an attempt was made to turn the revolutionary United Irishmen to Napoleon's cause. The crushing of their uprising at Vinegar Hill in June 1798 did not deter the French, who landed on the Irish coast two months later. Although these invaders fled when attacked by the Royal Navy, the British government was alarmed about the Irish Parliament's inability to maintain order.[20]

To remedy this, Prime Minister Pitt proposed no less than a formal political union between Britain and Ireland, whereby the Irish Parliament would be absorbed by its British counterpart. At that time, Sydney's cousin Charles Cornwallis was lord-lieutenant in Dublin. To give effect to Pitt's plan, Cornwallis set out to convince the Irish Parliament that it should vote itself out of existence. Among Ireland's largely Catholic population, there was strong support for a political union because most Catholics thought that the Irish Parliament, which was dominated by a Protestant minority, would never extend their civil rights. Cornwallis thought that union could be achieved 'without very great difficulty'. However, key Protestant MPs put up stiff resistance and Cornwallis was forced to use all his executive powers of patronage to buy enough votes to support a motion, whereby the Irish Parliament abolished itself. 'I despise and hate myself every hour', Cornwallis wrote, 'for engaging in such dirty work and am supported only by the reflection that without a union, the British Empire must be dissolved'.[21]

Finally, on 6 February 1800, the Irish Commons voted for union, followed five days later by the Irish House of Lords. The British Parliament resolved likewise. And as a result, the Irish Parliament ceased to exist. Despite its ignominious demise, Ireland's legislature of 1783–1800 later became a model of sorts for many Commonwealth nations.[22]

[*Twenty-three*]

From Nabobs to Nootka

Prime Minister Pitt was acutely aware that the East India Company could make and break governments. Its sovereign rights over much of the sub-continent and its large private army effectively made it a state in its own right. And those members of the British Parliament who had spent time in India, known as 'nabobs', were capable of forming a powerful block vote. The key issue for Pitt was how to balance the public interest in both Britain and India against the company's affairs. With the Commons' numbers stacked against him until the general election of 1784, he took personal control of India politics both inside and outside the Parliament.[1]

During the constitutional showdown in December 1783, the House of Lords had supported the stand taken by the king and Pitt over India. The real contest now was in the Commons, which had supported Charles Fox's plan for a powerful body, independent of the cabinet, to take over the company's affairs. As home secretary, Lord Sydney was responsible for India, but as a member of the Lords he could not assist Pitt in the Commons. Responsibility for India there was taken on by one of Pitt's drinking companions, Henry Dundas, whose junior ministerial role as treasurer of the navy did not fully reflect this bluff Scottish lawyer's influence with the young prime minister.

Following Pitt's 1784 election triumph, Parliament adopted a watered-down version of his India Bill. '[It is] to give the Crown the power of guiding the politics of India', Pitt said, 'with as little means of corrupt influence as possible'. Although the company was left in charge of India's local government, its ultimate corporate governance was the responsibility of a newly created board of control. By virtue of his role as home secretary, Sydney was appointed president, but Dundas, a more junior board member, was in charge. 'The whole power resided with Dundas, who, having secretly concerted his measures with Pitt', Wraxall said, 'dictated his pleasure to the others on every point'. As a regular overnight guest at Dundas's Wimbledon home, the prime minister had his own room there. One observer noted of Dundas that 'there is no man who eats Pitt's toads with such zeal and attention'. A touch bitterly, Sydney told the prime minister that he was 'ready to abandon ... [Indian affairs] to the ambition of those who like the Department'.[2]

Nevertheless, the home secretary did play an important role in negotiations, which had begun two years earlier, leading to Charles Cornwallis's appointment as India's governor-general. Despite his defeat by General Washington at Yorktown, Cornwallis was highly regarded. 'Judgment with moderation, simplicity of manners and incorruptible integrity', Wraxall noted, 'were in Cornwallis united'. Indeed Cornwallis's reputation was such that he had first been approached to take on the government of India while still a paroled prisoner of the Americans, but as a parolee, he could not take up the post. It was not until after he was completely freed in September 1783, that he became eligible. By then, however, Charles Fox's push to take over the East India Company's affairs was approaching its climax. Cornwallis was so troubled by the 'violent animosities' this push aroused that he left London for his country estate in Suffolk to avoid voting on Fox's India Bill. Only the king's personal intervention persuaded him to attend the Lords just before Christmas to vote against it.[3]

Following his return to the home office on the change of government a few days later, Sydney approached Cornwallis about India. Reluctant to commit himself, Cornwallis confided to a friend that he did not think the new government would survive. Pitt and Sydney, who both desperately needed to develop a momentum in Indian affairs to ensure the government's future, therefore decided to send another senior general to Madras immediately, to be followed by a commander-in-chief later on.[4]

Even though the 1784 election had put the future of the government beyond doubt, Cornwallis still became irritated by reports 'all over the Kingdom' that he would accept the job of commander-in-chief. 'The more I turn it in my mind the less inclination I feel to undertake it', he said, 'to abandon my children and every comfort on this side of the grave'. Cornwallis was particularly concerned that he would have 'neither power to model the army or correct abuses' if he did say yes. And having been defeated by George Washington, he fretted about the risk 'of being beat by some nabob and being disgraced to all eternity'.[5]

Undeterred, Sydney again approached his cousin, who stressed the importance of being given full civil and military command. Sydney's reply that 'he was sure Mr Pitt would wish to give both' did little to reassure Cornwallis. As he saw it, Pitt had become too close to the East India Company, being indebted to it for his initial appointment as prime minister. To Sydney's assurance that the company wanted him to go to India, Cornwallis replied: 'how precarious their favours must be'.[6]

During the 1784 election campaign, Pitt had received substantial donations from the company. Its nabobs subsequently polled well and the prime minister now felt pressured by the 'enlarged ranks of the Bengal squad' in the Commons. Before long Pitt's new bill, to reform the civil and military government of India by placing control in the hands of a governor-general, was under attack. On the floor of the House, he was forced to water it down. 'If the Bill had been framed by the delinquents themselves', Charles Fox charged, 'it could not ... have been more ... clearly calculated to perpetuate the abuses'. With his worst fears about the governor-general's lack of power being realized, Cornwallis again left London for his country estate as the eviscerated bill made its way to the House of Lords. Although critical of Sydney 'as a man of business', Cornwallis nevertheless gave his cousin his proxy vote in the Lords. Cornwallis's inconsistency may have been triggered by General Clinton, who was at that time criticizing Cornwallis for his march into Virginia. 'If my plans had been adopted', Clinton alleged, 'America would have been now at our feet'.[7]

Pitt's watered-down India Bill came before the House of Lords on 29 July 1784. To answer criticism that the government was rushing it forward, Sydney stressed 'the advanced stage of the season, the urgency of the business and the notoriety of [its] principles'. He then sent a copy to Cornwallis who was still in Suffolk. 'The East India Company are really desirous to trust their affairs to you', Sydney advised, 'and the Ministry go ... still farther beyond them'. Nevertheless, Cornwallis remained unimpressed. After noting that 'the Commander-in-Chief has no more military patronage than any other member of [his] Council', he told Sydney he would not go out to India unless this was fixed up. But Pitt's deal with the nabobs tied Sydney's hands; he could not make the changes Cornwallis demanded. So the home secretary cast around for alternative candidates, sounding out Sir Guy Carleton, who declined to serve under the company, and the governor of Madras, Lord Macartney, who demanded the same terms as Cornwallis.[8]

After Pitt's bill became law, Cornwallis's concerns about military patronage were highlighted when the East India Company nominated Lieutenant-General Robert Sloper to be the senior general in Madras. Although his government had reservations about Sloper's suitability, the prime minister told Sydney that any plans to overrule the company 'could not be taken'. Sloper went to India; behind the scenes, the government's doubts remained; and during September and October 1784, Sydney contracted with his spymaster, William Clarke, at the rate of five shillings a day to have 'one man at the East India House for the purpose of bringing a daily account of the proceedings of the Directors'.[9]

While Cornwallis was unhappy about India, he was still interested in obtaining office. He had ambitions to be placed in command of either Plymouth or the Tower of London. He missed out on both, and when he expressed his disappointment, Sydney explained that it was because the government still hoped he might accept India. Now accusing Sydney of 'bombast flummery', Cornwallis complained to the prime minister:

> As every transaction relative to myself with the present Administration has passed through Lord Sydney and as I have no reason to be satisfied with his Lordship's conduct towards me, I feel an inclination to state to you the occurrences that have happened to me with my feelings on them.

After reciting a litany of grievances, Cornwallis continued: 'the apologies made to me by Lord Sydney have only added insult to injury'. He concluded, 'I am sorry to say it of one whom I have sincerely loved [they] were of so disingenuous a nature that I do not care to think of them'. This was harsh criticism coming from a member of the House of Lords, who could have made a real impact in debates on the India Bill, but who had instead chosen to sit them out at his country estate.[10]

What followed was a long and heated meeting between Cornwallis and the prime minister in the second week of November 1784. Soon afterwards, Pitt proposed that Cornwallis take command of the Tower of London after all. Cornwallis declined, saying that, though he had no initial objection:

> Now it was known that there had been a negotiation; that it was not originally intended; and that it did not come as a spontaneous mark of the King's or Mr Pitt's personal regard or attention to my services, it would rather be construed into a political bargain.[11]

The prime minister quite properly trusted that both their characters 'were above such imputation' and again offered Cornwallis the Tower. After taking some hours to consider it, he accepted, erasing from his mind 'every idea that [he] could ever have been slighted by Mr Pitt', and writing a letter 'of the same sort to Lord Sydney...[that] all is forgot and forgiven'. Within a month, it appears that Cornwallis was well settled, writing that he had 'no desire to exchange the Tower for any other Government'.[12]

However, in February 1785, Cornwallis was yet again 'most violently attacked to take the Governor-Generalship'. If he agreed to go, Pitt said, the India legislation would be amended to answer his objections. Pitt now accepted what Sydney had long understood but had been powerless alone to change – that Cornwallis would not go to India unless the governor-general was empowered to override his Council. But it was not until a year later that Cornwallis could write:

> The proposal of going to India has been pressed upon me so strongly with the circumstance of the Governor General's being independent of his Council...and having the supreme command of the military that much against my will and with grief in my heart, I have been obliged to say yes.[13]

Finally, at 11.00 a.m. on 30 April 1786, Cornwallis was able to inform Lord Sydney from Portsmouth that 'we shall certainly sail tomorrow morning if the wind continues fair'. In fact Cornwallis was taking a risk. The bill giving him the powers he wanted was still before Parliament where Edmund Burke called it a 'libel' on the British constitution. Only later, while Cornwallis was on the high seas, did the bill become law.[14]

Meanwhile, on 13 June 1785, the governor of the East India Company's possessions in Bengal, Warren Hastings, had arrived back in England, exciting the attention of Charles Fox and Edmund Burke. A few months earlier, the opposition had attacked Henry Dundas in the Commons over alleged Indian 'debts of corruption' totalling 2,000,000 pounds. Dundas was accused of allowing these debts to be paid without inquiry, in return for support from the 'Arcot Group' of nabobs during the 1784 election. 'So absurd...did these accusations appear and with such ridicule...did the [Commons] consider [them]', Wraxall said, 'that the Treasury Bench remained silent'. In the Lords, Sydney simply said that it was 'not wise or necessary' to investigate them so soon after the passage of Pitt's India Bill.[15]

Unfortunately for Warren Hastings, this outcome enraged Fox and Burke, who remained determined to embarrass the government over India. They now alleged that Hastings' financial neglect as governor of Bengal had left his subordinates 'free to plunder', also accusing him of 'tyrannical conduct'. Far from being dishonest, Hastings had nevertheless been 'credulous to the highest degree, alarmed by every idle report and wholly diffident in himself' – he had been unable to see the wood for the trees. Sensing trouble ahead, the prime minister now became a regular attendee at board of control meetings.[16]

At about the same time, a movement was formed in Calcutta to demand the same rights for India under the British constitution as those enjoyed by the Americans under theirs. Indian petitions seeking concessions such as trial by jury began to swamp Sydney's office from early 1786. And concern grew within the ministry that a rights debate on the sub-continent might run out of control, just as it had in the American colonies. All the while, Fox and Burke continued their parliamentary campaign for an inquiry into Warren Hastings. At first, the prime minister backed Hastings, but on 13 June 1786 Pitt 'astonished' everyone by voting to support one of the charges: that a fine Hastings had levied on one Cheyt Singh was exorbitant. The prime minister's intervention was enough to convince the Commons to support this charge. '[Pitt] 'was happy to let Fox and the Opposition expend energy on Hastings', Wraxall said, 'rather than [the government]'. Even so, there was to be a nasty surprise for Lord Sydney.[17]

One of Warren Hastings' strongest parliamentary defenders was Major John Scott, who argued that the East India Company's governor had been 'the saviour of our possessions in the East'. To counter this, Fox's supporter Richard Sheridan claimed that 'an extraordinarily large diamond [had] been sent to Mr Hastings and presented to His Majesty' on 14 June. Being the day after Pitt had voted against Hastings on the Singh charge, Sheridan was inferring that the former governor had made a clumsy attempt to bribe the king to intervene. Unnerved, Scott then disclosed that, on 2 June, Hastings had given him a 'bulse' (packet) to pass on to Lord Sydney so it could be presented to George III. This bulse, which contained the diamond, was a gift to the king from a powerful Indian prince, the Nizam of Hydrabad, and its arrival in England had been delayed by a ship-wreck. Because it was not clear that the bulse had contained anything of value, Scott said, he had not passed it on to Sydney until 13 June, the day before Sydney in turn delivered it to the king. So although the timing of the presentation was unfortunate, it was not sinister. Even so, this did not stop *The Times*, *The Morning Herald* or *The Public Advertiser* from implying that the diamond was a bribe, an inference Scott asked Sydney to publicly deny. 'The story does not contain a word of truth', Sydney wrote to the editors. 'I never was in the house of Mr Hastings in my life nor ever had the least conversation with him on the subject of the diamond'.[18]

Although this denial eased the pressure on the government, it did not reverse the damage done to Hastings among the reading public. And thanks in no small part to the prime minister's intervention and to Scott's sloppy defence, the House of Commons duly impeached the company's viceroy. As preparations were made for Hastings' trial in the House of Lords, Pitt and Sydney checked the government's files for any correspondence which might embarrass them. What they found, they claimed, 'was so unconnected with anything that can affect Mr Hastings that there was no need to lay it before Parliament'. Egged on mainly by Henry Dundas, Hastings' ordeal continued in fits and starts until finally, a decade later, he was acquitted of all charges – after spending 100,000 pounds on his defence.[19]

In September 1786 Charles Cornwallis arrived in India. He immediately noted that a number of questionable alliances had embroiled the British in disputes between various native princes. The East India Company's man in

Madras, General Sloper, had allowed one of his officers, a Captain Monson, to sign up with the Nizam of Hydrabad. Complaining to Sydney, Cornwallis likened this to taking sides in a local dispute with the equivalent of 10,000 men. Keen to exert his new authority, Cornwallis demanded that Sloper, a man 'who never took any steps to discipline the Army', be sacked. And so the Company's hand-picked general was recalled. More generally, Cornwallis was confronted by what he described as 'a system of the dirtiest jobbery'. To tackle this corruption, he separated the local judicial and revenue collection systems and brought the administration of 'natives of influence' under close British supervision.[20]

George III and the East India Company each had separate armies in India, which the British government thought should be merged in the interests of efficiency. Responsibility for this was given to Cornwallis, who attempted to reconcile the company's concern about losing the power to appoint its own officers, with the king's demand that his officers be senior to company officers of the same rank. The home secretary's proximity to the king gave him influence on military matters, and Sydney had regular correspondence with Cornwallis about issues as arcane as 'advanced brevet rank'. However, the difficulty of reconciling the 'jealousies' the merger aroused led Cornwallis to conclude that, in the short term, he would do better by restoring the tent allowance, which had been paid to front-line soldiers in both armies, before being abolished by his predecessor.[21]

In 1787, Lord Sydney issued the king's command to prepare for war with France over a dispute about Holland. Cornwallis was directed to plan an assault on Trincomali, in what is now Sri Lanka. India was to be reinforced by four of the king's regiments – news the East India Company received 'with thankfulness'. Sydney assured Cornwallis that these regiments were first class and that their 'corps of European officers will see with pleasure the prospect which [Indian service] opens to them'. All the jealousies about rank between the king's officers and the company's officers were, however, reignited, and as soon as the threat of a war with France had passed the East India Company declined to receive the regiments, 'because of the injury done to their officers'.[22]

This threat of war convinced the British government to introduce the East India Declaratory Bill to remove any doubt that the expense of raising, transporting and maintaining troops in India could be offset by Indian revenues.

In the House of Lords, the lawyers did most of the running, while Sydney and his opposition counterpart, Lord Stormont, confined themselves to the question of whether the company or the government had been responsible for the delay in embarking the king's four regiments. The passage of this bill, the historian Vincent Harlow later said, 'transferred the power of the sword in India from the Company to the Crown'.[23]

Sydney's mostly official correspondence with Cornwallis still had space for family gossip. When their cousin George jumped two ranks in the peerage from Viscount to Marquess Townshend, his son, now known as the Earl of Leicester, was unhappy, as Sydney explained tongue in cheek:

> Poor Leicester... is now as miserable as possible that [his father] has chosen his own name for his new title [rather than 'Marquess of – ']. He has fretted himself ill with vexation. His reasonings to one who is not versed in Dugdale and other great authors on heraldry are totally unintelligible.[24]

After the war scare with France subsided, 'the tranquility of Hindustan', as Cornwallis put it, 'was undisturbed'. This allowed for the development of trading opportunities between China and the north-west coast of America. Ironically, one impediment to trade growth was the East India Company, which held the chartered rights to all British trade between the Cape of Good Hope and Cape Horn. Another was the reluctance of the Chinese to trade their tea for anything other than bullion. For their part, the British wanted to create a 'triangular trade' in goods with India and China. Charles Cathcart was appointed Britain's ambassador to Peking. Sydney, aware that Cathcart had previously worked for the East India Company, instructed him to concentrate on government business. The company did not like this. It had previously worked with Whitehall to establish Penang as a half-way house between India and China for the protection of British merchants; it no doubt felt that its concession agreement with the local Sultan there, which recognized it as 'guardian of the seas', would now be at risk. As the company saw it, a pattern seemed to be emerging where the British government was everywhere nibbling away at its charter.[25]

James Cook's voyaging had highlighted the commercial possibilities of Nootka Sound near modern day Vancouver, which was rich in furs and whale products. A group of merchants proposed to Lord Sydney that trade via the Straits of Magellan be opened up with the north-west coast of America and East Asia, especially Japan. Keen to assist, the government pressured the East India Company to give its required permission. In August 1785, a clearly reluctant company wrote to the home secretary:

> After due investigation of the scheme proposed … to send an adventure to the North West Coast of America [under Captains Nathaniel Portlock and George Dixon] to procure furs to be disposed of at or near the Japanese islands, [the Company had] agreeable to the wishes and recommendation of Government, agreed to grant a license to trade within the Company's limits under certain limitations.

These limitations were designed to protect the company's tea trade, but the scheme's promoters were nevertheless given permission to set up factories along the North American coast.[26]

Arriving at Nootka via Cape Horn in July 1786, Portlock and Dixon were astonished to be met by a party of Englishmen who had sailed from India via China and then across the Pacific – with the blessing of the government in Bombay. Portlock and Dixon then continued towards Japan, but upon arriving at the Sandwich Islands (Hawaii) they decided to return to Nookta. A year later, Sydney followed up with secret instructions for one of the First Fleet convict transports to New South Wales to return via Nootka and China. Although this plan had to be abandoned near Tahiti following an outbreak of scurvy, the British visits to the North American west coast had not gone unnoticed by the Spanish. In May 1789, they arrested some of the British ships then at Nootka and claimed possession of the entire area. When news of this filtered back to London, Prime Minister Pitt described Spain's claim to exclusive rights in the Pacific as absurd. The British government mobilized its fleet and issued an ultimatum, whereupon Spain backed down. In December 1790, Pitt was accused of warmongering over Nootka, prompting Sydney, who was by then retired from the ministry, to spring to his defence. 'Ministers must be strangely changed in their dispositions since I had the honour to sit among them', he told the House of Lords, 'if they are now disposed to involve their country in a war'. Having been a key participant in the original decision to allow the expedition to Nootka in 1785, Sydney knew in 1790 that the British government was simply maintaining a claim to a share of Pacific commerce, not looking for a war in Europe.[27]

[*Twenty-four*]

⸻ Loyalists transform Canada ⸻

Upon his appointment as home secretary in July 1782, Tommy Townshend assumed responsibility for what remained of British North America. Apart from Charleston, New York and Savannah, which were soon to be surrendered to the newly created United States, his portfolio included the provinces of Newfoundland, Nova Scotia, Quebec and St John, which were to remain in British hands. The total population of these four provinces, which were later to form part of Canada, was overwhelmingly French-speaking.

By far the largest province was Quebec, where 150 years of French rule had ended just 22 years earlier. Only ten percent of the more than 100,000 people who lived there spoke English. But the 90,000 French speakers had remained loyal to Britain during the American Revolutionary War, even though France had sided with the rebels. This was because few Quebecois had ever visited France and the British had tolerated French Catholicism and civil law, first recognized by George Townshend after the battle of Quebec. However, following the American Revolution, a dramatic influx of English-speaking colonists who had remained loyal to George III quickly raised the political temperature.[1]

Within the United States, many loyalists flocked to those areas still under Britain's control; and Tommy Townshend was reminded of his promise that Britain would look after colonists who had fought for the king, if the American states ignored Congress's recommendation to respect their rights. It soon became clear that those states would take a hard line, and the refugee tide swelled as loyalists were run off their properties. One eviction notice read: 'John Bates now or formerly of White Plains... did with force and arms adhere to the enemies... of New York... wherefore his land is forfeit'. Englishmen were also hard hit, including Robert, Lord Fairfax, a distant relative by marriage of

George Washington. At the age of 80, Fairfax was forced to vacate Leeds Castle in Kent. 'The loss of my property in Virginia... is too great for me to bear', he wrote to Tommy, 'and has brought me into the greatest distress.'[2]

The home secretary needed no reminding from Admiral Digby in New York that the loyalists were desperate. Benjamin Franklin's son, William, formerly the governor of New Jersey, was now president of the Board of Associated Loyalists. He and his colleagues, including William Smith, the former chief justice of New York, and John Penn, the former governor of Pennsylvania, lobbied Tommy ceaselessly. And when Tommy handed their petition to George III, he replied: 'my heart bleeds for them'. Other loyalists sought revenge. The Earl of Dunmore, also a former governor, proposed a scheme for 'pushing' loyalist settlements 'up the Mississippi and Ohio' to Canada. Then, with help from the Indians, he would 'drive the thirteen United Provinces into the sea'. The American turncoat, Benedict Arnold, also wanted to keep fighting. As late as August 1782 he requested the Home Office to supply him with a 40-gun frigate which he would 'man and sail without any expense to Government'.[3]

One New York-born loyalist, James Mario Matra, who had sailed with James Cook on the *Endeavour*, suggested that Botany Bay in what is now Australia might be a suitable spot for refugees fleeing his birth place. But at that time there were not enough ships to take them 900 miles to Halifax, Nova Scotia, let alone 12,000 miles around the globe. In any event, many wanted to resettle as close to their old communities as possible. It was therefore Tommy's job to provide the physical, political and legal infrastructure to accommodate them.

Tommy's first crisis was to persuade the British commander in New York, Sir Guy Carleton, to remain at his post to supervise the evacuation. A previous home secretary had commissioned Carleton to restore peace and grant 'a pardon to the revolted provinces in America', but when it became clear that the negotiations would take place in Paris, Carleton refused to be 'a mere Inspector of Embarkations' and resigned. With no doubt that Carleton was the best person on either side of the Atlantic to oversee the withdrawal, Tommy appealed to the general's vanity. Calling it 'the great and complicated business of evacuation', Tommy convinced him to remain in New York. And Carleton became the last British officer to leave, in late November 1783. On the final day, British sailors greased a flagpole flying the Union Jack. It took the Americans two hours to get it down, delaying George Washington, who refused to enter the city while the British flag flew.[4]

As a result of the evacuation process supervised by Carleton during 1782–83, the overwhelmingly French population of British North America was joined by tens of thousands of loyalist refugees. Over 6,000 travelled overland to Quebec while an estimated 30,000 came by sea to Nova Scotia. During the Paris peace talks, the boundary between the United States and British North America in this area had been hotly contested. At Henry Strachey's insistence on Tommy's behalf, the proposed American boundary had been pushed back to the St Croix River. As a result, land around the St John River, described by a 1783 survey as having 'a most fertile soil' and being 'perfectly secure against the Indians', was included in Nova Scotia. This area became a preferred destination for many of the loyalists, a number of whom had arrived from New York on the 32 ships of the 'Spring Fleet'.

Governor John Parr, who ruled Nova Scotia's 20,000 inhabitants, was soon struggling to cope with the 30,000 new arrivals. Described by his biographer 'as a short man with sharp features and a brisk, strutting gait', Parr was a stickler for formalities and had 'the tetchy stubbornness of an independent but narrow mind long accustomed to military discipline'. Complaints about severe shortages of food, shelter and clothing during the winter of 1782–83, soon grew to include demands for land grants. As the months passed, the loyalist leaders' calls for a separate government in the Bay of Fundy area grew ever louder. Although temperamentally suited to deal with the initial emergency, Parr struggled to accommodate the loyalists' political demands.[5]

Sir Guy Carleton arrived back in London in early 1784 and Tommy, by now Lord Sydney, turned to him for advice. Nova Scotia must be divided, Carleton said, to create a new province. So as soon as the 1784 election had settled the Pitt government's parliamentary ascendancy, Sydney set about reorganizing Britain's remaining North American colonies. On 10 May cabinet agreed to Sydney's proposal that the St John River area be separated from Nova Scotia to form a new province. At the same time, the islands of Cape Breton and St John (now Prince Edward Island) would be annexed to what remained of Nova Scotia. Then, on 18 June, after the Board of Trade had reported on the detailed administrative arrangements, the separation was ordered. At Sydney's request, the new province was created by a decision of the executive, not Parliament. This suited most MPs who thought that previous parliamentary interference had led to the American Revolution.[6]

The new province, called New Brunswick, was created out of western Nova Scotia, which had been settled by approximately 14,000 loyalists. This province and what remained of Nova Scotia were granted new legislatures, while the new governments of Cape Breton and St John were each to be presided over by a lieutenant-governor. As such, they would be 'sub colonies' answerable to Governor Parr of Nova Scotia. On 20 August 1784, Lord Sydney organized a cabinet meeting to approve Parr's revised commission, and the following day the new governor of New Brunswick, Colonel Thomas Carleton, set sail with it arriving off Halifax in late November.

The value of Colonel Carleton's prior experience in Canada had been diminished by clashes with his commander, but whatever reservations Sydney had were offset by the fact that the new governor was Sir Guy Carleton's younger brother. A strong supporter of the loyalists, the younger Carleton described them as being 'distinguished by [their] services and sufferings'. Still, it took a year for him to issue writs for New Brunswick's first election, and during the election itself, troops had to be called in to quell a riot. Although Sydney supported Carleton's handling of this unrest, he was critical of the governor's delay in calling the election, which he believed had been the main cause of the trouble. Once this unpleasantness was over, New Brunswick grew rapidly; its Assembly soon developed a robust reputation, representing a politically sophisticated population that had long been schooled in the hurly-burly of American politics.[7]

Apart from Quebec, which was more authoritarian, the standard pattern of British colonial government was built around a governor, an appointed Council and an elected Assembly. While this was fine in theory, the reality on Cape Breton Island was rather different. With a total population of just over 1,000 in 1784, it struggled even as a sub-colony. Nevertheless, it received a full brace of colonial officers, led by Joseph Frederic Wallet Des Barres. Appointed by Lord `vdney, this 62-year-old lieutenant-governor, who was to live to be 102, was largest landholder in the Maritime Provinces, and no one knew the Island better. Described by his biographer as 'pigheaded, irascible and litigious', Des Barres soon fell out with his superiors in Halifax, especially when he accused the government there of being jealous of his efforts to develop the Island. To please his colonial master in London, he named the provincial capital he was laying out 'Sydney', and in the summer of 1785, six companies of the 33rd Regiment were tasked to build the new town out of the wilderness. One settler described the surrounding scene: 'Looking up and down... [Sydney] harbour', he said, 'the eye cannot but delight in the graceful curve of the shores and the beauty of the stream which loses itself on one side amidst sloping woods'. The Island's office-bearers included an attorney-general and a Council appointed by Des Barres. On 17 August 1785 they joined the chief justice, who was 'dressed in scarlet robes trimmed in ermine and full bottomed wig', for the opening of the Supreme Court, 'a shell of a house... fitted up for the occasion'. At the time, the town consisted of just two principal streets and, apart from the soldiers, not more than two dozen families.[8]

During Canada's severe winters, Cape Breton Island was difficult to resupply. As a result, Des Barres pledged his own credit for many of the island's necessities and began to interfere with the military supply chain, infuriating senior officers. Some of the lieutenant-governor's more dubious appointments also had him offside with his chief secretary, Abraham Cuyler, a proud, jealous and ambitious loyalist who, at 28, had been mayor of New York. As a result, a number of complaints were sent to the Home Office and the consequences were severe. Lord Sydney recalled Des Barres, castigating his 'disposition to encourage... disunion of affection between Cape Breton and Nova Scotia' and doubting 'the rectitude of his conduct or at least his prudence and discretion'. It mattered not that the lieutenant-governor's departure was 'deeply regretted' by many locals or that he had named his sub-colony's capital in honour of the secretary of state. In 1788 it must have further galled Des Barres to learn of a royal visit to Sydney, during which the future King William IV dined at Cuyler's house. 'We had a good dinner', Des Barres's nemesis noted, 'and got outrageously drunk, Prince and subject'.[9]

After his recall, Des Barres began to lobby the home secretary, using the pseudonym 'Speculator'. He was particularly critical of one of his successor's first Ordinances – 'to dispossess... proprietors who settled lands during the Des

Barres administration'. At issue were many longstanding but unclaimed land grants, which had been cancelled and redistributed to newly arrived loyalists. The original grantees had been required to re-register their claims to keep them alive, but some, including Des Barres himself, had failed to meet the deadline. So their grants were cancelled and reissued to new arrivals. Despite Des Barres's tardiness, Lord Sydney did recommend payment of some of his compensation claims; these were, however, disputed by the Treasury after Sydney's retirement and only ever part paid.[10]

The affairs of Saint John, later renamed Prince Edward Island after the future Queen Victoria's father, were just as tangled – over the issue of quit rents. Those who could not pay this land tax had their properties disposed of cheaply to purchasers who included Lieutenant-Governor Walter Patterson. A man who possessed 'an amazing cleverness ... mixed with an equal proportion of folly and madness', one contemporary said, 'Patterson rose from nothing and would have done extremely well had he known when to stop'. Before long, the legality of Patterson's bargain buying was questioned by the former owners who complained to the British government. In July 1783 a draft bill annulling these purchases was sent out from London and Patterson was instructed to recommend its adoption by the local Assembly. Instead, the lieutenant-governor purported to dissolve this body, which he well knew would pass the bill, and when his enemies were elected to the new Assembly, he persuaded his allies in St John's Council to withhold the bill. Inheriting the mess, Lord Sydney dispatched a gun boat to seize all the paperwork Patterson and his Council had relied on. The lieutenant-governor remained defiant, and not long afterwards he suspended Saint John's chief justice, replacing him with three of his own supporters. Unhappy with Patterson's ongoing misbehaviour in office, which included further manipulation of the Assembly, Sydney recalled him in June 1786.[11]

American federal authority remained weak during Lord Sydney's time as home secretary, with Thomas Jefferson complaining to George Washington in 1784 about 'the crippled state of Congress'. Two years earlier, the British governor of Quebec, Frederick Haldimand, had been approached by a number of Vermonters who wanted 'immediate recognition of Vermont as a British Province'. Their leader, Ethan Allen, had fought bravely against the British, but he now disliked the American authorities even more, because they wanted to incorporate Vermont within New York. The status of Vermont was further complicated because its residents relied on Canada's waterways to get their goods to market. 'Vermont must either become annexed to Canada', Haldimand said in 1783, 'or become mistress of it'. Mindful that there were over 100,000 Vermonters, Sydney replied that it would be inconsistent with the American peace treaty to interfere openly. 'But it would be difficult to refuse to take them under our protection', he said, 'should they determine to become subjects of Great Britain'. The prime minister was also wary. 'A commercial intercourse with ... [the Vermonters] might open a channel of trade with the United States', Pitt told Sydney, 'which might clash with any system to be adopted by them'.[12]

The potential volatility of this situation was highlighted in 1787 when the Americans put down a rebellion against taxation in nearby Springfield, Massachusetts. This underscored their ability to strike out against dissent. So while the home secretary allowed Haldimand's successor, Lord Dorchester, to pass local laws to regulate trade with Vermont, there was a trade ban on many goods. And when Dorchester agreed to Ethan Allen bringing naval stores into Quebec in return for goods such as furs, he earned Sydney's displeasure. However, it was difficult for the home secretary, three thousand miles away in London, to place limitations on the governor's discretion. Vermont's relationship with Quebec continued to splutter along in this fashion until, in 1791, it was admitted as the fourteenth state of the Union.[13]

Lord Sydney's concern for American sensibilities over the terms of the peace treaty diminished in direct proportion to the distance of a dispute from the major centres of population in the United States. While problems relating to Vermont were on balance to be avoided, it was a different story further west. Under the peace treaty of 1783, the United States obtained all the land south of the Great Lakes, including the Forts of Detroit, Mackinac, Niagara and Oswego each of which Britain agreed to evacuate 'with all convenient speed'.[14]

In 1782, while the American peace negotiations were still underway, Lord Sydney had received correspondence from the British commander in Detroit warning that the local Indians would go to war to stop American settlers seizing their land. 'On the friendship of the Indians at Detroit', he warned, 'depends the safety of the trade and posts in that quarter'. Sydney had gone to some effort to ensure that the Mohawk chief, Joseph Brant, was paid 1,500 pounds for his war service and he had also sent the chief a telescope as a personal gift. Such connections, together with a fear that a British withdrawal would be followed by a great Indian war, were relied upon by those who argued that the forts should not be handed over. But, as the home secretary explained, he had another reason to hold on to them:

> The seventh Article of the Peace treaty stipulates that the Forts shall be evacuated with all convenient speed but no certain time is fixed and as America has not on her part complied with even one Article of the Treaty, I think I may ... delay the evacuation of those posts.

Sydney was especially angry about America's failure to comply with the articles relating to loyalists. He was in no hurry to comply with the seventh article, and nor were his successors. It was not until 1796 that Detroit and the three other forts were handed over to the United States.[15]

[*Twenty-five*]

— Dorchester upon the spot —

Confronting Lord Sydney when he returned to the Home Office in December 1783 was a dispatch from the British governor of Quebec, Frederick Haldimand. Although he was Swiss born, General Haldimand had served the British government in North America for almost three decades and his advice was highly regarded. The Quebec Act, which Sydney had opposed nine years earlier, was Haldimand's top priority. If the home secretary wanted the French population to remain 'dependent', Haldimand said, this legislation, which continued Quebec's system of French government, must remain in place. He warned of a growing body of English-speaking Quebecois who were demanding its repeal.

Using the very arguments Sydney himself had used in 1774, this vocal English minority agitated for an elected Assembly, 'indifferently composed'. But what would this mean, the French speakers demanded to know, in a province where there were twenty of them for every English speaker. Would the English settle for majority French rule? Or would they attempt to limit the vote to an English-speaking oligarchy? A proposal to allow the Assembly to raise taxes was also criticized. 'Would the imposition of taxes add three months to our summer and make our rivers navigable for the whole year', the French speakers asked, before answering their own question with a resounding 'no'. They demanded no change until their communities were 'legally called together … so the unanimous wish of our people can be transmitted'. With the loss of the American colonies over parliamentary taxation still a recent memory, Sydney was reluctant to upset them.[1]

§

During the evacuation of New York, the home secretary had emphasized the importance of the British commander, Sir Guy Carleton, being able to make decisions 'on the spot'. After returning to London at the beginning of 1784, Carleton recommended the appointment of a governor-general for all British North America, with the provincial governors reporting directly to him. Accepting this advice, Sydney explained that 'vesting certain powers in a person to be upon the spot ... [would] avoid the tedious delay of continual recourse to [London]'. He never doubted that Carleton was best suited for the role. But in addition to the new position, Carleton wanted a peerage – a demand that was just 'too high' for the cabinet, which refused him in June 1784, thereby stalling any progress. Carleton was furious. 'The present Ministers ... [are] not competent', he fumed. 'Lord Sydney ... [is] incapable and so too ... Carmarthen ... [while] Mr Pitt ... [is] too young'.[2]

Meanwhile, Governor Haldimand had also returned to London, leaving Lieutenant-Governor Henry Hamilton in charge of Quebec. Haldimand had done so with reluctance because he and Hamilton had been at loggerheads over the province's direction. '[Haldimand] gave the helm into the [French party leader's] hand', Hamilton complained, 'but would not trust me with the management of an Oar'. Unlike Haldimand, who tried to maintain the status quo, Hamilton encouraged the English speakers' petitions, thereby infuriating the French. Pressure now grew for Quebec to be split so that the western or upper districts of the province would have a lieutenant-governor of their own, under English rather than French law.[3]

All the while, Sydney remained keen to appoint Carleton as governor-general with the widest powers. Carleton continued to rebuff him. The general's good friend, William Smith, the former chief justice of New York, recorded in his diary:

> [Carleton] has been ill used and not recompensed ... he delivered himself freely and resentfully and said Ministers made it inconsistent with his honour to serve the nation. He gave me liberty to say so to Lord Sydney and that his objection removed, he would go out.

Sydney was delighted that his preferred candidate, 'the fittest of all men for the management of American and Canadian affairs', was still interested in the job, but he was concerned that the priggish Carleton was too sensitive to perceived slights. '[He] had a jealousy in his nature', Sydney said, 'and carried his claim to confidence too high whenever he was trusted'. Still, Sydney was motivated to get something sorted out. In a meeting with William Smith on 16 April 1785 the home secretary requested an urgent decision from Carleton. 'Time pressed', Sydney said. 'There were Petitions now on the table of both Houses from Canada…[and] something must be done…[because] Canada was divided by parties'.[4]

Unimpressed, Carleton continued to demand a peerage. When Sydney repeated the cabinet line that this was 'impossible', Carleton called him a 'trifler'. As for the permanent head of the Home Office, Evan Nepean, he was a 'liar'. In fact Sydney was anything but a trifler, warning the prime minister that Quebec's future was now precarious. 'I cannot help dreading that Cabinet will separate without a decision on that point', he said, 'upon which in my humble opinion depends whether Canada will remain ours a twelvemonth longer or not'. Sydney told Pitt that Lieutenant-Governor Hamilton had openly led an 'English party' against Governor Haldimand in Quebec's Legislative Council, and since Haldimand's return to London Hamilton had counteracted his 'every measure'. The final straw was the lieutenant-governor's ordinance providing for juries in civil cases.[5]

Having fought so hard in opposition against the Quebec Act because it did not provide for juries, Sydney's targeting of Hamilton reeked of hypocrisy, but as a senior minister, he had come to realise the danger of agitating ancient hatreds between the French and Anglo-Celts. He was no doubt sobered by their relative strengths: of the English speakers, 6,000 had settled in Quebec before the American war and another 6,000 loyalists had arrived since; by contrast, the French speaking population now totalled approximately 100,000. With these figures in mind, Sydney moved against Hamilton over juries, convincing the prime minister to replace him with a colonel called Hope.[6]

For Sydney, Henry Hope was never more than a stop-gap leader, and he continued to press for Carleton's appointment. 'If a Governor General of all that remains of British possessions in North America can now be appointed', he told Pitt, 'Sir Guy Carleton is in my opinion…infinitely preferable to any other person'. So Sydney kept negotiating. Carleton would, however, only accept if his friend William Smith was appointed chief justice of Canada. Originally nicknamed 'Patriotic Billy' for his opposition to the Stamp Act, Smith had later come to advise the American turncoat Benedict Arnold in his negotiations with the British. It was said that Smith could be 'secured by an application to his ambition'. Aware of Smith's reputation as an able lawyer 'of great intrigue and subtlety ... if he could be trusted', the home secretary decided to overlook his shortcomings. And so, at the end of August 1785, Sydney obtained Sir Guy Carleton's agreement to be governor-general. There was no public announcement because of a cabinet dispute over Carleton's commission. 'All sticks with the Attorney General', Smith said. 'Lord S. is not well pleased with Mr Attorney'.[7]

Hamilton's sacking had angered his English-speaking supporters who continued to bombard London with demands 'to be governed by British laws'. While Colonel Hope struggled 'by moderation and impartiality ... to promote [Quebec's] tranquility', the Pitt government scrambled to respond to Thomas Powys MP, who put up a Quebec Bill which proposed representative government and jury trials in civil cases. The prime minister replied that General Carleton would have to investigate and report first and the bill was duly voted down. Still, the debate had smoked Prime Minister Pitt out and forced him publicly to confirm Carleton's vital role. On 16 April 1786, Lord Sydney was finally able to send Carleton's commissions to the king for signature.[8]

It was soon clear that the cabinet had watered down the idea of a governor-general with a supreme commission operating at all times across all of British North America. The lawyers had had their way after the solicitor-general advised that Carleton 'could not command out of his province in the others' and the lord chancellor refused to affix the seals to a commission which he thought was unconstitutional. As a result, Carleton ended up with separate commissions as captain-general and governor-in-chief of each province. And while the governors of those provinces were downgraded to lieutenant-governors, they still had full power when Carleton, who was to reside in Quebec, was not actually in their province. In practice, the lieutenant-governors continued to correspond directly with Sydney as Carleton became preoccupied by Quebec's constitutional challenges.[9]

Sydney had persevered to ensure Carleton's appointment in Canada just as doggedly as he had pursued Cornwallis to accept the government of India. Still the powers granted to these two viceroys were very different. In Carleton's case, the extreme sensitivity of the lawyers to constitutional innovation in colonies populated largely by people of European origin had won out over Sydney's idea of one man 'on the spot'. But any concerns Carleton may have had were offset by news that he would be granted a peerage. With a total annual income of 5,000 pounds, including sundry pensions he was already entitled to, the newly created Lord Dorchester arrived at Quebec on 23 October 1786.[10]

How qualified was the man who had control of all British colonies in America apart from the West Indies? During an earlier term as governor of Quebec, he had stopped the American invasion of Canada. Later on, he had been Britain's last commander-in-chief in New York. There he had handled the evacuation and resettlement of loyalists with great skill. But those achievements were soon overshadowed by his slow progress in reforming Quebec, and historians are divided about his competence. While Helen Manning said that 'Dorchester was in many ways eminently fitted to the task', Vincent Harlow argued that Lord Sydney 'blundered in bringing Carleton back again'.[11]

The home secretary had instructed Lord Dorchester to find out as quickly as possible 'the real sentiments of… [Quebec's] inhabitants [about reform]… and point out what may with propriety and good policy… be done'. To do this, Dorchester set up a number of Legislative Council committees. But he inherited all the feuding between the English and French factions on the Council. Indeed William Smith used his position as chairman of the Council's law and justice committee to shamelessly side with the English faction, describing the French as 'slaves in polity… their morals trifling and insincere'. In late 1786 he overturned a lower court's finding that French law applied to a case involving English-speaking litigants. Contrary to the Quebec Act, Smith applied English law. 'The lower Court's opinion', he said in his capacity as chief justice, 'alarmed and disgusted all the English inhabitants and appeared to be… as ill founded as it was dangerous'.[12]

Smith next bombarded the Legislative Council with draft ordinances, one of which attempted a legal partition of Quebec by proposing that English law apply to the upper part of the province. Dorchester refused to allow these proposals to be considered. On 13 February 1787, the English faction complained to the Home Office. 'We have not as yet debated on any one Ordinance', they said.

'The Chief Justice has proposed three: they lie on the table'. A month later, Smith and eight of his supporters signed a protest against the Council's refusal to support his ordinance for 'the better administration of justice'. Six weeks after that the attorney-general threw his weight behind Smith by appearing at the bar of the Council to criticize Quebec's law and justice system. Meanwhile, Frederick Haldimand's contacts in the province had kept him informed. On 10 June he warned Sydney about 'the confusion reigning' in Canada. 'The Chief Justice is unmasked as a fool', he said, 'and Dorchester observes a silence so profound that the friends of Government do not know what to think'. The home secretary's reply was as embarrassing as it was inadequate. '[I] never had a good opinion of Smith', Sydney said, 'but... Dorchester had asked for him and made himself responsible for his conduct'.[13]

On 13 June 1787 Dorchester bundled up the Legislative Council's conflicting reports with a covering dispatch to the Home Office. 'One [party was] zealous for English law and... an Assembly', he said, '[while] the other was not less anxious to maintain the present form of Government'. Dorchester noted that the English party had recently been swelled by loyalists, but he urged caution in a province 'where nine tenths of the people are ignorant of... an Assembly'. Even so, he had no policy proposals of his own, admitting that he was 'at a loss for any plan likely to give satisfaction'.[14]

Sydney's official response was to assure Dorchester that the cabinet did not intend any immediate changes to the constitution. He exhorted the governor to prevent the 'violent proceedings among the servants of the Crown which cannot fail of weakening the Government'. But in a private letter to Dorchester the home secretary really let fly: 'The disputes in the Council are extremely disgusting not to say disgraceful', he said, '[because] it is impossible for any government to subsist under such circumstances'. Accusing the attorney-general of 'extremely improper' conduct, Sydney charged that he was 'very unfit to continue in office' and sacked him not long afterwards.[15]

The bundle of conflicting reports Dorchester had submitted included a petition from western loyalists. In it, they proposed that 'the blessings of the English Constitution' be extended to those living in the area 'from Point au Baudet on Lake St Francis westward as far as Niagara'. This prompted Sydney to suggest that a dividing line might be possible between the English and French speakers:

All the disputes tend to a division of the Province into two with a Lieutenant Governor to each under the Governor. Give me your thoughts on that subject as well as upon any other plan of adjusting the differences subsisting in the Province and unfortunately among officers of the Crown.

In weighing up the pros and cons of this division, Sydney said, Dorchester was better able 'to form a decisive opinion upon the spot than we can here'. But the opinions of the French speakers must be respected, he continued, 'Otherwise under the shew of giving a free Constitution we are really practicing tyranny'.[16]

As the government waited for Dorchester's further advice, Thomas Powys once again took up the cause of English-speaking Quebecois in the Commons. Again Powys proposed an assembly for Quebec. Again the ministers responded that not enough information had been received from the province to 'determine the merits of an Assembly'. And again the vote went the government's way. Powys' reputation as an independent MP who had helped pressure George III to recognise the United States was by now a distant memory. 'The reason why the honourable gentleman stood degraded', one of Powys colleagues said, 'was that he had become a partisan'. Whatever his motives, Powys remained a thorn in the government's side over Quebec.

In so far as Dorchester had any ideas of his own, they were directed to the creation of an Upper House rather than an Assembly. He proposed that the king should reward his faithful colonial servants by reserving a portion of every major land release for them. '[This would] create and strengthen an Aristocracy... on this continent', he said, 'where all Governments are feeble and the general condition of things tends to a wild democracy'. Dorchester's obsession with aristocracy had first manifested itself some years earlier when he gave credence to a rumour that many Americans wanted 'a Prince of the Blood of England' to be their king. It had continued with his preoccupation over his own title. And now it formed the basis of his limited reform plan. Although Sydney did initiate a generous system of land grants to former soldiers who became known as United Empire Loyalists, he would not countenance the creation of an aristocracy.[17]

Sydney was concerned that Dorchester's proposed aristocracy would inflame the House of Commons. In September 1788, he commandeered a packet-boat to send out a special dispatch. In it, the governor was again pressed for his advice, but this time, it was for his opinion on specific proposals. Sydney had decided to seize the initiative before any further parliamentary assault by his opponents. The home secretary began by noting that 'it had been in contemplation to propose to Parliament a division of... [Quebec]'. In the newly settled western areas of the province, largely populated by loyalists, it was proposed to grant land according to English law, using Nova Scotia and New Brunswick as precedents. But Sydney needed to know 'how far it may be practicable or expedient or whether any other line or mode of separation would be preferable'. As to the French-speaking remainder of the province, he made it clear that no change to the existing constitution was contemplated. The government was ready to act, Sydney said, as soon as Dorchester's favourable advice was received.[18]

In his reply of 8 November, Dorchester cautioned against a division of the province. 'It is by no means at present', he said, 'either in the interests of the new or ancient districts'. But should it be divided, he continued, 'I see no reason why the inhabitants of those western districts should not have an Assembly... or the English system of laws'. Then he set out a 'proposed line of division', similar to the modern Quebec/Ontario boundary.[19]

Meanwhile, in late October 1788, George III had begun to show the first signs of madness which soon plunged Britain into a constitutional crisis. As home secretary, Sydney became deeply involved in helping the prime minister manage this gathering storm. So any further work on Quebec was postponed, and it did not resume until after Sydney's retirement in June 1789. Still, as the historian Vincent Harlow later acknowledged, the British government had decided by then to divide the province, granting an Assembly to Upper Quebec, while retaining the French system for the remainder. It took Sydney's successor, William Grenville, a further two years to finalize the Canada Act of 1791, albeit one that introduced representative government into both parts of Quebec, while applying English and French law respectively in the areas Sydney had proposed.[20]

Sydney had begun the political process leading to the Canada Act of 1791 and had been instrumental in securing the land to make it work. At Paris in 1782 his representative, Henry Strachey, had obtained this key part of Upper Canada, bounded by the French, Ottawa and St Lawrence Rivers and the Great Lakes of Ontario, Erie and Huron, following last-minute bargaining with the

Americans. These water boundaries encouraged trade and communication. And, as the Canadian historian Norman Macdonald put it, 'millions of rich acres were available for the surplus population of Great Britain'.[21]

[*Twenty-six*]

~ Nelson, Bligh and Phillip ~

During Lord Sydney's time as secretary of state, the Home Office was a government clearing house. Its jurisdiction included overseeing of naval officers involved in trade regulation, secret service and special projects. As a result, Sydney crossed paths with three men who left their mark on history – Horatio Nelson, William Bligh and Arthur Phillip.[1]

Until 1776, the thirteen American colonies had collectively been one of the largest importers of British goods. After the revolution, there had been high hopes on both sides that American ships and goods would receive the same preferential treatment from Britain as British ships and goods. However, the peace treaty did not cover trade and although the British proposed an Intercourse Bill to give preference to American goods, no such advantage was proposed for American ships. Most affected was the West Indian trade, which Sydney described as follows:

> To the West Indies from New England ... [exports] of timber, livestock, salted provisions and dried fish. Flour, Indian corn &c. from the southern States as well as onions, apples, cider and potatoes ... These [are] run in small vessels between New England and the West Indies their return being sugar, coffee, cocoa and rum for home consumption ... The trade is chiefly barter.

During his first term as home secretary, Sydney had pushed for a policy to meet the United States halfway. 'Ships laden with provisions for the West Indies bona fide disposing of them there and wanting a freight to Europe', he said, '[should be able] to lade such ships only as are bound for Great Britain giving bond for the performance of the voyage'.[2]

Sydney's successor abandoned the Intercourse Bill, preferring direct negotiations with the Americans, but these talks failed over the West Indian trade because Britain was worried that her European competitors would use the American flag as a flag of convenience. Britain abandoned the negotiations and proceeded to enforce her Navigation Acts. As a result, the trade in goods between the United States and the West Indies was reserved for British subjects using British-owned and British-built vessels, manned by British crews. This policy was designed to encourage a 'nursery for seamen' to protect Britain's 'Empire of the Oceans' and to make up for the loss to Britain of an estimated 18,000 American seamen, who were now citizens of a foreign nation. Even so, Britain's governors in the West Indies were sympathetic to local businessmen and turned a blind eye to their trade with the Americans. Horatio Nelson, who was already displaying that combination of courage and impetuosity which would later make him famous, was therefore dispatched to enforce the law.[3]

Upon returning to the Home Office in December 1783, Lord Sydney assumed ministerial responsibility for the Navigation Acts and for orders issued by his predecessor. These were intended to prohibit American shipping from any involvement in West Indian trade. Six months later, when Nelson arrived at Barbados in command of the 28-gun frigate *Boreas*, he witnessed American ships stevedoring without interference. 'The [British] Admiral and all about him are great ninnies', Nelson said. The commander-in-chief, Admiral Sir Richard Hughes, excused himself by saying that he did not have copies of the Navigation Acts. Nelson therefore supplied them. The young captain was passionate about enforcing these Acts because he believed they underwrote the Royal Navy's manpower in wartime. And he was concerned about the United States' territorial intentions. 'If once the Americans are admitted to any kind of intercourse with these Islands', he said, 'they will first become carriers and next have possession of [them] if we are ever again involved in a French war. I am all for doing my duty... to suppress the admission of [these] foreigners'.[4]

Admiral Hughes thought differently as did the governor of Antigua, General Sir Thomas Shirley. 'Old respectable officers of high rank, long service and of a certain life', Shirley said, 'are very jealous of being dictated to in their duty by young gentlemen whose service and experience do not entitle them to'. Hughes ordered Nelson to abide by the governor's unofficial policy of admitting American vessels to port. 'Our commander ... is led by the advice of the Islanders to admit the Yankees to a trade', Nelson observed, '[or] at least to wink at it'. One of the loopholes the Americans exploited was to claim a ship was in distress, thus allowing its cargo to be unloaded. The governor and his customs officers would allege that they were unable to examine the vessel themselves. They would accept the Americans' claims of distress, according to Nelson, 'sworn as the sea phrase is through a nine inch plank'.[5]

Made aware of this evasion, Lord Sydney said that while enforcement of the Navigation Acts should not be 'oppressive', generally speaking 'American ships should not have any intercourse with our West India Islands'. A petition from the local Assembly to relax the rules for Americans was met with the firm response that 'all his [Majesty's] orders which were received by his Governors would be strictly obeyed'. Unlike many others, Nelson was in no doubt where he stood:

> Whilst I have the honour to command an English Man of War, I never shall allow myself to be subservient to the will of any Governor nor cooperate with him in illegal acts ... They shall make proper application to me for whatever they want to come by water.[6]

Nelson's two strongest supporters in the West Indies were his fellow officers, the brothers Wilfrid and Cuthbert Collingwood. The latter was to serve as Nelson's second-in-command at Trafalgar. Their regular reports kept the home secretary abreast of problems with colonial officials, especially Governor Shirley and his customs officers. Although Nelson had the power to ask why vessels were registered as British when they were foreign-built and operated entirely by foreigners in contravention of the Navigation Acts, it seemed to be no deterrent. 'The illegal acts [by the King's Customs Officers] of granting Registers to Americans', he reported, 'are carried on with great confidence'.[7]

Meanwhile the West Indian colonists put it about that Nelson 'was injuring the Colony and that ... [Sydney] never intended to hinder Americans from coming into their ports with any trifling excuse'. Now under enormous pressure, the young captain wrote direct to the home secretary, on 20 March 1785, to explain himself. Whenever he excluded an American vessel, Nelson said, it unloaded its cargo in another port, claiming that it was leaking or had sprung a mast 'or some excuse of that sort'. Just the day before, the master of an American brig, allegedly in distress, had become infuriated when Nelson told him not to come ashore until his vessel had been surveyed. A malicious story soon swept the island that Nelson intended to 'turn him out of Port' when he was in imminent danger of sinking. 'My name is most probably unknown to your Lordship but my character as a man, I trust, will bear the strictest investigation', Nelson said. 'My greatest ambition is to receive approbation for my conduct.'[8]

Although Nelson was the captain of a warship, his challenge to British colonial authority required the constant backup of dispatches from the Home Office. These, though, were often delayed by the long Atlantic voyage. At one point a rumour reached Lord Sydney that Nelson had died; the news that the deceased was in fact Wilfrid Collingwood took months to reach London. Delays like this placed Nelson at a dangerous disadvantage after prosecutions he instigated resulted in forfeiture orders against a number of vessels. The masters of these vessels retaliated with legal action of their own, whereupon Nelson took the unusual step of petitioning the king. 'The masters have been instigated to procure divers Writs for the arrest of your Memorialist', Nelson explained, 'under pretence of their having been assaulted and imprisoned by him to the amount of 4,000 pounds damages'. To avoid being arrested, Nelson said, he had been 'obliged to keep himself confined to his ship'. This confinement, which impaired his health, he likened to that imposed on a 'close prisoner', and thanks to communication delays, it had lasted for eight weeks, undermining the enforcement of British government policy. 'If Ministers do not support me', Nelson said, 'may they find the want of officers to support them'.[9]

Delayed dispatches may have given Sydney a distorted view at times of just what Nelson was up against in the West Indies, but he remained steadfast in his determination 'to secure the whole of this freight to Great Britain'. And when Sydney finally learned of Nelson's predicament, he acted decisively. He waived aside the colonists' complaints and strongly backed the young captain. Nelson in turn was grateful:

> This Packet has brought a letter from Lord Sydney signifying his Majesty's approbation of my conduct and orders for the Crown Lawyers to defend me

at his expense from all Civil prosecutions and in case of [an] unfavourable decree advising me to Appeal. When Ministers support good officers they will ever find alert and good ones.

Following this show of ministerial support, Nelson continued to seize American vessels. He also had the satisfaction of seeing the introduction of reforms to give other naval captains 'great additional powers enough to carry on the business of... the Nation without interruption'. As a consequence, it was claimed that 'the whole [West Indian] freight... [was] retained by Great Britain', even though, in reality, policing the Navigation Acts continued to be hit and miss.[10]

One West Indian merchant, Michael Keane, seemed unfazed by the home secretary's enforcement of the Acts and sent him a gift of chocolate rolls. These, however were seized in transit by customs officers, prompting Keane to write:

So trifling a matter as a dozen grounds of chocolate as to prevent a family who may not be able to procure such at any price in England... I can never think to be a prejudice to His Majesty's revenue... I will... procure 100lbs of the best species of Cocoa... and your Lordship's Housekeeper might manufacture as good chocolate as that made here.

A sweet tooth did not get in Sydney's way when it came to supporting the enforcers of the Navigation Acts. Dirty and difficult work that it was, Nelson saw it as vital to maintaining the strength of the British navy. When years later, Nelson was inducted as a viscount, he was 'supported' into the chamber of the House of Lords by Admiral Lord Howe and John Thomas Townshend, second viscount Sydney.[11]

Lobbying by West Indian colonists was not limited to opposing the Navigation Acts. A West India committee of planters and merchants had approached the celebrated botanist Sir Joseph Banks to introduce the breadfruit plant to their Islands, as a ready source of slave food. Banks had tasted this plant, a native of the Pacific Islands, and the lobbyists believed that as a friend of George III, Banks could obtain a vessel to courier specimens to the West Indies. A shortage of shipping during the American war prevented this proposal being pursued, but finally, in 1787, the British government resolved to take action.[12]

Responsibility for the operation, which was of special interest to the king, fell within the home secretary's portfolio. Serious consideration was given to instructing Captain Arthur Phillip, who was about to leave for New South Wales, to send one of his First Fleet ships on this task, but Banks thought that the specialized transport required was likely to be better fitted out in England than Botany Bay. On 5 May 1787 the home secretary issued instructions to the Admiralty: 'A vessel of proper class...for this service', Sydney directed, '[was] to be fitted with proper conveniences for the preservation of as many of the trees as can be taken on board, giving command of her to some able and discreet officer'. The vessel was to sail to the Society Islands where James Cook had reported that the best plants grew and take a selection of them to the West Indies. A botanist, David Nelson, and a gardener, William Brown, were to choose the plants and care for them during the voyage. Sydney's matter-of-fact commands obscured what was a tricky logistical exercise, using a small ship to take large living plants half way around the world. 'The difficulty of carrying plants by sea is very great', Banks warned, 'as a small sprinkling of salt water or of the salt sea which fill the air even in a moderate gale will instantly destroy them if not immediately washed off with fresh water'.[13]

After imposing an upper limit of 250 tons, the Admiralty began an immediate search for a vessel 'of proper class'. From a short list, Sir Joseph Banks and David Nelson chose the cutter *Berthia*, which was duly purchased for 1950 pounds. This ship of 230 tons, Sydney was advised soon afterwards, was 'fitting out...under the direction of Sir Joseph Banks'. On 6 August Lieutenant William Bligh, who had returned from Jamaica the previous day, thanked Banks for nominating him to command it. By 14 August work to sheath this vessel's hull in copper, shorten its masts and alter its accommodation to fit 45 people was complete. Despite this progress, Sydney wrote to Banks with just a hint of irritation at being informed rather than consulted:

> The Admiralty have I understand purchased a vessel for the purpose of conveying the breadfruit tree...to be commissioned in...a few days, to be called the *Bounty* and to be commanded by Lieutenant Bligh...As I am totally unacquainted with the Instructions...to be given to Nelson and Brown the two gardeners who are to collect the trees and be entrusted

with their care and management ... on board the ship, I shall think myself particularly obliged to you if you will prepare such Instructions as you may judge requisite for their guidance.[14]

A cloak of secrecy shrouded key aspects of the expedition from other senior ministers as well. On 7 September the secretary at war, Sir George Yonge, noted after a visit to the *Bounty* that Bligh 'knew little or nothing of the object of his voyage'. In a letter to Banks, however, Bligh cast Yonge's visit in a different light. 'As I never heard you mention Sir George', Bligh wrote, 'I have avoided answering any direct questions'.[15]

Bligh was more forthcoming about his ambitions for promotion. As the leader of this unique expedition, he hoped to be made a master and commander or even a post-captain, following the precedent set by John Hunter who had recently gone out to Botany Bay in the *Sirius*. But the Admiralty did not oblige, which Bligh thought was 'a violation of all justice and respect'. One of his supporters, Lord Selkirk, noted that without a promotion Bligh could not command a larger vessel. 'The establishment of Bligh's vessel is that of a Cutter', Selkirk said. '[It] is highly improper for so long a voyage [with] only 24 able seamen and 21 of all others without a Lieutenant or any Marines'.[16]

In mid-September 1787 Bligh took his leave of Lord Howe at the Admiralty. But it was not until 24 November, after he had moved the *Bounty* to Spithead, that he received his final orders from Admiral Hood. Bligh was angry with those who had delayed him:

> If there is any punishment that ought to be inflicted on a set of men for neglect I am sure it ought to be on the Admiralty for my three weeks detention at this place during a fair wind which carried all outward bound ships clear of the Channel but me who wanted it most.

Thanks to this delay, Bligh and his crew took a terrible beating trying to round Cape Horn to reach the Pacific directly. After two attempts they gave up, travelling east via the Cape of Good Hope instead. It is difficult to say whether this experience contributed to the mutiny on 28 April 1789, just weeks after the *Bounty* had been loaded with hundreds of breadfruit plants. Bligh had become obsessed with the condition of the plants in their 774 pots, 39 tubs and 24 boxes. At one stage, he threatened to make some of his crew jump overboard, bellowing that they were 'infernal scoundrels, blackguards, liars, thieves, a disgrace to the service and damn'd long pelts of bitches'. These tongue lashings did not affect the loyalty of the botanist David Nelson, who along with seventeen others, turned his back on the mutineers, electing to accompany Bligh in the *Bounty's* 23-foot launch. It was a different story, though, with the gardener, William Brown, who remained aboard the *Bounty* with Fletcher Christian and the rest of the crew.

When Bligh and his party arrived in Batavia at the end of their epic 3,900 mile open-boat voyage he was in no doubt about what could have prevented the mutiny. 'If I had been equipped with more officers and marines', Bligh wrote, 'the piracy could never have happened'. While Lord Sydney bore the ultimate responsibility in cabinet for the preparations, he had relied upon the Admiralty experts to choose 'a vessel of proper class'. In selecting a cutter rather than a larger vessel capable of carrying marines, the Admiralty experts had failed to choose a vessel which was fit for purpose. William Bligh would later be involved in another mutiny, but this time it was to be a whole colony, which had been founded by Arthur Phillip.[17]

According to some, links between the families of Arthur Phillip and Lord Sydney may have stretched back to 1709 when Sydney's grandfather, Charles second Viscount Townshend, assisted Palatine refugees from the lower Rhine to migrate to Britain. Among them apparently was the family of Arthur Phillip's father, Jacob, who hailed from Frankfurt. However, although Townshend continued to assist these refugees after their arrival in London, there is no suggestion that he was personally acquainted with Phillip's family. There is also nothing to support an assertion made in the *London Observer* that Phillip was Lord Sydney's 'cousin'.[18]

After seeing active service during the Seven Years' War, Phillip had developed a reputation as a 'discreet' naval officer who could speak French and German. In 1774 he had volunteered to serve in the navy of Britain's ally Portugal, seeing action against Spain in South American waters. In command of a frigate, Phillip had led a successful attack on a much larger Spanish battleship. Some years later, the *St James Chronicle* suggested that Phillip had also been employed to convey 400 convicts from Lisbon to Brazil, but there is no hard evidence of this. Whatever the case, Phillip returned to Britain in 1778 with a ringing endorsement from the Portuguese who singled him out from the other seconded British officers:

> This officer is most honourable and meritorious ... his health is very delicate but he never complains excepting when he has nothing to do ... He is one of the officers of the most distinct merit ... well up in every branch of the Military profession ... an officer of education and principle ... clean handed ... very brave ... no flatterer ... but without temper or want of respect.[19]

Corroborating these endorsements, the British ambassador reported that Phillip 'had served in the Brasils with great zeal and honour'. Among other things, Phillip had acted as a diamond courier, keeping extensive journals which described the South American diamond-mining and cochineal industries. Some journal entries reveal how diamonds were smuggled by the miners and how the mines, being located close to colonial borders, created tensions between Portugal and Spain. Others describe how a valuable red dye, cochineal, was extracted from a cactus-dwelling insect 'from which the Spaniards draw great profit'. Phillip bred this insect in his cabin. 'Before the fly appears', he wrote, 'if you press the shell in which it lays hid, it stains the fingers of a fine purple'. [20]

Despite his fine record with the Portuguese, Phillip saw only intermittent active service when he returned to the British navy during the American Revolutionary War. But after Spain joined the rebels' side and attacked the British garrison at Gibraltar, he was sought after for his combat experience against the Spanish navy off South America. Keen to ease the pressure on Gibraltar's besieged garrison, Prime Minister Shelburne was eager to open up another front against the Spaniards. And on 10 July, his first day at the Home Office, Sydney was confronted by a number of plans to 'distress' Spain elsewhere. To this end, a British naval officer, John Blankett, had proposed an 'expedition against Buenos Aires and the South Seas conditionally' to attack Spain's South American colonies. The force suggested was for:

One ship of 64 guns, 4 of 50, 2 frigates, 2 sloops and 2 cutters 10 ships coppered (North County Barks recommended) for the transporting of 2,000 soldiers… the ships of war to take on board 300 soldiers in order to give good room in the transports… On success at the river Plate, such force might be sent as reinforcement to India or to the South Seas.[21]

Already in possession of Phillip's reports of his South American service, Sydney sought his advice on Blankett's plan. With just a hint of irritation at the influence one of his junior captains was now having on the Home Office, the first lord of the admiralty wrote to Sydney on 25 September 1782:

If you have nothing further for Captain Phillip we shall send him to his ship… The memo intrusted you with in relation to the Southern expedition if it is to take place should come from you as the ships commands to the Admiralty to collect and order to fit for Secret Service.[22]

As it turned out, the Royal Navy was unable to assemble an invasion force within the government's time-frame. A squadron of four ships was brought together instead and Phillip was appointed captain of one of the larger vessels, the 64-gun *Europe*. This squadron set sail for South America on 16 January 1783, but soon afterwards it was hit by a violent storm in the Bay of Biscay, forcing all but one of the ships to return to England. The *Europe*, however, sailed on. It was not until after Phillip had entered the South Atlantic that he learned the war with Spain was over, but still he continued, reaching India on 18 July 1783.[23]

Although Blankett's original plan had envisaged reinforcing India 'on success at the river Plate', it is not clear why the *Europe* had sailed on. Phillip, so his commissary Edward Spain claimed, had wanted to delay returning to England, knowing that with the war now over, he would be put on half pay, but after falling out with Phillip over a promotion, Spain's word was suspect. Phillip's biographers, George Mackaness and Alan Frost, agree that while details of his mission have never been revealed, it was 'a secret expedition of some importance'. It appears that Phillip's talents as a 'discreet' naval officer had once again been utilized.[24]

Even though Europe was at peace when Lord Sydney returned to the Home Office in December 1783, he encouraged the Secret Service to continue its espionage, engaging Arthur Phillip to spy on the French, following his return from India in May 1784. According to the Secret Service accounts which now form part of Lord Sydney's papers at the Clements Library, Phillip was paid 150 pounds on 11 November that year 'to enable him to undertake a journey to Toulon and other parts of France for the purpose of ascertaining the Naval force and stores in their arsenals'.[25]

When Phillip was appointed to command the First Fleet to Botany Bay in mid-1786, the first lord of the admiralty told Sydney that, from the little he knew of the appointee, he would not have chosen him for such a complex task. But Sydney already knew that Phillip was one of the most talented and versatile officers ever to wear a Royal Navy uniform.[26]

[*Twenty-seven*]

Sydney, the soft touch

In late April 1776 the *Virginia Gazette* announced the arrival of the ship *Jenny* from England. The British convicts she carried were to be the last of over 50,000 transported to the American colonies before revolutionary hostilities forced the suspension of further shipments. Under the pre-war system, the British government had delivered convicts to ship-owners who contracted to transport and sell them, for the term of their sentences, to colonial farmers. The government's responsibility ceased once they were secured on board their transports. In 1751, Benjamin Franklin had threatened to trade rattlesnakes for such felons. When he and his fellow rebels signed the Declaration of Independence, the British had no choice but to halt transportation to the revolting colonies.[1]

To secure the swelling ranks of convicts who could no longer be sent to Maryland and Virginia, the North government decided to confine them in ship-hulks moored on the River Thames. During a debate on a bill requiring such convicts to raise gravel from the river, Tommy Townshend was loud in his criticism of the plan. 'Robberies were increased instead of being diminished', he thundered, 'and scarcely a night passed in which there were not robberies … in Park Lane and … pistols heard'. Still, the legislation passed, and in August 1776 the hulk *Justitia* was duly loaded with felons.[2]

More hulks and many more convicts followed. And by 1779, one quarter of them were dying in the cramped and filthy conditions. A parliamentary committee, led by Sir Charles Bunbury, investigated. Apart from recommending that the hulks be cleaned up, the committee asked whether transportation to West Africa might be a solution. The optimistic reply of one witness was that, in the process of building a self-supporting African settlement, not more than twenty percent of the convicts would die in the tropical climate. After noting that transportation to America was no longer an option, the committee recommended:

> That the sending of atrocious criminals to unhealthy places where their labour may be used and their lives hazarded, in the place of better citizens, may in some cases be advisable and in the instance of capital respites is indisputably just.[3]

By now, Britain was at war with France and Spain, as well as with the American rebels. In December 1780, the Dutch joined in too. On the Gold Coast of West Africa, in an area which is now part of Ghana, the British had thirteen forts; the Dutch had twelve. To attack these, the British raised a force of 200 volunteers, but most were soon redeployed to America – to be replaced, so their commander said, 'by convicts ... taken out of ... Newgate and the Hulks'.[4]

It was not until February 1782, however, that these convict soldiers saw action, attacking the main Dutch fort. Quickly forced into a 'precipitate retreat', many of them either deserted to the enemy or just disappeared. According to the local British governor, those who remained were 'miserable and filthy'. Although he had been appointed secretary at war in March 1782, wartime communications with Africa were such that Tommy Townshend only received first news of this debacle shortly before his transfer to the Home Office, four months later. By contrast, in his new job, where his office and the Law Courts were a stone's throw from each other, Tommy quickly became aware that judges had started to impose the sentence of transportation to Africa.[5]

Tommy Townshend had had a longstanding interest in 'law and order', and in 1764 he had written to his uncle in France: 'If you can bring over any regulations for the police they will be extremely acceptable as the good people of London have taken much of late to house breaking'. Now home secretary, Tommy found public order in an even worse state. He wrote to London's lord mayor and magistrates demanding more frequent court sittings. 'The strictest ... warrants for the search and apprehension of rogues and vagabonds', he directed, '[are] to proceed with vigour'.

It was the home secretary who bore ultimate responsibility for housing the extra convicts generated by this crackdown and Tommy Townshend mulled over his options. These included a continuation of the hulks, a new form of penitentiary or transportation out of Britain. Since 1779, conditions on the hulks had improved, and the previous government had entered into a preliminary contract, at a cost of 210,000 pounds, for massive penitentiaries to be built alongside the Thames. Even so, Tommy was leaning towards a renewal of transportation and, in September 1782, a Commons committee noted that 'new measures were about to be taken...which made the building of the Penitentiary Houses less necessary'.[6]

The revolted American colonies remained off limits. Under pressure from the rising tide of convicts, Tommy Townshend therefore decided that transportation to the African forts would resume. Although the home secretary ignored protests from the Company of Merchants trading with Africa, who were part-owners of these forts, he did limit the number of convicts by choosing a small ship, the *Den Keyser*, to transport them. With Britain's war still raging against France, Spain and Holland, the *Den Keyser* set sail on 6 November 1782. Tommy had assumed that many of the felons aboard her would become convict soldiers, and after being offloaded at various British forts, most of them were placed on soldiers' half pay. The company's attitude, meanwhile, had mellowed and it accepted further shipments of convict soldiers until it became aware, in late 1784, that an Anglo/Dutch peace treaty had been struck. The total number of British convicts shipped to Africa during this time numbered little more than 100, making virtually no impact on Britain's crowded jails.[7]

Just days after Tommy Townshend was created Lord Sydney in March 1783, he went into opposition. With an American peace treaty all but ratified, the new home secretary, Lord North, contracted with one George Moore to transport a number of criminals to America. As before the war, the government took no further interest in these convicts and was unaware that Moore had entered into a fraudulent enterprise with a Maryland trader. This fraud involved changing the name of the ship from the *George* to the *Swift*, calling the convicts indentured servants and listing the ship's destination as Nova Scotia, knowing all along that its captain would falsely claim a shortage of supplies as an excuse to dock in Maryland. By the time Moore's deception came to the attention of an outraged Maryland Legislature, most of the convicts had been landed and on-sold. Meanwhile, still unaware of the scam, Lord North had delivered Moore another batch of convicts.[8]

From time to time, Parliament was required to renew its transportation legislation. On 19 December 1783, as it was considering whether to do so, Lord North, who as home secretary had carriage of that business, entered the Commons chamber at 3.00 p.m. To everyone's surprise, he made straight for the opposition benches where word quickly spread that George III had sacked him, Charles Fox having just suffered the same fate. As the two of them sat side by side discussing what to do about that 'school-boy' William Pitt, the transportation debate continued, leading to the re-emergence of Sir Charles Bunbury's transportation committee. Three days later, Lord Sydney returned to the Home Office.[9]

The king's sacking of Fox and North ushered in three months of bitter parliamentary brinkmanship as they tried every tactic to bring down the new government. Even modest transportation reforms to iron out legal anomalies were threatened. Some convicts imprisoned on hulks had been sentenced 'to raise sand in the river', while others, who had been sentenced 'to transportation to America', could not be ordered to do any work. Nevertheless, a bill requiring all such convicts to do their fair share only narrowly avoided defeat. A lone private member's proposal to send convicts to New Zealand was not taken seriously.[10]

Among the papers waiting for Lord Sydney when he returned to the Home Office was a plan drawn up by James Mario Matra, a native-born New Yorker with loyalist sympathies. Having seen Botany Bay with James Cook in 1770, Matra suggested that loyalists could start a settlement there. Emphasizing the proximity of New Zealand's flax and timber, he claimed they were suitable for 'naval equipments'. He referred to the prospects of a China trade, to a fur trade between north-western America and Asia and to a British wool trade to Japan and Korea. He pointed out Botany Bay's strategic potential in relation to Java, Manila and Spanish America. And he claimed that he had the support of Sir Joseph Banks who had seen it too. Unimpressed, Lord North had ignored this plan when it had been submitted to him in late August 1783.[11]

Now it was Lord Sydney's turn. As he was establishing New Brunswick to accommodate the loyalists, the object of Matra's plan appeared to be of little interest to him, but the plan itself appealed as offering a possible destination for convicts sentenced to transportation; he took it seriously. In early April 1784, with a volatile parliamentary session behind him, Sydney made it his business to meet Matra, who noted what was said as follows:

> When I conversed with Lord Sydney on this subject, it was observed that New South Wales would be a very proper region for the reception of criminals condemned to transportation. I believe that it will be found that in this idea good policy and humanity are united.

Five years earlier, when Sir Joseph Banks had been asked by the Bunbury committee to nominate a 'distant part of the globe' where a convict colony might be established, he had suggested Botany Bay was 'the place...best adapted'. Whether or not Sydney had this evidence in mind, he was the first minister to propose Botany Bay for this purpose.[12]

Matra began reworking his Botany Bay plan to focus on transportation. In doing this, he distinguished between the old American system where convicts had been sold into private servitude, and an African scheme where they did public work. But the critical question of just how convicts might first be sent to New South Wales, when no one was there who could contract to receive them, remained unanswered. All the same, Matra supported a parliamentary recommendation that legislation permitting transportation to America be amended 'to authorize the same to any part of the globe'.[13]

At the end of July 1784 the government introduced a bill 'to reduce the several [transportation] statutes into one Act'. The hulks would be integrated into a new transportation system under which the cabinet rather than Parliament would nominate where convicts were to be sent. This time, there was no opposition from Charles Fox. Perhaps he realized that with the ministers choosing the destination, the opposition would be free to criticize any delay in making the choice as well as the choice itself. As home secretary, Lord Sydney now bore the full weight of political responsibility within cabinet for choosing a suitable place 'either within his Majesty's Dominions or elsewhere'.[14]

Although interested in Matra's revised plan, the home secretary had remained concerned that there was no one in New South Wales capable of receiving convicts. And after returning to the Home Office, he had continued to focus on those destinations where private contractors could on-sell convicts to colonists.

Unaware of the *Swift* scam, Sydney took over North's second contract with George Moore and a number of convicts were duly delivered up for transportation to America. When their ship, the *Mercury*, arrived in Maryland, the Americans refused to let it dock, remembering Moore's earlier deceit with the *Swift*. The *Mercury* then made for the Hondo River in what is now Belize, where British settlers reluctantly accepted her convict cargo as logwood cutters. For a time, Sydney was fired up by the Hondo's potential as a convict destination, but with only 30 families in the settlement, its ability to absorb convicts was severely limited. When Sydney arranged with Moore to ship a further 29 convicts to the Hondo aboard the *Fair American*, the British settlers threatened violence if these felons were landed, and they were taken to the Mosquito Shore, now part of Honduras and Nicaragua, instead. There the small logging community was just as unenthusiastic. When word of this reached London, Sydney reluctantly accepted that these small Central American settlements did not offer a solution to his ever-growing convict problem. Moreover, in other colonies which had remained loyal, such as Nova Scotia, there was an equally hostile reaction.[15]

Sydney's dilemma throughout the 1780s was best summed up by a *Times* letter-writer 'Hampden' whose *nom de plume* celebrated John Hampden, a parliamentary hero who had been killed during the English civil war. On 17 May 1785 Hampden wrote:

> The character of Lord Sydney ... flows from the purest principles of the constitution ... When in opposition ... it did not arise from party motives or personal considerations but from a constitutional spirit of opposing whatever ... was dangerous to that just equilibrium of power which preserves alike the prerogative and dignity of the Crown and the authority and interest of a free people. And in power his Lordship is acting from the same principles.

Hampden contrasted this with the glaring defects in penal administration where 'darkness and terror seize the imagination and convey the horrid ideas of a county prison'. He hoped that 'the accomplishments of Lord Sydney will rectify the defects of office which discredit his Department and disgrace the nation'.[16]

Although the code of laws Sydney introduced in 1785 'for putting the Magistracy and Police … on a more respectable and salutary footing' suggested a hard-line approach, he nevertheless felt that he owed a duty of care to all British subjects being dealt with by the criminal justice system. During his long career he had repeatedly shown compassion. In opposition, he had sponsored a bill for the licensing and inspection of private mad-houses by the Royal College of Physicians. And decades before the advent of the M'Naghten Rules which laid down a test for criminal insanity, he had accepted Margaret Nicholson's unfitness to stand trial for the attempted assassination of George III with a blunt knife.[17]

As home secretary, Sydney was responsible for submitting all pleas for mercy to the king, after obtaining reports from the judges and adding his own comments. The day before the execution of William Holloway, who had been sentenced to hang for highway robbery, Sydney intervened. 'In consideration of his former good character and the probability of it being his first offence', Sydney said, '[Holloway] might be an object of his Majesty's royal clemency on condition of transportation for life'. The home secretary also acted to defer executions if the king was unavailable. Thus he postponed Catherine Hyland's execution for coining (counterfeiting), the penalty for which was being burned alive. On the king's return, Sydney submitted that the evidence showed she should be punished for the lesser crime of uttering false coin and transported for life. At times, his compassion tested George III's patience. When Sydney 'very reluctantly applied' to the king for a determination of the respite he had himself given to a convict sentenced to death for forgery, his Majesty replied testily:

> There cannot be the smallest reason for any farther delay as to the law taking its course on George Owen; the former respite was not improper but the affidavit not having been attended to with proofs it makes the execution of this unhappy convict absolutely necessary as an example that by such wicked means men under condemnation will not escape.

Sydney was once even castigated by a minister of religion. 'I am told that you have now obtained a pardon for a man convicted of the horrid crime of wilful murder', the Reverend Charles Hardy said. 'Do I now live in a country where a Secretary of State can in effect annul our laws?' To many, Sydney was a soft touch.[18]

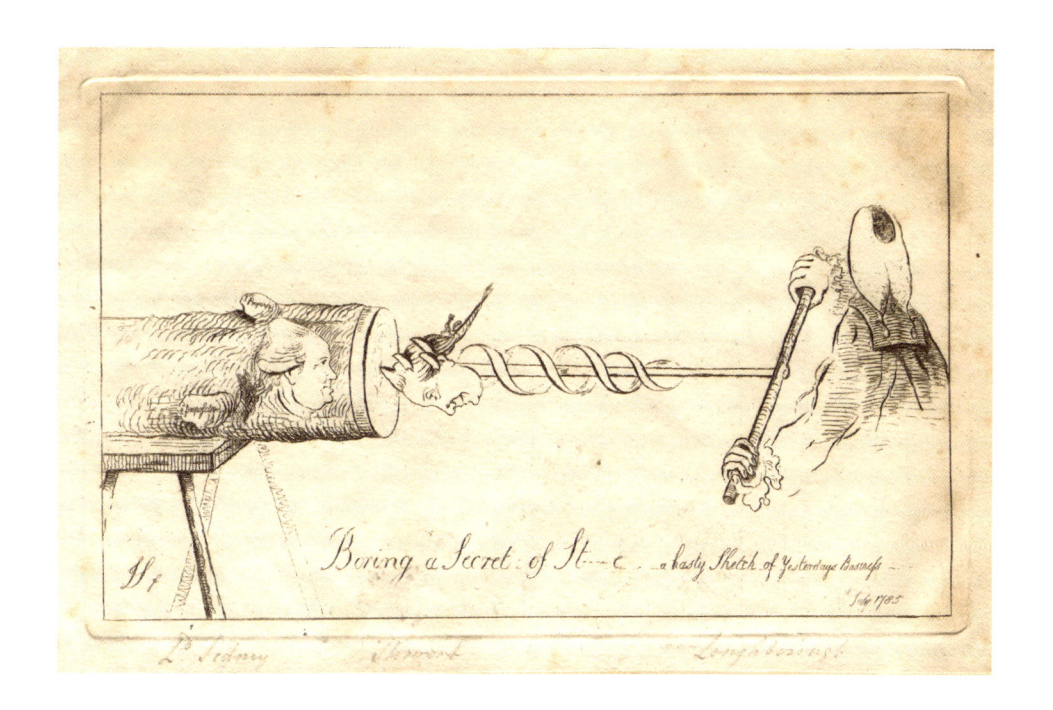

Sydney and Stormont in 1785 (National Portrait Gallery, London)

Here Lord Sydney in the form of a capped pole is being bored by Lord Stormont in the form of a large auger. As the 'shadow' home secretary, Stormont clashed repeatedly with Sydney in the House of Lords, in this case over Britain's commercial relations with Ireland. In 1788–89, they had heated confrontations over the madness of George III.

General Sir Guy Carleton in 1786 (Library and Archives Canada)

After repelling an American invasion of Canada during the revolutionary war, Carleton supervised the withdrawal of British troops and loyalists from the newly independent United States. Lord Sydney's pick to be governor-in-chief of what remained of British North America the 'priggish' Carleton struggled to manage political tensions in Quebec.

The Coming of the Loyalists, 1783 (Library and Archives Canada)

This is an idealised image of some of the 30,000 loyalists who arrived in Nova Scotia during 1783–84. Many settled in an area which, thanks to the efforts of Lord Sydney and Henry Strachey, had remained part of British North America. To accommodate their political demands, Sydney created the colony of New Brunswick.

Instructions to the Treasury 18 August 1786

(National Archives, UK)

Immediately after the British cabinet accepted his recommendation that convicts be sent to Botany Bay, Sydney instructed the Treasury lords to 'forthwith' provide for the First Fleet. Extracts from Sydney's letter of instruction, which triggered the first European settlement of what is now Australia, are reproduced here.

> Whitehall 18th August 1786
>
> My Lords,
>
> The several Goals and Places for the Confinement of Felons in this Kingdom being in so crowded a State

> I am therefore commanded to signify to your Lordships His Majesty's Pleasure, that you do forthwith take such Measures as may be necessary for providing a proper Number of Vessels for the Conveyance of 750 Convicts to Botany Bay, together with such Provisions, Necessaries and Implements for agriculture as may be requisite for their Use after their arrival.

> In the mean time, I am only to recommend it to your Lordships to cause every possible Expedition to be used in preparing the Shipping for the reception of the said Convicts and for transporting the Supplies of Provisions and Necessaries for their use to the place of their destination.
>
> I am,
> My Lords,
> Your Lordships
> most obedient
> humble Servant
> Sydney

The First Parliament of Botany Bay 1786 (National Library of Australia)

The decision to send convicts to Botany Bay was ridiculed by many. In this caricature, 'The First Parliament of Botany Bay in High Debate' which appeared in the *Hibernian Magazine*, the Speaker sits in a tree surrounded by unruly convicts, some drinking and brandishing cudgels. In the background, bodies hang from gallows.

Landing at Botany Bay (National Library of Australia)

Published in 1786, this cartoon depicts Britain's opposition leaders and the Prince of Wales landing at Botany Bay, with convicts in the launch behind. Lord North, wearing a blue sash, and Charles Fox, dressed in armour, are holding the prince aloft. Throwing rocks and discharging imaginary arrows from the hill behind, are two Aborigines.

Black-eyed Sue and Sweet Poll, 1792 (National Library of Australia)

In this cartoon, Black-eyed Sue and Sweet Poll take leave of their lovers who are going to Botany Bay. According to *The Times*, and contrary to the impression given here, the flattering descriptions of Botany Bay's climate 'had induced a great number of the lower ranks…to accompany the felons'.

	Brought over	5443 3 9
Aug.t 12	Mr Johnstone employed for the purpose of ascertaining and watching the motions of persons engaged by the French Minister, particularly Madme d'Eon	20
26	Thomas Green for Services performed	3 3
30	Joseph Hinson as full compensation, in lieu of a Pension of £200 per annum, which had been given to him for intercepting the Dispatches of Doctor Franklin & others to Congress, during their residence at Paris	1000
Sept.r 24	Mr Jas Johnstone for Services performed	20
Octo.r 5	J Dumaresq, one quarters Pension	50
15	Mr Jas Johnstone for Services performed	20
29	Thos Green Do	5 5
Nov.r 11	Captain Phillip to enable him to undertake a Journey to Toulon & other parts of France for the purpose of ascertaining the Naval Force, and Stores in the Arsenals	150
16	Thomas Green for Services performed	4 4
29	Mr James Johnstone Do	20
Decem.r 2	Will.m Alvey for discovering the overtures which had been made to him by Mr John Brunner, a Foreigner, with a view to his procuring from the Office of Ordnance Copies of the Contracts for Stores, the prices and quantity of each article in Store	10
		6745 13 9

Secret Service Accounts (W. L. Clements Library, Michigan)

Lord Sydney was responsible for the Secret Service which spied on Britain's enemies, including France. In this extract from the Secret Service Accounts, Captain Arthur Phillip was paid 150 pounds on 11 November 1784 for travelling 'to Toulon and other parts of France for the purpose of ascertaining the naval force and stores in their arsenals'.

Governor Arthur Phillip (Mitchell Library, Sydney)

The first lord of the admiralty made it clear that he would not have chosen Captain Phillip to be the first governor of the convict colony in New South Wales. But Lord Sydney, who selected Phillip, had come to admire his work as a part time spy and never doubted that he was the best person for this unprecedented mission.

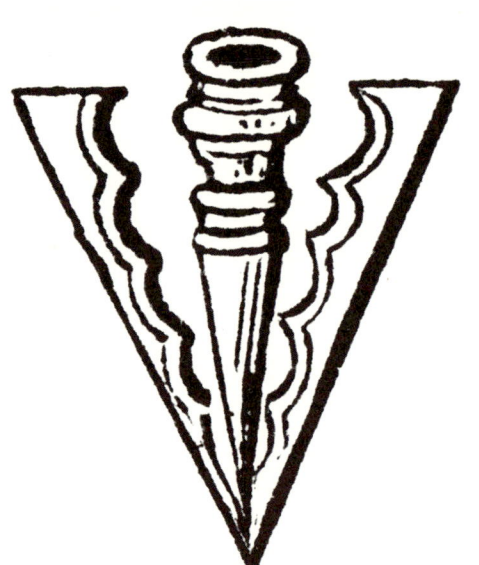

View of Sydney Cove in 1794
(Mitchell Library, Sydney)

Sydney Cove, around which the Sydney metropolitan area later grew, was named by Arthur Phillip in honour of Lord Sydney on 23 January 1788. 'It has the best spring of water', Phillip said. '[And] ships can anchor so close to the shore that at a very small expense, quays may be made at which the largest ships may unload'.

A Pheon or Broad Arrow (public domain)

Algernon Sidney and his younger brother, Henry, both had pheons incorporated in their coats of arms. After Henry became master-general of ordnance, pheons were used to mark all government property. So when convicts landed at Botany Bay 'all covered in broad arrows' they literally bore the Sidney family's mark.

Ben-nil-long in 1798 (National Library of Australia)

Originally captured by Governor Phillip so he could learn the local Aborigines' language and customs, Bennelong accompanied Phillip back to England in 1792. He was presented to George III and spent time with Lord Sydney and his family, before returning to Sydney Cove in 1795. Bennelong was the first Australian born adult to make this return trip.

> Copy of a letter from a Native of Botany Bay / to Mr Phillips
> Lord Sydney's Steward / being returned to his own country
> after he had resided a short time in England.

Sidney Cove
New S. Wales Aug.st 29
1796

Sir/ I am very well. I hope you are very well. I live at the Governor's. I have every day dinner there. I have not my wife: another black man took her away: we have had murry✗ doings: he spear'd me in the back, but I better now: his name is now ✗ſarroway. all my friends alive & well. not me go to England no more. I am at home now. I hope Sir you send me anything you please Sir. hope all are well in England. I hope Mrs Phillips very well. you nurse me Madam when I sick. you very good Madam: thank you Madam, & hope you remember me Madam, not forget. I know you very well Madam. Madam I want Stockings. thank you Madam; send me two pair stockings. you very good Madam. Thank you Madam. Sir, you give my duty to L.d Sydney. Thank you very good my Lord. very good: hope very well all family. very well. Sir, send me you please some Handkerchiefs for Pocket. you please Sir send me some shoes: two pair you please Sir.

Bannolong

✗ meaning bad.   ✗ they frequently change their names

Bennelong's thankyou letter (National Library of Australia)

On 29 May 1796, Bennelong sent a letter to Lord Sydney's steward, Mr Phillips. Addressing Phillips' wife, Bennelong said: 'You nurse me Madam when I sick. You very good Madam'. He continued: 'Sir you give my duty to Ld Sydney. Thank you very good my Lord very good: hope very well all family. Very well'.

Deputy Judge Advocate David Collins (National Archives of Australia)
Ignoring the first lord of the admiralty's objections, Sydney ensured that the convict colony would have a civil court. In July 1788, Collins presided over the first case. It involved two convicts who successfully sued the captain of a convict transport for lost property. In England, they would have been barred from taking such an action.

The Great Seal of NSW – 1790 (Mitchell Library, Sydney)

On 21 May 1790, Lord Sydney was present at a Privy Council meeting presided over by George III during which a great seal was approved for the NSW Government. It depicted 'convicts landed at Botany Bay; their fetters taken off and received by Industry sitting on a Bale of Goods' – a symbol of hope and redemption.

[*Twenty-eight*]

Transportation where?

With the Americas now ruled out as a convict destination, Lord Sydney again turned to the Company of Merchants trading with Africa, pressuring them 'to receive and dispose of…Twenty Men Convicts in the safest and best manner'. The company, however, drove a hard bargain, demanding that the government pay for the ongoing upkeep of these men, whose labour the merchants would enjoy without charge. A commercial dispute over their transport, the *Recovery*, cost the government still more. In the end, the convicts were parcelled out among Britain's forts. The cost involved, combined with the high mortality rate, made Sydney realise that the West African Gold Coast was as unsuitable for transportation as the Americas.[1]

What Sydney was searching for was a scheme which would better fit with his 'constitutional spirit', as Hampden had put it, while at the same time allowing for the transportation of greater numbers of convicts. And so he looked again at a proposal, which had first been put to the Bunbury committee in 1779, for a convict settlement to be established on Lemane Island about 400 miles up the River Gambia. This idea had received fresh impetus from John Barnes, a merchant who had lived and traded in this area, which was located on Africa's Atlantic coast, approximately 1,125 miles west-north-west of the Gold Coast. The island's fertile soil, Barnes said, would easily support 4,000 people, who could govern themselves through an elected chief and council. Only a single guardship down river, he claimed, would be needed to prevent their escape.[2]

As the home secretary continued to weigh up Africa as a convict destination, James Matra referred his New South Wales' plan to Charles Fox, but the opposition seemed uninterested. Matra had a reputation for double-dealing, praising Fox to his face and calling him 'a dangerous man' behind his back. After an approach from the De Lancey brothers, who wanted their loyalist kinsmen resettled in New South Wales, Matra again approached the Home Office. In doing so, he took up a suggestion from the attorney-general, Pepper Arden, that ships engaged in the China tea trade could help offset the cost of convict transports to Botany Bay. Now the Home Office began to listen.[3]

The next cabinet meeting had to deal with more pressing Home Office business – a threatened Spanish attack on British colonists in Central America. But at the meeting after that, in December 1784, Sydney proposed 'a settlement upon the coast of New South Wales... as an asylum for some of the American loyalists... and also a place for the transportation of young offenders whose crimes had not been of the most heinous nature'. It was Sydney's variation of Matra's plan. Conscious of the vast distances involved, cabinet wanted the first lord of the admiralty to investigate further, and on Boxing Day Sydney delivered his working papers to Lord Howe, who soon voiced concern. 'The length of navigation subject to all the retardments of an India voyage', Howe said, 'do not, I must confess, encourage me to hope for a return of the many advantages in commerce or war which Mr M. Matra has in contemplation'.[4]

Being a junior minister, the attorney-general was not privy to cabinet discussions about Matra's plan. Still, Arden's interest in the plan grew, fuelled by a procedural crisis in his courts. Despite a new form of sentence which left it to 'the King in Council to declare the place to which the convicts... sentenced [to transportation] should be sent', some judges were still sentencing them to Africa. Others were refusing to order transportation at all; for them, a sentence which did not specify a destination was too uncertain. More and more convicts ended up being sentenced to imprisonment in the already overcrowded county jails. Under increasing pressure, the attorney-general sent the home secretary a plan drawn up by a senior captain, Sir George Young. Like Matra, Young stressed the advantages of trade, especially with China, that a settlement at Botany Bay would bring. 'Upon a cursory view... [Young's plan is] the most likely method of effectually disposing of the convicts', Arden said, 'the number of which requires the immediate interference of Government'.[5]

The attorney-general's support for Lord Sydney's modification to Matra's plan – to focus on convicts rather than loyalists – was useful. And so too was Sir George Young's proposal, because his hands-on experience of the India and

China runs meant he could answer Lord Howe's concerns. But Young, who had close ties to the King through his captaincy of the royal yacht, prefaced his advice with the bold introduction: 'had I command of this expedition'. Like Matra before him, who wanted to be the governor of any new colony, Young's plan was about getting a job.[6]

For the next few weeks, Sydney weighed up whether to choose Botany Bay, or Lemane Island in the Gambia River. Then, on 9 February 1785, he ordered that Lemane be occupied – in anticipation of 200 convicts being sent there to form their own settlement. The plan he adopted was to provide these felons with supplies after which they would then 'left to themselves', except for a guardship down river to deter escapees. In light of the arrangements later made for the First Fleet to Botany Bay, Sydney now appears naïve to have thought that convicts could be left to their own devices in this way, but the plan fitted the theory underpinning the new Transportation Act where convicts were pardoned conditionally on not returning to Britain during their term of transportation. This concept of convicts as settlers also fitted the home secretary's liberal approach: they 'would not be bound in servitude'.[7]

However, in March 1785, Sydney's old friend and now political enemy Edmund Burke did him what, with the benefit of hindsight, was a favour, although that was certainly not Burke's intention, nor was it how Sydney saw it at the time. In politics, what goes around often comes around: Sydney, who had loudly attacked Lord North's convict policy from the relative safety of opposition, now found himself under attack from Burke over the 'melancholy situation' of those sentenced to transportation. That Sydney was now in the House of Lords was little comfort to him as Burke let fly in the Commons on 16 March:

> What was to be done with these unhappy wretches; and to what part of the world was it intended they should be sent. He hoped it was not to Gambia... where all life dies and all death lives.

When Burke was told point-blank that no contract had yet been entered into for sending these convicts to the coast of Africa, he remained suspicious. And on 11 April he claimed in the House that 75 convicts 'might sail before morning'.

Knowing full well that Sydney had only deferred transportation to Africa 'until [the end of] the ... sickly season', when it would begin, Prime Minister Pitt relied on a technicality, accusing Burke of pre-empting a report to Parliament. Furious at being side-tracked in this way, Burke now supported Lord Beauchamp's call for a select committee to inquire into 'the manner in which the Government intended to dispose of felons under sentence of transportation'. Within days, a select committee was up and running with Lord Beauchamp as chairman.[8]

Beauchamp's committee duly sat between 26 April and 3 May. In his evidence, the permanent head of the Home Office, Evan Nepean, acknowledged that many places for transportation had been suggested; he conceded that the government 'preferred [Lemane] to every other plan though [it] was not finally resolved on'. Pressed further, he admitted that '200 convicts were to be sent ... [there] in a transport or two chartered for that purpose'. Next to give evidence was the African merchant John Barnes, who proudly claimed the credit for proposing Lemane. 'In different conversations with Lord Sydney', Barnes said, 'the plan had been formed'. Talking up his recommended choice, Barnes claimed that Lemane was a fertile, healthy place where the natives were friendly. For Sydney, the embarrassment of knowing that his African plan had been disclosed was offset by Barnes's evidence that it was a good choice.[9]

But then things took a turn for the worse. Two African traders, an African army surgeon, and the seafarers Sir George Young and Commodore Edward Thompson tore the plan to pieces. They said it was likely to start a war with the natives, lead to escapes and cause many deaths from sickness and starvation. The evidence of two MPs with experience in Africa was just as damning. All this was reported to the House by Lord Beauchamp on 9 May. What Beauchamp did not report to the House was that just days earlier his committee had begun the second stage of its hearings, this time examining James Matra and Sir Joseph Banks, among others, about the suitability of New South Wales as a convict destination. The committee also directed its chairman 'to apply to Lord Sydney ... for copies of all plans which have been submitted to Government for the transportation of criminals which might be attended to with no public inconvenience'. Now under great pressure, Sydney played loose with the truth. 'Different ideas had been suggested', he said, 'but they were either made in conversation or appeared from the nature of them unworthy of the attention of the Committee and... no such plan as was required existed in his office'. Despite strong evidence to the contrary, the committee took this answer no further except to testily observe that they had 'no materials to proceed upon' other than those provided by the witnesses. Perhaps Chairman Beauchamp's manners, described by Wraxall as 'noble yet ingratiating', help to explain why.[10]

Indeed on 29 June 1785 an apparently exasperated Beauchamp admitted to the House of Commons that as chairman of the transportation committee he should have stated some place for the settlement of convicts. 'But a particular circumstance occurred during the sitting of the committee', he said, 'that rendered it improper for him to mention it at the time'. By then he had heard evidence from Matra and Banks strongly supportive of New South Wales. Questioned about Botany Bay's suitability as a site for a convict colony, Matra replied that '500 [convicts] might go with safety'. However, while this evidence apparently found its way into Home Office files, it was not included in Lord Beauchamp's later report to the House. Perhaps embarrassed, Beauchamp never did explain why. The most likely answer is that Sydney had leaned on Beauchamp to recommend an African destination because, as the committee itself pointed out, 'criminals are being condemned to be transported... [to Africa] at every sessions', and Sydney was concerned that convicts sentenced to transportation to Africa could not lawfully be sent to Botany Bay.[11]

Beauchamp delivered his report to the House on 28 July 1785. First of all, the report rejected the idea that convicts could be 'settled' without strict government supervision. Then it prioritized its list of places to search for a suitable location. Africa was first, followed by British North America, and then by 'such other parts of the globe as have already or which may be taken possession of... without violating the territorial rights of any European State'. From this process only one option emerged – Das Voltas Bay on the south-west coast of Africa. It was claimed by no other state and, according to sketchy accounts, contained plenty of 'wood, water, antelopes and wild fowls'. After noting that a settlement there would provide Britain with a staging port for Indian commerce, the committee effectively endorsed Das Voltas Bay by nominating Commodore Thompson, whose proposal it was, to be put in charge. Although the home secretary had been leaning towards Africa too, he refused to commit to Das Voltas Bay without further investigation. In August he directed Commodore Thompson to go there in the sloop *Nautilus*, to select 'a proper spot for the making of a settlement if… judged expedient'.[12]

As he waited for Thompson to report back, the political pressure on Sydney grew. According to *The Times*, jailers everywhere complained about 'the numerous convicts in custody for transportable offences who… [were] becoming daring and outrageous'. In February 1786 the prime minister admitted in the Commons that 'great difficulty lay in fixing upon a fit place for the transportation of convicts'. Responding to a complaint from Lord John Cavendish about overcrowding in Derby's county jail, Sydney noted that many of the inmates had been sentenced to transportation to Africa. 'This was the wish of many others', he continued, '[because] no climate is worse than a jail'. While acknowledging his critics' claims that Africa might be 'impracticable', it was still his solution. And intelligence from Paris that the Comte de La Perouse was about to set out on a voyage to the South Seas, during which he would set up a convict colony in New Zealand, did not change Sydney's mind.

A year passed before the *Nautilus* finally returned from Africa, on 23 July 1786, under the command of Thompson's nephew. The commodore was dead. And those who remained had found 'no bay, river or inlet but only a steep barren rocky shoreline… without… a drop of fresh water or… a tree'. It was now almost a year and a half since Edmund Burke had asked in the Commons, 'to what part of the world was it intended [the convicts] would be sent?' The home secretary desperately needed an answer without the very long delay involved in yet another survey.[13]

In recommending Botany Bay on the New South Wales coast for a convict colony, Lord Sydney placed great weight on James Matra's evidence to the Beauchamp committee, which had found its way into Home Office files. When asked on 9 May 1785 whether the government would run any risk in sending convicts there 'without further examination… of that country', Matra had replied, 'I think they would not'. On the following day Sir Joseph Banks had suggested Botany Bay 'was in every respect adequate to the purpose', both men having been there with James Cook in 1770. Lord Sydney's mind was made up by Matra's evidence that no further examination of New South Wales was needed, or really possible, given the urgent need for action. Africa was unsuitable and North America was unwilling. And so by a process of elimination driven by the political need to do something, the Pitt government adopted Sydney's recommendation, nominating New South Wales as the place to which convicts would be sent under the Transportation Act of 1784. While no minutes of this historic decision are known to survive, there can be no doubt that a cabinet resolution based on Sydney's recommendation was made – because the Transportation Act required it. Joining in the immediate chorus of criticism, Nathaniel Wraxall described the choice as 'beneath the disquisition of reason and below the efforts of ridicule'. Only years later would he finally acknowledge that New South Wales was 'better calculated [than Africa] for every object of policy and punishment without losing sight of humanity'.[14]

[*Twenty-nine*]

⸺ The First Fleet ⸺

Lord Sydney's instruction to the Treasury to 'forthwith' provide 'a proper number of vessels for the conveying of 750 convicts to Botany Bay' was brusque. Issued on 18 August 1786, less than a month after the *Nautilus* returned from Africa, its businesslike language obscured the fact that never before in history had such an enterprise been attempted. This may have been the home secretary's intention. Still harbouring strong reservations about Botany Bay, the last thing Sydney wanted to emphasise was the unprecedented scope of his order. Almost as if to bolster this choice, an accompanying document, Heads of a Plan, noted that 'it may be remiss to remark [on Botany Bay's] 'considerable advantage... to us as a naval power'. However, when the first lord of the admiralty received his copy of the plan, there is no evidence to suggest that he was any more impressed with this naval argument than he had been in December 1784.

Although Sydney had relied on Matra and Banks in choosing Botany Bay, he remained sceptical about some of their claims. In 1770 they had described the land there as rocky, swampy and sandy; later they had changed their stories – Matra claiming that all European produce would grow there, and Banks telling the Bunbury committee that the convicts would be able 'to maintain themselves... after the first year'. Concerned that these later claims were exaggerations, the home secretary directed that two years' supplies be provided.[1]

The Transportation Act of 1784 stipulated that convict overseers 'could inflict... such moderate punishment... as may be inflicted by law on persons committed to a House of Correction'. Regardless of where they were sent, the convicts had substantial rights under British law, just as their overseers had substantial responsibilities. When Sydney had sent convicts to Africa and the Americas, the assumption was that there would always be settlers or the commanders of forts to receive them. And for a while, relaxed standards were excused by wartime conditions. Lemane, it is true, would have been different, but Sydney now seemed to accept that his proposal to leave unsupervised convicts there had been ill-advised and unworkable. As he now saw it, the Transportation Act imposed on both him and all who carried out his orders a duty of care to the convicts, albeit a primitive one by modern standards. At Botany Bay, where there were no European colonists or forts, this duty of care would be onerous.[2]

Sydney himself was now responsible for both the voyage and the settlement, right down to itemized lists of 1,000 panes of glass, fishing hooks and nails. Other stores included 1045 rations. 'Allowing for deaths and disasters during the passage', the chief clerk said, '1000 rations... will be sufficient'. In fact, there were to be only 25 deaths during the voyage. The stores issued to male convicts included two jackets, three trousers, four woollen drawers and three shirts. To identify them as government property, they were stamped with pheons (broad arrows). These devices had been used by Algernon Sidney in his coat of arms over a century earlier and Algernon's younger brother Henry had later incorporated them in his official seal. In 1693, after Henry became master-general of ordnance in charge of government supplies, these arrow heads were used to mark all government property. The convicts who arrived at Botany Bay in clothes 'all daubed with broad arrows' literally bore the Sydney family's mark.[3]

The Heads of a Plan drew heavily on a number of sources, including submissions by James Matra, Sir George Young and the attorney-general, but not all their ideas were taken up. There was no reference to trade, except for the colony's own needs. And neither Matra nor Young were selected for command. As a consolation, Matra was appointed British consul at Tangier. From there, he reported to the home secretary about the caravan trade 'to Tambuctoo', while Young became a commissioner of Thames Navigation and, later on, a full admiral. John Blankett was apparently the Admiralty's choice, but his chances with Lord Sydney had probably been cruelled by his failed plan to attack Spanish South America in early 1783.[4]

The Beauchamp committee had stressed that the success of a convict colony in a far-away place would depend on the wisdom of the person in charge, who should have 'the most absolute control'. This was taken up in the Heads of a Plan, which provided that 'the whole regulation... of the settlement should be committed to ... a discreet officer'. Specifically, the naval commander on the voyage out would, upon arrival, be the governor. On 31 August 1786, Lord Sydney sent a copy of this document to the Admiralty, with a covering letter directing that a ship of war, commanded by such an officer, be made available 'with all possible expedition'. A requisition was also made for 160 marines, whose commanding officer would double as lieutenant-governor. But all personnel, from the governor down, would be subject to the home secretary's direction.

Sydney's letter suggests that he was leaving it up to the Admiralty to choose the governor, but this was not so. The person chosen, Arthur Phillip, had never been fully appreciated by the Admiralty, despite his long and meritorious naval service; his exotic looks did not help. Of less than average height with an olive complexion, a long hooked fleshy nose and dark eyes which had a hint of the orient about them, the only thing Phillip shared in common with the typical British naval officer was a sharp and powerful voice. Behind the scenes, it was Sydney who had chosen Phillip, leaving the admiralty chief, Lord Howe, nonplussed:

> The settlement of the convicts as you have determined being a matter so immediately connected to your Department, I could never have a thought of contesting the choice you would make of the officer to be entrusted with the conduct of it.
>
> I cannot say from the little knowledge I have of Captain Philips [*sic*] would have led me to select him for a service of this complicated nature. But as you are satisfied of his ability and I conclude he will be taken under your direction I presume it will not be unreasonable to move the King for having his Majesty's pleasure signified to the Admiralty for these purposes as soon as you see proper that no time may be lost in making the requisite preparations.[5]

Arthur Phillip was Sydney's man.

This fact is not universally accepted and some have suggested that the treasury secretary, George Rose, chose Phillip. But Rose's own published diaries make no reference to Phillip and nor does Rose's biographer. By contrast, Phillip's letters to the home secretary indicate a longstanding friendship. Writing to Sydney six months after arriving at Botany Bay, the governor requested that 'his compliments may be made acceptable to Lady Sydney and family', at the same time expressing sorrow that he had not been able 'to procure any small birds for Miss Townshend to whom your Lordship will please make my compliments'. This is the letter of a friend, not merely of someone flattering his patron.[6]

On 5 September 1786 the Navy Office responded to the Heads of a Plan. Its claim that the shipping requested could 'be got ready in six weeks' soon proved to be optimistic, however. At the beginning of December, Phillips' flagship *Sirius* was still not ready, while the transport, *Alexander*, continued to have security problems. Only two cross-bars secured by a 'common staple and padlock' secured her main hatch, which 'might with great ease be broke open'. Meanwhile, it had taken the Admiralty until 12 October to formally nominate the *Sirius* as the ship of war, with Phillip as its commander. Having no second thoughts about this officer, who he had already effectively chosen, Sydney issued Phillip's first commission as governor that same day. It was a simple document, which the historian Alan Atkinson has observed made Phillip 'look more like the governor of a fort than the governor of a colony'.[7]

In effect, Phillip's first commission was a holding document, which gave him the authority to get the First Fleet ready. This he proceeded to do with great energy, improving the transports' security and obtaining better medical supplies. He also lobbied on the marines' behalf for an alcohol allowance. Just as Phillip realized that extra work was required to prepare the fleet, so Sydney realized that more had to be done to establish the legal framework for a settlement of conditionally pardoned convicts. Gone were the days when it was thought that they could be left to their own devices at remote places like Lemane Island. Accordingly, the home secretary focused on a second commission containing more checks on the governor, as well as on legislation which balanced military authority with the introduction of civil government. At least one of Sydney's cabinet colleagues, Lord Howe, expressed surprise. Convicts and soldiers alike should be subject to military law, he said. And why was a deputy judge advocate needed to preside at court hearings between convicts?[8]

As Sydney's framework became increasingly complex, so the staff establishment grew. To the original list of a governor, lieutenant-governor, commissary of stores, surgeon, two mates and a chaplain were added a deputy judge advocate, provost marshal, surveyor of lands and an agent. Such people were necessary to give effect to Sydney's goal of emancipating the convicts and settling them as free men and women at the earliest opportunity. Recognizing that Phillip's responsibilities would now be more onerous, Sydney doubled his salary to 1000 pounds per year.[9]

To secure the services of the *Alexander* and other merchant transports like her, advertisements had been placed in London's papers, and on 14 September *The Times* turned them into a story about the government's plan for Botany Bay. With the full scope of his project now emerging in the press, the home secretary wrote to the East India Company. Acknowledging that Botany Bay fell within its chartered territory, Sydney asked for the company's 'concurrence' to his Heads of a Plan. '[It was] a means of preventing the emigration of our European neighbours to that quarter', he claimed, 'which might be attended with infinite prejudice to the Company's affairs'. Although the prime minister and home secretary were on the company's board of control, they did not want to upset the multinational which had put them into office in December 1783. After due consideration, the company gave its concurrence, on condition that the transports would be sailing under its license.[10]

On 24 October a number of senior appointments were settled. Although he had 'failed to impress' Lord Sydney, and was later described by one of his lieutenants as being 'without exception the most disagreeable commanding officer I ever knew', Major Robert Ross was appointed lieutenant-governor on the recommendation of Evan Nepean, who had served with him during the American revolutionary war. By contrast, the deputy judge advocate, David Collins, was probably the home secretary's choice, his grandfather Arthur Collins having published the Sidney Papers some years earlier. On 15 December cabinet authorized the appointment of John Hunter to command the *Sirius* at sea whenever the governor was required to remain ashore. As a volunteer, Hunter had helped prepare the *Sirius* and there was no shortage of others willing to make the long voyage. According to *The Times*, the flattering descriptions of Botany Bay's climate 'had induced great numbers of the lower ranks ... to accompany the felons'. Most of the convicts chosen were under 30. And while some preferred hanging, others deliberately committed crimes to be sent to Botany Bay.[11]

The merchant transports were comparatively new ships which were hired under contracts drawn up with 'meticulous care'. The masters of these vessels, the *Alexander, Borrowdale, Charlotte, Fishburn, Friendship, Golden Grove, Lady Penhryn* and *Scarborough*, were placed under Arthur Phillip's command. Sir George Young's proposal to save money by using China ships was adopted. 'We have taken up the *Scarborough*, *Lady Penhryn* and *Charlotte* to bring home teas at the rate of 10 pounds per ton builders measurement', the East India Company's directors noted, 'provided that they do not sail from Canton with less than eight men and a boy for each 100 tons'. In fact the *Lady Penhryn* had been taken up for a great deal more, with secret instructions to sail for Canton via Nootka Sound (near modern Vancouver) to trade furs.[12]

The arrangements with the East India Company meant that the government would not have to pay for the return of three empty convict transports because they would be full of tea. 'A very considerable saving would arise to the public', Sydney said, 'in the freight of these vessels'. For its part, the company would not have to pay for empty transports all the way to China because for much of the way they would be full of convicts paid for by the government. Such was the true importance of the China trade to the first settlement of New South Wales. Apart from this, Phillip was ordered to prevent foreign trade 'by every possible means', and there was to be a ban on building merchant ships, except those necessary for the essential provisioning of the settlement. Java, Botany Bay's nearest European settlement, also imposed trade limitations – the Dutch factor (agent) there would not permit any foreign trade until he had been bribed. According to one old salt, 'about 10 pounds in addition to some English beer (perhaps a few dozen) will satisfy him'.[13]

Filling the transports with convicts, many of whom had been pardoned on condition that they would be transported to a place visited only once by Europeans, was a serious legal business. The warrants to do so were signed by the secretary of state. One of them, dated 3 January 1787, directed the superintendent of convicts on the hulks, Duncan Campbell, to 'forthwith deliver to … Mr William Richards shipbroker … and Mr Duncan Sinclair, master of the transport ship *Alexander* … the convicts now in your custody'. As contractor for the voyage, Richards was one of Sydney's most important appointments. But only occasionally did the home secretary intervene in the selection of convicts and their kin; and then only in the most extraordinary circumstances.

At Plymouth, the master of the hulk *Dunkirk* refused to let the baby son of a female convict on board. The jailer, John Simpson, who had delivered mother and child from Norwich prison on the assumption that both of them were to be sent to Botany Bay, dashed off, babe in arms, to London. There he proceeded to lobby the home secretary on the steps to his office. Initially sceptical, Lord Sydney's sympathy was aroused when told that the baby's mother, Susannah Holmes, was contemplating suicide. Upon being informed that the father, Henry Cable, a fellow Norwich jail inmate, wanted to marry Susannah and go to Botany Bay too, Sydney, the soft touch, decided that something must be done. He directed that both Cable and the infant join Susannah at Plymouth. Simpson rode back to Norwich with the baby, collected Cable and then escorted them both to Plymouth. 'In total', Simpson said, 'I travelled with [the baby] in my lap upwards of seven hundred miles'. Soon the press got hold of the story. Public sympathy for the Cables was such that clothes and books to a value of 20 pounds were donated for their use at Botany Bay.[14]

At the opening of Parliament on 23 January 1787, George III referred only briefly to the 750-odd convicts, many of whom were already aboard their ships. 'A plan has been formed ... for transporting a number of convicts to ... [reduce] the crowded state of the jails', the king said, 'and Parliament would take such farther measures as may be necessary'. One of these was the New South Wales Judicature Bill to establish a criminal court, which being non-controversial, passed both Houses within a month. Although the court was to be constituted by military officers, it was to apply the ordinary criminal law. As Sydney had hoped, the convicts would be treated by the courts as English civilians and not be subjected to military law. By a separate warrant, a civil court was also set up.[15]

From the beginning, the home secretary had insisted on generous rations for the marines and convicts alike. 'Few ... soldiers going out on foreign-service ... were ever better if so well provided for', the *Lady Penrhyn's* surgeon said, 'as these convicts are'. Further, Sydney sought out the surgeon general to ensure that all necessary instruments and medicines were included. The home secretary's 'humanity' in providing extra medical supplies was acknowledged by John White, who was to be the colony's principal surgeon. Sydney felt the need to emphasise, that the extra wine was to be administered only to the sick.[16]

All the while, Arthur Phillip's agile mind had been full of requests, sparking a frenetic correspondence with the secretaries of the Admiralty, Home Office and Treasury. Most problems were solved satisfactorily and those that were not ended up on the home secretary's desk. When Phillip expressed concern that the number of transports allocated to the First Fleet was an insufficient 'quantity of tonnage' for the number of convicts to be transported, Lord Sydney did not hesitate to 'cause another vessel to be taken up'. And the *Prince of Wales* was added to the fleet. On another occasion when Phillip was having trouble with the Navy Board over supplies for the marines, Sydney intervened to ensure that they were provided by the First Fleet's private contractor.[17]

By mid-March 1787, when all the convicts had been embarked, Phillip and his deputy, Major Ross, were seeing the same things differently. Some convicts had by now been aboard their transports for almost three months. And while Ross had 'great pleasure' in reporting that they all appeared to be 'perfectly satisfied and obedient', Phillip saw room for improvement. He ordered fresh clothes for all and requested that the *Alexander* be thoroughly cleansed. 'If the evils complained of were now neglected', he said, 'it may be too late hereafter'. Acting promptly, the home secretary saw to it that alternative accommodation for the *Alexander's* convicts was found so that she could be disinfected. Then Sydney reviewed all the correspondence between Phillip and the bureaucrats, giving the governor permission to convert a transport into a hospital ship should 'disease render it absolutely necessary'. As was customary for senior commanders many months sailing distance from London, Phillip was also allowed a wide discretion to act 'until his Majesty's pleasure be known'. And he was given permission to resettle somewhere else on the New South Wales east coast if Botany Bay was found to be unsuitable.[18]

Being so far away from London and without any council to advise him, the governor's powers at Botany Bay would be unprecedented. A commission dated 2 April 1787 allowed him to administer oaths, appoint justices, pardon and reprieve, levy forces for defence, proclaim martial law and punish offenders. And just over three weeks later came more instructions. The first draft of these had directed that 'the laws against blasphemy, profanity, adultery, fornication, polygamy, incest … swearing and drunkenness were to be vigorously executed'. But this was soon toned down to 'the due observance of religion and good order'. Pursuant to Phillip's second commission, convicts could be emancipated and discharged. The governor was instructed to grant land to any who were – 30 acres for a single man, 20 more for a married man and still 10 more for each child. He was also directed to settle Norfolk Island 'to prevent it being occupied by any other European power.[19]

In line with Sydney's enlightened defence of the Carribs fifteen years earlier, Phillip was ordered to treat the Aborigines with respect:

> [He was] to endeavour by every possible means to open an intercourse with the natives and to conciliate their affections enjoining all subjects to live in amity and kindness with them ... If anyone shall wantonly destroy them or give them any unnecessary interruption in the exercise of their several occupations ... you [will] cause such offenders to be brought to punishment according to the degree of the offence.

However, there was no mention of any treaty with them because the lands they occupied had, in British eyes, belonged to the Crown since James Cook first claimed possession of them seventeen years earlier.[20]

In early May 1787 there was some final unpleasantness concerning the lieutenant-governor, Major Ross. Whereas Phillip was concerned about 'supplying both marines and convicts', Ross's priority was always for the welfare of his men, sometimes at the convicts' expense. Just days before the fleet set sail, Ross insisted on the 'usual supply' of alcohol for his marines. The home secretary thought that this was ill advised. However, upon learning of Phillip's fear of the 'very disagreeable consequences' if Ross's demands were not met, Sydney relented. Still, it was John Hunter rather than Ross who was issued with the dormant commission to succeed Phillip, should he become incapacitated. Sydney had a low opinion of the lieutenant-governor.[21]

Finally, on 10 May, Phillip signalled the First Fleet to get under way, but he was foiled by what in the eighteenth century verged on mutiny – today, an industrial dispute. 'The seamen on board several of the transports, refusing to get their ships under sail', he reported, 'put me under the disagreeable necessity of ordering eight men to be taken out of the *Fishburn*'. Those sailors had refused to unmoor their ship, and it was not until three days later, after the *Fishburn's* master paid those who remained '3 guineas a piece', that the fleet finally set sail. There was more trouble on 20 May over a convict plan to seize the *Scarborough*, but this conspiracy was foiled and the ringleaders were transferred to the *Sirius*. By that evening, about 100 leagues clear of the English Channel, Phillip was confident enough to allow his escort frigate, the *Hyena*, to return to port. At last, the First Fleet was on its own – to make its way half way around the world, a voyage of 16,000 miles, at the speed of a man walking.[22]

From Teneriffe, on 10 June, Phillip reported that the convicts were in better health than they had been when the fleet left England. And from Rio de Janiero on 2 September he advised that only fifteen convicts and one marine's child had died so far. Two months later, the fleet reached the Cape of Good Hope. 'All the ships were very amply supplied with soft bread, vegetables and fresh meat', Phillip said, 'and there are very few sick at present'. On 12 November 1787, Phillip left the Cape, embarking on a voyage a part of which had never before been sailed by Europeans. Many of the transports strung out behind his flagship were now so crammed with livestock that they resembled little Noah's Arks.[23]

[*Thirty*]

─ Sydney Cove ─

After splitting from the rest of his fleet in the *Supply* to make faster time, Governor Phillip arrived safely at Botany Bay on 18 January 1788. But when he and Lieutenant King went ashore, Aborigines confronted them. 'They called to us in a menacing tone', King said, 'at the same time brandishing their spears'. The Aborigines were keen to assert their possession over a place which soon left the Europeans less than enthused. As Phillip saw it, Botany Bay lacked an adequate fresh water supply and was badly exposed to high winds. 'If we had stayed [there]', one officer noted, 'it would have been the grave of us all'. It was clear too that Matra and Banks had misrepresented the quality of the soil. 'Upon first sight one would be induced to think this a most fertile spot', a ship's surgeon said. 'But upon nearer inspection ... the soil is not fit for the vegetation of anything'. And within days, Phillip was in search of a better place.[1]

On 21 January the governor led a small band of explorers out of Botany Bay in three open boats. Once clear of the bay's low sandstone cape, they made for Port Jackson, nine miles to the north, which had been named by James Cook but not entered by him. As the Europeans hugged the coast, the Aborigines shouted from the cliff tops – 'Walla Walla' (Go Away) – the same cry that had greeted Cook eighteen years earlier. Entering Port Jackson in the early afternoon, Phillip described what he saw as 'the finest harbour in the world'. To no avail, the Aborigines continued shouting as the boat crews separated to examine the harbour's inlets.

After a night sleeping on the beach at Camp Cove, Phillip pushed on and explored the inner harbour. As he later told Lord Sydney, he soon came upon a cove that:

had the best spring of water and in which…ships can anchor so close to the shore that at a very small expense quays may be made at which the largest ships may unload. This cove, which I honoured with the name of Sydney, is about a quarter of a mile across and half a mile in length.[2]

Many years later, Phillip's boat-keeper, Jacob Nagle, recalled landing on the western shore, not far from a run of fresh water. While the others explored this stream, Nagle waited by his boat and began fishing:

I hove my line over…[and] hauled up a large black bream…The Governor coming down very much pleased with this cove…observed the fish I had ketched…'Recollect' said he 'that you are the first white man that ever caught a fish in Sidney Cove where the town is to be built.

In London that same evening, Lord Sydney held a dinner at his townhouse in Grosvenor Square, Mayfair, one of London's most exclusive addresses. Sydney's guests included His Royal Highness the Duke of York, Prime Minister Pitt and George, Marquess Townshend. But whatever honour those gentlemen did Sydney that night, it was nothing compared to Arthur Phillip's gesture of naming Sydney Cove after the home secretary, even though it took fourteen months for this news to reach him.[3]

On 23 January Phillip returned to Botany Bay, where he was met by a chorus of concern about the exposed coast line, poor soil and lack of fresh water. Acting on the discretion Sydney had given him, he promptly ordered the fleet to relocate. On 25 January the ships weighed anchor, but they were then hit by a massive thunderstorm and only the *Supply*, with the governor aboard, was able to work its way to open water and reach Sydney Cove. There, at dawn the next day, the Union Jack was raised and 'possession was taken for His Majesty'. Meanwhile, back at Botany Bay, the remainder of the fleet weighed anchor for a second time. As if to underscore the danger of the bay's prevailing winds, the *Fishburn* soon collided with the *Prince of Wales*, destroying some of her sails, before running into the *Charlotte* and destroying woodwork on her stern. In all, it took the *Fishburn* six hours to 'turn out' of Botany Bay and she did not arrive at Port Jackson until 4 pm. As this all-day parade of damaged vessels dropped anchor again after a short sail up the coast, each ship's master signed off his logs: 'moored in Sydney Cove, Port Jackson'. Phillip's name for 'the place now destined for...the reception of the new settlement' had already taken hold.

After a miserable few days at Botany Bay, the first fleeters were in awe of their new surroundings. According to Lieutenant Smyth:

> The finest terraced lawns and grottos...in any nobleman's grounds... cannot excel in beauty those [that] nature now presented...The...flight of numerous parraquets, lorrequets, cockatoos and macaws, made all around appear like an enchantment; the stupendous rocks from the summit of the hills down to the very water's edge...forming the most commodious quays by the water, beggared all description.[4]

The female convicts remained aboard their transports for the next few days, while their male counterparts undertook the back-breaking work of clearing enough timber to pitch tents for all. Then on 6 February, in anticipation of a formal ceremony the following day during which the governor's commission would be read out, the women disembarked. 'While they were on board ship', Captain Watkin Tench observed, 'the two sexes had been kept most rigorously apart; but when landed, their separation became impracticable'. Some of them had not been ashore for more than a year. 'Their old habits of depravity', Tench noted drolly, 'were beginning to recur'. Indeed it was not long before they were all swept up in a drunken orgy. And as night fell the wild scenes were illuminated by the lightning of a violent thunderstorm.

Next day, the bleeding, bruised and mud-stained revellers watched as the marines received the governor 'with flying colours and a band of music'. After the deputy judge advocate had read the governor's commission, Phillip let fly at the sorry rows of hung over convicts:

> If they attempted to get into the women's tents of a night there were positive orders for firing upon them...if they did not work they should not eat...In England thieving poultry was not punished with death but here where a loss of that kind could not be supplied...stealing...would be punished with death...they would never be worked beyond their abilities but every individual should contribute his share.[5]

Opinion about the governor's speech was divided. One officer described it as a 'harangue', another as a 'pointed and judicious speech'. Whatever, they agreed that Phillip's commission, which left him entirely to his own judgment with no Council to advise him, was more 'unlimited' than any other ever granted to a British governor. And it was not long before his powers were put to the test when a number of convicts chose to ignore his warning about thieving. At the end of February, three members of a gang who had repeatedly robbed the stores were condemned to death. All were marched to a hanging tree where their leader, Thomas Barret, was executed. After being given an overnight reprieve, the others were secured in neck-halters and marched back to their place of execution, but at the last possible moment, Phillip commuted their sentences. 'In the hopes that his leniency would not be abused', a marine said, 'His Excellency was pleased to order one only for execution'. In fact Phillip was to be much tougher on the marines: two years later, he hanged six for the repeated theft of stores they were supposed to be guarding.[6]

To everyone's astonishment, two French ships under the command of the Comte de La Perouse had arrived at Botany Bay on 24 January. Phillip's instructions had directed him to settle Norfolk Island, 1000 miles to the northeast, to prevent it being occupied by a European rival; on 14 February a settling party led by Lieutenant King was dispatched. Mirroring his own instructions, Phillip told King not to permit trade with any passing ships. The French, meanwhile, had remained peaceably at Botany Bay until 10 March when they sailed off, never to be heard from again.

The only trade allowed had been prearranged between the home secretary and the East India Company to mutually offset costs by using convict transports to carry tea from China to England. To execute this plan, the *Charlotte*, *Scarborough* and *Lady Penhryn* departed Sydney Cove in early May 1788. While the first two sailed a direct route north to Canton, the *Lady Penhryn* set off across the Pacific towards Nootka Sound, near modern day Vancouver. Her captain, William Sever, was following secret orders to pick up a cargo of furs before re-crossing the Pacific to China. However, an outbreak of scurvy at Tahiti forced Sever to abandon this plan and alter course for Canton. There the *Lady Penhryn* rejoined the *Charlotte* and the *Scarborough*, and there the three ships remained until the end of the year. It was not until May 1789 that the first of them arrived back in

England. By the time the *Lady Penhryn* made landfall, she had sailed a round trip of 44,840 miles.[7]

Meanwhile, on 15 May 1788, the governor completed his first major dispatch to the home secretary. 'Our situation though so very different from what might be expected', he reported, 'is nevertheless the best that offered'. Clearing the land to plant crops, he continued, required immense effort. Any plants which began to grow were immediately attacked by armies of ants and 'field mice'. He also noted that although he had not had to fire on the Aborigines, La Perouse had been less fortunate, and this had soured relations for everyone. The governor estimated that the total Aboriginal population on the coastal strip stretching from Botany Bay via Port Jackson to Broken Bay was not less than 1,500 – the Europeans were significantly outnumbered. Nevertheless, the Aborigines kept their distance, remaining both threatening and elusive. On New Year's Eve 1788 Phillip resorted to kidnapping a native to learn his language. Initially greatly distressed, Arabanoo was soon dining heartily at the governor's table. After first wiping his hands on his chair, he quickly learned to use a towel, as Tench noted, 'with great cleanliness and decency'. Still, some of the colonists' customs appalled him, including the severe flogging of convicts who had provoked an Aboriginal attack at Botany Bay. When Phillip attempted to use Arabanoo to talk to other Aborigines, they shunned both men. Indeed the Europeans and the Eora people never were reconciled. What gave the colonists the upper hand was a fatal epidemic, probably smallpox, which ravaged the Aborigines in April 1789, reducing their numbers around Sydney by half. Arabanoo himself was a victim and a distressed Phillip had him buried in the grounds of Government House.[8]

The governor was an active explorer of a continent full of natural features to name after his patrons. Looking west to what are today known as the Blue Mountains, Phillip named the northernmost Carmarthen Hills after the foreign minister and the southernmost, Lansdowne Hills, after a former prime minister. A mountain in between was called Richmond Hill after the lord privy seal. Consistent with this approach, Phillip addressed his dispatch to the home secretary from 'Sydney Cove', concluding with an apology. 'My situation at present does not permit me to begin so long a letter again', he said, 'the canvas house I am under being neither wind nor water proof'.[9]

Since his first appointment in 1786 Phillip had demonstrated his willingness to co-operate with marines and convicts alike, and after arriving at Botany Bay, he extended this approach to the Aborigines, as he had been instructed to. When a convict returned to camp dangerously wounded by a spear, Phillip was careful to ask whether he had given the Aborigines any provocation. Lieutenant-Governor Ross, however, continued to set a different example. It was bad enough that his marines refused to oversee the convicts, despite having agreed to do so in exchange for a special discharge after three years' service. But within just eight weeks of arriving at Sydney Cove, Ross had so mishandled a court martial that five of his officers who comprised the court were themselves arrested by him. Such an outcome was disastrous in a tiny community. Phillip stepped in to sort out the mess and was soon congratulated by the arrested officers for reconciling this 'unfortunate difference of opinion'. Despite this, the lieutenant-governor's sense of entitlement continued to get the better of him. Some months later, as the colony's rations began to run dangerously short, Ross complained of being served 'with no more butter than the convicts', a stark contrast to Phillip who willingly accepted the convict ration.[10]

Phillip's dispatch of 15 May to the home secretary did not immediately go anywhere. It was not until mid-July that the next available ships were sufficiently repaired to make the return voyage. As their departure date drew near, there was a flurry of letter writing. The governor knew that it would be some time before he would get another chance. While his dispatches were matter-of-fact and positive, Phillip repeatedly stressed that further supplies would be needed for up to five years. Being so far away from stores at Batavia and the Cape of Good Hope, and with the *Sirius* being the only sizeable vessel at his disposal, he emphasized the risk of relying on just a few ships to resupply him from London. Nevertheless, the governor was optimistic enough to enclose a plan of the town to be built around Sydney Cove. 'The temporary buildings are marked in black', he said, '[and] those intended to remain in red'. He outlined his proposals for a government house and law courts, as well as a hospital, storehouse and barracks. And he proposed a minimum allotment of 60 feet by 150 feet for each dwelling house to ensure 'uniformity in the buildings' and to 'prevent narrow streets'. For the time being, farmers, builders and overseers should be sent to the colony, he said, in preference to further boat loads of unskilled convicts.[11]

On 1 July 1788 Sydney's decision to provide for civil law in the colony, an arrangement which had raised Lord Howe's eyebrows, was put to its first test when Henry Cable sued the master of the *Alexander*, Duncan Sinclair. On behalf of Susannah, whom he had married in the colony's first wedding ceremony, and on behalf of their infant son Henry, Cable claimed damages for the loss of clothes donated to them before they left England. Headed up by the colony's deputy judge advocate, David Collins, the court heard that while the Cable family had travelled out on the *Friendship*, a parcel of sewn hessian matting containing their donated clothes and books had been placed in the *Alexander's* after-hold. Many people, including convicts, had access to this area. The hessian matting had broken open during the voyage, the *Alexander's* steward said, and only the books could later be found. On 5 July the court awarded the Cables fifteen pounds' damages. Because they were convicts who had originally been sentenced to death, Cable and his wife would have been prevented from suing in England, but in the colony's new civil court, a different precedent was set – the first of many in this unique society of convicts and their kin.[12]

[*Thirty-one*]

— First news of Phillip —

Still coming to terms with a court order which required him to pay civil damages to convicts, Captain Sinclair boarded the *Alexander* for the return voyage to England. On 14 July 1788, he set sail accompanied by the *Borrowdale, Friendship* and *Prince of Wales*. At Governor Phillip's suggestion, this little convoy planned to make firstly for the Cape of Good Hope, via Batavia. But the vessels became separated off Lord Howe Island and the masters of the *Prince of Wales* and *Borrowdale* elected to change course, for a run across the South Pacific to Cape Horn. In early October, Captain Hunter did likewise after the governor dispatched him to the Cape of Good Hope to obtain urgent supplies. Sailing via Cape Horn in the *Sirius*, which leaked so badly that 12 inches of water had to be pumped out every two hours, Hunter returned to Sydney in April 1789, having sailed around the world, much of it a white-knuckle ride in the roaring forties.[1]

If 1788 had begun well at Sydney Cove with just about everyone on the First Fleet landing in good health, it ended shamefully when 100 starving convicts arrived at the settlement of Sydney on Cape Breton Island in British North America. They had been brought over from Ireland in the *Providence*, whose owners had contracted with the lord mayor of Dublin to take them to Nova Scotia. However, after being refused entry there, these scantily clad felons had been forced to walk through snowdrifts to Sydney, where they remained under the care of the local authorities, before being absorbed into the community. Although Irish politicians exercised considerable independence following Lord Sydney's reforms in 1783, the Home Office maintained ultimate responsibility for Ireland's affairs. And after another attempt to send Irish convicts to North America (this time to Newfoundland) ended in disaster, the

British government stepped in to redirect such felons to New South Wales, beginning with the Third Fleet in 1791.[2]

Meanwhile, speculation about Phillip's fate had begun in the London press as early as September 1788. *The Times* assured it readers that there was no cause for alarm, given the 'extreme distance of New South Wales'. Interest in the First Fleet's story was widespread. Both the governor and Captain Tench had left London with contracts to publish their stories. Phillip's book was to be based on his official dispatches, which were now aboard the *Alexander*. But Tench's manuscript was being carried by the *Prince of Wales*, which returned first, making landfall off Falmouth on 22 March 1789. A few days later, almost identical news items were carried by the *London Chronicle* and *The Times*:

> *Sirius* and *Supply* with the transports... have made good their voyage to Botany Bay. Of this important arrival, intelligence has been brought by the *Prince of Wales*... The dispatches for Government are not yet arrived... Only forty appear to have died and to compensate for this loss, forty two infants were born... when the *Prince of Wales* quitted Jackson's Bay... a very fine crop of grain presented to the eye.[3]

The generally positive news about Botany Bay spread quickly. 'It is much to be feared that Botany Bay will operate as an encouragement', *The Times* said, 'instead of proving a terror to the commission of crimes'. As Lord Sydney waited anxiously for the appearance of Phillip's official dispatches, Tench's book appeared for sale on 24 April 1789. Bearing the title *A Narrative of the Expedition to Botany Bay*, it was 150 pages long and retailed for 3 shillings and 6 pence. An immediate bestseller, it was to be printed in three editions before the year was out and translated into French, German and Dutch. Sydney must have taken a deep breath reading Tench's opening words. 'On offering this little tract to the public', Tench said, 'it is equally the writer's wish to conduce to their amusement and information'. As he read on, Sydney would have been relieved to see Tench's cryptic conclusion that 'if only a receptacle for convicts be intended, this place stands unequalled'.[4]

The First Fleet had done little, however, to ease Britain's overcrowded prisons. In Newgate Jail, the distemper was so bad that the windows of the Old Bailey courtroom next door had to be kept open during the winter of 1788–89. Well aware that the First Fleet had contained many more male convicts than females, the home secretary had already issued orders to prepare 200 women for transportation, should Phillip's dispatches prove positive. The First Fleet contractor, William Richards, was re-employed and by mid-April 1789 well over 100 females were aboard the convict transport, *Lady Juliana*. As he had done with the First Fleet, Sydney took an interest in their welfare, making sure that the Treasury complied with Richards' request for extra tea, sugar, soap and linen, just in case any of his charges were pregnant.[5]

News from those aboard the *Prince of Wales*, reordered Sydney's priorities. Even without the benefit of Phillip's official dispatches, it was clear that the governor had used up a great part of his supplies and was in immediate need of further food, tools, clothing and medicines. So Sydney directed the Admiralty 'forthwith' to make a special storeship available and the *Guardian* was chosen. By now aware that Phillip would struggle to support any more large shipments of convicts, Sydney limited their number on the *Guardian* to just 25 – either builders or those who 'understood farming'. The only other passengers were ten overseers. The *Lady Juliana's* hold was altered to carry extra provisions.[6]

As it turned out, the *Scarborough*, one of the ships tasked to return via Canton, and the *Fishburn*, which had not left Sydney Cove until mid-November, both beat the *Alexander* home. The latter did not arrive back in England until 25 May 1789, its ten-month voyage home having physically distressed its crew. Indeed a further week passed before the home secretary finally received the governor's official dispatches and Phillip's publisher had something to send to the printer. By contrast, the *Scarborough*'s return voyage 'freighted with teas' was a complete success and the East India Company resolved 'to take up' five more Botany Bay transports 'to bring home teas from China'.[7]

Just days after receiving Phillip's official dispatches, Lord Sydney retired as home secretary to be replaced by the prime minister's first cousin, William Grenville. Governor Phillip would remain unaware of this change for almost a year and would still be addressing his dispatches to Lord Sydney as late as 15 April 1790. Meanwhile, at Sir Joseph Banks' request, Grenville had delayed the departure of the *Guardian* to allow for the fitting of special equipment to carry plants. Finally she set sail in mid-September, five months having passed since Sydney had issued his order to prepare her 'forthwith'. However, on 23 December, disaster struck when she hit an iceberg off Cape Town and had to be written off.[8]

The ambitious young Grenville, who would later become prime minister himself, was keen to impress his cabinet colleagues. Described by Nathaniel Wraxall as being 'devoid of elegance or grace... [and] destitute of suavity', Grenville grimly focused on two priorities: shipping more convicts and cutting costs. Ignoring Governor Phillip's warnings, Grenville wrote to the Treasury on 6 July 1789, directing that a thousand convicts were to be sent immediately to New South Wales, 'with least expense to the public'. The First Fleet's contractor, William Richards, was replaced by one of London's largest slaving firms, Camden, Calvert and King. Although Sydney had used Anthony Calvert to ship twenty-two convicts to West Africa aboard the *Recovery* in 1785, the voyage had passed without incident, in part because the government had paid a reasonable rate. The difference now was that while Richards had been paid 54,000 pounds, Calvert's firm bid just 22,370 pounds to prepare the larger Second Fleet. And the consequences were disastrous. When this fleet arrived at Sydney Cove on 24 July 1790, the convicts 'were almost half dead [and] very few could stand'. In fact, out of a total of 1006 convicts carried in three transports, 267 died, a mortality rate later confirmed as the highest in the history of transportation. By contrast, the female convicts aboard *Lady Juliana*, which had arrived just three weeks earlier, were 'healthier and happier than they had ever been in their lives'.[9]

Meanwhile, unaware of the human cost of his penny pinching, Grenville had directed the Treasury to plan for a Third Fleet, again 'with the least expense'. While the death-rate turned out to be less than that suffered by the Second Fleet, it was still twice that of the First. In consequence, the government finally turned again to Sydney's man, William Richards. In 1793, he transported more than 700 convicts, suffering only a single death. Despite this, William Grenville had the temerity to say of Lord Sydney that he had been 'unequal to the most ordinary business of his office'. In fact, the penal colony in New South Wales would have failed had Sydney organized the First Fleet in the same way that Grenville organized the Second.[10]

It took some time for the struggling settlement at Sydney Cove to absorb the shock arrival of the Second and Third Fleets. But by 1792 Governor Phillip was able to report that 'material difficulties were diminishing'. Moreover the long-term effects of transportation were largely positive. Phillip noted that many convicts behaved 'better than ever could be expected', including James Ruse, who founded the Australian wheat industry. As for Henry Cable, he established an inn called 'The Ramping Horse' from which he ran the colony's first stage-coach. He then went on to be appointed the colony's chief constable, before being dismissed for illegally importing pigs. Later, after amassing a trading fortune, he transferred his property to his son, to avoid paying a 12,000 pound debt to one of his business partners – a fellow ex-convict.[11]

Following his retirement, Lord Sydney continued to receive letters from Arthur Phillip at Sydney Cove. In one, the governor asked Sydney to lobby his son-in-law, Lord Chatham, who was then first lord of the admiralty, about promoting him to the substantive rank of commodore. In another, he asked the former home secretary to support his application for leave to settle his 'private affairs'. Phillip also kept Sydney abreast of developments, including the establishment of 'a spermaceti whale fishery' and the beginnings of the new town called 'Parramatta'. Apart from Phillip, Sydney kept in touch with other First Fleet officers, among them John Hunter, Phillip Gidley King, Henry Waterhouse and John Shortland. In 1797, King sent Sydney a Waratah plant in a small grated box while Governor Hunter copied him in on some of his dispatches to Home Secretary Portland. So it was that the former home secretary's support and encouragement of the colony continued until his death in 1800.[12]

With the exception of Sir Joseph Banks and the staff at the Home Office, Sydney continued to be one of the best-informed people in Britain about the goings on around the cove named after him. On 30 April 1796, Waterhouse told him with considerable understatement that 'the Governor and the Corps do not appear to be in perfect harmony'; twelve years later, this so called 'Rum Corps' would overthrow the colony's fourth governor, William Bligh. As for Governor Hunter himself, his biggest news was verification 'of a conjecture … in my Journal … [that] a straight may separate Van Dieman's Land from New Holland' – George Bass and Matthew Flinders had circumnavigated what is now Tasmania.[13]

It was the former deputy judge advocate David Collins who wrote what many consider to be 'the earliest historical account of settlement in Australia'. And it was particularly appropriate that in 1798, he dedicated his book to Lord Sydney:

> The benevolent mind of your Lordship led you to conceive this method of redeeming many lives that might be forfeit to the offended laws but which being preserved under salutary regulations might afterward become useful to society.[14]

[*Thirty-two*]

— Madness and regency —

It all began in the summer of 1788 when the king suffered a bilious attack which confused his doctor, Sir George Baker. Similar attacks occurred spasmodically until the third week of October. Then, after riding all day in wet stockings, George III began to suffer 'an agitation and flurry of the spirits'. At midnight, Baker sent an urgent note to Prime Minister Pitt that 'His Majesty is bordering on delirium' – a message of such grave constitutional consequence that Pitt arrived on Baker's doorstep at 2.00 a.m. For a couple of weeks thereafter, the king tried to keep up appearances, but people became concerned after he appeared in a deranged state at an official levee. This concern turned to alarm during a dinner at Windsor when his Majesty seized the Prince of Wales by the collar and hurled him against a wall. Before long, George III was giving orders to imaginary people and awarding the highest honours to his most junior staff.[1]

In Baker's opinion, his Majesty was now 'under an entire alienation of the mind', which meant that there was no head of state. In 1783 Britain had had a king but no prime minister. Now it had a prime minister but no king. George III was physically alive but constitutionally he might as well have been dead. There were longstanding rules for the appointment of a regent following the death of a monarch whose heir was under age. There were no rules, however, where a king had gone mad but might later recover, and while it was clear that the king's constitutional stand-in would be the 26-year-old Prince of Wales, the manner and timing of his appointment were unclear. These it seemed were matters for Parliament.[2]

Putting aside all other business, the prime minister personally managed this crisis. He was supported by the lord chancellor who provided the legal advice and the home secretary who was responsible for the king's official correspondence. 'A disorder about the middle of yesterday attacked his Majesty's head', Sydney said shortly after the king assaulted the prince, 'and the case ... is full of extreme danger'.[3]

When his father attacked him, the prince had burst into tears, and for a short time, he remained genuinely concerned about the king's illness. But as the advantages of being regent dawned on the prince, his attitude changed. In the House of Lords five years earlier he had supported Charles Fox's India Bill – a measure which had been bitterly opposed by the king, leading to Fox's dismissal as prime minister and to his replacement by young William Pitt. The prince had also taken up womanizing and gambling with Fox while the prince's residence, Carleton House, had become a meeting place for Fox's supporters. George III's heir was a supporter of his political enemy who was ever on the lookout for an opportunity to get back at the king who had sacked him and the prime minister who had replaced him.[4]

Admitting that he was 'rather too fond of wine and women', the prince had secretly married a Catholic widow in 1785. This marriage to Maria Fitzherbert endangered the prince's claim to the throne under the Act of Settlement. By the end of the following year, his gambling debts had reached the staggering sum of 150,000 pounds. On 20 April 1787, the prince arranged for his financial needs to be raised in Parliament. But this triggered oblique references to the Fitzherbert marriage. Ten days later Fox lied to the House, denying the marriage to protect the prince's status as heir apparent. Thereafter, the king's heir was in Charles Fox's political pocket.[5]

By mid-November 1788, it was clear that if the prince was appointed regent, he 'would dismiss Pitt without hesitation' – there being little doubt that he would have the power to do so. But any decision to appoint the prince depended upon whether the king might recover his sanity and if so, how long this might take. The prince had his physician, Dr Richard Warren (who also treated Charles Fox), interposed at Windsor to treat the king. Needless to say, Warren thought that George III's madness was permanent while others, including the prime minister's doctor Anthony Addington, thought there was a prospect of recovery; for the present, they all agreed that the king was totally incapable. Ominously for Pitt, the prince began to avoid him. Instead, he dealt with the government through Lord Chancellor Thurlow, who many suspected 'was about to rat'.

Finally, on 24 November, Pitt and Sydney had a long conference with the prince at Windsor. However, this resolved nothing and when the cabinet next met its members had 'the longest faces', with Sydney's the longest of all.[6]

As home secretary, Lord Sydney was the cabinet minister most closely involved in the king's private affairs and he received regular reports about the king's treatment. 'A warm bath was used yesterday... which [his Majesty] was much pleased with', one report said. 'He is much better than he was a week ago [but] he doesn't gain the ground we all hoped for'. Sydney's family pestered him for news. It mattered not that his daughter Mary was married to the first lord of the admiralty: her father seemed to know more than her husband, who was the prime minister's brother. 'What account [have] you received this morning from Windsor', she demanded of Sydney on 16 November. 'Pray heaven it may be favourable'. Days later, the home secretary was advised that the king should be moved to Kew. It would provide the 'air and exercise necessary for [his] cure', the physicians said.[7]

The Times had predicted that the prince would be proclaimed regent when Parliament next sat on 20 November, but that day passed uneventfully because the king was incompetent to notify any parliamentary business. Then, in anticipation of the next sitting day, the prime minister and cabinet cross examined the king's doctors on oath. While they agreed that the king was incapable, all except Warren believed that his recovery was more probable than not. On 4 December, Parliament was duly informed and further adjourned. With both government and opposition now manoeuvring to gain an advantage, Sydney recalled the accession of George III in 1760. 'I am old enough to have [seen]... a demise of the Crown', he said, 'an event which does not bring the virtues of men more into light than their contrary qualities'.[8]

The king had already been examined by five doctors. Nevertheless, on 5 December Dr Francis Willis was called in. Although considered by many to be a quack, Willis had successfully treated other patients exhibiting the king's symptoms. Known for his aggressive approach, which included restraining his Majesty in a straight-jacket, Willis was optimistic about his patient's prognosis, predicting recovery within three months. The wily young Pitt used this to play for time, planting in wavering MPs' minds the suggestion that the king would soon be able to hold them to account if they backed Fox and the prince.

Before long, Dr Willis was entrenched as the king's primary doctor and Lord Sydney saw to it that Willis's son, John, also a doctor, had access too. Soon an order appeared, pinned to the chimney in the royal pages' room, directing that 'no person should be admitted into his Majesty's apartment' without the Willis doctors' permission. Those most committed to the king's early recovery, upon which the government's future depended, now monopolized access to their royal patient.[9]

Later, during intense cross-examination of Dr Francis Willis by members of Charles Fox's opposition, Sydney's role in entrenching the Willis doctors was exposed. What Fox and his allies probably never found out, though, was that Sydney had put them under Secret Service surveillance. On 6 December 1788 a detective tailing one of Fox's principal lieutenants, Richard Sheridan, reported:

> Mr Sheridan went out on foot to ... Mrs Fitzherbert's ... thence to Mr Foxes ... thence to the Duke of Devonshire's ... thence to Mr Foxes to dinner ... at half an hour after eight o'clock the Duke of Portland and Lord Longborough came to Mr Foxes ... At ten o'clock Lord North came and staid till a quarter of twelve left Mr Sheridan there at half after one o'clock, the Prince of Wales [and] the Duke of York ... was at Mrs Fitzherberts at half after one o'clock morning.[10]

On reading this, Sydney was no doubt reminded of the royal marriage rumours which, if proved, would destroy the prince's chances of being regent. Soon afterwards, the prime minister and home secretary received letters claiming that the prince and Mrs Fitzherbert were husband and wife, but if the ministers had firm proof, they chose not to act on it.[11]

When Parliament next met on 8 December, the government again stalled for time, appointing one committee to question the doctors and another to research previous regencies. A member of both committees, Sydney was an old hand at regency politics, having helped to undermine Prime Minister Grenville over a botched Regency Bill. Even so, the hunt for precedents uncovered nothing useful, and while most of the doctors maintained that the king would recover, they still could not say when. Meanwhile the opposition had attempted to seduce some government MPs but soon found that there were 'fewer rats than could be expected'. The parliamentary stalemate continued.[12]

Nowhere were the battle lines more clearly drawn in the Lords than between the home secretary and his opposition counterpart, Lord Stormont. 'Even his enemies admitted...[Stormont] to possess application', Wraxall said. 'Whenever he rose in the...[Lords] he displayed a thorough acquaintance with the subject...together with great passion of language and force of argument'. In 1785 a cartoon had depicted Stormont in the form of an auger attempting to bore into Sydney in the form of a log. Two years later, *The Times* noted that they had equalled each other during a debate about whether a postage stamp was a tax. 'I insist', said Stormont, 'that the postage of letters is not a tax because you may return the letter'. 'On the same principle', Sydney replied, 'I insist the duty on post horses is not a tax because you may return the post horses'. Now the regency debate generated similar clashes. The prince was heir apparent, Stormont said, and therefore had an immediate right to assume power. Any other assumption 'must lead to a republic'. To this Sydney replied that during the king's illness, 'no person however distinguished his birth had a legal claim to assume it as a matter of right'. Algernon Sidney had fought and died for the proposition, finally settled at the end of the seventeenth century, that Parliament had the ultimate right to determine who wore the Crown. Although Sydney's hot temper had mellowed in the Upper House, anything which cast a shadow over his martyred kinsman's work could still rile him. And infuriated by Stormont's trivialisation of this issue, Sydney threatened him to a duel:

> The temper of the House...ill became the solemnity of the subject...at such a awful moment...He knew not what offence he had given...but...there were other ways of settling differences between one gentleman and another...He thanked heaven warm as he was by nature that his warmth seldom lasted long.[13]

Passions ran just as high outside Parliament. Writing to his cousin Charles Cornwallis, Sydney identified those whom he thought most responsible. 'The ladies are as usual at the head of all animosity', he said, 'and distinguished by caps, ribands and other ensigns of party'.[14]

Thanks to Pitt's delaying tactics, it was not until 19 December that the Commons agreed the king's illness prevented him from 'attending to public business'. But disagreement remained over how this 'defect' might be remedied.

While the opposition said a simple parliamentary resolution acknowledging the prince's right to stand in would do, Pitt again played for time, arguing that legislation was necessary. Charles Fox then claimed that the prince had a 'divine right' to be regent. It was an assertion which would have appalled Algernon Sidney and it surprised many of Fox's friends. Pursuing power ahead of principle for the second time in five years, Fox had again gone too far. The government's view that legislation was needed won the day, and a conference with the House of Lords was agreed upon, to determine the next step.[15]

To negotiate with its Commons counterpart, the Lords nominated a committee. On it, Lord Sydney argued that legislation was required to appoint a regent while George, Marquess Townshend claimed that the prince had an immediate entitlement to the position. This debate was resolved the home secretary's way on 29 December and so the regency dispute duly spilled over into the New Year. During January, the doctors were re-examined with some of their evidence bordering on farce. There were disagreements about whether the king had 'a very good night' or just a 'good night', about whether blistering was a proper treatment, about whether his Majesty had been given *King Lear* to read in an attempt to upset him and about whether he should have been allowed a razor to shave himself.[16]

As the government's leader in the Lords, Sydney liaised with Pitt to ensure that any parliamentary decision to appoint the prince would be delayed – at least until Dr Francis Willis's forecast of a full recovery after three months had been tested. What followed was a protracted debate about the principles which should underpin any offer to the prince. In the end, the government prevailed with terms which would prevent the prince, as regent, from appointing any peers or disposing of any of the king's property. And control of his Majesty's 'Royal Person' would be the queen's responsibility. An opposition attempt to place a time limit on these restrictions was rejected because at the end of it, as Sydney said, 'His Majesty though not yet recovered might be on the point of perfect recovery'. It was not until the end of January that Parliament agreed to resolutions offering the prince the regency. And if he accepted, the precise terms then had to be settled in legislation.[17]

George III's ongoing disability meant that he was unable to determine pleas for clemency. As the king's adviser on such matters, the home secretary now found himself in a dilemma. Should such pleas await the king's recovery? Or should the law take its course? Two prisoners had been 'butchered' at a public execution, Lord Porchester charged, because the king, as the 'fountain of mercy', had been unable to consider their reprieve applications. Responding to these 'violent allegations', Sydney explained that the Crown law officers had signified 'their thorough conviction that the persons under sentence were beyond all question, guilty'. But as someone who took pride in his reputation for being compassionate when it came to clemency pleas, Sydney would have been embarrassed by Porchester's conclusion: '[The Ministers] had arrogated to themselves offices which they had no right to hold', he said. 'They were clinging to office to the last moment'.[18]

It fell to the home secretary to communicate Parliament's offer to the prince, but the prince's relations with the government were by now so strained that Sydney had to prevail upon one of the prince's friends to do so. With that out of the way, the nation waited. 'Sydney moved to adjourn till tomorrow', *The Times* reported on 30 January, 'and said he hoped the answer from his Royal Highness would…enable the House to proceed on Saturday'. Pitt, meanwhile, was contemplating a return to legal practice.[19]

The prince accepted Parliament's resolutions on 31 January. Although most of his powers as acting head of state would be limited, there would be no limitation on his power to sack the government. But legislation was still required before he could take over, and in the interim the Pitt ministry remained in office. On 5 February, a Regency Bill was introduced into the Commons and Edmund Burke now confidently asserted that the king was 'insane'. The next day, however, his Majesty asked Dr Willis whether Parliament was sitting. On being told that it was, the king replied that, as he had previously adjourned it, the sitting was 'totally illegal'. This exchange suggested that the king was recovering and it corroborated the most recent medical reports. The government managed to spin out debate for another week before the bill finally passed the Commons. Only a Lords' vote stood between the prince and power. With Dr Willis's three-month deadline for recovery fast approaching, public attention was equally focused on the king's residence at Kew and on the Lords' chamber. There, the high drama was parodied in the *Incantation*:

1st Witch: Thrice the doctors have been heard
2nd Witch: Thrice the Houses have conferred
3rd Witch: Thrice has Sydney cocked his chin
4th Witch: Jenky cries 'Begin, Begin' ... [20]

The Regency Bill was introduced into the Lords on 13 February. The very next day, *The Times* claimed: 'The King is recovered from his late melancholy indisposition'. However, this turned out to be premature. The latest medical advice to Sydney suggested only that the king was in 'amendment' and then 'convalescence'. Debate on the Regency Bill proceeded through 16, 17 and 18 February. When Lord Stormont attempted to lift the limitations on the regent's powers by claiming that they would 'cripple government most dangerously', Sydney's response was firm. 'The Regent was left with all the great power of Government', he said, 'and the restrictions imposed were ... only provided with a view to his Majesty's temporary illness'.[21]

The opposition next pushed to have the custody of his Majesty's person transferred from the queen to the prince, no doubt intending to break the Willis family's monopoly on the king's treatment. This prompted Sydney to perform a delicate political balancing act. After describing the prince as a person 'of high character, of amiable manners [and] greatly beloved', he noted that the queen had never meddled in politics in 27 years. 'Why would she change her house into a house of faction', Sydney asked, 'for the purpose of opposing her own son?' And why change now when even the prince's doctor, Richard Warren, was reporting that the king was steadily improving. Such questions helped to give the government some much needed momentum.

Soon afterwards, the Lords were formally advised that the king was in convalescence. The Regency Bill was adjourned to 24 February, and following further advice to Sydney that there was 'an entire cessation of his Majesty's illness', the bill was put off again. Finally on 10 March Parliament was informed that the king was 'happily recovered', whereupon the bill was withdrawn altogether.[22]

Dr Francis Willis's prognosis had proved to be uncannily accurate. 'The King's recovery happened critically about three or four days at most before the Prince was to ... [be] Regent', one observer said, '[whereupon] Charles

Fox would have been fixed on the Treasury Bench'. It had been such a close run thing that a special medal had already been struck – 'Prince Regent, born 12 August 1762, appointed February 1789'. Privately furious that Pitt had 'attempted to destroy my rights', the prince publicly expressed his joy at the king's recovery. And Lord Stormont did likewise, telling the Lords that he felt 'a degree of joy nearer to his heart' than at any other time in his life. Writing to Charles Cornwallis, an angry Sydney let fly. 'Gratitude was not ... to be expected from Stormont', he said, '[and I will] not dwell upon the filthiest conduct of North who ... [joked] about the King's misfortunes'.[23]

In Ireland, it had been a different story. Because the king was seen as anti-Catholic, the prince was popular there. Thanks largely to Lord Sydney's Judicature Act of 1783, the Irish Parliament was independent, and it took immediate steps to offer the regency of Ireland to the prince, with no strings attached. So the Pitt government told its lord-lieutenant, Buckingham, not to agree to any Irish regency 'varying one iota from that adopted here', otherwise it would 'dissolve the Union of the two Kingdoms'. To avoid this, Lord Sydney directed Buckingham to dissolve the Irish Parliament itself. Buckingham refused, claiming that his powers had been 'annihilated' by the king's disability. The Irish Parliament therefore continued to sit and resolved in mid-February 1789 to invite the prince 'to assume the Government of Ireland unconditionally during the King's illness.' But the lord-lieutenant then refused to transmit this resolution to the prince. The Irish Parliament declared Buckingham's conduct unconstitutional and appointed its own 'Ambassadors' as its messengers. However, their arrival in London on 27 February coincided with the news that the king was in 'complete recovery'. They were too late.[24]

To celebrate the withdrawal of the Regency Bill, Lord Sydney held a ball at his London house. As his 200 guests arrived at Grosvenor Square, 'the face of joy smiled on every countenance'. And the crowds in the surrounding streets were so large that the prime minister's carriage was forced to a stop at the 'head of the Haymarket'. Pitt therefore stepped into White's Club where he 'supped' for an hour and a half only to find when he re-emerged that his carriage had not been able to move an inch. On 11 March, *The Times* reported on the home secretary's ball:

> The females [of Sydney's family] … were some of the most lovely in the world. The supper consisted of everything valuable and in season; there was a clockwork piece of confectionary that had a fine effect, the star in the middle moving in regular motion and displaying various colours.[25]

Within the week, it was business as usual at the Home Office, with Sydney submitting pleas to the king 'relative to the convicts ordered for execution tomorrow'. At the same time, plans were underway for a Thanksgiving service at St Paul's on 23 April. When that day dawned, huge crowds lined the route to the cathedral. After the crush outside his house on 11 March, Sydney had issued special regulations that 'no hackney coach be permitted on any pretence whatsoever to be drawn within those parts of the city to be enclosed with bars and chains'. Any coachman who did so, Sydney warned, would lose his license. The day passed without any major trouble. The massive crowds sang 'God Save the King' and while they 'huzza'd Mr Pitt, they hooted and hissed Mr Fox'. The only sour note was the sight of the king's sons talking throughout the Service – 'so indecent it was shocking'.[26]

[*Thirty-three*]

~ A GOOD RETREAT ~

Although slavery had long been illegal in England, British ship owners were allowed to continue the trade between Africa and America. But at the beginning of 1788 the British Parliament was swamped with petitions claiming this trade was inhuman. These petitions had been triggered by something new in eighteenth century politics – a small band of vocal idealists who challenged the morality of a particular line of business, thereby spawning a popular political movement. On 21 May, a member of the Commons, Sir William Dolben, introduced a bill to limit the number of slaves per vessel. But even though this bill acknowledged a continuation of slavery, it drew fierce criticism from slave merchants, who feared for their profit margins, and they had strong cross-factional support in Parliament. For many, slavery in other parts of the world, including Britain's West Indian colonies, was acceptable, just as cheap third world labour is now. Was not that champion of liberty, Thomas Jefferson, a slave owner? Nevertheless, with Prime Minister Pitt's support, Dolben's bill passed the Commons on 18 June.[1]

When this bill reached the Lords, it was clear the ministers there were hopelessly split, especially over a clause which made the bill retrospective. The Duke of Richmond was in favour. Lord Chancellor Thurlow was against. And Lord Sydney argued for a postponement, claiming that the 'humanity' of the slave merchants could be relied on for 'a few months longer'. He particularly regretted the introduction of the bill so late in the session – and its retrospective effect. In New South Wales, the one colony Sydney had established from the ground up, there was to be no slavery. As Governor Phillip put it: 'there can be no slavery in a free land and consequently no slaves'. But in many older British colonies, slavery was a long-established fact of life. Sydney was no doubt mindful of the indignation Dolben's bill would cause among West Indian colonists whose affairs came within his portfolio. During a heated cabinet meeting at the height of debate in the Lords, the prime minister said that if the bill was defeated, he could not 'continue' the ministers who opposed it. This did not deter Lord Chancellor Thurlow who abused his position as chairman of the Lords' debate to intervene with invective and contempt, spurning Sydney's apparent equivocation. 'Of a dark complexion and ... with a severe and commanding demeanour', Wraxall said, 'Thurlow impressed his auditors with awe before he opened his lips'. In the end, Sydney's loyalty to Pitt prevailed. 'As ... [the bill] has been brought in', Sydney said, 'it should receive from him no further opposition'. And having finally made up his mind, he went further, actively rounding up support for the prime minister. The bill, heavily amended, finally passed the Lords by the wafer-thin margin of just two votes.[2]

Meanwhile, a flood of petitions opposing the reform of slavery laws had flooded the Parliament. With business worth 1,000,000 pounds at risk, the Liverpool merchants claimed that 'the trade of the town would be ruined'. Nevertheless, Sir William Dolben pressed on, introducing a fresh bill to incorporate the Lords' amendments. After passing the Commons, this bill was approved by the Lords on 11 July, with Lord Thurlow watching on in 'indignant silence'. Although further reforms were then sidelined by the regency crisis, the prime minister's narrow win on Dolben's bill had begun the process that eventually led to the abolition of slavery. Ironically, it had been a reluctant home secretary who had cast one of the pivotal votes which kept the bill alive.[3]

In May 1789, with the regency crisis safely out of the way, William Wilberforce reopened the slavery debate in the House of Commons. As the West Indian colonists saw it, their wealth was now being further threatened. This placed great pressure on the home secretary. Apart from anything else, each colony had its own local government, its own colonial legislature and its own slave laws. And in London Lord Sydney was the minister responsible for the lot. As his father's parliamentary secretary, John Townshend, had collated all the local laws regulating slaves in Antigua, the Bahamas, Dominica, Grenada, Jamaica, Montserrat, Nevis, Saint Vincent, St Christopher and Tortola. They were all different. All would have to be nullified by Britain before slavery was abolished.

The great size of this political task can be measured by the fact that Britain's slave ships were not outlawed for another eighteen years and slaves within the British Empire did not all become free for another half century.[4]

At the end of May, as Lord Sydney contemplated further bruising battles with West Indian colonists, Liverpool merchants and some of his own cabinet colleagues over slavery, he decided that he had had enough. Having reluctantly returned to the Home Office in December 1783, he negotiated the terms of his departure with Prime Minister Pitt, and on 4 June 1789, he delivered up his seals of office to the king. As Pitt's biographer Stanhope put it, 'Lord Sydney did not retire from Downing Street without some substantial tokens of [the Prime Minister's] ... friendship and esteem'. He was advanced in the peerage from baron to viscount and he was appointed chief justice of Eyre, a sinecure Charles Cornwallis had held some years earlier. By now this office was worth 2,500 pounds a year, prompting Sydney to write to his cousin: 'I have it on better terms following the precedent of my immediate predecessor who understood a bargain better than your Lordship'. Cornwallis also received a letter from Charles Townshend. 'You will see from the papers', he said, 'that my brother has made a good retreat from the vexations of this world'. This retreat included Sydney's son John, who upon leaving the Home Office was made a lord of the admiralty. There he joined his brother-in-law John Pitt, second Earl of Chatham, who had been appointed first lord in 1788.[5]

After being formally introduced to the House of Lords as Viscount Sydney of St Leonards on 17 June, the former home secretary and his family left for Weymouth and a seaside holiday with the royal family. 'Our company consists of the Howe family, the Sydneys, the Courtowns and Lord and Lady Chesterfield', Queen Charlotte said, 'all our friends and very sincere ones too'. At Weymouth, the king bathed regularly; a machine followed him into the sea, filled with fiddlers who played *God Save the King* as he 'took the plunge'. But Lady Sydney drew the line at going sailing with Princess Augusta. In London, meanwhile, the prime minister had received letters threatening the king. However, Pitt decided not to inform his Majesty. Instead he wrote to Sydney, telling him to be on the lookout for suspicious characters at Weymouth, while the Secret Service attempted to trace the letters through the Post Office. Other less eventful visits to the royal family at Weymouth continued throughout the 1790s.[6]

This close relationship with the king's immediate family had begun through Lady Sydney's relatives and had blossomed after she and her sister, Lady Courtown, were appointed ladies-in-waiting to the queen. It had been further nurtured by Lord Sydney, whose official dealings with the king had sparked a friendship between them – their daughters also becoming friends. Following his Majesty's recovery from madness in 1789, the queen had crept up behind Sydney's eldest daughter, Georgiana, at a public celebration and 'tapped' her on the bottom. 'I started round', Georgiana gushed, 'and to my astonishment saw the Queen who laughed and said "I believe you never was whipped by a Queen before" '. Later on, Georgiana, who never married, became the state housekeeper at Windsor Castle. Over the years, she was presented with many tokens of royal gratitude, including a cameo portrait of the king in a 'gold entwined snake mount with ruby eyes'.[7]

For some time after his retirement, Lord Sydney was kept busy by Home Office matters. From India, he received private letters from Charles Cornwallis who, in his capacity as governor-general there, also mentioned affairs of state. 'Though I cease to be of the number of HM's Ministers', Sydney replied, 'I thought it my duty to come up to London to lay before HM some parts of … your letters'. Another correspondent who raised portfolio business was Margaret Nicholson. Years earlier, Sydney had committed her to an asylum for trying to assassinate the king with a blunt knife. 'Poor Margaret Nicholson', *The Times* reported in 1791, 'still continues writing letters to Lord Sydney'. Although he was no longer a cabinet minister, Sydney remained an active member of the Privy Council. And on 21 May 1790, he was present at a meeting to approve a great seal for the government of New South Wales. It depicted 'convicts landed at Botany Bay; their fetters taken off and received by Industry sitting on a Bale of Goods'.[8]

Sydney's visitors and friends continued to include people of all ranks. Admirals and lieutenants, governors and penniless loyalists all beat a path to his door. But none came from so far away or from such a different background as the Australian Aborigine, Bennelong. Originally kidnapped by Governor Phillip in December 1789 to help the European colonists learn Aboriginal words and customs, Bennelong volunteered to accompany Phillip to London in December 1792. Arriving in England in May 1793, he was presented at court and saw a great deal of the Sydney family before returning to New South Wales two years later – the first Australian-born adult to make this return trip. The former home secretary looked after Bennelong for some of his stay and his guest was warm in his appreciation, even writing a thank you letter to Sydney's steward, Mr Phillips. Bennelong and Lieutenant Henry Waterhouse, who accompanied him back to New South Wales, were fond of all the family, especially Sydney's daughter Harriet. On board the *Reliance* for their return to the antipodes, Waterhouse sent his best wishes to her, 'as well as those of Bennelong who is well'.[9]

In a letter to Charles Cornwallis at the beginning of 1789, Sydney had commented on the 'complete ferment' in France. Even though it was impossible to predict how events would now unfold, he welcomed the push for a more representative form of government there. And he noted the change that had come over the French press. '[They] have as much of the spirit of freedom as any we have read in our own history', he said, 'or seen in our own times'. However, the storming of the Bastille, which took place six weeks after Sydney's retirement, changed everything. By the beginning of 1790, Sydney was describing a very different situation to Cornwallis:

> The state of our neighbours is ... most extraordinary ... they seem to be forming a constitution which they boast is to be freer than ours ... They have read too many ... opposition pamphlets of this country, from the revolution to the present day and cannot ... easily separate the corn from the chaff. Insurrections happen frequently but at present the bourgeoisie of Paris seem to govern France. No taxes are paid and that seems the circumstance which the multitude look upon as the real test of liberty.

In contrast, England remained at peace, its inhabitants pleased with the spectacle presented by their 'rival neighbour'. Sydney himself was wary. 'French politics go on progressively toward republicanism in the first instance, anarchy in the second and what the chapter of accidents may produce in the last', he said. 'The French army is in a strange state'.[10]

By November 1792, that chapter of accidents had transformed France into an aggressive nation that threatened Europe. 'Lewis the fourteenth ... did not aim more openly and avowedly at universal dominion in Europe', Sydney said, 'than the French politicians do at present'. While he applauded those who struggled to free France from oppression, Sydney hated the Jacobins. He dismissed those French veterans of the American Revolutionary War who claimed that, then as now, they were motivated by revolutionary sentiment. 'They were animated by the same spirit as the ... Ministers who sent them to America', he said, 'the earnest desire to diminish the power of Great Britain'. And they would have been even more enthusiastic had their mission been to make the French king's brother 'absolute monarch of America'.[11]

Early in 1793, the French guillotined their king and declared war on Britain. But in the House of Lords, Lord Lauderdale among others objected to the Pitt government's mobilization plans and especially to its description of the growing conflict as a 'just and necessary war'. An angry Sydney promptly joined the fray. 'A certain description of men', he thundered, 'made it a rule to object to every measure which would strengthen this country against its avowed enemy'. The threat of French invasion was such that the government decided to arm the counties by private subscription. Although there was strong parliamentary opposition to this, Sydney and his cousin George Marquess Townshend were in rare agreement. Such a measure was necessary 'to support a war waged against the most blood thirsty, inhuman and savage set of beings that ever disgraced human nature'.[12]

Sydney's own County of Kent was especially vulnerable to a French attack, being located closest to the French coast. So the former home secretary answered the local sheriff's requisition for prominent landholders 'to stand forward in a Constitutional manner in defence of King and Country'. At Maidstone on 8 April 1794, a meeting of the county's leading citizens set up a defence fund and called for the creation of volunteer troops of yeomanry. Sydney subscribed 100 pounds to the fund and set about underwriting the Chislehurst troop, one of the first. Manned principally by local parishioners, it was captained by Sydney's eldest son, John, whose younger brother, William, acted as his lieutenant.[13]

Much of the fighting during 1794 took place in the English Channel where Sydney's old cabinet colleague, Admiral Howe, won the battle of the 'Glorious First of June'. Sydney's first news of this battle, 'one of the most obstinate actions ever fought', was from his friend and First Fleet protégé Henry Waterhouse. Along with Matthew Flinders, he had been aboard the *Bellerophon,* which had engaged a French battleship. '[After] an hour and twenty minutes...we were disabled', Waterhouse wrote, 'and Admirals Bowyer and Pasley...each lost a leg'. In a parliamentary vote of thanks to Lord Howe, Sydney spoke fulsomely of the navy's efforts. Not as lucky as Waterhouse was Watkin Tench, recently returned from Sydney Cove. On 6 November 1794, Tench was made a prisoner of war after the French captured his ship, the *Alexander*. Again, Sydney first heard this from Waterhouse, now aboard the *Reliance*. Five line-of-battle ships and two frigates had chased the *Alexander*, Waterhouse said, and although 'she was a fine 74, well manned', she was no match for such overwhelming strength.[14]

Concern about French aggression abroad was matched by fears about subversion in England. In 1792 a cabinet minister claimed that under the mask of reform the London Corresponding Society had really been intent upon undermining the British government. In the society's defence, an opposition member pointed out that during the 1780s Thomas Townshend and the former prime ministers, Portland and Rockingham, had been among its members. Explaining himself to the House of Lords, Sydney readily admitted that this had once been so, but the society had since changed, and he now dissociated himself from what had become 'a seditious and traitorous conspiracy directed to the subversion of authority'.[15]

In January 1796, Sydney received a report of radical activity in his own back yard at the Crown Alehouse, Chislehurst, where ten men from the London Corresponding Society tried to stir up trouble. The report said:

> The men read several books and offered them to persons they found in the alehouse... They said they could raise fifty thousand men in a few minutes but did not say for what purpose... They said that if the price of provisions could not be attained by fair means, it must be by foul... They wanted men to form a committee at Chislehurst... They offered liquor to those who would take it... They said soldiers were enemies of liberty.[16]

The London Corresponding Society had itself been subverted. Once upon a time Sydney might have welcomed its members to Chislehurst, but by 1796, they were more likely to be met by John Townshend's troop of yeomanry. In the House of Lords, Sydney backed the government's tough line, supporting a continuation of the Habeas Corpus Suspension Act to allow people suspected of subversion to be held indefinitely. 'Strong measures [are needed] to repress the new doctrines', he said, 'which… threatened the Constitution'. Such was this threat that Sydney supported suspending a key part of the constitution in order to save it. He illustrated the consequences of doing nothing by referring to Genoa, which he had visited in his youth. Then 'one of the most happy countries in Europe', Genoa was now in a 'deplorable situation', he said, racked by revolution.[17]

[*Thirty-four*]

Give me my draught

Sydney's concern about the turmoil in Europe was offset by his satisfaction at seeing his children settle down. Apart from Mary, who had married Lord Chatham, Frances married Lord Dynevor; and according to Charles Cornwallis, 'Lord and Lady Sydney were in great joy at Harriet's marriage to Lord Dalkeith'. But Sydney went overboard in April 1790 when describing the marriage of his eldest son, John, to Sophia Southwell, daughter of the member for Gloucestershire:

> My son has just entered into the holy state of matrimony with a very pretty and very amiable girl … She is fortunate in being married to the best tempered young man breathing … It is hardly modest [for me to say so] … but something is due to a young man whose whole life has been one continued scene of attention to his parents.

However within five years, Sophia was dead. Left to bring up two daughters on his own, John did not remarry until 1802. Meanwhile, after working for his father at the Home Office and then with his brother-in-law at the Admiralty, John had moved to the Treasury Board in 1793. First elected to the Commons as the member for Newport in 1786, he had transferred to his father's old seat of Whitchurch in 1790. Up to that time, there is no record of him speaking in the House. Thereafter, his political career continued to be modest – his final appointment being that of lord of the bedchamber, which involved waiting on the king as his Majesty dressed and ate in his rooms.[1]

For Sydney's second son, William, the road to the Commons proved a little more difficult. In January 1791, Sydney's uncle George Selwyn died, leaving a vacancy in his seat of Luggershall. This he had held on and off for over 40 years without ever making a speech in the House – being best remembered there for his ability to imitate Lord North's snoring. Sydney knew that an effort would be required to replace such a member. This involved marshalling so called 'faggots', being votes created by allotting people property to give them the status of electors. On 1 February, *The Times* reported on William's progress:

> The sober orderly and industrious poor of … Luggershall return their sincere thanks to Mr Everett for the fat ox of 50 score given them by Lord Sydney, the two hogsheads of beer by the Hon Mr Townshend and the 500 faggots by Mr Charles Townshend [Sydney's brother]. It is rather surprising that there should be 500 faggots left in Luggershall … as every faggot … was given away to gentlemen of a certain description previous to the last general election.[2]

Indeed a number of faggot voters, who had received their property conveyances on the morning of the election and then had them cancelled after the poll closed, were later ruled ineligible to vote. Charles Townshend's faggots were out and the election was thrown wide open. 'This decision operates directly against Lord Sydney's interest', *The Times* reported, 'and will occasion either a fresh election or the sitting member to be thrown out'. As a result, William did not become the member for Luggershall, although family tensions over the constituency went on for years. In 1799, Sydney wrote to his son John: 'I hope William will in future be more punctual in the delivery of letters [in Luggershall] … otherwise a great deal of money is uselessly thrown away'. William, who never married, did finally get to sit in the Commons the following year. After his father's death and John's elevation to the House of Lords, William came to represent Whitchurch, remaining a modest member until his death in 1816. His sister, Lady (Mary) Chatham, noted: 'he has no turn for political business.'[3]

Sydney's youngest son, Horatio, became an ensign in the Foot Guards in 1795. He saw active service during the Peninsula war and was later severely wounded at the battle of Quatre Bras in 1815. The following year, Horatio succeeded his brother William as member for Whitchurch. Like him, Horatio never married or made any mark in Parliament. He later joined his sister Georgiana at Windsor Castle, where he became lieutenant-governor of the Round Tower, responsible for defending the Castle 'against all enemies, whether foreign or domestic'.[4]

And what became of Sydney's cousins? George Marquess Townshend was made a field marshal in 1796. Although he lived until 1807, finally dying at the then ripe old age of 83, his career after his return from Ireland in the early 1770s had been something of an anticlimax. As for Charles Cornwallis, he became a marquess in 1792. Following his time as lord-lieutenant of Ireland and a short stint in cabinet as master-general of ordnance, he returned to India in 1805. There he died two months later, a pro-consul to the end. Time if not distance had brought the three cousins closer together and when Cornwallis was criticized in the House of Lords, Viscount Sydney and Marquess Townshend strongly defended him.[5]

Sydney remained a regular attendee at the Lords. And although he professed 'never to read the newspapers', he was an active participant in debates on the navy, Ireland and wars touching France, India and Spain. If there was a common theme to Sydney's speeches, it was loyalty to his former ministerial colleagues. In March 1795, the Earl of Guilford, formerly Prime Minister North, moved for an inquiry on 'the state of our allies, the conduct of the Government towards the neutral powers and the domestic situation of the country' – the very sort of motion Sydney himself would have moved against North during the American war. But Sydney would have none of it now, in relation to France. He must oppose North's motion, he said, 'as tending to weaken us' in our war with an ancient enemy.[6]

On 3 May 1797, in what was his last recorded contribution to a Lords' debate, Sydney spoke in defence of his old cabinet colleague, Lord Howe, who was under pressure over a navy mutiny about pay. Nicknamed 'Black Dick' by his sailors on account of his swarthy complexion, Howe 'wished for the sake of the service [that] the business had never been brought under discussion'. And Sydney supported him. 'All discussion upon a subject of so great delicacy', he said, 'could do no good and might produce much harm'. The mutiny, which occurred at the height of the war with France, was settled when Howe was rowed around the fleet, ship by ship, to announce a pay rise for all ranks.[7]

Throughout his career, Sydney had been a combative politician. But he did not hold a grudge and kept up a wide circle of friends on both sides of Parliament. During the American war, Sydney and John Cavendish had been close allies in their lonely battle against the North government. But when

North was finally toppled in 1782, these allies were soon at loggerheads over the American peace treaty and Cavendish later lost his seat, a victim of the Pitt government's landslide win in 1784. Still, following Cavendish's death in 1796, Sydney wrote to his own son, John:

> I am indeed... extremely concerned for the death of Lord John Cavendish. He was one of my oldest and most intimate friends... Politics had separated us for some years past but had not diminished my regard and friendship for him and I flatter myself that I still possessed... his good will.[8]

During the late 1790s, Sydney was reminded about the rebirth of Britain's empire, which he himself had done much to trigger; in 1798, his East Smithfield estate had to be split up for a new dock at Wapping to accommodate the explosive growth in British shipping. Sydney complained in vain to the prime minister that a wall around this new dock would prevent 'any communication' between the two parts of his now divided property. Other reminders were more pleasant, including those about two towns which bore his name. From Sydney in Cape Breton, he received a painting bearing the dedication: 'This view of Sydney in the Island of Cape Breton is most humbly dedicated to the Rt Hon Lord Viscount Sydney... by his... very obliged humble servant John Holmes... Provost Marshall of Cape Breton, 24 August 1799'. And from Sydney in New South Wales, he received a letter dated 10 September 1799 form Henry Waterhouse who hoped to visit him the following July:

> This Colony is in a very flourishing state... Benalong [sic] is well but as great a savage as ever, he is scarcely ever engaged in a battle but he gets wounded, he constantly desires to be remembered to your Lordship and family.[9]

Sydney was never to see Waterhouse again. On 30 June 1800, he went for his usual morning stroll around his Frognal estate, returning via a pond in his garden to visit his ducks. After entering his parlour, Sydney asked his servant to bring him his pen so he could write to his lawyer. *The Annual Register* reported what happened next. 'After writing, "sir I shall be", his Lordship fell down in a fit. His eldest son who was with him called for assistance but to no purpose; the last words his Lordship spoke were "give me my draught"; in three minutes afterwards he expired'. Sydney's widow, Elizabeth, survived him by a quarter of a century, dying in her ninetieth year.[10]

Following Sydney's death, his eldest son John, now second Viscount Sydney, married Caroline Clements in 1802. And their son, John Robert, was born three years later. Educated in the family tradition at Eton and Cambridge, John Robert entered royal service, becoming lord steward of Queen Victoria's household, ultimately responsible for her Majesty's private investments. The family kept up an interest in New South Wales, and a 'View of Sydney and the Governor's House 1846' was hung proudly at Frognal. Earl Sydney, as John Robert became in 1874, died in 1890 and the Sydney title died with him. The Earl's estate passed to his nephew, Hon. Robert Marsham-Townshend, and was finally auctioned off in 1915 at the height of World War I. Frognal was soon turned into a military hospital, accommodating wounded soldiers from all over the Empire, including Australian veterans of the Gallipoli campaign. Continuing Lord Sydney's association with Australia, his distant relative William Philip Sidney, Viscount De L'Isle, was governor-general from 1961 to 1965.

During his long career, Sydney was overshadowed by giants including William Pitt, Charles Fox and Edmund Burke. Yet, after a pedestrian start, he proved himself to be a courageous and ultimately effective opponent of Lord North's wartime government. Moreover, as home secretary, he made key contributions which helped to entrench British rule in India, bring the first whiff of self-government to Ireland, set a basis for co-operation with the United States and, above all, shape the beginnings of modern Canada and Australia. Sydney's term as a minister is therefore important in tracing the early development of the modern English-speaking world, despite the scant regard most historians have had for him.

What would that martyred champion of liberty, Algernon Sidney, have made of the home secretary's decision to give the first governor of the convict settlement, which in effect bore Sidney's name, greater power than any other British governor? Beheaded just over a century earlier for asserting that 'all just magisterial power is from the people', Sidney would no doubt have been horrified. However, that first governor's powers have to be understood against the difficulties involved in establishing a remote penal colony. What is therefore remarkable is Sydney's insistence, over objections from Lord Howe, that military law would not apply to the convicts and that a separate court would be set up to hear civil cases. It is the *Cable case*, where convicts successfully sued the master of a First Fleet transport for their lost luggage, which demonstrates the spirit of Algernon Sidney in his distant nephew's decision-making. As the great martyr put it in *Discourses Concerning Government*, 'the rigour of the law is to be temper'd by men of known integrity and judgment'. [11]

[Notes]

Each numbered note covers all the material in the main text back to the previous numbered note. Some notes cover one paragraph. Others cover more than one. The first instance of an abbreviation is shown in bold.

Preface

1. Thomas Townshend Jr [**TT**] to Richard Oswald [**Oswald**] 26 July 1782, Volume 70, Shelburne Papers, William L. Clements Library, University of Michigan, Ann Arbor, Michigan [**Clements Library**].
2. A. Frost, *Botany Bay The Real Story,* Black Inc., Collingwood, Victoria, 2011 [**Frost BB**] p. 138; L. Namier and J. Brooke, *The House of Commons 1754–1790*, Her Majesty's Stationery Office, London, 1964 [**Namier**] Volume III, p. 554; I.K.R. Archer, 'Townshend, Thomas' *Oxford Dictionary of National Biography*, Oxford University Press, 2004 [***ODNB***], Volume 55, pp. 166–69; A. Atkinson, *The Europeans in Australia*, Oxford University Press, Melbourne, 1997, Volume I [**Atkinson**] p. xv and following.

Chapter 1

Republicans and royalists

1. J. Carswell, *The Porcupine – The Life of Algernon Sidney*, John Murray Ltd, London, 1989 [**Carswell**] pp. xii, 233; *The Very Copy of a Paper etc.* was published in London and endorsed 'Printed for R.H.J.B. and J.R. and are to be sold by Walter Davis in Amen Corner MDCLXXXIII'.
2. Carswell, p. 227; J. Rosenheim, *The Townshends of Raynham*, Wesleyan University Press, Middletown, Connecticut, 1989 [**Rosenheim**] p. 60; E.A. Webb, *The History of Chislehurst*, George Allen, London, 1899 [**Webb**] p. 157; M. Scorgie & P. Hudgson, 'Arthur Phillip's Familial and Political Networks', *Journal of the Royal Australian Historical Society*, Volume 82, Part 1, June 1996 [**Scorgie & Hudgson**] pp. 24–25.
3. A genealogical Table of the Townshend Family, Charles Townshend Papers, 296/6/7, Clements Library; Rosenheim, pp. 19, 22, 45, 60.
4. A. Fraser, *Cromwell Our Chief of Men*, Granada, London, 1981 [**Fraser**] p. 282; Carswell, pp. 90, 118; J. Scott, 'Sidney, Algernon', *ODNB*, Volume 50, p. 540.
5. Carswell, pp. 184, 203, 206, 211, 213, 222, 226; R. Filmer, *Patriarcha*, London, 1680.
6. A. Sidney, *Discourses concerning Government Published from an Original Manuscript of the Author*, London, MDCXCVIII [**Sidney**] pp. 8, 12, 54, 59, 70, 300, 305, 354, 399, 406, 413.

7   C. Van Doren, *Benjamin Franklin*, Penguin Books, New York 1991 [**Van Doren**] p. 191; Carswell, pp. 240–41; M. Peterson, *Thomas Jefferson Writings*, Library of America, New York, 1984 [**Jefferson's Writings**] pp. 479, 744; Jefferson to Mason Weems, 13 December 1804, Library of Congress website www.loc.gov/exhibits/jefferson/jeffdec.html [accessed 26 June 2006]; C.F. Adams, *The Works of John Adams*, Little Brown and Co., Boston, 1856 [**Adams' Works**] Volume 10, p. 410; Sidney, p. 166; B. Franklin, *Poor Richard's Almanac*, Ballantine Books, New York, 1977, p. 39.

8   T. Harris, *Revolution and the Great Crisis of the British Monarchy 1685–1720*, Allen Lane, London, 2006, pp. 3, 271; D. Hosford, 'Sidney, Henry', *ODNB*, Volume 50, pp. 552–53; T. Claydon, 'William III', *ODNB*, Volume 59, p. 83; Carswell, p. 234.

9   Rosenheim, pp. 108, 110, 119; S. Wade Martins, *Turnip Townshend*, Poppyland Publishing, Norwich, 1990 [**Wade Martins**] p. 16.

10 Wade Martins, pp. 30, 36; B. Williams, *The Whig Supremacy 1714–1760*, Oxford at the Clarendon Press, 1949, pp. 3–4; Rosenheim, p. 210; W. Knittle, *Early 18th Century Palatine Emigration*, Genealogical Publishing Co., Baltimore, 1997 [**Knittle**] pp. 57, 60, 257; Atkinson, p. 28.

11 Wade Martins, p. 39; L. Colley, *Britons*, Pimlico, London, 2003 [**Colley**] p. 46; Rosenheim, p. 231; Charles Townshend, second Viscount to first Earl Cadogan, 3 March 1716, Box III, Sydney Papers, Clements Library; R. J. White, *The Age of George III*, Walker and Co., New York, 1968 [**White**] p. 29; D.L. Kier, *Constitutional History of Modern Britain*, A.C. Black, London, 1957 [**Kier**] p. 298.

12 S. Taylor, 'Walpole, Robert', *ODNB*, Volume 57, p. 80; L. & M. Frey, 'Townshend, Charles, second Viscount', *ODNB*, Volume 55, p. 142; Wade Martins, p. 59; Rosenheim, pp. 233, 236.

13 'An undated letter also unsigned, in TT's hand, addressed to My Lord', *Osborn Files* 37.230–37.271, Beinecke Rare Book and Manuscript Library, Yale University [**Osborn Files**].

14 Wade Martins, pp. 80, 93; White, p. 10.

Chapter 2

Young Tommy Townshend

1   *Gentleman's Magazine*, Volume 3, February 1733, p. 100; *ODNB*, Volume 55, p. 166; Namier, Volume III, p. 554; I.K.R. Archer, 'Townshend, Thomas', *ODNB*, Volume 55, pp. 166–69.

2   Namier, Volume III, pp. 220, 554; Webb, p. 163.

3   Webb, pp. 159, 161–63; J.H. Jesse, *George Selwyn and his Contemporaries*, Bickers and Son, London, 1882 [**Jesse**] Volume I, pp. 1, 10–11;

4   Webb, p. 164; Namier, Volume I, p. 219; 21 page letter in Latin to George III [**GIII**] from Hon. T. Townshend Sr [**TT Sr**] n.d., Sydney Papers, Box XVII, Clements Library; Letters from Dr Conyers Middleton to TT Sr, 1736–45, in Knight Frank and Rutley, *The Sydney Collection Catalogue*, Dryden Press, London, 1915 [**Sydney Catalogue**] Lot 1820, p. M2; H. Walpole, *Memoirs of the Reign of King George III*, Richard Bentley, London, 1845 [**Walpole's Memoirs GIII**] Volume IV, p. 314; Clause of a Bill regulating the sale of wine, Sydney Papers, Box XVII, Clements Library; Fragment of a biographical sketch of TT Sr 1701–1780, Sydney Papers, Box VIII, Clements Library.

5   Namier, Volume III, p. 554; *ODNB*, Volume 55, p. 142; Copy of a poem to Henry Pelham, n.d., Sydney Papers, Box XVII, Clements Library; Webb, pp. 163, 278.
6   Jesse, Volume I, p. 35; TT to TT Sr, 1765, Osborn Files; Much of the information for this paragraph was kindly provided by the Eton archivist in emails dated 15 and 16 September 2004.
7   C.V.F. Townshend, *The Military Life of Field Marshal Marquess Townshend*, John Murray, London, 1901 [**Townshend**] pp. 6, 27, 73.
8   Townshend, pp. 83, 100; Lord Edmond Fitzmaurice, *Life of Shelburne*, Macmillan, London, 1875 [**Fitzmaurice**] Volume I, p. 61; *Gentleman's Magazine*, Volume 15, December 1745.
9   F. McLynn, *1759*, Pimlico, London, 2004, p. 207; Townshend, pp. 114, 117; Namier, Volume III, pp. 539, 548; Lord Rosebery, *Chatham His Early Life and Connections*, A.L. Humphreys, London, 1910 [**Rosebery/Chatham**] p. 214; J. Owen, *The Rise of the Pelhams*, Methuen and Co., London, 1957 [**Owen**] pp. 284–85; Webb, p. 165; S. Ayling, *The Elder Pitt*, Collins, London, 1976 [**Ayling/Pitt**] p. 107.
10 Webb, pp. 163–64; *ODNB*, Volume 55, p. 166; Commons debate on the Quebec Bill, 3 June 1774, R. Simmons, ed., *Proceedings and Debates of the British Parliament Respecting North America 1754–1783*, Kraus International Publications, Millwood, New York, 1982 [**Simmons**] Volume V, p. 60.
11 *ODNB*, Volume 55, p. 166; P. Langford, *A Polite and Commercial People*, Oxford University Press, New York, 1992 [**Langford**] pp. 312–13; TT to TT Sr, 29 July 1753, Osborn Files; TT to TT Sr, 13 October 1753, Osborn Files; L. Picard, *Dr Johnson's London*, Phoenix Press, London, 2003 [**Picard**] pp. 26–27.
12 TT to TT Sr, 24 January 1754, Osborn Files; Portrait of the young Thomas Townshend 1733–1800 held in the Mitchell Library.

Chapter 3

THE PARLIAMENTARY APPRENTICE

1   Namier, Volume 1, pp. 30–31, 47, 301–02, 519; Letter from Grove to TT Sr, 14 September 1752, Sydney Papers, Box VI, Clements Library.
2   Namier, Volume 1, pp. 2, 514; L. Namier, *The Structure of Politics at the Accession of George III*, Macmillan, London, 1929 [Namier S], Volume 1, p. 96; J. Ehrman, *The Younger Pitt, Years of Acclaim*, Constable, London, 1984 [Ehrman] pp. 28–30; Report of the Committee appointed to inspect the several houses and other buildings adjoining Westminster Hall and the two Houses of Parliament and the offices thereunto belonging; presented by Sir Peter Burrell, 22 July 1789. Ordered to be printed 16 February 1790; W. Hague, William Pitt the Younger, Harper Perennial, London, 2005 [Hague] Illustration: 'Pitt addressing the Commons'.
3   Namier, Volume 1, p. 98; The King's Message, 3 June 1754, Journals of the House of Commons, Reprinted by Order of the House of Commons, 1803 [JHC] Volume 27, p. 8; B. Connell, The Plains of Abraham, Hodder and Stoughton, London, 1959 [Connell] pp. 22–23, 30; F. Anderson, Crucible of War, Faber and Faber, London, 2000 [Anderson] p. 7
4   Namier, Volume I, p. 57, Volume II, p. 120, Volume III, pp. 420, 538–56; Owen, pp. 128–29; R. Pares, King George III and the Politicians, Oxford at the Clarendon Press, 1959 [Pares] p. 4; H. Walpole, Memoirs of the Reign of George II, Henry Colburn, London, 1846 [Walpole's Memoirs GII] Volume I, p. 378.

5   Langford, pp. 391–92, 397, 404; R. Keverne, Tales of Old Inns, Collins, London, 1951, p. 89; Thomas Bingham to TT, 2 March 1755, Sydney Papers, Box VI, Clements Library.
6   Namier S, Volume 1, p. 253; Namier, Volume 1, pp. 62–63; Walpole's Memoirs GII, Volume III, pp. 279–80; J.S. Watson, The Reign of George III 1760–1815, Oxford at the Clarendon Press, 1976 [Watson] pp. 2, 141; ODNB, Volume 55, p. 166; Webb, p. 165.
7   J.C.D. Clark, The Memorials and Speeches of James 2nd Earl Waldegrave 1742–1763, Cambridge University Press, Cambridge, 1988 [Waldegrave's Memorials] p. 277; Rosebery/Chatham, p. 387; Walpole's Memoirs GII, Volume I, p. 72; George Prince of Wales to George II, 12 July 1756, in B. Dobree, The Letters of King George III, Cassell, London, 1968 [GIII's Letters] pp. 8–9; S. Ayling, George III, Collins, London, 1972 [Ayling/GIII] p. 39; C. Hibbert, George III A Personal History, Penguin, London, 1999 [Hibbert/GIII] pp. 3, 22–25; W.R. Anson, Autobiography of the Duke of Grafton, Kraus Reprint, Millwood, New York, 1973 [Grafton's Autobiography] p. 11; George P. to Bute, 25 September 1758, in GIII's Letters, p. 13.
8   Walpole's Memoirs GII, Volume I, p. 399, Volume II, pp. 288, 317, 370; Anderson, pp. 68, 104, 171; Rosebery/Chatham, p. 398; R. Holmes, Redcoat, Harper Collins, London, 2002 [Holmes] p. 41.
9   Ayling/Pitt, pp. 184, 263; Anderson, p. 175; N. Wraxall, Historical Memoirs of my Own Time, Keegan Paul, London, 1904 [Wraxall HM] p. 258; T.H. Escott, Gentlemen of the House of Commons, Hurst and Blackett, London, 1902 [Escott] Volume II, p. 202; Namier, Volume I, p. 220, Volume III, pp. 549–50.
10 The Statutes at Large from the Thirtieth Year of the Reign of King George II to the End of the Second Year of the Reign of King George III, p. 457; Walpole's Memoirs GII, Volume III, pp. 279–80; Debate on Bill on Members' Qualifications, 2 May 1760, JHC, Volume 28, p. 903.
11 Anderson, pp. 212–13, 299; Ayling/Pitt, p. 271; C. Ross, Correspondence of Charles 1st Marquess Cornwallis, John Murray, London, 1859 [Cornwallis's Correspondence] Volume I, p. 7; Viscount Brome (Cornwallis) to TT, 2 September 1758, Cornwallis's Correspondence, Volume I, p. 7; Walpole's Memoirs GII, Voulme III, p. 199; Namier, Volume III, pp. 552–53; Ayling/Pitt, p. 256; P. Macksey, The War for America, University of Nebraska Press, Lincoln, 1964 [Macksey] p. 49.
12 Connell, p. 181, Anderson, p. 232.

Chapter 4

Cousin George and the conquest of Quebec

1   ODNB, Volume 55, p. 144; Jesse, pp. 160–61; H. Fielding, The History of Tom Jones, a Foundling, Penguin Books, London, 2005, p. 651; Jesse, Volume I, pp. 111–12; Wraxall HM, p. 107; ODNB, Volume 55, p. 156; Waldegrave's Memorials, p. 276; Townshend, p. 130.
2   Connell, p. 137; Walpole's Memoirs GII, Volume III, p. 34; Townshend, p. 134.
3   Langford, p. 334; Walpole's Memoirs GII, Volume II, p. 99; Ayling/Pitt, pp. 190, 212,217; Anderson, p. 213; Townshend, p. 316; Connell, p. 183; G. Townshend to Pitt Sr, 27 August 1758, in Executors of John, Earl of Chatham, eds., Correspondence of William Pitt Earl of Chatham, John Murray, London, 1838 [**Chatham's Correspondence**] Volume I, p. 121.

Notes

4   Anderson, pp. 213–14; B. Willson, *The Life and Letters of James Wolfe*, William Heinemann, London, 1909 [**Wolfe's Letters**] pp. 380, 410–11; Connell, pp. 181, 183–84; Townshend, p. 146.
5   Townshend, pp. 153–55, 209.
6   C.P. Stacey, *Quebec 1759*, Robin Brass Studio, Toronto, 2002 [**Stacey**] p. 59; Connell, p. 195; Wolfe's Letters, pp. 421, 459; Townshend, pp. 169, 173–74, 183, 193–96.
7   Stacey, p. 106; Connell, pp. 199–200; Wolfe's Letters, pp. 448–50.
8   Connell, p. 213; Wolfe's Letters, pp. 466–68.
9   Stacey, p. 122; Connell, pp. 223–24; Wolfe's Letters, pp. 484–85.
10 Connell, pp. 230–31, 236–37; Stacey, p. 137, 139–43; Wolfe's Letters, p. 489.
11 Stacey, p. 151; Connell, pp. 242–43.
12 Stacey, pp. 162–64.
13 Anderson, p. 362; Wolfe's Letters, p. 495; Townshend, p. 237.
14 Connell, pp. 247–48; Stacey, p. 164; Anderson, pp. 364–65; Townshend, p. 240.
15 Anderson, pp. 368,377; Walpole's Memoirs GIII, Volume I, p. 24, Volume III, p. 222.
16 G. Warburton, *Conquest of Canada*, Richard Bentley, London, 1857 [**Warburton**] p. 208; Anderson, p. 363; Connell, pp. 247, 258; Wolfe's Letters, p. 495; Townshend, p. 231; Stacey, p. 169; G.N.D. Evans, *Allegience in America – the Case of the Loyalists*, Addison Wesley, Reading Massachusetts, 1969 [**Evans A**] pp. 7–8.
17 Lord John Russell, ed., *Memorials and Correspondence of Charles James Fox*, Richard Bentley, London, 1853 [**Fox's Memorials**] Volume I, pp. 107–08.

Chapter 5

George III and Tommy's Whig inheritance

1   P. Thomas, *King George III and the Politicians 1760 – 1770*, Manchester University Press, Manchester, 2002 [**Thomas**] p. 36; Ayling/Pitt, p. 262–63; Waldegrave's Memorials, p. 213; Earl of Albemarle, *Memoirs of the Marquess of Rockingham*, Richard Bentley, London, 1852 [**Rockingham's Memoirs**] Volume I, p.1; Grafton's Autobiography, p. xi; Rockingham's Memoirs, Volume I, p. 3.
2   GIII's Letters, pp. 19–20; Walpole's Memoirs GIII, Volume I, pp. 8–9.
3   Jesse, Volume I, p. 316; J. Norris, *Shelburne and Reform*, Macmillan, London, 1963 [**Norris**] p. 177; Simmons, Volume I, pp. 390–93; Stacey, p. 151.
4   Walpole's Memoirs GIII, Volume I, pp. 34–35; Chatham's Correspondence, Volume II, pp. 142–43.
5   Ayling/Pitt, pp. 297–98; Chatham's Correspondence, Volume II, p. 174; GIII's Letters, p. 19; J. Adolphus, *The History of England*, John Lee, London, 1840 [**Adolphus**] Volume I, pp. 68–69; Ayling/Pitt, p. 299; Rockingham's Memoirs, Volume I, p. 78; J. Young to TT, 22 January 1762, Sydney Papers, Box VII, Clements Library; Chatham's Correspondence, Volume II, p. 178; GIII's Letters, p. 21.
6   Townshend, pp. 285–320; Wolfe's Letters, pp. 295–96; Epitaph intended for Lieut Col Henry Townshend who died 24 June 1762, Aet 26, Sydney Papers, Box VII, Clements Library.
7   Fitzmaurice, Volume I, pp. 137, 151–52; Ayling/Pitt, pp. 305–06; 309
8   Chatham's Correspondence, Volume II, pp. 194, 198; Walpole's Memoirs GIII, Volume I, pp. 97, 198–99, 226, 233; Ayling/Pitt, p. 280; Thomas, p. 77; List of the Minority, 9 December 1762, Parliamentary History, Volume XV, p. 1272

9   Walpole's Memoirs GIII, Volume I, pp. 200–01, 233–34; Thomas, p. 78; P.D.G. Thomas, 'Townshend, Charles', *ODNB*, Volume 55, p. 146; Namier, Volume III, p. 543, 552; M.J. Powell, 'Townshend, George, 1st Marquess Townshend', *ODNB*, Volume 55, p. 157.
10 Thomas p. 79; D.H. Watson, 'The Rise of the Opposition at Wildman's Club', *Bulletin of the Institute of Historical Research*, 1971, Volume 44, p. 57; GIII's Letters, p. 23; Thomas, p. 79; Jesse, Volume I, p. 317.

Chapter 6

THE AMERICAN STAMP ACT

1   Thomas, pp. 42, 84–85; Ayling/Pitt, p. 312; Thomas, p. 103; Walpole's Memoirs GIII, Volume II, p. 70; Namier, Volume II, p. 539.
2   G.S. Wood, *The American Revolution*, Weidenfield & Nicholson, London, 2003 [**Wood**] p. 9; Fitzmaurice, Volume I, p. 247.
3   Thomas, p. 104; White, p. 89; C.L. Mowat, *East Florida as a British Province 1783–1784*, University of Florida Press, Gainsville, 1964 [**Mowat**] p. 10, Connell, p. 171.
4   Chatham's Correspondence, Volume II, p. 339; Thomas, pp. 84, 109; Van Doren, p. 321.
5   Simmons, Volume II, pp. 9, 15, 30, 51; Walpole's Memoirs GIII, Volume II, p. 68.
6   J. Fortescue, *Correspondence of King George III*, Frank Cass, London, 1967 [**GIII's Correspondence**] Volume I, pp. 73–75, 82, 115; Thomas, p. 116; Walpole's Memoirs GIII, Volume II, pp. 107–08, 147, 180; Namier, Volume III, p. 554; Grafton's Autobiography, p. 31.
7   Walpole's Memoirs GIII, Volume II, 197 Volume III, pp. 185, 189, 193; Thomas, pp. 107, 118–19; Namier, Volume III, p. 554; TT to TT Sr, 5 July 1765, Osborn Files, Beinecke Library.
8   Grafton's Autobiography, p. 54; Memo in TT's hand, 7 October 1765, Sydney Papers, Box VII, Clements Library.
9   Thomas, p. 129; Summary of Gage's Letters 23 September to 8 November 1765, Sydney Papers, Box VII, Clements Library.
10 Walpole's Memoirs GIII, Volume II, pp. 218–20.
11 Namier, Volume III, p. 554; G III's Letters, pp. 35–36.
12 Namier, Volume III, p. 554; Walpole's Memoirs GIII, Volume II, pp. 260, 262, 278.
13 Walpole's Memoirs, GIII, Volume II, pp. 278, 298, 301; *Parliamentary History of England from the Earliest Period to 1803*, T.C. Hansard, London, 1814 [**Parliamentary History**], Volume XVI, p. 165; Simmons, Volume I, pp. 311–13; Thomas, pp. 137–38.

Chapter 7

COUSIN CHARLES AND HIS TEA TAX

1   L. Namier and J. Brooke, *Charles Townshend*, Macmillan, London, 1964 [**Namier B**] pp. 47, 69; Walpole's Memoirs GII, Volume I, pp. 340–41; Namier, Volume III, p. 542; M. Bateson, *Changes in the Ministry 1765–1767*, Longmans Green, London, 1898 [**Bateson M**] p. 25; *ODNB*, Volume 55, p. 147.
2   Rockingham's Memoirs, Volume I, p. 250; Walpole's Memoirs GIII, Volume II, p. 313; Bateson M, pp. 54–55.

3 Bateson M, pp. 55, 80, 115; Rockingham's Memoirs, Volume I, p. 330; Walpole's Memoirs GIII, Volume II, p. 315; R. Browning, 'Holles, Thomas Pelham–', *ODNB*, Volume 27, p. 722.
4 Bateson M, pp. 81, 88, 93; *ODNB*, Volume 55, p. 166.
5 J. Brooke, *Chatham Administration*, Macmillan, London, 1956 [**Brooke C**] pp. 10–11, 55–56; Walpole's Memoirs GIII, Volume II, p. 358; Namier, Volume III, p. 554.
6 Brooke C, pp. 72–74; Robert Gosling to TT, receipt dated 5 March 1763, Sydney Papers, Box VII, Clements Library.
7 Thomas, p. 167–68, 170; Walpole's Memoirs GIII, Volume III, pp. 23–25.
8 Walpole's Memoirs GIII, Volume III, p. 41; Rosebery/Chatham, p. 310; GIII's Correspondence, Volume I, p. 495; Ayling/Pitt, p. 370; GIII's Letters, p. 50; W.J. Smith, ed., *The Grenville Papers*, John Murray, London, 1852 [**Grenville's Papers**] Volume IV, p. 220; NamierB, p. 158.
9 Parliamentary History, Volume XVI, p. 144; Ayling/Pitt, p. 340.
10 Namier, Volume III, p. 547; Grafton's Autobiography, pp. 126–27.
11 Walpole's Memoirs GIII, Volume II, pp. 418–19, 423; Grafton's Autobiography, p. 122; GIII's Letters, p. 46; Thomas, p. 170.
12 Thomas, pp. 571–72; Chatham's Correspondence, Volume III, pp. 184–85.
13 Namier, Volume III, p. 548; Walpole's Memoirs GIII, Volume III, p. 100; Thomas, pp. 189–90; Wood, pp. 29–31; Fitzmaurice, Volume II, p. 125; D. Boorstin, *The Americans The Colonial Experience*, Phoenix Press, London, 2000, p. 320.
14 Thomas, p. 206; Wood, p. 34; Grafton's Autobiography, pp. 229–30, 234.
15 Simmons, Volume III, p. 227.
16 Thomas, p. 233; V. Harlow, *The Founding of the Second British Empire 1763–1793*, Longmans Green, London, 1964 [**Harlow Volume II**] p. 43; Wood, pp. 36–37; GIII's Letters, pp. 99–100.
17 Wood, p. 37; Adolphus, Volume II, p. 73; Simmons, Volume IV, pp. 169–70, 193–94.
18 Wood, p. 45; Simmons, Volume III, p. 92.

Chapter 8

WILKES AND LIBERTY! – TOMMY'S DEFENCE OF DISSENT

1 Wood, p. 20; White, p. 64.
2 Namier, Volume III, p. 639; Thomas, p. 73; Walpole, Memoirs GIII, p. 177.
3 Walpole's Memoirs GIII, Volume I, pp. 274–75; Thomas p. 98.
4 Thomas, pp. 98–99; Walpole's Memoirs GIII, Volume I, p. 277–80.
5 Thomas, p. 100; Walpole's Memoirs GIII, Volume I, pp. 316, 322, 330.
6 Walpole's Memoirs GIII, Volume I, p. 350;
7 Walpole's Memoirs GIII, Volume I, pp. 355–61.
8 Walpole's Memoirs GIII, Volume I, pp. 361–64; NamierB, p. 114; Thomas, pp. 100–02.
9 Chatham's Correspondence, Volume III, p. 285; Holmes, p. 90; Chatham's Correspondence, Volume III, p. 285; Walpole's Memoirs GIII, Volume III, pp. 140–41.
10 Chatham's Correspondence, Volume III, pp. 306–07, 319; Thomas, pp. 187, 189; Namier, Volume III, p. 640; Walpole's Memoirs GIII, Volume III, pp. 185–86, P. Durrant, 'Fitzroy, Augustus Henry, third Duke of Grafton, *ODNB*, Volume 19, pp. 924–29.
11 Brooke C, p. 359; The Oath of a Privy Councillor, Sydney Papers, Box XVII, Clements Library; Thomas, p. 188.

12. Undated and unsigned letter in TT's hand addressed to My Lord, Osborn Files; Walpole's Memoirs GIII, Volume III, p. 226; T. Copeland, ed., *The Correspondence of Edmund Burke April 1744 – June 1768*, Cambridge University Press, 1958 [**Burke's Correspondence Volume I**] p. 355; Jesse, Volume II, p. 324; Namier, Volume III, p. 355.
13. Walpole's Memoirs GIII, Volume III, p. 226; Doggerel referring to the Duke and Duchess of Bedford and to Richard Rigby, n.d., Sydney Papers, Box XVII, Clements Library; Namier, Volume III, p. 555; Brooke C, p. 362.
14. Grenville's Papers, Volume IV, p. 375; Chatham's Correspondence, Volume III, pp. 338, 344; GIII's Letters, p. 58; Walpole's Memoirs GIII, Volume III, p. 226.
15. Walpole's Memoirs GIII, Volume II, p. 413; Thomas, pp. 200–203.
16. Thomas, pp. 203–04; Walpole's Memoirs GIII, Volume III, pp. 257–58; Namier S, Volume I, p. 96; Namier, Volume I, p. 331; D.A. Winstanley, *Lord Chatham and the Whig Opposition*, Cambridge University Press, 1912 [**Winstanley**] p. 330; Chatham's Correspondence, Volume III, p. 357.
17. Rockingham's Memoirs, Volume II, pp. 212–13; Undated Letter of John Wilkes, in the Sydney Catalogue, Lot 1824, p. 164; Namier, Volume III, p. 639.
18. Chatham's Correspondence, Volume III, p. 379.

Chapter 9

Opposition

1. Chatham's Correspondence, Volume III, pp. 359–60.
2. Winstanley, p. 288; Namier, Volume III, p. 555; L. S. Sutherland, *The Correspondence of Edmund Burke July 1768 – June 1774*, Cambridge University Press, 1960 [**Burke's Correspondence Volume II**] pp. 88, 90–92.
3. Parliamentary History, Volume XVI, pp. 737–40; Walpole's Memoirs GIII, Volume IV, 54.
4. Walpole's Memoirs GIII, Volume IV, pp. 70, 78–79, 86.
5. Fitzmaurice, Volume I, p. 300, Volume II, p. 216; Chatham to TT, November 1770, Pitt Papers, Clements Library; Thomas, p. 229; Chatham's Correspondence, Volume IV, p. 32; Winstanley, pp. 374, 404, 407, 412–13; Parliamentary History, Volume XVI, p. 1121.
6. Winstanley, pp. 415–19.
7. Winstanley, pp. 422–25; Parliamentary History, Volume XVI, pp. 1162, 1199, 1211, 1262–63; Simmons, Volume IV, pp. 169–70; Namier, Volume III, p. 555; GIII's Correspondence, Volume II, p. 227; Chatham's Correspondence, Volume IV, p. 127.
8. Winstanley, p. 433; Parliamentary History, Volume XVI, pp. 1329–1330; Walpole's Memoirs GIII, Volume IV, p. 231; Namier, Volume II, pp. 683–85, Volume III, pp. 390–96.
9. Burke's Correspondence, Volume II, pp. 368, 371; Parliamentary History, Volume XVII, pp. 568, 717, 1363, 1397, 1400; P. Langford, 'Burke, Edmund', ODNB, Volume 8, pp. 820–41.
10. Parliamentary History, Volume XVII, pp. 568–69, 573, 722–23, 730; H. Walpole, *The Last Journals of Horace Walpole During the Reign of George III from 1771–1783*, John Lane, London, 1910 [**Walpole's Journal**] Volume I, p. 181; *Historical Records of New South Wales*, Volume I, Part 2, Government Printer, Sydney, 1892 [**HRNSW**] p. 89.
11. Walpole's Journal, Volume I, p. 25; Parliamentary History, Volume XVII, pp. 311, 315, 1057.
12. Parliamentary History, Volume XVII, pp. 1055–56; Wraxall HM, p. 88; Walpole's Journal, Volume I, pp. 307–08.

[13] Parliamentary History, Volume XVII, p. 1057; J. Lynch, *Dr Johnson's Dictionary*, Atlantic Books, London, 2004 [**Johnson's Dictionary**] p. 5; Fox's Memorials, Volume 1, p. 100.
[14] *Boswell's Life of Johnson*, Heron Books, London, 1960 [**Boswell**] Volume II, p. 538; F.F. Moore, *The Life of Oliver Goldsmith*, Constable, London, 1910 [**Moore FF**] pp. 442–43; P. Masson, *The Miscellaneous Works of Oliver Goldsmith*, Macmillan, London, 1871, p. 595.
[15] Moore FF, p. 446; Boswell, Volume II, p. 538; S. Gwynn, *Oliver Goldsmith*, Thornton Butterworth, London, 1935, p. 268; Jesse, Volume I, p. 132, Wraxall HM, p. 365; Lord Rosebery, *Pitt*, Macmillan, London, 1892 [**Rosebery/Pitt**] p. 46; Escott, Volume II, p. 233; Ehrman, p. 184; C.M.H. Clark, *A History of Australia*, Melbourne University Press, 1962, Volume I [**Clark CMH**] p. 68.
[16] Norris, pp. 188–90; Hibbert, GIII, p. 144; Boswell, Volume II, p. 225.
[17] Namier, Volume III, p. 556.

Chapter 10
The dye is cast

[1] GIII's Correspondence, Volume III, p. 131.
[2] P. Reynolds, *Sir Guy Carleton*, William Morrow and Co., 1980 [**Reynolds**] pp. x, 48; Wood, p. 22; J.D. Driscoll, *United States Constitution California*, California Legislative Assembly, 1971 [**U.S. Constitutional Documents**] p. 15; Parliamentary History, Volume XVII, pp. 1357–58.
[3] Parliamentary History, Volume XVII, p. 1376.
[4] Walpole's Journal, Volume I, p. 372; Parliamentary History, Volume XVII, pp. 1397, 1400.
[5] Namier, Volume I, pp. 73–80; *ODND*, Volume 55, p. 167; U.S. Constitutional Documents, p. 16; GIII's Letters, p. 108; TT Sr to the Vice Chancellor of Cambridge, April 1774, Osborn Files.
[6] Namier, Volume I, pp. 73–80, 514–19; Volume II, p. 120.
[7] Reynolds, pp. 56–59.
[8] Wood, p. 51; GIII's Correspondence, Volume III, pp. 154, 159.
[9] Simmons, Volume V, pp. 315–16; Fitzmaurice, Volume II, p. 311; Parliamentary History, Volume XVIII, p. 353; Chatham's Correspondence, Volume IV, p. 104; Langford, p. 538.
[10] Namier, Volume I, pp. 96, 159, 514; C. Moore, *The Loyalists*, McClelland and Stewart, Toronto, 1994 [**Moore L**] p. 43; Wood, pp. 39–40; Kier, p. 352.
[11] Parliamentary History, Volume XVII, pp. 1064, 1074.
[12] Wood, p. 43; A. de Tocqueville, *Democracy in America*, Penguin, London, 2003 [**Tocqueville**] p. 52; Rockingham's Memoirs, Volume II, p. 279; Boorstin, p. 156; Sidney, p. 399.
[13] Parliamentary History, Volume XVIII, p. 392; GIII's Correspondence, Volume III, p. 184.
[14] Parliamentary History, Volume XVIII, pp. 387, 573; GIII's Letters, p. 108; Van Doren, p. 567.
[15] Wood, p. 52; GIII's Correspondence, Volume III, pp. 207–08; Fitzmaurice, Volume II, p. 310.
[16] Wood, pp. 51–52; Macksey, p. 73.
[17] Wood, p. 53; Macksey, pp. 39, 60; Sir George Yonge to TT, 8 July 1775, Sydney Papers, Box VIII, Clements Library.
[18] GIII's Correspondence, Volume III, p. 269; GIII's Letters, p. 114; Namier, Volume III, pp. 390–95.

19. H. Bicheno, *Rebels and Redcoats*, Harper Collins, London, 2003, p. 13; Macksey, p. 61; Parliamentary History, Volume XVIII, pp. 831, 1331;
20. Mackesy, pp. 71–7, 74, 77; Parliamentary History, Volume XVIII, pp. 1234–38.
21. Macksey, pp. 83, 87; Walpole's Journals, Volume II, pp. 68, 83; R. Russell, 'Where is George III's Head?' *The Sons of the American Revolution Magazine*, Winter, 1998; Simmons Volume VI, p. 595.

Chapter 11

AT WAR WITH AMERICA

1. T. Fleming, *The Man from Monticello*, William Morrow and Co., New York, 1969 [**Fleming**] p. 68; Jefferson's Writings, p. 479; Carswell, p. 213; *Chambers Dictionary of Quotations*, Cambridge University Press, Cambridge, 1996, p. 402.
2. Jefferson's Writings, pp. 1500–01; Sidney, pp. 5, 17; Carswell, p. 213; Fleming, pp. 61–62.
3. Wood, p. 43; Fleming, p. 64; Parliamentary History, Volume XVIII, p. 1331.
4. Colley, p. xv.
5. Macksey, p. 33; W. Isaacson, *Benjamin Franklin*, Simon and Schuster, New York, 2004 [**Isaacson**] pp. 308–09; Namier, Volume III, pp. 538, 549; Walpole's Journal, Volume I, p. 512; Cornwallis's Correspondence, Volume I, pp. 11–13.
6. Macksey, pp. 34, 93, 97; D. H. Fisher, *Washington's Crossing*, Oxford University Press, Oxford, 2006, p. 115; Cornwallis's Correspondence, Volume I, p. 24.
7. Fitzmaurice, Volume III, pp. 1, 3–4; Parliamentary History, Volume XVIII, p. 1448; A.G. Olson, *The Radical Duke*, Oxford University Press, London, 1961 [**Olson**] p. 170; TT to Chatham, 18 November 1776, Sydney Papers, Box VIII, Clements Library.
8. Namier, Volume 1, pp. 138, 144, Volumes 2 and 3 for individual political biographies of these commanders; TT to Clinton, 5 November 1776, Clinton Papers, Box XVIII, Clements Library.
9. Parliamentary History, Volume XIX, pp. 4, 18, 51.
10. Cornwallis's Correspondence, Volume I, p. 30; Bicheno, p. 73; Macksey, pp. 58, 112, 129; A. T. Mahan, *The Influence of Sea Power on History*, Dover Publications, New York, 1987 [**Mahan**] p. 343.
11. Reynolds, pp. 113–14; Macksey, pp. 108, 114–15; Jesse, Volume III, p. 206.
12. Macksey, pp. 131, 133, 141; Wood, p. 79; Bicheno, pp. 100–01.
13. Fitzmaurice, Volume III, p. 11, Parliamentary History, Volume XIX, pp. 457–58; GIII's Correspondence, Volume III, p. xvi; Adolphus, Volume II, p. 498.
14. GIII's Correspondence, Volume III, pp. 503–04, Volume IV, p. 15; Parliamentary History, Volume XIX, p. 694, 700–01, 708.
15. GIII's Correspondence, Volume IV, pp. 27, 31, 35; Fitzmaurice, Volume III, pp. 15–16; Parliamentary History, Volume XIX, p. 787.
16. GIII's Correspondence, Volume IV, pp. 55, 58.
17. Jesse, Volume III, pp. 261–62; TT to Clinton, 31 March 1778, Clinton Papers, Box XXXII, Clements Library; TT to Clinton, 23 December 1780, Clinton Papers, Box CXXXIV, Clements Library.
18. Fitzmaurice, Volume III, pp. 25–30; Chatham's Correspondence, Volume IV, p. 513; Ayling/Pitt, pp. 424–25; Parliamentary History, Volume XIX, pp. 1080, 1082, 1088; Walpole's Journal, Volume II, pp. 260–61; W. Lowe, 'Lennox, Charles, third duke of

Richmond', *ODNB*, Volume 33, pp. 361–65; L. G. Marshall, *Charles James Fox*, Penguin, London, 1997, pp. 25–27, 33–34; Hibbert GIII, p. 233.

[19] Fitzmaurice, Volume III, p. 26; Ayling/Pitt, p. 425; Parliamentary History, Volume XIX, p. 1225; Note on the file marked TT to TT Sr, 13 May 1778, Pitt Papers, Box 1, Clements Library; W. Churchill, *A History of the English Speaking People*, Cassell, London, 1957, Volume III, p. 124; TT to TT Sr May 1778, Sydney Papers, Box VIII, Clements Library; TT to TT Sr, 15 May 1788, Sydney Papers, Box VIII, Clements Library; TT to TT Sr, 13 May 1778, Pitt Papers, Box 1, Clements Library; Lady Chatham to TT, 18 May 1778, Pitt Papers, Box 1, Clements Library; Langford, p. 83; Barnard, Edward ALS to TT 26 May 1778, Sydney Papers, Box VIII, Clements Library; *ODNB*, Volume 43, pp. 951–61.

[20] Macksey, p. 220; U.S. Constitutional Documents, pp. 24, 31.

Chapter 12

AT WAR IN PARLIAMENT

[1] Macksey, p. 160; Walpole's Journal, Volume II, p. 223.
[2] Walpole's memoirs, GIII, Volume I, p. 97; Wraxall HM, p. 227.
[3] Parliamentary History, Volume XIX, pp. 454, 458; Macksey, p. 223; GIII's Letters, p. 132.
[4] GIII's Correspondence, Volume IV, pp. 112–13; Macksey, p. 199; Mahan, p. 359; Wraxall HM, p. 319.
[5] Parliamentary History, Volume XIX, pp. 1131–33; GIII's Correspondence, Volume IV, p. 130.
[6] Fox's Memorials, Volume I, p. 197; GIII's Correspondence, Volume IV, pp. 134–35; Parliamentary History, Volume XIX, p. 1136.
[7] Mahan, pp. 364–65; Macksey, pp. 222, 273, 275–76; A. Lambert, *War at Sea in the Age of Sail*, Cassell, London, 2000 [**Lambert**] p. 134; R. Harvey, *A Few Bloody Noses*, The Overlook Press, New York, 2003, p. 299.
[8] TT to TT Sr, 15 May 1778, Sydney Papers, Box VIII, Clements Library; Namier, Volume II, p. 144; Parliamentary History, Volume XIX, pp. 1213–16; Macksey, p. 238; Burgoyne to TT, 18 October 1779, Sydney Papers, Box VIII, Clements Library.
[9] Lambert, pp. 135–36; GIII's Correspondence, Volume IV, p. 294; Macksey, pp. 203, 239; Namier, Volume III, p. 246; Jesse, Volume III, p. 303.
[10] Jesse, Volume III, p. 331; Namier, Volume III, p. 246; GIII's Correspondence, Volume IV, pp. 225–27.
[11] Macksey, pp. 239, 242; GIII's Correspondence, Volume IV, pp. 231, 281; Namier, Volume III, p. 247.
[12] Parliamentary History, Volume XX, pp. 174, 187.
[13] Parliamentary History, p. 187, 189; GIII's correspondence, Volume IV, pp. 295, 298.
[14] Parliamentary History, Volume XX, p. 399; GIII's Correspondence, Volume IV, p. 297; Macksey, p. 321.
[15] Macksey, p. 244; Namier, Volume II, pp. 648, 650.
[16] Parliamentary History, Volume XX, p. 731.
[17] Parliamentary History, Volume XX, pp. 732, 748–49; GIII's Correspondence, Volume IV, pp. 269, 337; Cornwallis's Correspondence, Volume I, p. 42.
[18] Parliamentary History, Volume XX, pp. 801–03, 816–18; Macksey, p. 152.
[19] Parliamentary History, Volume XX, pp. 828–31, 854, 876.

20. Parliamentary History, Volume XX, p. 918.
21. Parliamentary History, Volume XX, p. 919, Macksey, pp. 264–65; GIII's Correspondence, Volume IV, pp. 366, 374.
22. Grafton's Autobiography, p. 306; Lambert, p. 137; Macksey, pp. 250, 281, 289; GIII's Correspondence, Volume IV, p. 388.
23. Macksey, pp. 289, 297; Rockingham's Memoirs, Volume II, p. 379; Fox's Memorials, Volume I, p. 230; Jesse, Volume IV, pp. 229, 232, 239; Adolphus, Volume III, p. 48.
24. Macksey, pp. 65, 275–78; Lambert, pp. 138, 140.

Chapter 13

BRITAIN ON THE BRINK

1. GIII's Correspondence, Volume IV, pp. 497–99.
2. Parliamentary History, Volume XX, pp. 1104, 1150; GIII's Correspondence, Volume IV, p. 503; A Merchant to TT, 27 November 1779, Sydney Papers, Box VIII, Clements Library.
3. Bicheno, p. 227; Lambert, p. 138; A Merchant to TT, 27 November 1779, Sydney Papers, Box VIII, Clements Library.
4. Norris, pp. 111–13; S. Ayling, *The Life and Times of Charles James Fox*, John Murray, London, 1991 [**Ayling/Fox**] p. 75; Walpole's Journal, Volume II, p. 23; Grafton's Autobiography, p. 308; H. Dickinson, 'Wyvill, Christopher, *ODNB*, Volume 60, pp. 717–21.
5. Norris, pp. 116–20; Fitzmaurice, Volume III, p. 71; Parliamentary History, Volume XX, p. 399; W.T. Laprade, *Parliamentary Papers of John Robinson*, Royal Historical Society, London, 1922 [**Robinson's Papers**] pp. 9–17; Parliamentary History, Volume XXI, p. 909; Namier, Volume I, pp. 54–55.
6. Hibbert, GIII, p. 208; Walpole's Journal, Volume II, p. 364; Namier, Volume II, p. 367; Parliamentary History, Volume XXI, pp. 72–73.
7. Parliamentary History, Volume XXI, pp. 195, 199; Norris, p. 121.
8. Parliamentary History, Volume XXI, pp. 279–80; D. Limon, ed., *Erskine May's Treatise on the Law, principles and proceedings of Parliament*, London, 1997, p. 676.
9. Parliamentary History, Volume XXI, pp. 80, 82; Fitzmaurice, Volume III, p. 79; Walpole's Journals, Volume II, p. 391; Norris, p. 129; GIII's Correspondence, Volume V, p. 40; Namier, Volume II, p. 367.
10. Parliamentary History, Volume XXI, pp. 412, 503; Namier, Volume II, p. 680; Fitzmaurice, Volume III, p. 73; GIII's Correspondence, Volume V, p. 52.
11. C. Haydon, 'Gordon, Lord George' *ODNB*, Volume 22, p. 895; Parliamentary History, Volume XXI, pp. 654–56; Namier, Volume II, p. 514.
12. Namier, Volume II, p. 514; Wraxall HM, pp. 196–203.
13. Wraxall HM, pp. 206–09; Adolphus, Volume III, p. 145; Namier, Volume II, p. 514.
14. Fitzmaurice, Volume III, p. 83; Olson, pp. 48, 56; I. Christie, *The End of North's Ministry 1780–1782*, Macmillan, London, 1958 [**Christie**] p. 24; Macksey, p. 362; J.J. Edwards and R. Pares, 'The Marquis of Rockingham and Lord North's Offer of a Coalition June–July 1780', *The English Historical Review*, Volume LXIX, 1954 [**Edwards/Pares**] p. 391.
15. GIII's Correspondence, Volume IV, p. 542; Macksey, p. 341; GIII's Correspondence, Volume V, p. 40; Namier, Volume III, p. 154; GIII's Correspondence, Volume V, p. 96; Walpole's Journal, Volume II, p. 423.

[16] GIII's Correspondence, Volume V, pp. 97–99; Parliamentary History, Volume XX, p. 1105; Pares, p. 399; Hibbert, GIII, p. 234.
[17] Robinson's Papers, p. 33; Christie, pp. 98, 101, 104, 117; Namier, Volume II, p. 120.
[18] Namier, Volume I, pp. 81–82, 219, Volume II, pp. 145, 650, Volume III, pp. 10, 431; Jesse, Volume IV, p. 77.
[19] Wraxall HM, p. 337; Fox's Memorials, Volume I, p. 260; Macksey, p. 378.
[20] Parliamentary History, Volume XXI, p. 891; Cornwallis's Correspondence Volume I, p. 92.

Chapter 14

COUSIN CORNWALLIS AND YORKTOWN

[1] Cornwallis's Correspondence, Volume I, pp. 3, 11, 13–14.
[2] Macksey, pp. 159, 342; GIII's Correspondence, Volume IV, pp. 542–58.
[3] Cornwallis's Correspondence, Volume I, pp. 46, 54–55; Bicheno, p. 185.
[4] Cornwallis's Correspondence, Volume I, pp. 59, 61, 67.
[5] Cornwallis's Correspondence, Volume I, pp. 66, 71.
[6] Cornwallis's Correspondence, Volume I, pp. 77–78, 82–83.
[7] Cornwallis's Correspondence, pp. 85–87; Macksey, p. 407; Bicheno, p. 201.
[8] Cornwallis's Correspondence, pp. 86–87, 93; Macksey, p. 409.
[9] Cornwallis's Correspondence, Volume I, pp. 97, 111; Bicheno, p. 235; Macksey, p. 408.
[10] Parliamentary History, Volume XXII, p. 450; Cornwallis's Correspondence, Volume I, pp. 98–100.
[11] Cornwallis's Correspondence, Volume I, pp. 101–104; Bicheno, p. 235.
[12] Cornwallis's Correspondence, Volume I, pp. 106–07.
[13] Macksey, pp. 410, 412; Cornwallis's Correspondence, Volume I, pp. 109–10; Van Doren, p. 628; Mahan, p. 388.
[14] Lambert, p. 139; Macksey, p. 423–25.
[15] Cornwallis's Correspondence, Volume I, pp. 118–22; Macksey, p. 213.
[16] Cornwallis's Correspondence, Volume I, pp. 121–22; A. Lambert, 'Cornwallis, Sir William', *ODNB*, Volume 13, p. 489.
[17] Cornwallis's Correspondence, Volume I, pp. 123–24; Cornwallis to Clinton, Yorktown Virginia 12m 11 October 1781, Clinton Papers, Box CLXXX, Clements Library.
[18] Cornwallis's Correspondence, Volume I, pp. 125, 511–13; Great Britain, Army in America, 18 October 1781, Return of Army in Virginia, Clinton Papers, Box CLXXX, Clements Library; Macksey, p. 427.
[19] Cornwallis's Correspondence, Volume I, p. 516; Bicheno, p. 248; Macksey, p. 427; R. Leckie, *George Washington's War*, Harper Perenial, New York, 1993, p. 658; Clinton to Germain, 19 October 1781, Clinton Papers, Box CLXXX, Clements Library.
[20] Intelligence, 24 October 1781, Clinton Papers, Box CLXXX, Clements Library; Hood to Clinton, 25 October 1781, Clinton Papers, Box CLXXX, Clements Library.
[21] Cornwallis's Correspondence, Volume I, p. 127;
[22] Cornwallis to Clinton, extracts with annotations in Clinton's hand, 20 October 1781, Clinton Papers, Box CLXXX, Clements Library; Clinton to Shelburne, I July 1782, Sydney Papers, Box IX, Clements Library.
[23] Holmes, p. 23; I. Gruber, 'Clinton, Sir Henry', *ODNB*, Volume 12, p. 143; Giii's Correspondence, Volume V, pp. 339–40.

Chapter 15

OH GOD! IT'S ALL OVER!

1. Macksey, pp. 434–35.
2. Walpole's Journal, Volume II, p. 492; K.G. Davies, *Documents of the American Revolution 1770–1783*, Colonial Office Series, Irish University Press, Shannon, 1981 [**Davies**] Volume XXI, p. 136; Macksey, pp. 436, 454; Grafton's Autobiography, p. 314.
3. Fitzmaurice, Volume III, p. 124; C. Towse, 'Conway, Henry Seymour', *ODNB*, Volume 13, pp 49–57.
4. Fitzmaurice, Volume III, p. 123; GIII's Correspondence, Volume V, pp. 303–04; Macksey, p. 460; Christie, p. 270; Parliamentary History, Volume XXII, p. 741.
5. Christie, pp. 272, 283.
6. Davies, Volume XXI, pp. 1–2, 5; Moore L, p. 114; Chrisite, pp. 274, 277; Macksey, pp. 240, 462; Parliamentary History, Volume XXII, pp. 836–37.
7. GIII's Correspondence, Volume V, p. 326; Wraxall HM, p. 311; GIII's Correspondence, Volume V, p. 313
8. Adolphus, Volume III, p. 331; Parliamentary History, Volume XXII, pp. 1030, 1033–34, 1042; R. Thorne, 'Ellis, Welbore', *ODNB*, Volume 18, p. 262.
9. Parliamentary History, Volume XXII, pp. 1048–51; Fox's Memorials Volume I, pp. 277–78; GIII's Correspondence, Volume V, p. 373.
10. Namier, Volume I, p. 147, Volume II, p. 328; Parliamentary History, Volume XXII, p. 1083–84; N. Aston, 'Dolben, Sir William', *ODNB*, Volume 16, pp. 467–68.
11. Parliamentary History, Volume XXII, pp. 1084–85; Namier, Volume II, p. 394, Volume III, p. 320; GIII's Correspondence, Volume V, pp. 374–75.
12. Parliamentary History, Volume XXII, pp. 1086, 1101; GIII's Correspondence, Volume V, p. 376.
13. Parliamentary History, Volume XXII, pp. 1087, 1101, 1103.
14. GIII's Correspondence, Volume V, pp. 378–89.
15. Chrisite, p. 352; Parliamentary History, Volume XXII, pp. 1170, 1181.
16. GIII's Correspondence, Volume V, pp. 389, 392.
17. GIII's Correspondence, Volume V, pp. 392, 394, 397, 399; Namier, Volume I, p. 147; Wraxall HM, pp. 424–25.
18. Parliamentary History, Volume XXII, pp. 1214, 1217; Christie, p. 369.

Chapter 16

TOMMY RE-ENTERS THE MINISTRY

1. Wraxall HM, pp. 365–66; Parliamentary History, Volume XXII, pp. 1238–40; Fox's Memorials, Volume I, pp. 291–92; Namier, Volume III, p. 556.
2. Parliamentary History, Volume XXII, pp. 1336–44, Volume XXIII, p. 127; Fitzmaurice, Volume III, p. 162; Wraxall HM, p. 440.
3. Parliamentary History, Volume XXIII, pp. 128, 132, 134; The Fourth Report of the Commissioners Appointed to Examine, Take and State the Public Accounts of the Kingdom, 1781, Sydney Papers, Box XVII, Clements Library; The Examination of TT upon oath, 27 March 1781; Benbridge to TT, 18 October 1781, Sydney Papers, Box XVII, Clements Library.

4   Parliamentary History, Volume XXII, p. 1344.
5   Parliamentary History, Volume XXII, pp. 1344–45; B. Fergusson, *Advice to Officers of the British Army*, Jonathan Cape, London, 1946 (first published in 1782) pp. 14–15.
6   GIII's Correspondence, Volume V, p. 436; Macksey, p. 475; Rockingham to TT March to July 1782, Sydney Papers, Box IX, Clements Library; List of Transports, Army Victuallers and Store Ships at New York 16 January 1783, Shelburne Papers, Volume 68, p. 281, Clements Library; Moore L, p. 150.
7   Macksey, pp. 479–84; Boyd to TT, 25 July 1782, Sydney Papers, Box IX, Clements Library; Boyd to Hardy, 11 February 1782, Sydney Papers, Box IX, Clements Library; Boyd: representation to George III, 21 March, 1782, Sydney Papers, Box IX, Clements Library; Boyd to TT, 25 July 1782, Sydney Papers, Clements Library; Boyd to TT, 31 July 1782, Sydney Papers, Box IX, Clements Library; J. Falkner, 'Eliott, George Augustus', *ODNB*, Volume 18, p. 77; S. Handley, 'Boyd, Robert', *ODNB*, Volume 7, p. 46; GIII's Correspondence, Volume VI, p. 117; Parliamentary History, Volume XXIII, p. 303.
8   Fitzmaurice, Volume III, pp. 162, 210, 219, 221; Grafton's Autobiography, p. 323; Fox's Memorials, p. 435.
9   Grafton's Autobiography, p. 324; H. Furber, *Correspondence of Edmund Burke, July 1782– June 1789*, Cambridge at the University Press, 1965 [**Burke's Correspondence, Volume V**] pp. 8–9, 15, 24; Fitzmaurice, Volume III, 226.
10 Fitzmaurice, Volume III, p. 227; Ehrman, p. 83; GIII's Correspondence, Volume V, pp. 70, 79; Namier, Volume III, p. 300; Earl of Stanhope, *Life of Pitt*, John Murray, London, 1861 [**Stanhope**] Volume I, p. 83; Cornwallis to TT, 9 July 1782, Melville Papers 1600–1783, Clements Library.
11 R.R. Nelson, *The Home Office 1782–1801*, Duke University Press, Durham, North Carolina, 1969 [**Nelson RR**] pp. 4, 6–7, 13, 75; H. T. Manning, *British Colonial Government after the American Revolution 1782–1820*, Archon Books, Hamden, Connecticut, 1966 [**Manning**] p. 84.
12 Nelson RR, pp. vii, 8; Parliamentary History, Volume XXIII, p. 303; Sydney to Earl Ferrers, 2 November 1784, Osborn Files, Beinecke Library.
13 Memorandum to Mr Townshend, n.d., Shelburne Papers, Volume 72, p. 531, Clements Library; Establishment of the Office of His Majesty's Principal Secretary of State for the Home Department Oct. 1784, Sydney Papers, Box XII, Clements Library; Nelson RR, pp. 26, 32, 65; J.C. Sainty, *Office Holders in Modern Britain V Home Office officials 1782–1870*, Athlone Press, Bristol, 1975 [**Sainty**] p. 13; E. Sparrow, 'Nepean, Sir Evan', *ODNB*, Volume 40, pp. 425–26; G.S. Dugdale, *Whitehall Through the Centuries*, Theodore Brun Ltd, London, 1950, pp. 117, 136, Plates 63 & 64.
14 Nelson RR, p. 66; L.F.S. Upton, *The Diary and Selected Papers of Chief Justice William Smith*, The Champlain Society, Toronto, 1963 [**Smith's Diary**] Volume I, pp. 150, 152, Volume II, pp. 65, 102; F. Haldimand, *The Private Diary of General Haldimand*, www.canadiana.org/ECO [**Haldimand's Diary**] p. 133; A. Aspinall, *The later Correspondence of George III*, Cambridge University Press, London, 1962 [**GIII's Later Correspondence**] Volume I, p. 79.
15 Smith's Diary, Volume I, pp. 119,148, 150, 213, 242, Volume II, pp. 104–05, 114, 116; Haldimand's Diary, pp. 153, 171, 183, 205, 227, 229, 233, 247, 273; A. Atkinson, 'The First Plans for Governing New South Wales', *Australian Historical Studies*, Volume 24, Number 94, April 1990 [**Atkinson FP**] p. 39; Nelson RR, p. 32.

Chapter 17

THE AMERICAN PEACE TALKS

1. M. Skousen, ed., *The Compleated Autobiography by Benjamin Franklin*, Regnery Publishing, Washington D.C., 2006 [**Skousen**] p. 256; Fitzmaurice, Volume III, p. 188.
2. Fitzmaurice, Volume III, pp. 168, 196; Namier Volume II, p. 458
3. GIII's correspondence, Volume V, p. 488; R.B. Morris, *John Jay, The Winning of the Peace*, Harper and Row, New York, 1980 [**Jay's Papers**] Volume II, p. 239; Macksey, p. 474; Fitzmaurice, Volume III, pp. 188, 195; Oswald to Shelburne, 8 July 1782, Shelburne Papers, Volume 70, p. 39, Clements Library.
4. Report of the Committee of Merchants Trading to North America, 10 April 1782, Sydney Papers, Box IX, Clements Library; Davies, Volume XXI, pp. 108–11; Reynolds, p. 137.
5. AD 1782, Anno Vicesimo Secundo, George III CAPXLVI; Parliamentary History, Volume XXIII, p. 202; S.F. Beamis, *The American Secretaries of State and their Diplomacy*, Knopf, New York, 1927 [**Bemis**] Volume I, p. 47; TT to Shelburne, 27 July 1782, Sydney Papers, Box IX, Clements Library; S.M. Lee, 'Fitzherbert, Alleyne', *ODNB*, Volume 19, p. 871; M.A. Giunta, ed., *The Emerging Nation, Foreign Relations of the United States 1780–1789*, National Historical Publications and Records Commission, 1996 [**Giunta**] Volume I, pp. 460, 508, 555, 565; Walpole's Journals, Volume II, p. 566; J. Cannon, 'Petty, William', *ODNB*, Volume 43, pp. 952, 957; G. Smith and R. Davis, 'Grenville, Thomas', *ODNB*, Volume 23, pp. 747–48.
6. Giunta, Volume I, p. 690.
7. D. Hancock, 'Oswald, Richard', *ODNB*, Volume 42, p. 91; Giunta, Volume I, p. 480.
8. Giunta, Volume I, p. 480; Alleyne Fitzherbert to TT, 8 August 1782, Shelburne Papers, Volume 87, p. 185, Clements Library.
9. Giunta, Volume I, pp. 462–63; Fitzmaurice, Volume III, pp. 179–81; Van Doren, p. 673; W.S. MacNutt, *New Brunswick: a history, 1784–1867*, Macmillan, Toronto, 1984 [**MacNutt**] p. 13; U.S. Constitutional Documents, p. 30.
10. Giunta, Volume I, pp. 471–73, 505; TT to Oswald, 3 August 1782, Shelburne Papers, Volume 70, p. 83, Clements Library; GIII's Correspondence, Volume VI, pp. 95–96; TT to Oswald, 26 July 1782, Shelburne Papers, Volume 70, p. 75, Clements Library; E.R. Cohn, ed., *The Papers of Benjamin Franklin*, Yale University Press, New Haven, Connecticut, 2003 [**Franklin's Papers**] Volume 37, pp. 678–79; Franklin to TT, 4 November 1782, Shelburne Papers, Volume 70, p. 331, Clements Library.
11. Giunta, Volume I, pp. 482–83.
12. Giunta, Volume I, pp. 507–09, 520, 523; Isaacson, pp. 325, 408–09.
13. Giunta, Volume I, p. 509; Skousen, p. 259; Bemis, p. 66.
14. Fitzherbert to TT, 17 August 1782, Shelburne Papers, Volume 87, p. 190, Clements Library; GIII's Correspondence, Volume VI, pp. 108–10.
15. GIII's Correspondence, Volume VI, p. 118; Jay's Papers, p. 347; Parliamentary History, Volume XXIII, p. 203.
16. Giunta, Volume I, pp. 545–46.
17. TT to Oswald, 1 September 1782, Shelburne Papers, Volume 87, p. 89, Clements Library; Franklin's Papers, Volume 37, p. 713; Oswald to TT, 27 August 1782, Shelburne Papers, Volume 70, p. 186, Clements Library; Giunta, Volume I, pp. 527–28, 561; L.H. Butterfield, ed., *Diary and Autobiography of John Adams*, Belknap Press, Cambridge, Massachusetts, 1961 [**Adams's Diary**] Volume 3, p. 70; Isaacson, p. 397.

Chapter 18

Strachey strikes the peace with America

1. S.F. Bemis, *The Diplomacy of the American Revolution*, Indiana University Press, Bloomington, 1967, p. 223; Giunta, Volume I, pp. 527, 568.
2. Ashburton to Shelburne, 16 September 1782, Sydney Papers, Box X, Clements Library; GIII's Correspondence, Volume VI, p. 131.
3. Giunta, Volume I, pp. 593, 597, 604; Fitzmaurice, Volume III, p. 272; Jay's Papers, Volume II, p. 398; GIII's Correspondence, Volume VI, pp. 143–44, Simmons, Volume IV, p. 6.
4. Jay's Papers, Volume II, pp. 395–96, 398; Giunta, Volume I, pp. 589, 725.
5. Namier, Volume III, pp. 487–89.
6. TT to Oswald, 23 October 1782, Shelburne Papers, Volume 70, p. 319, Clements Library; Giunta, Volume I, 623.
7. Giunta, Volume I, pp. 622–23; Franklin to TT, 4 November 1782, Shelburne Papers, Volume 70, p. 331, Clements Library; Jay's Papers, Volume II, p. 411; Adams's Diary, Volume III, p. 46
8. Fitzherbert to TT, 30 November 1782, Sydney Papers, Box X, Clements Library; Oswald to TT, 5 November 1782, Shelburne Papers, Volume 70, p. 329, Clements Library; M.B. Norton, *The British Americans; the loyalist exiles in England 1774–1789*, Little Brown and Co., Canada, 1972 [**Norton**] p. 175.
9. Giunta, Volume I, p. 650; Skousen, p. 281; GIII's Correspondence, Volume I, p. 635; S.F. Bemis, *A Diplomatic History of the United States*, Holt Rinehart and Winston, New York, 1965 [**Bemis DH**] Map 5 'Boundary Claims and Settlement in the Anglo–American Negotiations of 1782'.
10. Davies, Volume XXI, p. 135; Jay's Papers, Volume II, pp. 398–99; Harlow, Volume II, pp. 294–95; GIII's Correspondence, Volume VI, pp. 155, 157; Taken from the Lord Chancellor Article 5, Sydney Papers, Volume I, Document 16, Clements Library; Giunta, Volume I, pp. 678–79
11. Strachey to TT, 8 November 1782, Shelburne Papers, Volume 70, p. 374, Clements Library; GIII's Correspondence, Volume VI, p. 159; Jay's Papers, Volume II, p. 430; Giunta, Volume I, pp. 677, 681; Nepean's Secret Service Accounts, 30 August 1784, Sydney Papers, Clements Library
12. Washington to Cornwallis, Capitulation Articles, Clinton Papers, Box CLXXX, Clements Library; Giunta, Volume I, pp. 597–600; 635, 643, 686–87.
13. G. Bancroft, *The American Revolution*, Little Brown, 1875, Volume IV, pp. 586–87; Giunta, Volume I, pp. 690–91; Adams's Diary, Volume 3, p. 81.
14. Bicheno, p. 254; Bemis, p. 101; Giunta, Volume I, pp. 700–01, Isaacson, p. 415. Henry Laurens also signed the Peace Treaty for the United States.
15. Giunta, Volume I, pp. 712, 718; Davies, Volume XXI, p. 143; Evans A, pp. 148–49.
16. Nepean to Oswald, 11 December 1782, Shelburne Papers, Volume 70, p. 426, Clements Library; Giunta, Volume I, p. 779.
17. Cornwallis's Correspondence, Volume I, pp. 135–36; D.R. Chesnut and C.J. Taylor, *The Papers of Henry Laurens 1778–1782*, University of South Carolina Press, Columbia, South Carolina, 2003 [**Laurens's Papers**] Volume 15, pp. xvii, 48, 521; Nepean to Oswald, 21 December 1782, Shelburne Papers, Volume 70, p. 427, Clements Library.

18 Cornwallis's Correspondence, Volume I, p. 135; Giunta, Volume I, p. 755; Bemis, p. 109; Grafton's Autobiography, p. 341; Bemis DH, p. 58; Jay's Papers, Volume II, p. 481; V. Harlow, *The Founding of the Second British Empire 1763–1793*, Longmans Green, London, 1952, Volume I [**Harlow, Volume I**] p. 406.

Chapter 19
Tommy's defence of the peace

1 Parliamentary History, Volume XXIII, pp. 206, 233, 247–49.
2 Nelson RR, p. 140; Fitzmaurice, Volume III, p. 259; Grafton's Autobiography, pp. 333, 335; Olson, p. 70.
3 Fitzmaurice, Volume III, p. 304; Mowat, p. 128; GIII's Correspondence, Volume VI, pp. 170, 182, 184, 192; Wraxall HM, p. 501; Duke of Buckingham, *Memoirs of the Courts and Cabinets of George III*, Hurst and Blackett, London, 1853 [**Buckingham's Memoirs**], Volume I, p. 89; Harlow, Volume I, p. 352; P.D. Nelson, *General Sir Guy Carleton, Lord Dorchester: soldier-statesman of early British Canada*, Associated University Presses, Cranbury, New Jersey, 2000 [**Nelson PD**] p.166.
4 Parliamentary History, Volume XXIII, pp. 264–65, 276, 286; Fitzmaurice, Volume III, p. 309; Ehrmann, p. 98; Norris, p. 263; GIII's Correspondence, Volume VI, p. 175; Wraxall HM, p. 338
5 Grafton's Autobiography, pp. 353, 361; GIII's Correspondence, Volume VI, pp. 205, 226–27, 232; Olson, p. 192; Fitzmaurice, Volume III, p. 339; Fox's Memorials, Volume II, p. 18.
6 Grafton's Autobiography, pp. 355–56; GIII's Correspondence, Volume VI, p. 237; Harlow, Volume I, p. 424; Wraxall HM, p. 504.
7 Grafton's Autobiography, pp. 357–59, 362; Parliamentary History, Volume XXIII, p. 462; Wraxall HM, pp. 506–07; D. Wilkinson, 'Bentinck, William Henry Cavendish Cavendish, third duke of Portland' *ODNB*, Volume 5, pp. 261–69.
8 Parliamentary History, Volume XXIII, pp. 380, 390–92, 394, 418, 420, 435.
9 Parliamentary History, Volume XXIII, pp. 437–38, 442, 444; Fox's Memorials, Volume II, pp. 16, 31; Grafton's Autobiography, p. 361.
10 Parliamentary History, Volume XXIII, pp. 443, 453, 455.
11 Parliamentary History, Volume XXIII, pp. 462, 464–66.
12 Parliamentary History, Volume XXIII, pp. 487, 493.
13 Buckingham's Memoirs, Volume I, p. 158; Norris, p. 267; Wraxall HM, pp.509–10; Stanhope, Volume I, p. 96.
14 Grafton's Autobiography, pp. 363–66; Fox's Memorials, Volume II, pp. 10–11; Parliamentary History, Volume XXIII, pp. 498, 502–03, 560–61; F. Haldimand to TT, 26 October 1782, Sydney Papers, Box X, Clements Library.
15 Parliamentary History, Volume XXIII, p. 571; GIII's Correspondence, Volume VI, p. 247; Fitzmaurice, Volume III, pp. 369, 384–85; Stanhope, Volume I, p. 103.
16 Stanhope, Volume I, p. 109; GIII's Correspondence, Volume VI, pp. 255–56; Webb, p. 157.
17 D. Hosford, 'Sidney, Henry', *ODNB*, Volume 50, pp. 552–53.
18 Great Britain Parliament, House of Lords, 8 March 1783, Lord Sydney's Introduction Fees receipted by H. Sutherland, Sydney Papers, Box X, Clements Library; Journal of the House of Lords [**JHL**] Volume 36, p. 608; Lady Chatham to TT, 2 March 1783, Sydney Papers, Box X, Clements Library; Ayling/Pitt, pp. 400–01.

[19] Chatham's Correspondence, Volume III, p. 65; Ayling/Pitt, pp. 326–27; Pitt to TT, 23 March 1780, Pitt Papers, Box I, Clements Library.

Chapter 20
ALOFT IN A STORM

[1] Stanhope, Volume I, p. 116; G. Tomline, *Memoirs of the Rt Hon William Pitt*, John Muray, London, 1821, Volume I, pp 155–56; Fox's Memorials, Volume II, p. 43; Grafton's Autobiography, pp. 369–70; C. Matheson, *The Life of Henry Dundas*, Constable, London, 1933 [**Matheson**] p. 92; GIII's Correspondence, Volume VI, pp. 261, 264; Fitzmaurice, Volume III, p. 375.
[2] GIII's Correspondence, Volume VI, pp. 276, 278–81, 286–87.
[3] Parliamentary History, Volume XXIII, pp. 658, 687; GIII's Correspondence, Volume VI, pp. 297, 300, 307, 309–12.
[4] GIII's Correspondence, Volume VI, p. 329; Fox's Memorials, Volume II, p. 65; Ayling/Fox], p. 111; Parliamentary History, Volume XXIII, p. 723.
[5] GIII's Correspondence, Volume VI, pp. 316–19; Giunta, Volume II, p. 177.
[6] Grafton's Autobiography, p. 381; Stanhope, Volume I, pp. 118, 126; N. Wraxall, *Posthumous Memoirs of his Own Time*, Richard Bentley, London, 1836 [**Wraxall PM**] p. 155; Parliamentary History, Volume XXIII, p. 1114; Ehrman, p. 43; Ayling/Pitt, pp. 400–01.
[7] Grafton's Autobiography, p. 380; GIII's Letters, p. 176; Reynolds, p. 148; Wraxall HM, p. 597; Giunta, Volume I, p. 932.
[8] Ehrman, p. 118; Parliamentary History, Volume XXIII, p. 1190–91; Anon, A letter to the Earl Shelburne on the Subject of Mr Secretary Townshend's Letter to the Chairman and Deputy Chairman of the East India Company, J. Debrett, London, 1783, p. 25; Stanhope, Volume I, p. 137.
[9] Buckingham's Memoirs, Volume I, p. 283; Stanhope, Volume I, pp. 138, 146; WraxalHM, pp. 599–601; R. Gore-Browne, *Chancellor Thurlow*, Hamish Hamilton, London, 1953 [**Gore-Browne**] p. 216; Namier, Volume II, p. 456.
[10] Parliamentary History, Volume XXIV, pp. 123, 157, 196; Robinson's Papers, p. xiii; Wraxall HM, pp. 610–11; Buckingham's Memoirs, Volume I, p. 285; Fox's Memorials, Volume II, p. 220; GIII's Correspondence, Volume VI, p. 474.
[11] Parliamentary History, Volume XXIV, pp. 197, 226; Fox's Memorials, Volume II, p. 221.
[12] Wraxall HM, pp. 621, 693; Parliamentary History, Volume XXIV, p. 227; Fitzmaurice, Volume III, p. 406; Temple to George Townshend, 19 December 1783, George Townshend Papers, Box 2, Clements Library.
[13] Wraxall HM, p. 623; GIII's Later Correspondence, Volume I, p. 12; Ehrman, p. 130; Buckingham's Memoirs, Volume I, pp. 290, 298; Stanhope, Volume I, p. 158; Fitzmaurice, Volume III, p. 410; Grafton's Autobiography, p. 387; White, pp. 181–82.
[14] GIII's Later Correspondence, Volume I, p. 6; Sydney to Shelburne, 24 December 1783, Sydney Papers, Box XI, Clements Library.
[15] Burke's Correspondence, Volume V, p. 61.
[16] Cornwallis's Correspondence, Volume I, p. 159; Namier, Volume II, pp. 120–21.
[17] Ehrman, p. 130; Olson, p. 77; Pitt to Sydney, 1786, Pitt Papers, Box II, Clements Library; Parliamentary History, Volume XXIV, pp. 523–24, Volume XXVII, p. 1293; Sydney to fourth Duke of St Albans, December 1787, Sydney Papers, Box XIV, Clements Library.

18. Ayling/Fox, p. 126; Parliamentary History, Volume XXIV, pp. 263–64, 268, 484, 494; Fox's Memorials, Volume II, p. 228; Wraxall HM, p. 627.
19. Sydney Catalogue, Lot 1897, p. 172.
20. Parliamentary History, Volume XXIV, pp. 523–25; Grafton's Autobiography, p. 386.
21. Stanhope, Volume I, Appendix vii, viii; GIII to Portland, 15 February 1784, Sydney Papers, Box XI, Clements Library; Portland to Sydney, 15 February 1784, Sydney Papers, Box XI, Clements Library; GIII's Later Correspondence, Volume I, p. 36; Cornwallis's Correspondence, Volume I, p 160.
22. Third Earl of Malmsbury, *Diaries and Correspondence of James Harris 1st Earl of Malmsbury*, Richard Bentley, London, 1845, Volume II, p. 4; Parliamentary History, Volume XXIV, pp. 713, 734, 744; Cornwallis's Correspondence, Volume I, p. 163; Bengal Narrative, East India House, 6 March 1784, East India Company Miscellaneous Documents, 1761–1776, Clements Library.
23. Cornwallis's Correspondence, Volume I, p. 160; Namier, Volume I, p. 91; Wraxall HM, pp. 343–44.
24. Fox's Memorials, Volume II, p. 247; Gore-Browne, p. 223; Kier, p. 380; Cornwallis's Correspondence, Volume I, p. 165; Stanhope, Volume I, pp. 204, 214.

Chapter 21

FAMILY AND FRIENDS

1. Stanhope, Volume I, pp. 282, 284.
2. Townshend, Frontispiece; D. McCulloch, *1776*, Penguin Books, London, 2005, image 38; Webb, facing page 166.
3. V. Gibbs, ed., *The Complete Peerage*, St Catherine Press, London, 1913 [**Gibbs**] Volume III, pp. 14–15; *ODNB*, Volume 55, p. 166; Jesse, Volume III, pp. 326, 331–32.
4. Namier, Volume III, p. 554; Picard, p. 156; Jesse, Volume III, p. 246.
5. Grenville's Papers, Volume III, p. 157; TT to Chatham, 18 November 1776, Sydney Papers, Box VIII, Clements Library.
6. Parliamentary History, Volume XVIII, Table of Contents; Jesse, Volume III, p. 325, Volume IV, pp. 328, 354; namier, Volume II, p. 120; TT to Clinton, 23 December 1780, Clinton Papers, Box CXXXIV, Clements Library.
7. GIII's Later Correspondence, Volume I, pp. 236, 254; Jesse, Volume III, p. 345; Sydney Catalogue, Lot 459, p. 39.
8. Sydney to Earl Ferrers, 2 November 1784, Osborn Files, Beinecke Library; JHC, Volume 44, p. 85; GIII's Later Correspondence, Volume I, pp. 76, 230, 257, 321.
9. Nelson RR, p. 8; Detective's report on the movements of Richard Brinsley Sheridan from noon till 1 30 a.m., 6 December 1788, Sydney Papers, Box XV, Clements Library; Nepean's Secret Service Accounts, 30 August and 28 December 1784, 1784–1787, Sydney Papers, Clements Library; GIII's Later Correspondence, Volume I, p. 591; A.P. Shy, *Guide to the Manuscript Collection of the William L. Clements Library*, G.K. Hall and Co., Boston, 1978, p. 136.
10. *The Times*, 15 May 1786, 23 January and 23 July 1787, 24 September 1789, 27 September 1790.
11. Stanhope, Volume I, pp. 81, 126, 377; Wraxall PM, Volume III, p. 129.
12. Stanhope, Volume I, p. 90; N.Wraxall, *A Short Review of the Political State of Great Britain*

at the Commencement of 1787, 7th edition with corrections, J. Debrett, London, 1787 [**A Short Review**] p. 24; Pitt to Sydney 1784, Pitt Papers, Box I, Clements Library; GIII to Sydney, 5 February 1784, Sydney Catalogue, Lot 1897, p. 172.

13   GIII's Later Correspndence, Volume I, pp. 138–39, 142; Draft Bill for Amending the Representation, Sydney Papers, Box XVII, Clements Library; Ehrman, p. 227.
14   GIII's Later Correspondence, Volume I, p. 659; Hague, p. 211; Gore-Brown, p. 225; Matheson, p. 121; Wraxall HM, p. 630; *The Times*, 24 January and 19 March 1787.
15   Grafton's Autobiography pp. 394–95; *The Times*, 18 December 1786 and 10 January 1787; Sydney to Jack Townshend, 7 October 1785, Osborn Files, Beniecke Library.
16   Nelson RR, pp. 15–16; Smith's Diary, Volume I, pp. xxi, 152, 154, 276, Volume II, pp. 59, 119.
17   John, Duke of Rutland, *The Correspondence of Pitt and Rutland 1781–1787*, William Blackwood, London, 1890 [**Rutland's Correspondence**] p. 20; F. Watson ed., *Historical Records of Australia*, Library Committee of the Commonwealth Parliament, 1914, Series I, Volume I, p. xvi.
18   Parliamentary History, Volume XXIII, p. 1190; Fox's memorials, Volume II, p. 254.
19   Kier, p. 437.

Chapter 22

THE GOLDEN AGE OF IRISH GOVERNMENT

1   *ODNB*, Volume 50, p. 553; M. Cronin, *A History of Ireland*, Palgrave, New York, 2001 [**Cronin**] p. 70.
2   Carswell, pp. 48–52; Cronin, pp. 78, 81; *ODNB*, Volume 50, p. 553.
3   *ODNB*, Volume 55, p. 141; Cronin, pp. 94, 96.
4   Cronin, p. 96; S. Gwynn, *Henry Grattan and his Times*, Harrap, London, 1939 [**Gwynn**] pp. 10, 35, 37, 85; *ODNB*, Volume 55, pp. 158–59; 'Protest of the Lords of Ireland', *Annual Register*, Volume 14, December 1771, p. 247; W. Flood, *Memoirs of the Life and Correspondence of Henry Flood*, John Cumming, Dublin, 1838 [**Flood's Memoirs**] p. 75; Earl of Rochford to George Townshend, 9 February 1771, George Townshend Papers, Box II, Clements Library.
5   Parliamentary History, Volume XX, p. 112; Ayling/Fox, p. 73; Gwynn, p. 51; Cronin, pp. 98–99.
6   H. Grattan, *The Speeches of Henry Grattan*, Longman, London, 1822 [**Grattan's Speeches**] Volume I, pp. 129, 131, 137; Gwynn, pp. 129, 132–33; Parliamentary History, Volume XXIII, p. 35.
7   6th of Geo. 1; Grattan's Speeches, Volume I, pp. 143–44; D. Madden, *The Select Speeches of Henry Grattan*, James Duffy, Dublin, 1845 [**Madden**] pp. xxxiii–iv; J. Kelly, 'Grattan, Henry', *ODNB*, Volume 23, pp. 365–73; J. Kelly, 'Flood, Henry', *ODNB*, Volume 20, pp. 155–59.
8   Gwynn, p. 152; Flood's Memoirs, pp. 157–58, 166.
9   R.W. Davis, 'Grenville, George Nugent Temple' and J.P. Jupp, 'Grenville, William Wyndham', both in *ODNB*, Volume 23 at pp. 727 and 749 respectively; Buckingham's Memoirs, Volume I, pp. 66–68, 73, 75, 78–79.
10 Buckingham's Memoirs, Volume I, pp. 80–82, 96–97.
11 Buckingham's Memoirs, Volume I, p. 104, 106–07, 124, 126.

12. Parliamentary History, Volume XXIII, pp. 326–28.
13. Parliamentary History, Volume XXIII, pp. 342, 723; Buckingham's Memoirs, Volume I, pp. 145, 224–25.
14. Buckingham's Memoirs, Volume I, p. 233; Parliamentary History, Volume XXIII, pp. 730–31.
15. Parliamentary History, Volume XXIII, pp. 732, 752–53; GIII's Correspondence Volume VI, p. 356.
16. Cronin, p. 100; Kier, p. 437; Harlow, Volume I, p. 547.
17. Rutland's Correspondence, p. 43; Harlow, Volume I, p. 564; GIII's Later Correspondence, Volume I, pp. 121, 124; *The Times*, 18 January 1786.
18. Harlow, Volume I, pp. 578–79, 591, 596, 607, 611, 615; Gwynn, pp. 199–200.
19. Nepean's Secret service Accounts, 1784–1787, Sydney Papers, Clements Library; *The Times*, 2 May and 7 July 1785; Sydney to Lord Chief Justice Clark, 28 November 1786, Osborn Files, Beinecke Library.
20. Cronin, pp. 107–08, 111–12; Cornwallis's Correspondence, Volume II, p. 347.
21. Cronin, pp. 114–15; Cornwallis's Correspondence, Volume III, pp. 8, 102.
22. Cornwallis's Correspondence, Volume III, pp. 181, 184; Cronin pp. 115–16; Harlow, Volume I, pp. 547, 648.

Chapter 23

FROM NABOBS TO NOOTKA

1. Harlow, Volume I, p. 63, 150–51, Volume II, pp. 137, 140; Buckingham's Memoirs, Volume I, p. 365; Parliamentary History, Volume XXIII, pp. 1405–06.
2. Wraxall PM, Volume I, pp. 162–63; Matheson, pp. 110, 121; Harlow Volume II, pp. 119, 129, 142, 244; Buckingham's Memoirs, Volume I, p. 364; C. Bayley and K. Prior, 'Cornwallis, Charles, first Marquess Cornwallis, *ODNB*, Volume 13, pp. 474–482.
3. Matheson, p. 117; Wraxall PM, Volume 2, p. 68; Cornwallis's Correspondence, Volume I, pp. 136, 152, 154.
4. Cornwallis's Correspondence, Volume I, pp. 155, 157, 167; Harlow, Volume II, p. 149.
5. Cornwallis's Correspondence, Volume I, pp. 167–68.
6. Cornwallis's Correspondence, Volume I, p. 168.
7. Harlow, Volume II, pp. 149–50, 152; Cornwallis's Correspondence, Volume I, pp. 170–71; Ehrman, pp. 189–91.
8. Parliamentary History, Volume XXIV, pp. 1290–91; Cornwallis's Correspondence, Volume I, p. 172–73; Harlow, Volume II, p. 209.
9. Pitt to Sydney, 16 September 1784, Sydney Papers, Box XIII, Clements Library; Pitt to the East India Company, 24 September 1784, Sydney Papers, Box XII, Clements Library; Ehrman, p. 452; Cornwallis's Correspondence Volume I, p. 159; Nepean's Secret Service Accounts, 28 December 1784, Sydney Papers, Clements Library.
10. Cornwallis's Correspondence, Volume I, p. 177, 179–80.
11. Cornwallis's Correspondence, Volume I, p. 181;
12. Cornwallis's Correspondence, Volume I, pp. 181–82.
13. Cornwallis's Correspondence, Volume I, pp. 184, 208.
14. Cornwallis's Correspondence, Volume I, pp. 209, 214; 26 Goe. III c. 16; Harlow, Volume II, p. 210.

Notes

15   C. Lawson, *The Private Life of Warren Hastings*, Macmillan, London, 1911 [**Lawson**] pp. 40, 45; Harlow, Volume II, pp. 171, 173, 175, 206; Parliamentary History, Volume XXV, p. 261.
16   Harlow, Volume II, pp. 160, 206, 210, Wraxall PM, Volume I, p. 261; P. Marshall, 'Hastings, Warren, *ODNB*, Volume 25, pp. 782–92.
17   Harolw, Volume II, pp. 211–12; Ehrman, pp. 445–47; Wraxall PM, Volume II, pp. 37, 151, 155.
18   Wraxall PM, Volume II, pp. 152, 156, 159; Parliamentary History, Volume XXVI, pp. 146, 165–67; *The Times*, 8 July 1786.
19   Wraxall PM, Volume II, p. 291; Pitt to Sydney, 21 January 1788, Pitt Papers, Box II, Clements Library; GIII's Later Correspondence, Volume I, p. 365; Matheson, p. 128; Lawson, pp. 119–20.
20   Cornwallis's Correspondence, Volume I, pp. 216–17, 219–20, 228; Matheson, p. 115; *ODNB*, Volume 13, pp. 474–82.
21   Harlow, Volume II, pp. 191–93; Cornwallis's Correspondence, Volume I, pp. 237, 240, 249, 329, 417; GIII's Later Correspondence, Volume I, pp. 370–71.
22   Cornwallis's Correspondence, Volume I, pp. 324–25, 336, 349–50, 354–55; Harlow Volume II, p. 165; Nelson RR, p. 140; White, p. 193.
23   Matheson, p. 128; Harlow, Volume II, pp. 197–98; Parliamentary History, Volume XXVII, p. 221.
24   Cornwallis's Correspondence, Volume I, p. 336.
25   Cornwallis's Correspondence, Volume I, p. 386; A. Frost, *The Global Reach of Empire*, Melbourne University Press, Melbourne, 2003 [**Frost GRE**] pp. 164, 173, 185–87; Harlow, Volume II, pp. 535, 560; Ehrman, pp. 419, 421, 423; Harlow and Madden, *British Colonial Develpoments 1774–1834, Select Documents*, Oxford at the Clarendon Press, 1953 [**Harlow and Madden**] p. 54.
26   Harlow, Volume II, pp. 419–20; Harlow and Madden, pp. 27, 29.
27   Harlow, Volume II, pp. 425, 442–43, 447–49; P. Fidlon, ed., *The Journal of Arthur Bowes Smyth*, Australian Documents Library, Sydney, 1979 [**Smyth's Journal**] pp. 86, 98; Frost GRE, pp. 226, 229; Parliamentary History, Volume XXVIII, p. 938.

Chapter 24

Loyalists transform Canada

1   Manning, p. 58; Harlow, Volume II, p. 695; K. Donovan, *Cape Breton at 200*, University College of Cape Breton Press, Sydney, N.S., 1985, p. 41; Reynolds, pp. 14, 55; Kier, p. 442.
2   Manning, pp. 34, 39; Giunta, Volume I, p. 699; Parliamentary History, Volume XXIII, p. 446; Moore L, p. 116; Evans A, pp. 24, 148; Norton p. 216; C. Royster, 'Washington, George', *ODNB*, Volume 57, p. 531; Fairfax, Robert, 7th Baron to Lord Sydney, 1st November 1786, Sydney Papers, Box XIII, Clements Library.
3   Digby to TT, 19 November 1782, Shelburne Papers, Volume 68, p. 365; Nelson PD, p. 154; Evans A, p. 46; Reynolds, p. 150; Copy to Alleyne Fitzherbert, 24 December 1782, Sydney Papers, Box X, Clements Library; GIII to Sydney, 25 September 1782, Sydney Catalogue, Lot 1888, p. 171; Earl of Dunmore to TT, 24 August 1782, Dunmore Papers, Clements Library; Benedict Arnold to Shelburne, 13 August 1782, Sydney Papers Box X, Clements Library.

[4] A. Frost, *The Precarious Life of James Mario Matra*, Miegunyah Press, Melbourne, 1995 [**Frost M**], pp. 1, 101; Reynolds, pp. 133, 137, 148; Davies, Volume XXI, pp. 111, 146; A.G. Bradley, *Sir Guy Carleton*, University of Toronto Press, Toronto, 1966 [**Bradley**] p. 212; G.P. Browne, 'Carleton, Guy, 1st Baron Dorchester' *Dictionary of Canadian Biography* [**DCB**] Volume V, 1801–1820, on line edition [accessed 11 September 2010].

[5] Manning, p. 34; Moore L, p. 169; E.C. Wright, *The Loyalists of New Brunswick*, Fredericton, New Brunswick, 1955 [**Wright**] pp. 37–38, 50, 59; MacNutt, p. 32; P. Burroughs, Parr, John, *DCB*, Volume IV, 1771–1800, on line edition [accessed 11 September 2010].

[6] Moore L, pp. 158–60,169; Davies, Volume XXI, p. 18; Nelson PD, pp. 174–75; Smith's Diary, Volume I, p. 61; Manning, pp. 35, 70, 75, 83; GIII's Later Correspondence, Volume I, p. 59; MacNutt, pp. 44–45.

[7] MacNutt, p. 41; Wright, pp. 142–43; A. Burt, *The Old Province of Quebec*, The Ryerson Press, Toronto, MCMXXXIII [**Burt**] pp. 424–25; GIII's Later Correspondence, Volume I, p. 79; W.G. Godfrey, 'Carleton, Thomas', *DCB*, Volume V, 1801–1820, on line edition [accessed 11 September 2010].

[8] Manning, p. 61; G. Evans, *Uncommon Obdurate*, University of Toronto Press, 1969 [**Evans UO**] pp. vii, 27, 35, 44, 48; C. Fergusson, *Uniake's Sketches of Cape Breton*, Nova Scotia Public Archives, Halifax, N.S., 1958 [**Uniake**], pp. 72, 76–77, 143; J. MacKinnon, *Old Sydney*, Global Haritage Press, Milton, Ontario, 2003 [**MacKinnon**] p. 12.

[9] Evans UO, pp.35, 48, 50–51, 54–55; Uniake, p. 145; MacKinnon, p. 17.

[10] Speculator A. to Sydney, I March 1789, Sydney Papers, Bov, XV, Clements Library; Evans UO, pp. 38, 40; MacKinnon, p. 17; Papers relating to J.F.W. Des Barres, *http://fortress.uccb. ns.ca/search/RPAC1923_7-16.html* [accessed 20 August 2005].

[11] N. Macdonald, *Canada 1763–1841 Immigration and Settlement*, Longmans Green, London, 1939 [**Macdonald**] pp. 105–06; H. Baglole, 'Patterson (Paterson) Walter', *DCB*, Volume IV, 1771–1800, on line edition [accessed 11 September 2010].

[12] Jefferson's Writings, p. 784; Davies, Volume XIX, p. 312; J. Duffy, *Ethan Allen and his Kin*, University Press of New England, Hanover, N.H., 1998 Duffy] pp. xxxii, 307; S.F. Bemis, 'Relations between the Vermont Separatists and Great Britain 1789–1791', *The American Historical Review*, Volume XXI [**Bemis VS**] pp. 547–48; A. Shortt and A. Doughty, eds., *Canadian Archives, documents Relating to the Constitutional History of Canada 1759–1791*, Part II, J. de L. Tache, Ottawa, 1918 [**Shortt**] pp. 733–34; Pitt to Sydney, 8 August 1785, Sydney Papers, Box XII, Clements Library.

[13] Nelson PD, pp. 196, 198.

[14] Moore L, pp. 177–78; B.L. Dunnigan, *King's Men at Mackinac*, Harlo Printing, Detroit, 1993, p. 16; Burt, p. 333.

[15] Davies, Volume XXI, pp. 125–26; Shortt, Volume II, pp. 805–09; Nelson RR, p. 75; Joseph Brant to Sydney, 4 November 1786, Michigan Papers, Volume I, 1759–1786, Clements Library; Burt, pp. 342, 344, 336; Nelson PD, p. 199; B.L. Dunnigan, *Detroit*, Wayne State University Press, Detroit, 2001, p. 102.

Chapter 25

Dorchester upon the spot

[1] S. Sutherland, P. and M. Tousignant, 'Haldimand, Sir Frederick', *DCB*, Volume V, 1801–1820, on line edition [accessed 11 September 2010; Shortt, pp. 735–37, 742–52, 758–62,

765–66; Harlow, Volume II, p. 743.
2. Smith's Diary, Volume I, pp. 59, 242; Nelson PD, pp. 175–77; Davies, Volume XXI, pp. 108–09, 132; Manning, p. 36; Sydney to Lord Kensington, 6 January 1784, Osborn Files, Beinecke Library.
3. Smith's Diary, Volume I, p. 182; Nelson PD, p. 178; Shortt, pp. 777, 780; Harlow, Volume II, p. 730; E. Arthur, 'Hamilton, Henry', *DCB*, Volume IV, 1771–1800, on line edition [accessed 11 September 2010].
4. Smith's Diary, Volume I, pp. 214–16.
5. Smith's Diary, Volume I, pp. 242, 260, Reynolds, p. 152; Harlow, Volume II, pp. 730–31; Shortt, p. 783.
6. Manning, p. 24; Shortt, p. 971; Harlow, Volume II, pp. 727, 731.
7. Harlow, Volume II, p. 731; Smith's Diary, Volume I, pp. xxii–xxiii, 276, 280, 291, Volume II, pp. xiii–xiv, 69; Nelson PD, p. 183; R. Calhoon, 'Smith, William', *ODNB*, Volume 51, pp. 364–66.
8. Shortt, pp. 767, 772, 794, 796–97, 801, 803–04; JHC, Volume 41, pp. 647–48.
9. Haldimand's Diary, pp. 143, 149; Burt, p. 429; Reynolds, pp. 152, 155; Shortt, pp. 813–15; Manning, pp. 36, 320.
10. Nelson PD, pp. 186–88; Shortt, p. 837; Manning, p. 37.
11. Harlow, Volume II, pp. 731–32; Manning, p. 321.
12. Shortt, pp. 841, 865; Smith's Diary, Volume I, p. xxiv, Volume II, p. 208.
13. Shortt, pp. 843, 850, 856, 873. Haldimand's Diary, p. 227.
14. Shortt, pp. 865–66, 946–47; G.P. Browne, 'Carleton, Guy, 1st Baron Dorchester, *DCB*, Volume V, 1801–1820, on line edition [accessed 11 September 2010].
15. Harlow, Volume II, p. 745; Shortt, pp. 863–64; Burt p. 444.
16. Shortt, pp. 864, 949.
17. Short, pp. 946–47, 955; Harlow, Volume II, p. 748; Carleton to Shelburne, 16 December 1782, Shelburne Papers, Volume 68, p. 277; Macdonald, pp. 51–52; Namier, Volume III, p. 322.
18. Shortt, pp. 956–58.
19. Shortt, p. 959; Macdonald, Annexed Map of Eastern Canada.
20. Harlow, Volume II, pp. 754, 757.
21. Macdonald, p. 85.

Chapter 26

NELSON, BLIGH AND PHILLIP

1. Manning, p. 84; Nelson RR, p. 132.
2. Ehrman, p. 95; Giunta, Volume I, pp. 697–701; Harlow, Volume I, pp. 450–51; Notes on the New England Trade, 1783, Sydney Papers, Box XI, Clements Library.
3. Harlow, Volume I, pp. 459, 461–62, 464, 476, 491; Adams's Diary, Volume III, p. 121; MacNutt, p. 35; Ehrman, p. 339; Watson, p. 15; Mahan, p. 344; Manning, pp. 258–60.
4. A. Lingelbach, 'The Inception of the British Board of Trade', *American Historical Review*, Volume XXX, July 1925, Number 4, pp. 704–05, 708; Manning, pp. 76, 80–81; List of Business of the Privy Council (after 1783) Sydney Papers, Box XI, Clements Library; T. Coleman, *Nelson The Man and the Legend*, Bloomsbury, London, 2002 [**Coleman**] p. 60; N.H. Nicholas, *The Dispatches and Letters of Vice Admiral Lord Viscount Nelson 1777–1794*, Henry Colburn, London, 1845 [**Nelson's Dispatches**] Volume I, pp. 112–114, 171, 173.

5   Nelson's Dispatches, Volume I, pp. 113, 115, 175; N. Rodger, 'Nelson, Horatio', *ODNB*, Volume 40, pp. 396–410.
6   Nelson's Dispatches, Volume I, pp. 115–16; Coleman, p. 68.
7   Nelson's Dispatches, Volume I, pp. 116–18; C.H.H. Owen, 'Collingwood, Cuthbert', *ODNB*, Volume 12, p. 670; N.A.M. Rodger, 'Nelson, Horatio', *ODNB*, Volume 40, p. 397.
8   Nelson's Dispatches, Volume I, pp. 129–31.
9   Coleman, p. 69; Nelson's Dispatches, Volume I, pp. 134–36; 138, 178.
10 A Comparative View of the Trade to Jamacia from the Continent of America in the Years 1784 and 1785 and before the War, Sydney Papers, Box XII, Clements Library; Manning, p. 260; Nelson's Dispatches, Volume I, pp. 141, 180–85, 186–97.
11 Michael Keane to Sydney, 27 July 1787, Sydney Papers, Box XIV, Clements Library; Nelson's Dispatches, Volume I, p. 114; A. Lambert, *Nelson*, Faber and Faber, London, 2004 [**Lambert N**] p. 229.
12 C. Alexander, *The Bounty*, Harper Collins, London, 2003 [**Alexander**] pp. 41–42; G. Kennedy, *Bligh*, Duckworth, London, 1978 [**Kennedy**] p. 15.
13 Alexander, p. 41; Kennedy, p. 17; Frost GRE, p. 203; Sir Joseph Banks, Instructions for the Vessel from Botany Bay, February 1787, Papers of Sir Joseph Banks, State Library of New South Wales [**Banks Papers**] series 45.03 CY 3004/9.
14 Kennedy, p. 19; Nepean to Fraser, 27 June 1787, PRO/FO/27/21; Bligh to Banks, 6 August 1787, Banks Papers, Series 46.02 CY3004/54; Sydney to Banks, 15 August 1787, Banks Papers, Series 45.08 CY 3004/28.
15 Sir George Yonge to Banks, 7 September 1787, Banks Papers, Series 45.08 CY 3004/28; Bligh to Banks, 15 September 1787, Banks Papers, Series 45.03 CY 3004/55.
16 Kennedy, p. 22; Bligh to Banks, 10 December 1787, Banks Papers, Series 46.16 CY3004/93; Lord Selkirk to Banks, 14 September 1787, Banks Papers, Series 45.11 CY 3004/40.
17 Kennedy, pp. 29–30, 36–37,112, 176, 352; Frost GRE, p. 204; W. Bligh, *A Narrative of the Mutiny on Board H.M. Ship Bounty*, George Nicol, London, 1790, pp. 6–7; Bligh to Banks, 13 October 1789, Banks Papers, Series 46.27 CY 3004/130; A. Frost, 'Bligh, William', *ODNB*, Volume 6, pp. 214–16; *Minutes of Proceedings of the Court Martial held at Portsmouth August 12, 1792 on Ten Persons charged with Mutiny on board His Majesty's Ship Bounty*, London, MDCCXCIV, p.2.
18 Knittle, p. 60; Atkinson, p. 28; G. Mackaness, *Admiral Arthur Phillip*, Angus and Robertson, Sydney, 1937 [**Mackaness**] pp. 2, 59.
19 A. Frost, *Arthur Phillip 1738–1814 His Voyaging*, Oxford University Press, Melbourne, 1987 [**Frost AP**] pp. 63, 98, 111; Mackaness, pp. 15–18.
20 Frost AP, pp. 90–91, 106, 109; Extract of the Journal of Captain Arthur Phillip – South America, Sydney Papers, Box XVII, Clements Library; Frost GRE, p. 98.
21 W. Danall's Memo, n.d., Sydney Papers, Box VIII, Clements Library; Copy Rio de Janeiro 1782 Apr 20 Extract Intelligence on revolt in Peru, Sydney Papers, Box IX, Clements Library; Frost GRE, p. 100; Blankett to Shelburne, Force proposed for an Expedition against Buenos Aires and to the South Seas conditionally, August 1782, Sydney Papers, Box X, Clements Library.
22 Keppel to TT, 25 September 1782, Sydney Papers, Box X, Clements Library; Frost AP, p. 114.

23 Frost AP, p. 115.
24 Mackaness, pp. 27–30; Frost GRE, p. 100; Frost AP, p. 115.
25 Nepean's Secret Service Accounts, 2 February, 7 March and 11 November 1784, Sydney Papers, Clements Library; Frost AP, p. 131.
26 Lord Howe to Sydney, 3 September 1786, Mackaness, p. 58.

Chapter 27

Sydney the soft touch

1 A. Roger Ekirch, 'Great Britain's Secret Convict Trade to America, 1783–1784', *American Historical Review*, Volume 89, Part 5, 1984 [**Ekirch**], p. 1286; W. Oldham, *Britain's Convicts to the Colonies*, Library of Australian History, Sydney, 1990 [**Oldham**], p. 32; A.G.L. Shaw, *Convicts and the Colonies*, Melbourne University Press, 1981 [**Shaw**] p. 35; G.B. Barton, *History of New South Wales*, Government Printer, Sydney, 1889 [**Barton**] Volume I, p. 15; Van Doren, p. 210.
2 Oldham, pp. 36–37; Parliamentary History, Volume XIX, p. 970.
3 Oldham, pp. 46, 49–50, 70–71.
4 Oldham, pp. 66, 68, 71–72.
5 Oldham, pp. 74–75; E. Christopher, *A Merciless Place*, Allen and Unwin, Sydney, 2010 [**Christopher**] p. 212
6 Jesse, Volume I, pp. 328–29; Nelson RR, p. 116; Sydney to the Lords of the Admiralty, 20 December 1785, HO 29/2; Frost GRE, pp. 147–48; Bunbury Committee Report, 22 March 1784, JHC, Volume 39, pp. 1040–41.
7 Oldham, p. 66, 80–81; Christopher, p. 213.
8 Ekirch, pp. 1285–91; Christopher, pp. 254–58; Oldham, pp. 84–87.
9 JHC, Volume 39, pp. 844, 982; Parliamentary History, Volume XXIV, p. 227.
10 Parliamentary History, Volume XXIV, p. 757; JHC, Volume 39, pp. 982, 1041.
11 A. Frost, *Convicts and Empire*, Oxford University Press, Melbourne, 1980 [**Frost CE**] p. 10; Frost M, pp. xi, 58–59, 102, 115; HRNSW, pp. 2–5.
12 A. Atkinson, 'Whigs and Tories' in G Martin, *The Founding of Australia*, Hale and Iremonger, Sydney, 1981 [**Martin**] p. 192; HRNSW, p. 6; Frost M, p. 116; JHC, Volume 37, p. 311.
13 HRNSW, pp. 6, 7.
14 Nepean to Stephens, 21 April 1784, ADM 1/4151; JHC, Volume 40, p. 380; Frost M, pp. 102–03; JHL, Volume 37, pp. 160, 163; *The Statutes at Large*, Volume 14, 1784, Chapter 56, Sections VIII and X, p. 594; Clark CMH, p. 92.
15 Oldham, pp. 87–94; Christopher, pp. 264–274, 286–288; Evan Nepean's evidence to the Beauchamp committee, 9 May 1785, JHC, Volume 40, p. 956.
16 *The Times*, 17 May 1785.
17 *The Times*, 26 February 1785, 10 August 1786; S. Lambert, *House of Commons Sessional Papers of the 18th Century*, Scholarly Resources Inc., Delaware, 1975 [**Lambert S**] Volume 24, p. 137; GIII's Later Correspondence, Volume I, pp. 240–41.
18 GIII'S Later Correspondence, Volume I, pp. 119, 209, 384; S. Hardy to Sydney, 17 February 1783, Osborn Files, Beinecke Library.

Chapter 28

Transportation where?

1. Christopher, pp. 288–299.
2. Oldham, pp. 69–70; 95–97
3. Frost M, pp. 98 103; HNRSW, pp. 8–9; William Pitt to Sydney, 14 October 1784, Pitt Papers, Box I, Clements Library; GIII's Later Correspondence, Volume I, pp. 110–11.
4. Frost M, p. 103; HRNSW, p. 10.
5. HRNSW, pp. 10–13; JHC, Volume 40, p. 954.
6. HRNSW, p. 12; Frost M, p. 120; A. Frost, 'Sir George Young', *ODNB*, Volume 60, p. 895.
7. John Blankett, Memorial re Establishing a Colony of Convicts on Madagascar, Sydney Papers, Box XVII, Clements Library; B. Reece, *The Origins of Irish Convict Transportation to New South Wales*, Palgrave, New York, 2001 [**Reece**] p. 70; G. Martin, 'The Alternatives to Botany Bay', Martin, p. 158; HRNSW, pp. 6–7; JHC, Volume 40, pp. 955–56, Atkinson, pp. 52–55, 208–09, 262.
8. Parliamentary History, Volume XXV, pp. 391–92, 430–31; Sydney to the Lords of the Treasury, 20 March 1785, TI/619; JHC, Volume 40, p. 870.
9. JHC, Volume 40, p. 870.
10. JHC, Volume 40, pp. 954–60; 1161; Wraxall PM, Volume I, p. 323; Frost BB, pp. 116–17; Frost M, pp. 118–21.
11. Parliamentary History, Volume XXV, p. 906; Frost BB, pp. 116–17; Frost M pp. 118–21; JHC, Volume 40, p. 1163.
12. JHC, Volume 40, pp. 1162–64; Frost GRE, p. 157.
13. *The Times*, 14 July 1785; Sydney to Lord George Cavendish, 20 May 1785, Osborn Files, Beinecke Library; Dorset to Carmarthen, 5 and 19 May, 19 June 1785, FO 27/16; Frost GRE, pp. 181–82; J. King, *In the Beginning*, Macmillan, Melbourne, 1985, pp. 69–71.
14. JHC, Volume 37, p. 311; Frost M, pp. 118–22, 246; Parliamentary History, Volume XXV, p. 391; A Short Review, pp. 77–78; Wraxall PM, Volume I, p. 288; Frost BB, p. 117.

Chapter 29

The First Fleet

1. Sydney to the Lords of the Treasury, 18 August 1786, TI/639; Mackaness, p. 60; JHC, Volume 37, p. 311; Manning Clark, 'The choice of Botany Bay', Martin, p. 66; HRNSW, pp. 1, 14–15; J.C. Beaglehole, *The Endeavour Journal of Joseph* Banks, Angus and Robertson, Sydney, 1962, Volume II, p. 57; Frost M, pp. 59, 111, 118–22; Howe to Sydney, 3 September 1786, HRNSW, pp. 22–23.
2. *The Statutes at Large*, Volume 14, 1784, Chapter 56, Sections VIII and X, p. 594
3. HRNSW, pp. 16–17; Carswell, front cover; J. Petersen, *Hyde Park Barracks Museum and Guidebook*, Historic Houses Trust, Sydney, 2003, p. 23; E. Cobham Brewer, *Dictionary of Phrase and Fable*, Henry Altemus and Co., Philadelphia, 1898, p. 303; S. Mourot, *This was Sydney*, Ure Smith, Sydney 1969, p. 30; Estimate of Provisions, n.d., TI/639.
4. HRNSW, p. 19; Frost M, pp. 123, 173; Frost AP, p. 142; *ODNB*, Volume 60, p. 895.

5   JHC, Volume 40, p. 1164; HRNSW, pp. 18, 21–23.
6   Mackaness, pp. 58–59; W.S. Campbell, 'Arthur Phillip', *Journal of the Royal Australian Historical Society*, Volume XXI, 1936, p. 264; L. Harcourt, *The Diaries and Correspondence of George Rose*, Richard Bentley, London, 1860; R. Thorne, 'Rose, George', *ODNB*, Volume 47, p. 745; HRNSW, pp. 179–80.
7   Navy Office to Secretaries Treasury, 5 September 1786, TI/639; Nepean to George Rose, 7 December 1786, TI/639; George Johnston to Phillip Stephens, 18 December 1786, TI/639; HRNSW, p. 24; Barton p. 496; Atkinson, pp. 64–65; JHC, Volume 40, p. 955; D. Clune and K. Turner, eds., *The Governors of New South Wales 1788–2010*, Federation Press, Sydney, 2009 [**The Governors**] p. 31.
8   HRNSW, pp. 30, 45–46; Atkinson FP, p. 40; J. Currey, *David Collins A Colonial Life*, The Miegunyah Press, Melbourne, 2000, p. 30.
9   HRNSW, pp. 19, 33; Atkinson, pp. 89–90.
10 A. Atkinson, 'Whigs and Tories and Botany Bay', Martin, pp. 190, 201, 207–08; *The Times*, 14 September 1786; A. Frost, 'The East India Company and the Choice of Botany Bay', Martin, pp. 230–31; R. Sinh, *Fort William – India House Correspondence*, National Archives of India, New Delhi, 1972, Volume X, 1786–88 [**Sinh**] p. 169.
11 Atkinson, pp. 64, 91; HRNSW, pp. 26–28, 36; Howe to King, 14 December 1786, PC 1/61; *The Times*, 18 December 1786; M. Gillen, *The Founders of Australia: A Biographical Dictionary of the First Fleet*, Library of Australian History, Sydney, 1989 [**Gillen**] p. 447; Manning Clark, 'The choice of Botany Bay', Martin, p. 74; G. Martin, 'A London Newspaper on the founding of Botany Bay, August 1786–May 1787', Martin, p. 175.
12 C. Bateson, *The Convict Ships 1787–1868*, Brown and Son, Glasgow, 1985 [**Bateson C**] pp. 12, 94; HRNSW, p. 13; Sinh, p. 169; Smyth's Journal, p. 86.
13 HRNSW, pp. 43, 87, 91; Sinh, pp. 27–28.
14 HRNSW, p. 44; M. Flynn, *The Second Fleet*, Library of Australian History, Sydney, 2001 [**Flynn**] p. 13; Gillen, p. 178; Atkinson, pp. 100, 116, 129; W.J.V. Windeyer, 'A Birthright and Inheritance', *Tasmanian University Law Review*, Volume I, 1958, p. 659.
15 Parliamentary History, Volume XXVI, p. 211; JHL, Volume 37, pp. 596, 598; 27 Geo. III c. 2; Clark CMH, Volume I, p. 81; Atkinson, p. 89.
16 Nepean to Steele, 4 September 1786, HO 36/5; Nepean to Rose, 1 November 1786, HO 36/5; A. Chisholm, ed., *Journal of a Voyage to New South Wales*, Angus and Robertson, Sydney, 1962 [**White's Journal**] p. 50; Smyth's Journal, 1 and 10 December 1787, pp. 46–47; Nepean to Steele, 28 November 1786, HO 36/5.
17 HRNSW, pp. 40, 48, 50, 54, 56, 82; Nepean to Rose, 13 December 1786, TI/639; Sydney to the Lords Commissioners of the Treasury, 22 December 1786, HO 36/5; Nepean to Rose, 17 January 1787, HO 36/5; Gillen, p. 429.
18 HRNSW, pp. 57, 59, 82–83; Sydney to the Lords Commissioners of the Admiralty, 19 March 1787, HO 29/2.
19 HRNSW, pp. 61–67, 89–90; Frost AP, p. 150; Memorandum Concerning Phillip's Draft Instructions, 25 April 1787, PC 1/62.
20 HRNSW, p. 89; P. Edwards, ed., *James Cook, The Journals*, Penguin Books, London, 2003, p. 170.
21 HRNSW, pp. 40, 50, 54, 57, 78, 84, 93, 101–02.
22 HRNSW, pp. 103–06; *Fishburn's* Log, ADM 51/4375.
23 HRNSW, pp. 105–06, 113–14, 119.

Chapter 30

SYDNEY COVE

1. HRNSW, pp. 105–06, 113–14, 119; Smyth's Journal, pp. 18, 29, 42, 57; *Prince of Wales* Log, ADM 51/4376; Clark CMH, Volume I, pp. 29, 31, 33; Mackaness, p. 105.
2. Although Phillip's book (*The Voyage of Governor Phillip to Botany Bay*, John Stockdale, London, 1789 [**Phillip's Voyage**] p. 47) nominates 22 January, it was not written by him but compiled and edited by others from his dispatches: J. Wantrup *Australian Rare Books*, Hordern House, Sydney, 2000 [**Wantrup**] p. 60. The more likely date is 21 January nominated by Hunter, Collins and King: J. Hunter, *An Historical Journal of the Transactions at Port Jackson and Norfolk Island*, John Stockdale, London, 1793 [**Hunter's Journal**] p. 43; B. Fletcher, ed., *An Account of the English Colony at New South Wales*, A.H. and A.W. Reed, Sydney, 1975, Volume I, p. 3; P.G. Fidlon ed., *The Journal of Philip Gidley King*, Australian Documents Library, Sydney, 1980 [**King's Journal**] p. 35; J.C. Dann, ed., *The Nagle Journal*, Weidenfield and Nicholson, New York, 1988 [**Nagle's Journal**], p. 94; Eldershaw, p. 101; Mackaness, p. 107; HRNSW, p. 122.
3. *The Times*, 23 January 1788; Nagle's Journal, p. 94.
4. There is some disagreement over whether the flag-raising occurred in the morning or the evening of 26 January, Lieutenant King's journal and notes contradicting each other – Mackaness, pp. 110–11; HRNSW, p. 122; Phillip's Voyage, p. 54; *Alexander's* Log, ADM 51/4375; *Golden Grove's* Log, ADM 51/4376; Smyth's Journal, p. 64; *Fishburn's* Log, ADM 51/4375; Mackaness, pp. 109, 111–12; Smyth's Journal, p. 63.
5. HRNSW, p. 85; Clark CMH, p. 88; Smyth's Journal, pp. 67–69; W. Tench, *A Narrative of the Expedition to Botany Bay*, J. Debrett, London, 1789 [**Tench's Narrative**] pp. 62–3.
6. Smyth's Journal, pp. 67–69; Tench's Narrative, pp. 66–67, 73; HRNSW, pp. 126, 299
7. Tench's Narrative, pp. 49, 95; HRNSW, pp. 89, 126, 136–38; A. Cavanagh, 'The Return of the First Fleet Ships', *Journal of the Australian Association for Maritime History*, Volume II, No. 2, 1989 [**Cavanagh**] p. 10; Smyth's Journal, pp. 86, 88, 127, 130, 144; *The Times*, 30 May 1789.
8. HRNSW, pp. 123–24, 128, 133; The Governors, pp. 40–41.
9. HRNSW, pp. 133, 136; The Governors, p. 40.
10. HRNSW, pp. 89, 138, 146, 162, 164; Howe to Sydney, 21 November 1786, ADM 2/1178; Sydney to Major General Carruthers, 8 October 1786, ADM 2/1177; Atkinson, p. 105.
11. HRNSW, pp. 127, 146–47, 151–52, 177; Gillen, pp. 428–29.
12. B. Kercher and B. Salter, eds., *The Kercher Reports*, The Francis Forbes Society for Legal History, Sydney, 2009, pp. 15–20.

Chapter 31

FIRST NEWS OF PHILLIP

1. Gillen, pp. 427–29; HRNSW, p. 178; Hunter, pp. 105, 130.
2. Reece, pp. 158–60, 163, 166, 191–2, 266.
3. *The Times*, 30 September 1788, 27 March 1789; T. Flannery, *Watkin Tench 1788*, The Text Publishing Company, Melbourne, 1966 [**Flannery**] p. 2; *Prince of Wales* Log ADM 51/4376; *The London Chronicle* 24 to 26 March 1789.

Notes   295

4   HRNSW, p. 178; *The Times*, 7 and 17 April 1789; Wantrup, pp. 54, 56; Tench's Narrative, pp. 138–39.
5   Flynn, pp. 16–17; Sydney to the Lords of the Treasury, 24 April 1789, HO 36/6.
6   Sydney to Admiralty Lords, 13 April 1789, ADM 1/4154; HRNSW, pp. 230–31.
7   *The Times*, 30 May, 1 June and 27 July 1789; Gillen, pp. 428–29; Wantrup, p. 61.
8   Mackaness, pp. 209, 261; HRNSW, pp. 248, 310–11, 329; Flynn, p. 25.
9   Grenville to Treasury Lords, 6 July 1789, HO 36/6; J. Ritchie, *The Wentworths Father and Son*, Melbourne University Press, 1999 [**Ritchie**] pp. 27, 40; HRNSW, pp. 147, 153, 213; HRNSW, Volume II, p. 768; Christopher, p. 290; Bateson C, p. 127; S. Rees, *The Floating Brothel*, Hodder, Sydney, 2002 [**Rees**] back cover; Wraxall PM, Volume I, p. 277; A. Frost, *The First Fleet The Real Story*, Black Inc., Collingwood, Victoria, 2011, p. 192.
10 Grenville to Treasury, 6 July 1789, HO 36/6; Flynn, p. 64; Frost CE, p. 6.
11 Frost AP, p. 192; Gillen, pp. xxxv, 62, 318; D.R. Hainsworth, 'Kable, Henry', *Australian Dictionary of Biography*, Volume 2, Melbourne University Press, 1967, pp. 31–32.
12 Phillip to Sydney, 26 July 1790, Dixson Library, MS. Q 162/1030 and /31; HRNSW pp. 329, 422; Phillip to Sydney, 24 March 1791, Dixson Library, MS. Q 162/1034; Phillip to Sydney, 11 November 1791, Dixson Library, MS. Q 162/1041 and /44; King to Sydney, 13 August 1797, Dixson Library 98 ZMS. Q522; HRNSW, Volume III, p. 214; Hunter to Sydney, 15 May 1798, Dixson Library, 98 ZMS. Q522; Waterhouse to Sydney, 10 November 1794, Dixson Library, 98 ZMS. Q522.
13 Waterhouse to Sydney, 30 April 1796, Dixson Library, 98 ZMS. Q522; Hunter to Sydney, 1 June 1799, MSQ 522; Hunter's Journal, p. 126.
14 Wantrup, p. 83; Currey, pp. 31, 154.

Chapter 32

MADNESS AND REGENCY

1   Buckingham's Memoirs, Volume I, p. 429; Diary of Sir George Baker, 21 and 22 October 1788, Royal College of Physicians Library, London [**Royal College of Physicians**]; HibbertGIII, pp. 258, 261, 263.
2   HibbertGIII, p. 261.
3   Nelson RR, p. 22; Buckingham's Memoirs, Volume I, pp. 437–38.
4   HibbertGIII, p. 261, C. Hibbert, *George IV*, Penguin, London, 1973 [**Hibbert GIV**] pp. 45, 51, 54–55, 60; Parliamentary History, Volume XXIV, pp. 160, 196.
5   Hibbert GIV, pp. 77, 80, 94–95, 97; Stanhope, Volume I, p. 77; C. Hibbert, George IV, *ODNB*, Volume 21, pp. 856–64.
6   Buckingham's Memoirs, Volume II, pp. 3–4, 8, 14–15, 24; Hibbert GIV, pp. 113, 266; GIII's Later Correspondence, p. xxxix; *The Times*, 24 November 1788.
7   Royal College of Physicians Library, Catalogue Numbers 3011/1 – 3011/44; To Lord Sydney, Report of the King's Treatment, n.d., Sydney Papers, Box XV, Clements Library; Lady Mary to Sydney, 16 November 1788, Sydney Papers, Box XV, Clements Library; Drs Warren, Baker, Pepys, Addington and Reynolds to Sydney, 27 November 1788, Royal College of Physicians, 3011/1.
8   *The Times*, 14 November 1788; JHC, Volume 44, p. 3; JHL, Volume 38, p. 266–68; Great Britain, Privy Council, Copy of the Resolution with the record of the examination

of the King's Physicians, 3 December 1788, Sydney Papers, Box XV, Clements Library; Buckingham's Memoirs, Volume I, p. 447.
9. HibbertGIII, p. 275; Hibbert GIV, p. 121; JHC, Volume 44, p. 8; JHC, Volume 44, pp. 57, 61, 70, 85; R. Porter, 'Willis, Francis', *ODNB*, Volume 59, pp. 377–78.
10. HibbertGIII, p. 265; Nepean's Secret Service Accounts, 31 December 1788, Sydney Papers, Clements Library; Detective's report on the movements of Richard Brinsley Sheridan, 6 December 1788, Sydney Papers, Box XV, Clements Library.
11. A Sincere Lover of Truth and Justice to Sydney, 22 December 1788, Osborn Files, Beinecke Library.
12. Namier, Volume III, p. 554; Parliamentary History, Volume XXVII, p. 658; Proposal for a Parliamentary Grouping of Independents, 1788, Sydney Papers, Box XV, Clements Library; Cornwallis's Correspondence, Volume I, p. 433.
13. *Morning Post*, 28 November 1788; GIII's Later Correspondence, Volume I, p. xxxix; Boring a Secret of St—e [**State**], 8 June 1785, no. 6796 in F.G. Stephens, *Catalogue of Political and Personal Satires in the Department of Prints and Drawings in the British Museum*, British Museum, London, 1870–1954; *The Times*, 26 May 1787; Parliamentary History, pp. 674–65; Sidney, p. 229; JHL, Volume 38, p. 276; Parliamentary History, Volume XXVII, pp. 676, 681; Wraxall HM, p. 306.
14. Cornwallis's Correspondence, Volume I, p. 406.
15. JHC, Volume 44, pp. 43–44; Buckingham's Memoirs, Volume II, pp. 39, 51–52; Carswell, p. 213.
16. JHL, Volume 38, pp. 331, 334; JHC, Volume 44, pp. 55, 68, 76.
17. W. Pitt Jr to Sydney, 1788/9, Pitt Papers, Box II, Clements Library; JHL, Volume 38, p. 339; Parliamentary History, Volume XXVII, pp. 1060–61.
18. Parliamentary History, Volume XXVII, pp. 1063–64.
19. Sydney to Lord Southampton, 29 January 1789, Sydney Papers, Box XV, Clements Library; Southampton to Sydney, 29 January 1789, Sydney Papers, box XV, Clements Library; Wraxall PM, Volume III, p. 297; *The Times*, 30 January 1789.
20. Prince of wales regent, Copy to Parliament, Sydney Papers, Box XV, Clements Library; JHL, Volume 38, pp. 341, 343–44; Medical Reports to Sydney, 2, 3, 4, 6, 7, 8, 9 and 10 February 1789, Royal College of Physicians, 3011/20–3011/27; JHC, Volume 44, pp. 97, 115; Hibbert, GIII, pp. 291–92; Gore-Browne, p. 275.
21. JHL, Volume 38, p. 353; *The Times*, 30 January 1789; Drs Warren and Gisborne to Sydney, 16 February 1789 and Drs Baker and Reynolds to Sydney, 17 February 1789, Royal College of Physicians, 3011/28 and 29; Hibbert, GIII, p. 294; Parliamentary History, Volume XXVII, pp. 1285, 1288, 1292.
22. Parliamentary History, Volume XXVII, pp. 1292–93; Drs Baker and Pepys to Sydney, 26 February 1789, Royal College of Physicians, 3011/39; JHL, Volume 38, p. 362.
23. Cornwallis's Correspondence, Volume I, pp. 407, 432, Volume II, p. 27; Wraxall PM, Volume III, pp. 264–65; 311; Parliamentary History, Volume XXVII, p. 1294.
24. Buckingham's Memoirs, Volume II, pp. 42–43, 74–75, 80, 93–94, 100, 108, 111–13; Wraxall PM, Volume III, p. 358.
25. Cornwallis's Correspondence, Volume I, p. 434; *The Times*, 11 March 1789.
26. GIII's Later Correspondence, Volume I, p. 402; Lambert S, Volume 66, pp. 247–55; HibbertGIII, p. 301; Buckingham's memoirs, Volume II, p. 152.

Chapter 33

A GOOD RETREAT

1. JHC, Volume 43, pp. 159, 493, 634; Hague, p. 294; Parliamentary History, Volume XXVII, p. 573; Wraxall PM, Volume III, p. 114; A. Hochschild, *Bury the Chains*, Houghton Mifflin Co., New York, 2005 [**Hochschild**] pp. 6–7, 110, 140, 139.
2. Wraxall PM, Volume III, pp. 117–18, 120, 123; Parliamentary History, Volume XXVII, p. 646; Ehrman, p. 394; Lord Walsingham to Sydney, 30 June 1788, Sydney Papers, Box XIV, Clements Library; Atkinson, p. 62; Wraxall HM, p. 324.
3. JHC, Volume 43, pp. 644–48, 651; JHL, Volume 38, p. 263; Wraxall PM, Volume III, p. 126.
4. Hochschild, pp. 110, 160, 307, 348; Lambert S, Volume 67, pp. 89–223; J. Wolffe, 'Wilberforce, William', *ODNB*, Volume 58, p. 884.
5. Pitt to Sydney, 14 May 1789, Pitt Papers, Box II, Clements Library; Buckingham's Memoirs, Volume I, p. 397; Stanhope, Volume II, pp. 35–36; *The Times*, 8 and 10 June 1789; Cornwallis's Correspondence, Volume II, p. 31, GIII's Later Correspondence, Volume I, p. 422; Cornwallis's Correspondence, Volume II, p. 5.
6. JHL, Volume 38, p. 455; GIII's Later Correspondence, Volume I, pp. xiii, 433; Pitt to Sydney, 11 July 1789, Pitt Papers, Box II, Clements Library; *The Times*, 29 August 1796.
7. Sydney Catalogue, Lot 477, p. 41; HibbertGIII, p. 302.
8. Cornwallis's Correspondence, Volume II, p. 29; *The Times*, 6 December 1791, HNRSW, p. 340; R. J. King, 'Etruria', *Journal of the Numismatic Association of Australia*, Volume 5, October 1990, pp. 3–8.
9. I. Brodsky, *Bennelong Profile*, Sydney University Co-op Bookshop, Sydney, 1973, p. 65; A. Atkinson, 'Bennelong', *ODNB*, Volume 5, p. 96; Atkinson, p. 150; Waterhouse to Sydney, 10 November 1794, Dixson Library MSQ 522.
10. Cornwallis's Correspondence, Volume I, p. 406, Volume II, pp. 30, 31, 39.
11. Sydney on the French character and the French role in the American Revolution, 20 November 1792, Sydney Papers, Box XV, Clements Library.
12. Lambert, pp. 154–55; *The Times*, 27 March 1794.
13. *The Times*, 14 April 1794; Webb, p. 168.
14. Lambert, p. 159; M. Estensen, *Matthew Flinders*, Allen and Unwin, Sydney, 2003, p. 37; Henry Waterhouse to Sydney, 2 June 1794, Dixson Library MSQ 522; Parliamentary History, Volume XXXI, p. 906; G. Edwards, *Watkin Tench Letters from Revolutionary France*, University of Wales Press, Cardiff, 2001, p. xviii; Waterhouse to Sydney, 10 November 1794, Dixson Library MSQ 522.
15. Parliamentary History, Volume XXXI, pp. 910, 912, 914.
16. Sydney's notes on reported radical activity at Chislehurst, January 1796, Sydney Papers, Box XVI, Clements Library.
17. Parliamentary History, Volume XXXI, p. 1296.

Chapter 34

GIVE ME MY DRAUGHT

1. Cornwallis's Correspondence, Volume II, pp. 40, 283; R. Thorne *The House of Commons 1790–1820*, Secker and Warburg, London, 1986 [**Thorne**] Volume V, p. 408; Webb, p. 168; Namier, Volume III, pp. 553–54.
2. Namier, Volume III, p. 420; Webb, pp. 161–62; Thorne, Volume II, p. 421; *Collins English Dictionary Complete and Unabridged*, Harper Collins, London, 2003, p. 585; *The Times*, 1 February 1791.
3. *The Times*, 9 April 1791; Thorne, Volume II, pp. 421–22; Sydney to John Thomas Townshend, 20 September 1799, Osborn Files, Beinecke Library; Webb, p. 168; Thorne, Volume V, p. 409.
4. Thorne, Volume II, p. 193, Volume V, p. 405; Webb, p. 168.
5. *ODNB*, Volume 55, p. 159; V. Gibbs, ed., *The Complete Peerage*, St. Catherine Press, London, 1913, Volume 3, p. 455; Hague, p. 368; *ODNB*, Volume 13, p. 481; Parliamentary History, Volume XXIX, p. 159.
6. *The Times*, 4 April 1791; Parliamentary History, Volume XXVIII, p. 938, Volume XXXI, p. 1452.
7. Parliamentary History, Volume XXXIII, pp. 474–77; Hague, p. 403.
8. Norris, p. 266; S.M. Farrell, 'Cavendish, Lord John', *ODNB*, Volume 10, p. 631; Sydney to John Thomas Townshend, 20 December 1796, Osborn Files, Beinecke Library.
9. Sydney to Pitt, 18 November 1798, Osborn Files, Beinecke Library; Sydney Catalogue, Lot 121, p. 15; Waterhouse to Sydney, 10 September 1799, Dixson Library MSQ 522.
10. Webb, pp. 37, 167.
11. Undated and unidentified newspaper clipping of the 1915 auction at Frognal, enclosed in the Dixson Library's copy of the Sydney Catalogue; Webb, p. 169; Sydney Catalogue; A.G. Butler, *The Australian Army Medical Services in the War of 1914–1918*, Volume II, Australian War Memorial, Canberra, 1940, pp. 823–24; A.C. Howie, ed., *Who's Who in Australia*, Information Australia, 1991, p. 8; *Sidcup and District Times*, 21 September 1885; Sidney p. 354.

Bibliography

The author's notes and research files are held by the Mitchell Library, State Library of New South Wales.

Primary Sources

Public Records Office, London

ADM 1/4151, 21 April 1784 to ADM 1/4154 13 April 1789
ADM 51/ 4375, Alexander's Log, Charlotte's Log & Fishburn's Log
ADM 51/4376, Golden Grove's Log; Prince of Wales Log
ADM 2 /1177, 8 October 1786 to ADM2/1178 21 November 1786
CO 201/2, Port Jackson 1786–1787
FO 27/16, 9 June 1785
HO 13/5, 19 September 1787
HO 28/5, 15 October 1785
HO 29/2, 20 December 1785 to 19 March 1787
HO 36/5, 4 September 1786 to17 January 1787
HO 36/6, 21 April 1789 to10 February 1790
PC 1/61, 14 December 1786 to PC1/62 25 April 1787
TI/619, 20 March 1785
TI/639, 18 August 1786 to18 December 1786

William L Clements Library, University of Michigan, Ann Arbor, Michigan

Charles Townshend Papers
Earl of Dunmore Papers
East India Miscellaneous Documents
Henry Clinton Papers
George Germain Papers
George Townshend Papers
Howe Brothers Papers
Lord Sydney Papers
Michigan Collection
Pitt Family Papers
Viscount Melville Papers
William Dowdeswell Papers
William Petty, Lord Shelburne Papers

State Library of New South Wales

Dixson Library, MSQ 522
Dixson Library, 98 ZMS.Q 522
Dixson Library, MSQ 162/1030,1031,1034, 1035,1041, 1044, 1046,1051
Papers of Sir Joseph Banks, Series 45. 03. CY

Beinecke Rare Book and Manuscript Library, Yale University Library, New Haven, Connecticut

The James Marshall and Marie-Louise Osborn Collection. Letters of Thomas Townshend 1st Viscount Sydney 1733–1800 contained in Osborn Files 37.230–37.271

Royal College of Physicians Library, London

Correspondence between GIII's physicians and Sydney, 27 November 1788 to 27 February 1789, Catalogue numbers 3011/1–3011/44

Parliamentary Papers

Journals of the House of Commons, Reprinted by Order of the House of Commons, 1803
Journals of the House of Lords
Parliamentary History of England from the Earliest Period to the Year 1803. T.C. Hansard, London, 1814
Report of the Committee appointed to inspect the several houses and other buildings adjoining Westminster Hall and the two House of Parliament and the offices thereto belonging; presented by Sir Peter Burrell, 22 July 1789, ordered to be printed, 16 February 1790
Lambert, S. (ed.), *House of Commons Sessional Papers of the 18th Century.* Scholarly Resources Inc., Delaware, 1975
Simmons, R. (ed.), Proceedings and debates of the British Parliament Respecting North America 1754–1783. Kraus International Publications, Millwood, New York, 1982
The Statutes at Large, House of Commons Papers, George III. Scholarly Resources Inc., Delaware, 1975

Newspapers and Journals

Annual Register, Volume 14, December 1771
Gentleman's Magazine, V/3, February 1733 to V/15, December 1745
The London Chronicle, 24 to 26 March 1789, Vol LXV, No5058
Morning Post, 28 November 1788
Sidcup and District Times, 21 September 1885
The Times, 18 January 1785, Issue 15, to 29 August 1796, Issue 3674

Memoirs, Letters and Other Documents

Adams, C. F., *The Works of John Adams*, Little Brown and Co., Boston, 1856
Albemarle, Earl of, *Memoirs of the Marquis of Rockingham*, Richard Bentley, London, 1852

Bibliography

Anson, W. R., ed., *Autobiography of the Duke of Grafton*, Kraus Reprint, Millwood, New York, 1973
Aspinall, A., ed., *Later Correspondence of George III*, Cambridge University Press, London, 1962
Beaglehole, J. C., ed., *The Endeavour Journal of Joseph Banks*, Angus and Robertson, Sydney, 1962
Bligh, W., *A Narrative of the Mutiny on Board His Majesty's Ship Bounty*, George Nicol, London, 1790
Buckingham, Duke of, *Memoirs of the Courts and Cabinets of George III*, Hurst and Blackett, London, 1853
Butterfield, L.H., ed., *Diary and Autobiography of John Adams*, Belknap Press, Cambridge Massachussetts, 1961
Chambers Dictionary of Quotations, Cambridge University Press, Cambridge, 1996
Chesnut, D.R. & Taylor, C. J., eds., *The Papers of Henry Laurens 1778–1782*, University of South Carolina Press, Columbia, S.C., 2003
Clark, J. C. D., ed., *The Memoirs & Speeches of James 2nd Earl Waldegrave 1742–1763*, Cambridge University Press, Cambridge 1988
Cobham Brewer, E. *Dictionary of Phrase and Fable*, Henry Altemus and Co., Philadelphia, 1898
Cohn, E. R., ed., *The Papers of Benjamin Franklin*, Yale University Press, New Haven, Connecticut, 2003
Collins English Dictionary, Complete and Unabridged, Harper Collins, London, 2003
Copeland, T., ed., *The Correspondence of Edmund Burke April 1744–June 1768*, Cambridge at the University Press, 1958
Dann, J. C., ed., *The Nagle Journal*, Weidenfeld & Nicholson, New York, 1988
Davies, K.G., ed., *Documents of the American Revolution, 1770–1783, Colonial Office Series*, Irish University Press, Shannon, 1981
De Tocqueville, A., *Democracy in America*, Penguin, London, 2003
Dobree, B., ed., *The Letters of King George III*, Cassell, London, 1968
Driscoll, J.D., *United States Constitution Califoirnia*, California Legislature Assembly, 1971
Edwards, G., ed., *Watkin Tench Letters from Revolutionary France*, University of Wales Press, Cardiff, 2001
Edwards, P., ed., *James Cook, The Journals*, Penguin Books, London, 2003
Executors of John, Earl of Chatham, eds., *Chatham Correspondence*, John Murray, London, 1838
Fidlon, P. G., ed., *The Journal of Arthur Bowes Smyth*, Australian Documents Library, Sydney, 1979
Fidlon, P. G., ed., *The Journal of Phillip Gidley King*, Australian Documents Library, Sydney, 1980
Fitzmaurice, Lord Edmond, *Life of Shelburne*, Macmillan, London, 1875
Flood, W., ed., *Memoirs of the Life and Correspondence of Henry Flood*, John Cumming, Dublin, 1838
Fortescue, J., ed., *Correspondence of King George III 1760–1783*, Frank Cass, London, 1967
Franklin, B., *Poor Richard's Almanac*, Ballantine Books, New York, 1977
Furber, H., ed., *Correspondence of Edmund Burke July 1782–June 1789*, Cambridge at the University Press, 1965
Gibbs,V., ed., *The Complete Peerage*, St Catherine Press, London, 1913
Giunta, M. A., ed., *The Emerging Nation, Foreign Relations of the United States 1780–1789*, National Historical and Public Records Commission, 1996

Grattan, H., *The Speeches of Henry Grattan*, Longman, London, 1822
Haldimand, F., *The Private Diary of General Haldimand*, www.canadiana.org/ECO
Harcourt, L. V., ed., *The Diaries and Correspondence of the Rt Hon George Rose*, Richard Bentley, London, 1860
Harlow, V. and Madden, F., *British Colonial Developments 1774–1834, Select Documents*, Oxford at the Clarendon Press, 1953
Historical Records of Australia, Series I, Volume I, Library Committee of the Commonwealth Parliament, 1914
Historical Records of New South Wales, Volume I, Part 2, Government Printer, Sydney, 1892
Howie, A.C., ed., *Who's Who in Australia, XXVII Edition*, Information Australia, 1991
Hunter, J., *An Historical Journal of the Transactions at Port Jackson and Norfolk Island*, John Stockdale, London, 1793
Jesse, J. H., *George Selwyn and his Contemporaries*, Bickers and Son, London, 1882
Kercher, B. and Salter, B., eds., *The Kercher Reports*, The Francis Forbes Society for Legal History, Sydney, 2009
Knight, Frank and Rutley, *The Sydney Collection Catalogue*, Dryden Press, London, 1915
Laprade, W. T., ed., *Parliamentary Papers of John Robinson*, Royal Historical Society, London, 1922
Limon, D., ed., *Erskine May's Treatise on the Law, Principles and Proceedings of Parliament*, Butterworths, London, 1997
Lynch, J., ed., *Samuel Johnson's Dictionary*, Atlantic Books, London, 2004
Madden, D. O., *The Select Speeches of Henry Grattan*, James Duffy, Dublin, 1845
Malmesbury, 3rd Earl of, ed., *Diaries and Correspondence of James Harris 1st Earl of Malmsbury*, Richard Bentley, London, 1844
Morris, R. B., *John Jay The Winning of the Peace*, Harper and Row, NewYork, 1980
Nicholas, N. H., ed., *The Dispatches and Letters of Vice Admiral Lord Viscount Nelson*, Henry Colburn, London, 1845
Peterson, M., ed., *Thoms Jefferson Writings*, Library of America, New York, 1984
Phillip, A., *The Voyage of Governor Phillip to Botany Bay*, John Stockdale, London, 1789
Ross, C., ed., *Correspondence of Charles 1st Marquess Cornwallis*, John Murray, London, 1859
Russell, Lord John, ed., *Memorials and Correspondence of Charles James Fox*, Richard Bentley, London, 1853
Rutland, John Duke of, *The Correspondence of Pitt and Rutland 1781–1787*, William Blackwood, London, 1890
Shortt A. & Doughty A.G., eds., *Canadian Archives, Documents Relating to the Constitutional History of Canada 1759–1791, Part II*, J.de L.Tache, Ottawa, 1918
Sinh, R., ed., *Fort William – India House Correspondence*, Volume X, 1786 –1788, National Archives of India, New Delhi, 1972
Skousen, M., ed., *The Compleated Autobiography by Benjamin Franklin*, Regnery Publishing, Washington D.C., 2006
Smith, W. J., ed., *The Grenville Papers*. John Murray, London, 1852
Stanhope, Earl of, *Life of Pitt*, John Murray, London, 1861
Stephens, F.G., *Catalogue of Political and Personal Satires in the Department of Prints and Drawings in the British Museum*, British Museum, London, 1870–1954
Stern, P. Van Doren, ed., *The Life and Writings of Abraham Lincoln*, The Modern Library, New York, 1940
Sutherland, L.S., ed., *The Correspondence of Edmund Burke July 1768 – June 1774*, Cambridge at the University Press, 1960

Tench, W., *A Complete Account of the Settlement at Port Jackson*, G. Nicol, London, 1793
Tench, W., *A Narrative of the Expedition to Botany Bay*, J. Debrett, London, 1789
Tench, W., *Letters written in France to a Friend in London between the Month of November 1794 and the Month of May 1795*, J. Johnson, London, 1796
Upton, L. F. S., ed., *The Diary and Selected Papers of Chief Justice William Smith*, The Champlain Society, Toronto, 1963
Walpole, H., *Last Journals of Horace Walpole during the Reign of George III from 1771–1783*, John Lane, London, 1910
Walpole, H., *Memoirs of the Reign of George II*, Henry Colburn, London, 1846
Walpole, H., *Memoirs of the Reign of King George III*, Richard Bentley, London, 1845
Willson, B., *The Life and Letters of James Wolfe*, William Heinemann, London, 1909
Wraxall, N., *Historical Memoirs of My Own Time*, Keegan Paul, London, 1904
Wraxall, N., *Posthumous Memoirs of his Own Time*, Richard Bentley, London, 1836

Secondary Sources

Adolphus, J., *The History of England*, John Lee, London, 1840
Alexander, C., *The Bounty*, Harper Collins, London, 2003
Anderson, F., *Crucible of War*, Faber & Faber, London, 2000
Anon, *A letter to the Earl of Shelburne on the subject of Mr Secretary Townshend's letter to the Chairman and Deputy Chairman of the East India Company*, J. Debrett, London, 1783
Archer, I. K. R., 'Townshend, Thomas', *Oxford Dictionary of National Biography*, Oxford University Press, 2004, [*ODNB*], Volume 55
Arthur, E., 'Hamilton, Henry', *Dictionary of Canadian Biography* [*DCB*] on line edition
Aston, N., 'Dolben, Sir William', *ODNB*, Volume 16
Atkinson, A., 'Bennelong', *ODNB*, Volume 5
Atkinson, A., *The Europeans in Australia*, Oxford University Press, 1997
Atkinson, A., 'The First Plans for Governing New South Wales', *Australian Historical Studies*, Volume 24, No. 94, April 1990
Ayling, S., *George III*, Collins, London, 1972
Ayling, S., *The Elder Pitt*, Collins, London, 1976
Ayling, S., *The Life and Times of Charles James Fox*, John Murray, London, 1991
Baglole, H., Patterson (Paterson), Walter, *DCB*, on line edition
Bailyn, B., *The Ideological Origins of the American Revolution*, Belknap Press, Cambridge, Masachussetts, 1992
Bancroft, G., *The American Revolution*. Little Brown, 1875
Barker, G. F. R., 'Robinson, Thomas, 2nd Baron Grantham', *ODNB*, Volume 47
Barton, G. B., *History of New South Wales*. Government Printer, Sydney, 1889
Bateson, C., *The Convict Ships 1787–1868*. Brown and Son, Glasgow, 1985
Bateson, M., *Changes in the Ministry 1765–1767*. Longmans Green, London, 1898
Bayley, C., and Prior, K., 'Cornwallis, Charles, first Marquess Cornwallis', *ODNB*, Volume 13
Bemis, S. F., *A Diplomatic History of the United States*, Holt, Rinehart & Winston, New York, 1965
Bemis, S. F., 'Relations between the Vermont Separatists and Great Britain 1789–1791', *The American Historical Review*, Volume XXI, 1916
Bemis, S. F., *The American Secretaries of State and their Diplomacy*, Knopf, New York, 1927

Bemis, S.F., *The Diplomacy of the American Revolution*, Indiana University Press, Bloomington, 1967
Bicheno, H., *Rebels and Redcoats*, Harper Collins, London, 2003
Boorstin, D., *The Americans The Colonial Experience*, Phoenix Press, London, 2000
Boswell, J., *Life of Johnson*, Heron Books, London, 1960
Bradley, A. G., *Sir Guy Carleton,* University of Toronto Press, Toronto, 1966
Brodsky, I., *Bennelong Profile*, Sydney University Co-op Bookshop, Sydney, 1973
Brooke, J., *Chatham Administration*, Macmillan, London, 1956
Browne, G.P., 'Carleton, Sir Guy, 1st Baron Dorchester', *DCB*, on line edition
Browning, R., 'Holles, Thomas Pelham–', *ODNB*, Volume 27
Burroughs, P., 'Parr, John', *DCB*, on line edition
Burt, A. L., *The Old Province of Quebec*, The Ryerson Press, Toronto, 1933
Butler, A. G., *The Australian Army Medical Services in the War of 1914–1918*, Australian War Memorial, Canberra, 1940
Calhoon, R., 'Smith, William', *ODNB*, Volume 51
Campbell, W. S., 'Arthur Phillip', *Journal of the Royal Australian Historical Society*, Volume XXI, 1936
Cannon, J., 'Petty, William', *ODNB*, Volume 43
Carswell, J., *The Porcupine–The Life of Algernon Sidney*, John Murray, London, 1989
Cavanagh, A. K., 'The Return of the First Fleet Ships', *Journal of the Australian Association for Maritime History,* Volume II, No 2, 1989
Chisholm, A., ed., *Journal of a Voyage to New South Wales*, Angus and Robertson, Sydney, 1962
Christie, I., *The End of North's Ministry 1780–1782*, Macmillan, London, 1958
Christopher, E., *A Merciless Place*, Allen and Unwin, Sydney, 2010
Churchill, W.L.S. *A History of the English Speaking People*, Cassell, London, 1957
Clark, C. M. H., *A History of Australia*, Melbourne University Press, Melbourne, 1962
Claydon, T., 'William III', *ODNB*, Volume 59
Clune, D., and Turner, K., eds., *The Governors of New South Wales 1788–2010*, Federation Press, Sydney, 2009
Coleman, T., *Nelson The Man and the Legend*, Bloomsbury, London, 2002
Colley, L., *Britons*. Pimlico, London, 2003
Collingridge, V., *Captain Cook*, Ebury Press, London, 2002
Connell, B., *The Plains of Abraham*, Hodder & Stroughton, London, 1959
Cronin, M., *A History of Ireland*, Palgrave, New York, 2001
Currey, J., *David Collins a Colonial Life*, The Miegunyah Press, Melbourne, 2000
Davis, R. W., 'Grenville, George Nugent Temple', *ODNB*, Volume 23
Dickinson, H., 'Wyvill, Christopher', *ODNB*, Volume 60
Donovan, K., *Cape Breton at 200*, University College of Cape Breton Press, Sydney, N.S., 1985
Duffy, J. J., *Ethan Allen and his Kin*, University Press of New England, Hanover, N.H., 1998
Dugdale, G.S., *Whitehall Through the Centuries*, Theodore Brun Ltd, London, 1950
Dunnigan, B. L., *Detroit*, Wayne State University Press, Detroit, 2001
Dunnigan, B. L., *King's Men at Mackinac*, Harlo Printing, Detroit, 1993
Durrant, P., 'Fitzroy, Augustus Henry, third Duke of Grafton', *ODNB*, Volume 19
Edwards, J.G., and Pares, R.,' The Marquess of Rockingham and Lord North's Offer of Coalition June–July 1780', *The English Historical Review*, Volume LXIX, 1954
Ehrman, J., *The Younger Pitt, Years of Acclaim*, Constable, London, 1984
Ekirch, A.R., 'Great Britain's Secret Convict Trade to America 1783–1784', *American Historical Review*, Volume 89, Part 5, 1984

Bibliography

Eldershaw, M. B., *Phillip of Australia*. Angus and Robertson, Sydney, 1972
Escott, T. H. S., *Gentlemen of the House of Commons*, Hurst and Blackett, London, 1902
Estensen, M., *Matthew Flinders*, Allen and Unwin, Sydney, 2003
Evans, G. N. D., *Allegience in America–The Case of the Loyalists*, Addison Wesley, Reading, Massachussetts, 1969
Evans, G.N.D., *Uncommon Obdurate*, University of Toronto Press, Toronto, 1969
Falkner, J., 'Eliott, George Augustus', *ODNB*, Volume 18
Farrell, S. M., 'Cavendish, Lord John'. *ODNB*, Volume 10.
Fergusson, C. B., *Uniake's Sketches of Cape Breton, Nova Scotia*, Public Archives of Nova Scotia, Halifax, N.S., 1958
Fergusson, B., *Advice to Officers of the British Army*, Jonathan Cape, London, 1946
Fielding, H., *The History of Tom Jones a Foundling*, Penguin Books, London, 2005
Filmer, R., *Patriarcha*, London, 1680
Firth, C. H., 'Sidney, Philip', *ODNB*, Volume 50
Fischer, D. H., *Washington's Crossing*, Oxford University Press, Oxford, 2006
Flannery, T., *Watkin Tench 1788*, The Text Publishing Company, Melbourne, 1996
Fleming, T., *The Man from Monticello*, William Morrow & Co., New York, 1969
Fletcher, B., ed., *An Account of the English Colony in New South Wales*, A.H.& A.W. Reed, Sydney, 1975
Flynn, M., *The Second Fleet*, Library of Australian History, Sydney, 2001
Fraser, A., *Cromwell Our Chief of Men*, Granada, London, 1981
Frey, Linda & Marsha, 'Townshend, Charles 2nd Viscount', *ODNB*, Volume 55
Frost, A., *Arthur Phillip 1738–1814 His Voyaging*, Oxford University Press, Melbourne, 1987
Frost, A., 'Bligh, William', *ODNB*, Volume 6
Frost, A., *Botany Bay The Real Story*, Black Inc., Collingwood, Victoria, 2011
Frost, A., *Convicts and Empire A Naval Question 1776–1811*, Oxford University Press, Melbourne, 1980
Frost, A., *The First Fleet The Real Story*, Black Inc., Collingwood, Victoria, 2011
Frost, A., *The Global Reach of Empire*, Melbourne University Press, Melbourne, 2003
Frost, A., *The Precarious Life of James Mario Matra*, The Miegunyah Press, Melbourne, 1995
Frost, A., 'Young, Sir George', *ODNB*, Volume 60
Gibbon, E., *The Decline and Fall of the Roman Empire*, Alfred A. Knopf, New York, 1993
Gillen, M., *The Founders of Australia: A Biographical Dictionary of the First Fleet*, Library of Australian History, Sydney, 1989
Godfrey, W.G., 'Carleton, Thomas', *DCB*, on line edition
Gore-Browne, R., *Chancellor Thurlow*, Hamish Hamilton, London, 1953
Gruber, I. S., 'Clinton, Sir Henry', *ODNB*, Volume 12
Gwynn, S., *Oliver Goldsmith*, Thornton Butterworth, London, 1935
Gwynn, S., *Henry Grattan and his Times*, Harrap, London, 1939
Hague, W., *William Pitt the Younger*, Harper Perennial, London, 2005
Hainsworth, D.R., 'Kable, Henry', *Australian Dictionary of Biography*, Volume 2, Melbourne University Press, 1967, pp. 31–32
Hancock, D., 'Oswald, Richard', *ODNB*, Volume 42
Handley, S., 'Boyd, Robert', *ODNB*, Volume 7
Harlow, V., *The Founding of the Second British Empire*, Longmans Green, London, 1952
Harlow, V., *The Founding of the Second British Empire*, Longmans Green, London, 1964
Harris, T., *The Great Crisis of the British Monarchy 1685 – 1720*, Allen Lane , London, 2006

Harvey, R., *A Few Bloody Noses*, The Overlook Press, New York, 2003
Haydon, C., 'Gordon, Lord George'. *ODNB*, Volume 22
Hibbert, C., *George III A Personal History*, Penguin, London, 1999
Hibbert, C., ' George IV', *ODNB*, Volume 21
Hibbert, C., *George IV*, Penguin, London, 1973
Hochschild, A., *Bury the Chains*, Houghton Mifflin Co., New York, 2005
Holmes, R., *Redcoat*, Harper Collins, London, 2002
Hosford, D., 'Sidney, Henry', *ODNB*, Volume 50
Isaacson, W., *Benjamin Franklin*, Simon and Schuster, New York, 2004
Johnson, S., *The False Alarm*, T.Cadell, London, 1770
Jupp, P. J., *Grenville*, 'William Wyndham', *ODNB*, Volume 23
Kelly, J., 'Flood, Henry', *ODNB*, Volume 20
Kelly, J., 'Grattan, Henry', *ODNB*, Volume 23
Kennedy, G., *Bligh*, Duckworth, London, 1978
Kenny, A., ed., *The Oxford History of Western Philosophy*, Oxford University Press, Oxford, 1994
Keverne, R., *Tales of Old Inns*, Collins, London, 1951
Kier, D. L., *Constitutional History of Modern Britain*, A. & C. Black, London, 1957
King, J., *In the Beginning*, Macmillan, Melbourne, 1985
King, R. J., 'Bahia Botanica y Liqueyos: Alexandro Malaspina and British Designs in the Pacific', *http://www.mala.bc.ca/-black/amrc/liq.htm*
Knittle, W., *Early 18th Century Palatine Emigration*, Genealogical Publishing Co., Baltimore, 1997
Lambert, A., 'Cornwallis, Sir William', *ODNB*, Volume 13
Lambert, A., *Nelson*, Faber and Faber, London, 2004
Lambert, A., *War at Sea in the Age of Sail*, Cassell, London, 2000
Langford, P., 'Burke, Edmund', *ODNB*, Volume 8
Langford, P., *A Polite and Commercial People*, Oxford, New York, 1992
Laslett, P., *Locke Two Treatises on Government*, Cambridge University Press, Cambridge, 2003
Lawson, C., *The Private Life of Warren Hastings*, Macmillan, London, 1911
Leckie, R., *George Washington's War*, Harper Perennial, New York, 1993
Lee, S. M., 'Fitzherbert, Alleyne', *ODNB*, Volume 19
Lee, S. M., 'Eden, William', *ODNB*, Volume17
Lingelbach, A. 'The Inception of the British Board of Trade', *American Historical Review*, Volume XXX, July 1925
Lowe, W., 'Lennox, Charles, third duke of Richmond', *ODNB*, Volume 23
Lowe, W. C., 'Gower, Granville Leveson', *ODNB*, Volume 23
Macdonald, N., *Canada 1763–1841 Immigration and Settlement*, Longmans Green, London, 1939
Mackaness, G., *Admiral Arthur Phillip*, Angus and Robertson, Sydney, 1937
MacKinnon, J.G., *Old Sydney*, Global Heritage Press, Milton, Ontario, 2003
Macksey, P., *The War for America*, University of Nebraska Press, Lincoln, 1964
McLynn, F., *1759*, Pimlico, London, 2004
MacNutt, W. S., *New Brunswick: a history, 1784–1867*, Macmillan, London, 1984
Mahan, A. T., *The Influence of Sea Power on History*, Dover Publications, New York, 1987
Manning, H. T., *British Colonial Government After the American Revolution 1782–1820*, Archon Books, Hamden, Connecticut, 1966
Marshall, P., 'Hastings, Warren', *ODNB*, Volume 25
Martin, G., *The Founding of Australia the Argument about Australia's Origins*, Hale and Iremonger, Sydney, 1981

Masson P., *The Miscellaneous Works of Oliver Goldsmith*, Macmillan, London, 1871
Matheson, C., *The Life of Henry Dundas*, Constable, London, 1933
Mitchell, L. G., *Charles James Fox*, Penguin, London, 1997
Montgomery of Alamein, *A History of Warfare*, Collins, London, 1968
Moore, C., *The Loyalists*, McClelland & Stewart, Toronto, 1994
Moore, F. F., *The Life of Oliver Goldsmith*, Constable, London, 1910
Morris, J., *Sydney*, Viking Press, Sydney, 1992
Mowat, C. L. *East Florida as a British Province 1763–1784*, University of Florida Press, Gainesville, 1964
Murot, S., *This was Sydney*, Ure Smith, Sydney, 1969
Namier, L. and Brooke, J., *Charles Townshend*, Macmillan, London, 1964
Namier, L. and Brooke, J., *The House of Commons 1754–1790*, Her Majesty's Stationery Office, London, 1964
Namier, L., *The Structure of Politics at the Accession of George III*, Macmillan, London, 1929
Nelson, P. D., *General Sir Guy Carleton, Lord Dorchester soldier-statesman of early Canada*, Associated University Presses, Cranbury, N.J., 2000
Nelson, R. R., *The Home Office 1782–1801*, Duke University Press, Durham, N.C., 1969
Norris, J., *Shelburne and Reform*, Macmillan, London, 1963
Norton, M. B., *The British Americans; The Loyalist Exiles in England 1774–1789*, Little Brown and Co., Canada, 1972
O'Brien, E., *The Foundation of Australia (1786–1800)*, Sheed and Ward, London, 1937
Oldham, W., *Britain's Convicts to the Colonies*, Library of Australian History, Sydney, 1990
Olson, A. G., *The Radical Duke*, Oxford University Press, London, 1961
Owen, C. H. H., 'Collingwood, Cuthbert', *ODNB*, Volume 12
Owen, J., *The Rise of the Pelhams*, Methuen and Co., London, 1957
Pares, R., *King George the Third and the Politicians*, Oxford at the Clarendon Press, 1967
Petersen, J., *Hyde Park Barracks Museum Guidebook*, Historic Houses Trust, Sydney, 2003
Picard, L., *Dr Johnson's London*, Phoenix Press, London, 2003
Porter, R., 'Willis, Francis', *ODNB*, Volume 59
Powell, M, J. 'Townshend, George, 1st Marquess', *ODNB*, Volume 55
Reece, B., *The Origins of Irish Convict Transportation to New South Wales*, Palgrave, New York, 2001
Rees, S., *The Floating Brothel*, Hodder, Sydney, 2002
Reynolds, P., *Sir Guy Carleton*, William Morrow, New York, 1980
Ritchie, J., *The Wentworths, Father and Son*, Melbourne University Press, 1999
Rodger, N. A. M., 'Nelson Horatio', *ODNB*, Volume 40
Rosebery, Lord, *Chatham his Early Life and Connections*, A.L. Humphreys, London, 1910
Rosebery, Lord, *Pitt*, Macmillan, London, 1892
Rosenheim, J., *The Townshends of Raynham*, Wesleyan University Press, Middletown, Connecticut, 1989
Royster, C., 'Washington, George', *ODNB*, Volume 57
Russell, R., 'Where is George III's Head?', *The Sons of the American Revolution Magazine*, Winter, 1998
Sainty, J. C., *Office Holders in Modern Britain Home Office Officials 1782–1870*, Athlone Press, Bristol, 1975
Schweizer, K.W., 'Stuart, John, 3rd Earl of Bute', *ODNB*, Volume 53
Scorgie, M. & Hudgson, P., 'Arthur Phillip's Familial and Political Networks', *Journal of the Royal Australian Historical Society*, Volume 82, Part I, June 1996

Scott, J., 'Sidney, Algernon', *ODNB*, Volume 50
Shaw, A.G.L., *Convicts & the Colonies*, Melbourne University Press, 1981
Shy, A.P., *Guide to the Manuscript Collections of the William L. Clements Library*, G.K. Hall, Boston, 1978
Sidney A. *Discourses concerning Government Published from an Original Manuscript of the Author*, London, 1698
Sidney, A., *The Very Copy of a Paper delivered to the Sheriffs upon the Scaffold on Tower-hill on Friday December 7, 1683 by Algernon Sidney Esq; before his Execution there*, Printed for R.H.J.B. and J.R., 1683
Smith, G.R., and Davis, R.W., 'Grenville, Thomas', *ODNB*, Volume 23
Sparrow, E., 'Nepean, Sir Evan', *ODNB*, Volume 40
Stacey, C.P., *Quebec 1759*, Robin Brass Studio, Toronto, 2002
Sutherland, S.R.J., and ors, 'Haldimand, Sir Frederick', *DCB*, on line edition
Taylor, S., 'Walpole, Robert', *ODNB*, Volume 57
Thomas, P., *George III King and Politicians 1760–1770*, Manchester University Press, Manchester, 2002
Thomas, P. D. G., 'Townshend, Charles', *ODNB*, Volume 55
Thorne, R., 'Ellis, Welbore', *ODNB*, Volume 18
Thorne, R., 'Montagu, Frederick', *ODNB*, Volume 38
Thorne, R., 'Pitt, Thomas', *ODNB*, Volume 44
Thorne, R., 'Rose, George', *ODNB*, Volume 47
Thorne, R.G., *The House of Commons 1790–1820,*. Secker and Warburg, London, 1986
Tomline, G., *Memoirs of Rt Hon William Pitt*, John Murray, London, 1821
Townshend, C. V. F., *The Military Life of Field Marshal Marquess Townshend*, John Murray, London, 1901
Towse, C., 'Conway, Henry Seymour', *ODNB*, Volume 13
Van Doren, C., *Benjamin Franklin*, Penguin Books, New York, 1991
Wade Martins, S., *Turnip Townshend*, Poppyland Publishing, Norwich, 1990
Wantrup, J., *Australian Rare Books 1788–1900*, Hordern House, Sydney, 1987
Warburton, G., *Conquest of Canada*, Richard Bentley, London, 1857
Watson, D. H., 'The Rise of the Opposition at Wildman's Club', *Bulletin of the Institute of Historical Research*, Volume 44, 1971
Watson, J., *The Reign of George III 1760–1815,* Oxford at the Clarendon Press, 1976
Webb, E.A., *The History of Chislehurst*, George Allen, London, 1899
White, R. J., *The Age of George III*, Walker and Co., New York, 1968
Wilkinson, D., 'Bentinck, William Henry Cavendish Cavendish, third duke of Portland', *ODNB*, Volume 5
Williams, B., *The Whig Supremacy 1714–1760*, Oxford at the Clarendon Press, 1949
Windeyer, W.J.V., 'A Birthright and Inheritance', *Tasmanian Law Review*, Volume I, 1958, p. 659.
Winstanley, D. A., *Lord Chatham and the Whig Opposition*, Cambridge at the University Press, 1912
J. Wolffe, 'Wilberforce, William', *ODNB*, Volume 58
Wood, G. S., *The American Revolution*, Weidenfield & Nicholson, London, 2003
Wraxall, N., *A Short Review of the Political State of Great Britain at the Commencement of 1787*, 7th edition with comments, J. Debrett, London 1787
Wright, E. C., *The Loyalists of New Brunswick*, Fredericton, New Brunswick, 1955

Index

Aborigines 226, 228, 232–3, 254
Act of Settlement 5, 242
Adams, John 3, 61, 120, 122, 125, 127–8, 139–40, 148
Addington, Anthony 242
Advice to Officers of the British Army 109
Africa 111–12, 203–05, 207, 211–18, 238, 251
Alexander 221–3, 225, 234–7, 251
Allen, Ethan 180–1
American Civil War 66, 116
American department 63, 102, 111
American Revolution 41, 175, 178
American Stamp Act 29–32, 34, 186
A Narrative of the Expedition to Botany Bay 236
Arabanoo 232
Arden, Pepper 212
Arnold, Benedict 93, 176, 186
Ashburton, Lord – *see* John Dunning

Baker, George 241
Banks, Joseph 196–8, 206–7, 214–16, 218, 228, 237, 239
Barnard, Edward 72
Barnes, John 211, 214
Barras, Jaques-Melchoir 95
Barret, Thomas 231
Bay of Fundy 126, 177
Beauchamp, Lord 214–16, 219
Bedford, 4th Duke of 43, 45
Bellamont, Lord 160
Bennelong 254–5
Berthia (later renamed *Bounty*) 197
Blankett, John 200, 219
Bligh, William 192, 197–9, 239
Bonhomme Richard 85
Bonnie Prince Charlie 9
Boreas 193
Borrowdale 223, 235
Boston Tea Party 34, 39, 59
Boswell, James 55–6

Botany Bay 4, 152, 176, 197–8, 202, 206–7, 212–13, 215–16, 218–19, 220, 222, 224–5, 228–33, 236–7, 254
Bougainville, Louis Antoine de 22–3
Boyd, Robert 109–11, 131
Boyne, battle of the 156
Braddock, Edward 15
Bramston, Sarah 9
Brown, William 197, 199
Brudenell, Lady Mary 149
British North America 117, 120, 155, 175, 177, 184, 186, 215, 235
Brodrick, George (later 3rd Viscount Middleton) 13
Brodrick, George (later 4th Viscount Middleton) 58, 66, 88
Brodrick, Harry (Henry) 89, 92, 96
Bunbury, Charles 203, 207, 211, 218
Bunker Hill, battle of 62
Burgoyne, John 67, 69–70, 76, 79–80
Burke, Edmund 49, 53–5, 57–8, 61–2, 74–5, 84–5, 87–8, 110, 132, 143, 168–9, 213–14, 216, 247, 263
Bute, 3rd Earl of 15, 24–8, 30, 41–2, 74

Cable, Henry 224, 234, 239, 264
Calvert, Anthony 238
Cambridge University 4, 7–8, 10–11, 90, 263
Camden, battle of 91, 93
Camden, 1st Earl 127
Canada 2, 17, 19, 21, 23, 26–7, 29, 59, 63, 68–9, 80, 85, 109, 115, 117, 119–20, 123, 125–6, 128, 154, 161, 175–6, 178, 181, 185–8, 190, 263
Canada Act 190
Canadian boundaries 117, 120, 123, 125–6, 134, 191
Cape Breton 177–9, 235, 262
Cape of Good Hope 172, 198, 227, 233, 235
Carleton, Guy (later Lord Dorchester) 57, 59, 68–9, 80, 85, 102, 109, 115, 167, 176–8, 184–7

Carleton, Thomas 178
Carlisle Peace Commission 72
Carmarthen, Marquess of 144, 148, 154, 184
Carribs 53, 226
Cathcart, Charles 172
Cavendish, Lord John 49–50, 110, 216, 261–2
Charles I 3, 53, 66, 142
Charles II 1–4, 131, 153
Charleston 87, 89–91, 97, 100–01, 109, 115, 175
Charlotte 223, 229, 231
Chatham, Lady – *see* Hester Grenville
Chatham, 1st Earl – *see* William Pitt
Chesapeake Bay 92, 95
Chesterfield, 4th Earl of 5, 16, 253
Chief Pontiac 29
Chief Joseph Brant 182
China tea trade 172–3, 212–13, 231, 237
Clare Hall 10, 90
Clark, Manning 55
Clarke, William 167
Clements, Caroline (John Thomas Townshend's second wife) 263
Clinton, Henry 67–8, 71, 76, 79, 89–96, 98–100, 102, 166
Clive, Robert 124
Coercive Acts 39–40, 56, 59, 61
Collingwood, Cuthbert 194
Collingwood, Wilfrid 194–5
Collins, David 222, 234, 240
Continental Congress, the first 58–9
Continental Congress, the second 62, 65, 68, 75, 117, 126
Convicts 111, 173, 200, 203–09, 211–27, 230–39, 250, 254, 263–4
Conway, Henry 35–7, 100, 102–04, 131
Cook, James 176, 197, 206, 216, 226, 228
Cooke, George 43–4
Cornwallis, Charles (later 1st Marquess Cornwallis) 17, 34, 66–8, 79–80, 89–99, 101–2, 111, 129, 143, 146, 149, 163, 165–72, 186, 245, 249, 253–5, 259, 261
Cornwallis, Elizabeth (mother of Charles Cornwallis) 17
Cornwallis, William (brother of Charles Cornwallis) 96
Corps Diplomatique 120
Cowpens, battle of 92
Cromwell, Oliver 2, 146

Culloden, battle of 10, 41
Cumberland, Duke of 9–10, 18, 20, 31, 34
Cuyler, Abraham 179

Das Voltas Bay 215
Declaration of Independence 64–5, 67, 114, 203
Declaration of Rebellion 66
Declaration of Rights 57–8
Declaratory Bill 33
de Grasse, Francois-Joseph 95
Den Keyser 205
de Rayneval, Joseph Gerard 115, 130
Des Barres, Joseph 178–80
D'Estaing, Charles 75–6, 79, 82
Detroit 181–2
Dettingen, battle of 9
Devonshire, 4th Duke of 16, 244
Discourses Concerning Government 3, 264
Digby, Admiral 176
Dixon, George 173
Dolben, William 103–04, 251–2
Dorchester, Lord – *see* Guy Carleton
Dundas, Henry 153, 164–5, 169–70
Dunkirk 224
Dunmore, 4th Earl of 176
Dunning, John (later 1st Baron Ashburton) 84–5, 113, 122
Dyke, John 152

East India Company 35–6, 39, 53, 140–1, 146, 151, 155, 164–7, 169–73, 222–3, 231, 237
East India Declaratory Bill 171
Eliott, George 109–11, 131
Elliot, Gilbert 104
Ellis, Welbore 102–03
Enabling Act 115–17, 119, 122
English Civil War 2, 54, 59, 63, 66, 116, 156, 208
Eton College 4, 7, 9–10, 72, 90, 150–1, 263
Europe 201
Evening Post 59
Exeter, Lady 150

Fair American 208
Fairfax, 7th Lord of Cameron 175–6
Falkland Islands 51
Ferrers, Lord 66
First Fleet 4, 173, 197, 202, 213, 221, 225–7, 230, 235–9, 256, 264

Fishburn 223, 226, 229, 237
Fitzherbert, Alleyne 116–18, 124–7, 130
Fitzherbert, Maria 242, 244
Flood, Henry 157–9, 162
Foulon Cove 21
Fox, Charles 71–2, 75, 78, 81, 84, 87–9, 100, 103, 105, 107–08, 110, 114–16, 120, 127, 130–5, 138–46, 151, 153, 155, 160, 162, 164–6, 169–70, 206–7, 211, 242–4, 246, 248, 250, 263
Fox, Henry 18, 25–7
Fox/North Coalition 138–40, 142–3, 146, 160
Franklin, Benjamin 3, 37–8, 40, 61, 65–6, 74, 95, 115, 117–21, 124–5, 127–9, 151, 176, 203
Franklin, William 66, 102, 176
Frederick, King of Prussia 16, 25–6, 42
French Revolution 2, 13
Friendship 223, 234–5
Frognal 8–9, 77, 150, 152, 262–3
Frost, Alan 201

Gage, Thomas 31, 39
Gates, Horatio 91
General Advertiser 77
Gentleman's Magazine 7, 9, 54
George 205
George I 5
George II 5, 9, 14–15, 19, 24
George III 24–28, 30–1, 41–2, 44, 46, 51, 53, 57, 59, 63, 65–6, 70–1, 75, 81, 87–8, 91, 100, 102, 105–06, 108, 110, 114–15, 119, 126, 130, 138–9, 141–2, 144, 151–3, 170–1, 175–6, 189, 190, 196, 206, 209, 224, 241–3, 246
George, Prince of Wales *see* George III
Germain, Lord George (formerly George Sackville) 17, 52, 63, 68–71, 75–6, 79–80, 85, 92–3, 101–03
Gibbon, Edward 41
Gibraltar 75, 82, 109–11, 129–31, 200
Gisors, Comte de 11
Glorious 1st June, battle of 256
Golden Grove 223
Goldsmith, Oliver 54–5
Gordon, Lord George 86–7, 151, 162
Gordon riots 87, 89
Gower, the Earl 144–5, 148
Grafton, 3rd Duke of 31, 34–7, 39, 44–6, 50, 104–05, 127, 130–2, 138, 143, 145

Grand Tour of Europe 11, 113, 154
Grantham, 2nd Baron 111, 113, 115, 128, 130, 143
Grattan, Henry 157–8, 162
Graves, Thomas 95–6
Great Lakes 126, 128, 181, 190
Great Seal of New South Wales 254
Greene, Nathaniel 92–4
Grenville, George 25, 28–33, 37–8, 42, 49, 50–1, 158
Grenville, Hester (later married to 1st Earl Chatham) 136, 158
Grenville, Thomas 114–16, 118
Grenville, William 158–60, 190, 237–8, 244
Guardian 237
Guilford Courthouse, battle of 89–90, 92, 94

Haldimand, Frederick 112, 180–1, 183–5, 188
Halifax 42, 62, 109, 176, 178–9
Hamilton, Henry 184–6
Hampden, John 208, 211
Hanover 5, 7, 9, 17, 25–6
Hardy, Admiral Charles 67, 82
Hardy, Reverend Charles 210
Harlow, Vincent 129, 172, 187, 190
Harrison, Audrey (later married to 3rd Viscount Townshend) 18, 34
Hartley, David 118
Hastings, Warren 140, 169–70
Heads of a Plan 218–19, 221–2
Holloway, William 209
Holmes, Susannah 224
Home Office 111–12, 124, 128, 153–5, 165, 176, 179, 183, 185, 187–8, 192–3, 195, 200–02, 204, 206–07, 212, 214–16, 225, 235, 239, 250, 253–4, 259
Hood, Samuel 46, 77, 95–6, 98, 198
Hope, Henry 185–6
House of Commons 2, 7, 10–12, 25–6, 41, 54, 59, 78, 81, 84, 137, 144, 159, 170, 189, 215, 252
House of Lords 4, 75, 102, 134, 136, 138–9, 142, 160, 163–4, 166–7, 170, 172–3, 196, 213, 242, 246, 253, 256–7, 260–1
Howard, Charles 106
Howe, Richard 79
Howe, William 63–4, 67–9, 79–80, 144, 148, 196, 198, 212, 220–1, 235, 253, 256–7, 261, 264

Hughes, Richard 193
Hunter, John 198, 222, 226, 235, 239
Hydrabad, Nizam of 170–1
Hyland, Catherine 209

India 24, 35–6, 124, 140–1, 145, 147, 155, 164–73, 186, 201–2, 212, 254, 261, 263
India Bills 142–3, 145, 164–7, 169, 242
Intercourse Bill 192–3
Ireland 2, 8, 45, 111, 143, 151, 154–63, 235, 249, 261, 263
Irish Judicature Bill 160
Irish Parliament 155–9, 161–3, 249

James II 4, 156
James River 94
Jay, John 118–25, 127–8
Jefferson, Thomas 3, 61, 65, 148, 180, 251
Jeffreys, Lord Chief Justice George 1, 3
Jenkinson, Charles 83
Jenny 203
Jesse, John 27
Johnson, Samuel 54–5
Johnstone, George 52
Jones, John Paul 83–4
Junius 51
juries 3, 39, 51–2, 57, 59, 169, 185–6
Justitia 203

Keane, Michael 196
Keppel, Augustus 67, 75–9, 87–8, 119, 127–8, 130–3
King Lear 246
King, Phillip Gidley 239
King's Mountain, battle of 91

Lady Juliana 237–8
Lady Penhryn 223–4, 231–2
Laffeldt, battle of 10
Lake Nipissing 123, 126
La Perouse, Comte de 216, 231–2
Later Correspondence of George III 151
Lauderdale, 8th Earl of 256
Laurens, Henry 129
Leicester, Earl of 172
Lemane Island 211, 213–14, 219, 221
Lexington, battle of 62, 82
Lincoln, Benjamin 97
London Corresponding Society 257

London Gazette 44, 111
London Observer 199
Loyalist refugees 131, 175, 177
Luttrell, Henry 46–7, 49

Mackaness, George 201
Madison, James 128–9
Manning, Helen 187
Mansfield, 1st Earl of 86–7, 158, 160
Marion, Francis 92
Marsham-Townshend, Robert 263
Maryland 13, 91, 203, 205, 208
Matra, James 176, 206–7, 211–16, 218–19, 228
Mercury 208
Middlesex 44, 46–8
Minden, battle of 17, 52, 68, 102
Minorca 15, 26, 82, 131
Mississippi River 23, 26, 28–9, 72, 123, 128, 176
Monckton, Robert 19–22
Monson, Captain 171
Montagu lodgings 112
Montcalm, Louis-Joseph de 19–22
Moore, George 205, 208
Morgan, Daniel 92
Morning Post 77
Mosquito Shore 208
Murray, James 19–23, 58

Nabobs 164, 166–7, 169
Nagle, Jacob 229
Nautilus 216, 218
Navigation Acts 70, 193–4, 196
Nelson, David 197, 199
Nelson, Horatio 192–6
Nepean, Evan 112–13, 185, 214, 222
New Brunswick 178, 190, 206
Newcastle, 1st Duke of (formerly Thomas Pelham-Holles) 4–9, 13–16, 19, 24–5, 27, 31, 35
Newfoundland 117, 120, 123, 175, 235
New Jersey 66–7, 91, 102, 176
New South Wales 155, 173, 197, 207, 211–12, 214–17, 223, 225, 236, 238, 251, 254–5, 262–3
New South Wales Judicature Bill 224
New York campaign 64, 67–8
Nicholson, Margaret 209, 254
Norton, Fletcher 49–50

North Briton 41–2
North, Lord Frederick 39, 43, 50, 57–60, 63, 70–1, 83, 85, 99–100, 103, 108, 132–4, 140, 144, 151, 205–6, 213, 244, 260, 263
Nootka Sound 172–4, 223, 231
Nova Scotia 19, 60, 62, 109, 117, 119, 123, 125–6, 128, 175–9, 190, 205, 208, 235

O'Hara, Charles 97
Olive Branch petition 62
Onslow, George 27, 31
Ontario 123, 126, 190
Oswald, Richard 115–28

Palliser, Hugh 67, 74, 77–9
Paris peace talks 114–15, 176–7
Parliamentary Register 99
Parr, John 177–8
Patriacha 3
Patterson, Walter 180
Penn, John 176
Pelham, Elizabeth (later 2nd Viscount Townshend's wife) 4, 7
Pelham, Henry 4, 8, 10, 13
Petersburg 93–4
Philadelphia 3, 58, 68, 76, 80, 90, 126, 128
Phillip, Arthur 4, 192, 197, 199–202, 220–3, 225–33, 235–9, 251, 254
Phillip, Jacob 199
Pitt, John, (later 2nd Earl of Chatham) 152, 253
Pitt, William, (later 1st Earl of Chatham) 10, 16–19, 23–8, 31–5, 55, 72, 136–7, 152
Pitt, William (the Younger) 108, 110, 113, 127–8, 131–2, 135–9, 141–8, 152–3, 155, 158–60, 162–70, 173, 177, 181, 184–6, 206, 214, 217, 229, 241–3, 245–7, 249–53, 256, 263
Poor Richard's Almanac 3
Porchester, 1st Baron 247
Port Jackson 228–30, 232
Portlock, Nathaniel 173
Portland, 3rd Duke of 87–8, 110, 132, 138–40, 145–6, 158, 160, 239, 244, 257
Powys, Elizabeth (later married Tommy Townshend) 149–50
Powys, Mary (later married 2nd Earl of Courtown) 149–51
Powys, Richard 149
Powys, Thomas 104, 150, 186, 189

Poyning's Law 157–8
Preston Pans, battle of 9
Prince of Wales 225, 229, 235–7
Proclamation line 29, 123
Providence 235

Quebec 17, 19–24, 29, 57–9, 68, 74, 112, 135, 175, 177–8, 180–1, 183–90
Quebec, battle of 19–23, 175
Quebec Bill 57–8, 186
Queen Anne 5
Queen Caroline 5, 7
Queen Charlotte 151, 253

Rawdon, Lord Francis 93
Raynham 4, 6, 8
Recovery 211, 238
Regency 30, 163, 244–7, 249, 252
Regency Bill 244, 247–8
Retaliation 55
Revolution of 1688 4, 53–4, 57, 63
Rhode Island 59–60, 82, 93, 95
Richards, William 223, 237–8
Richmond, 3rd Duke of 71–2, 87–8, 94, 127–8, 130–3, 143, 161, 251
Rigby, Richard 29, 44–5, 76, 108
Robinson, John 105, 142
Rockingham, 2nd Marquess of 31–2, 34–5, 45–6, 49, 51–2, 58, 67–8, 72, 87–9, 105, 107, 109–10, 114, 119, 124, 158, 257
Rodney, George 82
Rose, George 154, 220
Ross, Robert 220, 225–6, 233
Ruse, James 239
Rutland, 4th Duke of 144, 148
Rye House plot 1–3

Saintes, battle of the 129
Sandwich, 4th Earl of 71, 75, 79, 83–4, 87–8
Saratoga 69, 74, 76, 79–80, 92
Savannah 100, 109, 115, 175
Scadbury 7–8
Second Fleet 238
Secret Service 111, 151, 162, 192, 201–2, 244, 253
Selkirk, 4th Earl of 198
Selwyn, Albinia 7–9, 13
Selwyn, George 7, 13, 107, 149, 259
Selwyn, John 6–7, 12

Serapis 84
Seven Years' War 13, 26, 28, 42, 74, 108, 134, 136, 199
Sever, William 231
Shelburne, 2nd Earl of 29, 62, 72, 87, 89, 105, 107, 110, 112–17, 119, 123–4, 130, 132–3, 135, 137–9, 141, 143, 158–61, 200
Sheridan, Richard 88–9, 110, 170, 244
Shirley, Thomas 193–4
Shortland, John 239
Sidney, Algernon 1–3, 53–4, 61, 65, 135, 219, 222, 245–6, 263–4
Sidney, Henry 4, 136, 219
Sidney, Lucy 2, 4
Sidney, William (later Viscount De L'Isle) 263
Simpson, John 224
Sinclair, Duncan 223, 234–5
Singh, Cheyt 169–70
Sirius 198, 221–2, 227, 233, 235–6
Slavery 251–3
Sloper, Robert 167, 171
Smith, William 112–13, 154, 176, 184–8
Smyth, Lieutenant 230
South Carolina 87, 91
Southwell, Sophia (John Thomas Townshend's first wife) 259
Spain, Edward 201
St Augustine 100
St Croix River 126, 128, 177
St James Chronicle 199
St James's Coffee House 54
St John 175, 177–8, 180
St John River 126, 177
Stormont, 7th Viscount of 86, 172, 245, 248–9
Strachey, Henry 124–8, 177, 190
Stuart, Gilbert 148
Supply 228–9, 236
Swift 205, 208
Sydney Cove 229–33, 235, 237–9, 257
Sydney, Lady – see Elizabeth Powys
Sydney, 1st Viscount - see Tommy Townshend

Tarleton, Banastre 92
Temple, Lord George-Nugent-Temple (later 1st Marquess of Buckingham) 25
Temple, Lord Richard Grenville (later 2nd Earl Temple) 142–3, 158–60
Tench, Watkin 230, 232, 236, 257
Transportation Act 213, 217–19

Thatched House Tavern 49, 54
The Floridas 131
The Morning Herald 170
The Public Advertiser 170
The Times 152, 154, 162, 170, 216, 222, 236, 243, 245, 247–9, 254, 260
The World Turned Upside Down 97
Thompson, Edward 214–16
Thoughts on the Causes of the Present Discontents 53
Thurlow, 1st Baron 144, 148, 242, 251–2
Toronto 123, 126
Toulon 75, 202
Tower of London 42, 87, 129, 167–8
Townshend, Albinia (Tommy Townshend's sister who married 3rd Viscount Middleton) 9, 13, 150
Townshend, Charles (later chancellor of the exchequer) 11, 13, 17, 27, 31, 34–40, 43,
Townshend, Charles (later 2nd Viscount Townshend) 4–7, 156, 199
Townshend, Charles (later 3rd Viscount Townshend) 34, 144
Townshend, Charles (Tommy Townshend's brother) 9, 82, 149–50, 253, 260
'Townshend Duties' 38–9, 44
Townshend, Frances (daughter of Tommy Townshend who married 3rd Baron Dynevor) 149, 259
Townshend, George (later 1st Marquess Townshend) 911, 13, 18–25, 27, 31, 34, 43, 64, 66, 86, 88, 133, 139–40, 149, 157, 172, 175, 229, 246, 256, 261
Townshend, Georgiana (daughter of Tommy Townshend) 149, 254, 260
Townshend, Harriet (daughter of Tommy Townshend who married the Earl of Dalkeith) 149, 255, 259
Townshend, Henry (Tommy Townshend's brother) 9, 13
Townshend, Horatio (son of Tommy Townshend) 149–50, 260
Townshend, Horatio (later 1st Viscount Townshend) 1–2, 4
Townshend, John (son of 1st Marquess Townshend) 88, 139, 142, 147–8
Townshend, John Robert (son of John Thomas Townshend) 263
Townshend, John Thomas (son of Tommy

Townshend) 112–13, 149–50, 154, 196, 252–3, 256–7, 259–60, 262–3
Townshend, Mary (daughter of Tommy Townshend who later married 2nd Earl Chatham) 149, 152, 243, 259–60
Townshend, Mary (Tommy Townshend's sister) 9, 144, 149–50
Townshend, Roger (George Townshend's brother) 18–19
Townshend, 'Spanish' Charles 13, 66, 139, 142, 146
Townshend, Thomas (Tommy Townshend's father) 7–8, 10, 13, 17, 150, 257
Townshend, Tommy (later Lord Sydney) 2–7, 9–18, 24–36, 38–47, 49–64, 66–72, 74–90, 92–3, 95–6, 100–5, 107–20, 122–46, 148–90, 92–7, 199–226, 228–9, 234–40, 242–264
Townshend, William (son of Tommy Townshend) 149–50, 256, 259–60

United States of America 73–4, 90, 100, 115–17, 122–3, 127–9, 131, 134, 154, 175, 177, 181–2, 189, 192–3, 263
Ushant, battle of 77

Vellinghausen, battle of 25
Vermont 180–1
Virginia 13, 32, 91–5, 98, 117, 166, 176, 203
Virginia Gazette 203

Walpole, Dorothy (later 2nd Viscount Townshend's wife) 5
Walpole, Robert 4–6, 8, 28
Walpole, Horace 18–19, 23, 26–7, 31, 34–6, 38, 41–2, 45–6, 50, 55, 58, 69, 75, 116, 138, 141
Warburton, George 23
Warren, Richard 242–3, 248
Washington, George 13, 15, 29, 62, 64, 67–8, 71, 76, 90–1, 95–7, 100, 102, 127, 148, 165–6, 176–7, 180
Waterhouse, Henry 239, 255–7, 262
West Africa 26, 203–04, 211, 238
Whig party 4–5, 7, 9, 14–15, 24–5, 27, 31, 35, 71
Whitchurch 12, 14, 59, 88, 135, 150, 153, 259–60
White, John 224

Wilberforce, William 252
Wilhelmstaal, battle of 25
Wilkes, John 41–9, 68
William III 156
William IV 179
Williamsburg 94, 96
Willis, Francis 243–4, 246–8
Willis, John 244, 248
Wolfe, James 17, 19–23, 25–6
Wraxall, Nathaniel 86–7, 107–08, 131–2, 135, 139–40, 142, 144, 152–3, 165, 169, 215, 217, 238, 245, 252
Wyvill, Christopher 84

Yonge, George 63, 198
Young, George 212–14, 219
York, Duke of 229, 244
York River 94, 96–7
Yorktown, battle of 82, 90, 94–101, 127, 165